ISBN 978-1-332-76478-5
PIBN 10437065

CATALOGUE

OF THE

MANUSCRIPTS AND MUNIMENTS

OF

Alleyn's College of God's Gift

AT

DULWICH

BY

GEORGE F. WARNER, M.A.

OF THE DEPARTMENT OF MANUSCRIPTS, BRITISH MUSEUM

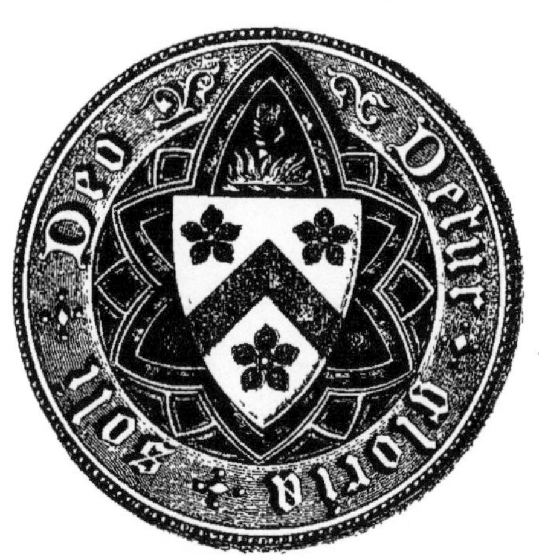

Published for the Governors by

LONGMANS, GREEN, AND CO.

1881

CORNELL
UNIVERSITY
LIBRARY

INTRODUCTION.

THE present Catalogue has been prepared in accordance with a resolution of the Board of Governors of Dulwich College. It consists of two parts. In the first are described the manuscript volumes[1] in the College Library, none of which were included in the recently-published catalogue of the printed books; in the second, all the documents in the Muniment Room bearing an earlier date than the death of the Founder as well as a few others of particular interest selected from those of a later period.

Several of the Manuscripts and the whole of the Muniments except nos. 65–72 belonged to Edward Alleyn, the actor, Founder of the College. The volumes numbered MSS. i.–vi. and xviii. are made up of letters and separate papers of all kinds, and their united contents are known as the 'Alleyn Papers.' Under this general term they include not only all that remains of Alleyn's own correspondence, but also that of his wife's stepfather, Philip Henslowe, which presumably came into his hands at the death of the latter in 1616. Apart from their value as materials for the Founder's biography, the extraordinary interest they possess in relation to the early history of the English drama and stage has long been

[1] Unfortunately the existence of the MSS. now numbered xviii.–xxxvi. was not known to me until the Catalogue was printed. They will be found described in an Appendix (p. 337).

recognised. In order that this special feature may be seen to advantage, everything which serves to illustrate it has accordingly been brought together in MS. i. In like manner MS. ii. contains the whole of the papers connected with the sports of the Bear Garden. The other volumes which certainly belonged to Edward Alleyn are numbered MSS. vii.–xi. They comprise the invaluable theatrical Diary of Philip Henslowe, a Memorandum-Book and a Diary of Alleyn himself, the Register of Dulwich College from its foundation, and a List of offices held under the Crown. Besides these, it is probable from their nature that MSS. xix. and xx. also formed part of the Founder's collection. The contents of the rest of the MSS. need not be here particularised. How and when some of them came to the College it is impossible to say; but several appear to have belonged at one time to the family of Hatton. With regard to the Muniments, these have been numbered from 1 to 594 in a consecutive series; but, for more convenient reference, they have also been divided into sections according to subject. Thus nos. 1–72, dated 1546–1662, relate exclusively to the Theatre and the Bear Garden; nos. 73–184, dated 1537–1626, to Bishopsgate, Southwark, Kennington, &c.; and nos. 185–594, dated 1323-1626, to Dulwich alone, including all the deeds connected with the foundation of the College. A fourth and last section is composed of a series of Court-Rolls of Dulwich manor. These are numbered independently from A to M, and extend in date, with several breaks in continuity, from 1333 to 1626.

The history of Alleyn's collection since his death in 1626 may be briefly told. The safe custody of the 'evidences' of the College was made the subject of special provision in the statutes, and they were no doubt deposited in the Treasure Chamber as a matter of course. But, with regard to the mass of private papers unconnected with the College and of no legal value, such precautions were not necessary, and there is no reason to believe that their preservation was directly due either to a deliberate intention on the Founder's own part or to reverence entertained for his memory by others. Whether they were from the first mixed up indiscriminately with the Muniments or remained, at Alleyn's death, in that part of the College buildings which he occupied, and which passed to successive holders of the office of Master, is altogether uncertain; but the whole extent of the care bestowed upon them by the College authorities for more than a century seems to have consisted in leaving them alone. The natural consequences of this neglect are everywhere seen in the marks which they bear of damp and decay, and there can hardly be a doubt that a large number of papers must have perished altogether.[1]

The first intimation that such relics existed is to be found in the *Biographia Britannica*, published in 1747. An earlier reference might have been looked for in John Aubrey's account of Dulwich College, printed after his death in the *Natural History and Antiquities of Surrey*, 1719 (below, p. 202); but, although the library and pictures are noticed, no mention is there made of any papers or other MSS. which had belonged to the Founder. William Oldys,

[1] The fate of some may be inferred from that of Norden's print of London, mentioned by Aubrey. To quote from Rich. Gough: 'Norden published also a view of London in eight sheets, having at bottom a representation of the Lord Mayor's shew, all on horseback, and the aldermen in round caps. Bagford says this view is singular, and was taken from the pitch of the hill towards Dulwich college going to Camberwell from London, about 1604 or 1606, and that he had not met with any other of the kind: he adds that he saw it on the staircase at Dulwich college, and that Secretary Pepys went afterwards to see it, and would have purchased it: but that since it is quite decayed and destroyed by the damp of the wall' (*British Topography*, 1780, vol. i. p. 747). The actual fall of the porch and Treasure Chamber in 1703 (p. 197) shows the lamentable state to which the fabric of the College had been reduced.

who wrote the life of Edw. Alleyn in the *Biographia*, was more inquisitive or more fortunate and drew from this source the greater part of his materials. His information was not obtained directly from the originals, but from the Master of the College and, more especially, from a letter addressed to him in 1745 by a 'learned and ingenious member.' To this letter he constantly refers, and its writer, the Rev. Tho. Waterhouse, who had been appointed usher as recently as 1744, deserves the credit of being the first Fellow on the Dulwich foundation who showed an appreciative interest in its manuscript treasures. At the same time, the particulars published related almost exclusively to Alleyn's own personal history, and it is evident, both from omissions and errors, that a large portion of the collection was still undiscovered or had been very superficially examined. The volume of which most use was made was Alleyn's Diary for 1617–1622, now MS. ix., and it is worth notice that this is expressly said to be the only one of its kind then extant.[1] Although it is probable enough that similar Diaries, after, if not before, the above period, had been left by Alleyn, the statement is so far satisfactory that it relieves the College in modern times from the suspicion of having allowed them to perish. Of Philip Henslowe Oldys knew so little that he wrote his name as Hinchtoe, and of his Diary he appears to have been wholly ignorant. Nearly forty years more, in fact, elapsed before this unique and most remarkable record of Elizabethan stage management was brought to light. Its discovery was announced by Edmond Malone at the end of his Historical Account of the English Stage (*Shakspeare*, 1790, vol. i.

[1] Malone, writing in 1780, says that he had enquired at the College for this Diary, but it had 'been lost within these few years' by the negligence of a former librarian (*Supplement to the Edition of Shakspeare published in* 1778, vol. i. p. 49). Fortunately at some time or other it was again discovered.

part ii. p. 288). To use his own words: 'Just as this work was issuing from the press, some curious manuscripts relative to the stage were found at Dulwich College, and obligingly transmitted to me from thence. One of these is a large folio volume of accounts kept by Mr. Philip Henslowe, who appears to have been proprietor of the Rose Theatre, near the Bankside, in Southwark.' Throwing, as they did, a flood of unexpected light on his subject, these new materials were of the highest importance to Malone; and, although, as he proceeds to say, it was too late to insert them in their proper places, he printed copious extracts from the Diary as an appendix, adding to them a few of the letters and papers in MS. i. and some curious theatrical inventories, the originals of which have since unfortunately disappeared. Shortly after Malone's publication, attention was again directed to the Dulwich collection by Daniel Lysons in his *Environs of London*, 1792, vol. i. p. 87. Though not free from errors, the account there given of Edw. Alleyn and his foundation was fuller and more accurate than any before it. This was mainly due to the facilities afforded the author for inspecting the MSS. at the College, whereby he was enabled not only to correct and supplement earlier writers, but to extract from Alleyn's Diary and other sources much interesting matter. Among the papers thus made known were some of the most important of those connected with the Bear Garden in MS. ii.; but the subject of Henslowe's Diary and the theatrical MSS. generally is passed over in silence. The reason of this is hard to understand, unless Lysons wrote, like Oldys, before they were found. This, however, could scarcely have been the case, since he refers to Malone's discovery of a note of Alleyn's marriage, by which he apparently means the entry in Henslowe's Diary quoted below, p. 6, note 1. The originals, as we know, were in the hands of Malone; but it is hardly credible that Lysons should have heard nothing about them at the College. It is, indeed, not wholly impossible that the authorities there had forgotten their existence; at the most, they had so little idea of their value, or such unbounded confidence in Malone, that he was actually permitted, it appears, to retain possession of them down to his death in 1812 (Collier, *Mem. of Edw. Alleyn*, p. 2). The greater part are said to have been then returned by the younger James Boswell, his literary executor; but some of the papers which he published as belonging to the collection are no longer to be found in it, and how many more disappeared, of which no record remains, it is impossible to say. The inventories mentioned above and an interesting agreement by Robert Dawes as a member of Henslowe's company in 1614 (*Shakspeare*, 1821, vol. xxi. p. 413) have been lost altogether, and the same is the case with the stage-plot of *Tamar Cam* (*ibid.* vol. iii. p. 356). Of the three other very curious plots printed by Malone the only one still at the College is that of *The Seven Deadly Sins*, now MS. xix. The plots of *The Dead Man's Fortune* and *Frederick and Basilea* by some means found their way into the library of Richard Heber, and, at its sale in 1836, they were bought for the British Museum, being now numbered Additional MS. 10449. It should be added that after Malone's death transcripts were found among his papers of a number of documents, in addition to the matter which he had actually printed. These transcripts, which included the valuable series of letters addressed to Henslowe by Rob. Daborne, the dramatist, were published by Boswell in his edition of Malone's *Shakspeare*, 1821, vols. iii. p. 343, xxi. p. 389.

The next writer who made an independent use of the Dulwich collection was Mr. John Payne Collier. The result of his earliest personal acquaintance with it was embodied in his *History of Dramatic Poetry*, &c., published in 1831, up to which time he had chiefly devoted his attention to Henslowe's Diary. In 1841 he produced his *Memoirs of Edward Alleyn*, a volume which had the honour of being the first of the series issued by the newly-formed Shakespeare Society. Its nature has been aptly described by Mr. Joseph Hunter[1] as 'a sylva of Alleyneana rather than a life of Alleyn'; but, in spite of many deficiencies, it contained a large amount of new facts and documents of the highest interest and value, with regard to both Alleyn himself and some of the most famous of his literary contemporaries. One disagreeable feature, which it has in common with other works of the same author, will have to be considered further on. The *Memoirs* were followed in 1843 by the *Alleyn Papers*, a thin volume edited by Mr. Collier for the same society. Its contents consisted solely of letters and papers, a number of which, such as the Daborne correspondence, were not entirely fresh matter. In the introduction were also included extracts from Alleyn's Memorandum-Book, now MS. viii. It should be observed that some of the documents published in this volume were at the time not at Dulwich, but in the possession of Mr. J. O. Halliwell. Their nature, however, leaves no room for doubt that they originally belonged to Alleyn's collection; and at a later period Mr. Halliwell with his usual liberality restored them to the College. They are now distributed through the volumes in their proper places, but a list drawn up by Mr. Halliwell will be found at the end of MS. iii. Mr. Collier's last Dulwich publication was *The Diary of Philip Henslowe*, Shakespeare Society, 1845, comprising all the matter in the MS. which has anything to do with the stage. The inventories of costumes, properties, and play-books, before alluded to,

[1] In the notes on Alleyn's life, forming part of his *Chorus Vatum Anglicanorum* (Brit. Mus. Add. MS. 24487, f. 166*b*), of which I have made frequent use.

were also included in an appendix; but, the originals being lost, these were taken just as they stood from Malone's *Shakspeare*, 1821, vol. iii. p. 308. Mr. Collier gives as his special reason for reprinting them that they had actually formed part of the Diary and had been abstracted since Malone's time. This, however, is an error, since Malone states (*op. cit.* p. 296) that they were found in a bundle of loose papers.

Through the medium of the works enumerated, and more particularly those of Mr. Collier, the collection was now fully made known;[1] and it need hardly be added that its custodians were at length thoroughly alive to the duty of preserving what was left of it intact. Though it could not atone for the scandalous neglect and apathy of earlier times, the care shown in this respect during the closing years of the old corporation left little to be desired. To the last two Fellows who held the office of Librarian, the Rev. John Image and the Rev. Charles Howes, Mr. Collier paid a fitting tribute in his several introductions; and it is the more to be regretted that some unscrupulous forger should have abused the opportunities, which their liberality allowed, by the introduction of spurious matter. Since the re-constitution of Alleyn's College under the Act of Parliament of 1857 the Manuscripts, which form part of the Library, have been in the official custody of the Rev. Dr. Carver, the first Master under the new scheme. The Muniments, on the other hand, which were formerly in the Treasure Chamber, are now deposited in the Muniment Room at the New College, where they are effectually secured from further harm. I may further mention that Dr. Carver

[1] As Mr. Collier has more than once reflected severely upon the inaccuracies of his predecessors, it is but fair to say that his own transcripts are far from immaculate, even when (as in MS. i. art. 136) he professes to be most exact. Even Malone hardly went so far as to transform the plain signature 'A Warwyke' (p. 85) into 'Edward Dyer.'

has had the good fortune to purchase back a few of the papers lost by his less careful predecessors, among them being an interesting series of suggestions made to Alleyn for his statutes by the Warden of Winchester College (p. 145). It is to be hoped that, if similar opportunities should occur, they will not be neglected.[1]

But, although now jealously preserved, the collection up to the present time has never been catalogued. The letters and papers also still remained in the utmost possible confusion; and it was necessary therefore, in the first instance, to reduce them to order. Their mutilated and fragmentary condition, and in many cases the absence of dates, made this a task of some difficulty; but all have now been carefully repaired and bound, and the contents of the several volumes, into which they are divided, have been chronologically arranged. One result is that some papers thought to be lost, as MS. i. art. 106, prove to be safe, while, on the contrary, others which survived to so comparatively recent a date as to be printed by Mr. Collier have to be reported as now missing. The other MSS., which already formed separate volumes, were in an almost equally dilapidated state. They have therefore been re-bound uniformly with the rest, care, however, being taken to preserve the old vellum covers of MSS. vii. and ix. The original design of the Catalogue was restricted to the manuscripts in the Library; but, on examination, their intimate connexion with the muniments made it advisable to include also a portion of the latter. All those deeds and other documents have accordingly been catalogued which were executed by Alleyn himself or in his own time, or which came to him on the acquisition o his estates. The few of a

[1] As recently as 1878 a slip cut from Henslowe's Diary was offered for public sale (see below, p. 163), containing autographs of Chapman and Dekker.

later date which have been added continue the history of the Fortune Theatre after his death till its final demolition.

The system upon which the Catalogue has been compiled is as follows :—With regard to the Alleyn Papers, every letter and paper, except in the case of a series to the same purport, has been separately described; references have been given when an article has already been printed; and explanatory foot-notes have been frequently subjoined. From their peculiar interest, the contents of MSS. i. and ii. claimed to be even more minutely treated. The descriptions therefore have often taken the form of a regular *précis*; and, if an important article has not been published or the published text is very inaccurate, it has been printed in full. This latter course has occasionally been adopted for other reasons; and in MSS. iii. and v. also a few articles have been dealt with in the same way. For MSS. vii.–xi., and for the rest of the MSS. not belonging to Alleyn's collection, a description in general terms, with the addition in some cases of a few extracts, has been deemed sufficient. The extracts from Alleyn's Diary are numerous. They form, however, a small portion only of the MS., in which even the most trifling payments are recorded from day to day; and all the entries selected possess some elements of interest. A good many of them have been printed or noticed elsewhere, but it has been in a loose and disconnected way, and the annotations, which they required and which here accompany them, will, it is hoped, be regarded as an additional reason for their reproduction. In cataloguing the muniments the descriptions have been made as concise as possible, but nothing worthy of notice has intentionally been omitted. The only exception is in the case of the Court-Rolls of Dulwich manor. The extreme dates of each of these have alone been given, a few general remarks upon them being reserved for this Introduction.

But, before I enter upon other matters, it will be convenient to collect some particulars of the life of Edward Alleyn, though, at the same time, much must necessarily be left to be supplied from the Catalogue itself or from what has already been written on the subject by others. The date of his birth on 1 Sept., 1566, is accurately fixed by his own entries of its recurring anniversary in his Diary; and his baptism on the day following is recorded in the parish register of St. Botolph's, Bishopsgate. Fuller's often-quoted statement that he was born 'near Devonshire house where now is the sign of the Pie' is fully confirmed by the mention of Pye Alley and Fisher's Folly, the old name of Devonshire House, in close connexion with his father's property. In the pedigree, signed by himself, in the Visitation of Surrey in 1623,[1] he appears as the son of Edward Alleyn, of Willen, co. Bucks, and of Margaret Townley, daughter of John Townley, of co. Lancaster. The paternal descent is so far borne out that a pedigree in the Visitation of Bucks in 1634 (Brit. Mus., Harley MS. 1234, f. 13) makes the elder Edward Alleyn to be the second son of Thomas Alleyn, of Willen and of Mesham, co. Bedford. On the other hand, even so experienced a genealogist as Mr. Joseph Hunter failed to trace the connexion between Margaret Townley and the Townleys of Lancashire;[2] and there is too much reason to suspect that it rested simply on imagination. This is not the less likely from the date of the pedigree, which was drawn out just before Alleyn's marriage with Constance Donne and about the time when he is known (p. 112) to have been desirous of 'sum further dignetie,' for

1 An authentic copy from the original in the Heralds' College is given by Hunter, Brit. Mus., Add. MS. 24487, f. 166*b*.

2 A John Townley, of Gray's Inn, was a tenant under Alleyn at Dulwich, but he does not address him (p. 99) as if he were a relative.

the attainment of which a good descent was probably of consequence.

The earliest mention in the Dulwich collection of Edw. Alleyn, the father, is in a bond dated 1555 (Mun. 77). He is there styled 'of London, yeoman,' as also in 1557 (Mun. 78). In subsequent deeds, the first of which records his purchase of a house in Bishopsgate in 1566 (Mun. 80), he uniformly appears as an 'innholder,' and he is so described in his will, dated 10 Sept., 1570 (Mun. 82). The statement made by Malcolm (*Londinium Redivivum*, 1802, vol. i. p. 345) and noticed by Hunter as 'a very curious fact,' that in the entry of his burial at St. Botolph's, on 13 Sept., 1570, he is called 'poete to the Queene,' may be readily dismissed. On referring to the register I found the word to be 'porter'; and the title 'one of the Queen's Maiesties porters' is given him in a document (p. 122) dated 1567.[1] In the pedigree of 1623, besides Edw. Alleyn, he has four other children, all sons, viz. John, William, Oliver, and Percival. Of the last three there is no mention in the collection; but in the register of St. Botolph's the baptism of William Allen is recorded on 13 Feb., 1567[8] and the burial of Oliver Allen on 13 Dec., 1563. Apparently the only one of the four brothers who grew up was John Alleyn, whose name frequently occurs in the Catalogue until after 1596. In that year he died, his property being administered by his widow, Margaret Alleyn. Whether his son, also named John, survived him is uncertain; but he too was already dead in 1623, without issue.[2] The elder John was senior to his brother Edward, and, as his baptism is not recorded in the parish register, was presumably born before

[1] A somewhat similar error was made by Mr. Collier (*Memoirs*, p. 155), in quoting from Alleyn's Diary the entry 'Goodman poet dind here.' It is really 'Goodman Pole' (cf. p. 176, below, 27 Aug.).

[2] A John Alleyn 'from Mr. Edward Alleyn his house at Dulwich' was buried at Camberwell, 31 Mar., 1614 (Blanch, *Hist. of Camberwell*, p. 177).

his parents settled in St. Botolph's. His wife's name being Margaret, it is not improbable that he was the John Allen whose marriage to Margaret Davie was registered on 21 Aug., 1580. In this case his mother-in-law, who is called Julian Crapwell (p. 256), must have had more than one husband.

Some time before 12 Feb., 1580, the widow of Edward Alleyn, the father, married again; for on that day she executed a deed (Mun. 84) as the wife of John Browne, who then and after is called a haberdasher. If we are to believe Mr. Collier and others who have followed him, he was an actor as well; but it is plain that he has been confounded with Robert Browne, and Mr. Collier's confident assumption that it was by his stepfather that Alleyn, to use Fuller's expression, was 'bred a stage player,' is, in fact, entirely unsupported. In default of evidence, both the reasons which led him to choose the profession and the date of his entering it must be left to conjecture. Unlike John Alleyn, who soon became, like his father, an innholder, he continued to be styled merely 'yeoman' and 'gentleman' during the whole of the period covered by the early deeds relating to the property they inherited in Bishopsgate; and it is a curious fact, not hitherto remarked, that on the first occasion on which he is credited with a profession it is that of a 'musicion' (Mun. 106). This was in 1595, by which time his reputation as an actor was fully established; and the designation is additional evidence that in the early theatre there was no strongly marked distinction between the stage and the orchestra. The probability is that he began to act when quite a youth, perhaps at the instigation of his elder brother, who, if not actually a performer, was in some way engaged in theatrical affairs. Edward Alleyn's name first occurs in a list of the Earl of Worcester's players in 1586 (*Shakespeare Soc. Papers*, vol. iv., 1849, p. 149); but the earliest document here connecting him with the stage is dated 1589 (p. 2). The position he ultimately achieved is sufficiently shown by the passage in T. Nash's *Pierce Pennylesse*, 1592, first quoted by Chalmers (Malone's *Shakspeare*, 1821, vol. iii. p. 503): 'Not Roscius or Æsope, those tragedians admyred before Christ was borne, could ever performe more in action than famous Ned Allen'; and, not to multiply references, the same flattering comparison is made by Ben Jonson in his well-known epigram addressed to Alleyn himself (Collier, *Memoirs*, p. 6).

On 22 Oct., 1592, Edward Alleyn married Joan Woodward, who was daughter by a former husband of Agnes, then wife of Philip Henslowe. Of the date of this marriage there is no question (p. 6, note 1); but it is singular that 'Mistris Allene' is named in a letter which was almost certainly written in Feb., 1591 or 1592 (p. 5). It is possible therefore that Joan Woodward was his second wife, and the tradition that the Founder was thrice married, formerly current at the College, but latterly discredited, may thus after all be correct. The close proximity of dates certainly need be no objection, if we may judge from the extreme haste with which he married again in 1623. The name and occupation of Joan Woodward's father, as well as the amount of property, if any, which she brought to her husband, have eluded discovery. What evidence there is, however, is decidedly against Mr. Collier's conclusions on the subject (*Memoirs*, pp. 15, 16). The entries in Henslowe's Diary, from which he assumes that Woodward was engaged in mining operations in Ashdown Forest, clearly relate to the family of Henslowe (p. 157, n. 1), and the parsonage of Firle came to Alleyn not with his wife, but by assignment from A. Langworth (Munn. 109, 144).

Not the least of the advantages which resulted to Alleyn

from his marriage was that it brought him into intimate relations with his wife's stepfather, Philip Henslowe.[1] Although the latter appears to have been servant to Agnes Woodward at the time he married her (*Memoirs*, p. 124), his origin was less obscure than has been generally supposed. In the Visitation of Sussex in 1634 (Harley MS. 1562, f. 114*b*) he is said to have been the fourth son of Edmond Hensley, or Henslowe, of Lindfield. The latter married Margaret Ridge, of the same county, and was, as we learn elsewhere (p. 157, n. 1), for a long period Master of the Game in Broil Park and Ashdown Forest. The pedigree in the volume quoted goes back as far as Edmond's great-grandfather, William Hensley or Hensleigh, of Devon, who, according to the Visitation of Devon in 1620 (*Harleian Society*, vol. vi., 1872, p. 123), married Joan, daughter and co-heir of William Whitfield. Philip Henslowe's name, which is spelt in a variety of ways, first occurs in the Catalogue in 1577 (p. 85), when he was already living in the Liberty of the Clink,[2] in Southwark, as he continued to do till his death. In 1584 (Mun. 86) and subsequently he is described as a dyer; but he seems to have acted also as a pawnbroker (p. 157) and to have engaged in sundry other trading speculations. In 1592 or 1593 he became a Groom of the Chamber to Queen Elizabeth, and in 1603 a Sewer of the Chamber to James I. Illiterate himself,

[1] In the Surrey Visitation pedigree Joan Alleyn is wrongly called Henslowe's own daughter, the name of Woodward being suppressed. The arms also there represented are *argent*, a chevron between three cinquefoils *gules*, for Alleyn, impaling *gules*, a lion passant gardant *or*, a chief *azure*, semé de fleurs de lis of the second. The latter coat, which should be that of Woodward, appears on a seal used by Henslowe (MS. ii. f. 51).

[2] In an assessment on the inhabitants of the Clink for a subsidy, 7 Aug., 1594, Henslowe was assessed on 10*l.*, and so in subsequent years down to 1609. Alleyn was assessed in 1594 on 5*l.*, and in 1598 on 12*l.* (Brit. Mus., Add. MS. 24487, ff. 168, 170). In 1612 Henslowe contributed 10*l.* towards a loan to the King, while Alleyn contributed 15*l.* (Add. MS. 27877, f. 140).

he has gained a permanent place in literary history through the preservation of the volume which recorded his receipts and transactions as a theatrical proprietor and manager at the most critical period of the developement of the English drama, although unfortunately there is nothing to show that he came into contact with its most illustrious exponent. His connexion with the stage, which probably began with his acquisition of the 'Little Rose' in 1585 (Mun. 15) and the erection or re-erection of a theatre on its site in 1587 (Mun. 16), has been fully discussed by Mr. Collier in the introduction to his edition of the Diary, and there is no occasion therefore to dwell upon it here. It is enough to say that from 1592, the year in which the Diary opens and in which Alleyn was married, Henslowe and he were united more or less closely in a theatrical partnership, which was only dissolved by the death of the former in 1616.

Edw. Alleyn, at the time of his marriage, was a member of the company known as the Lord Admiral's, and he still remained attached to it after it passed, on the accession of James I., to Henry, Prince of Wales. In 1593, however, when the plague was raging in London, he joined Lord Strange's company in a provincial tour, and to this we are indebted for the very interesting correspondence with his wife and her stepfather (p. 5). The letters on both sides bear pleasing testimony to Alleyn's amiable qualities and the affectionate terms upon which he lived with his 'mouse' and her family. In 1594–1597, as may be gathered from the Diary, he was again performing on the London stage; but, towards the close of the latter year, he is represented as having for some reason 'leafte playinge.' In confirmation of this temporary retirement he is found, both in June and September, 1598, staying with his wife at the house of Arthur Langworth at Broil, in Sussex, where Henslowe addressed to him the two letters on the subject of the Mastership of the Royal Game (pp. 15, 65) one of which contains so remarkable a notice of Ben Jonson. His next appearance is in connexion with the building of the Fortune Theatre, in Golden Lane, Cripplegate. A lease of the site was acquired by him on 22 Dec., 1599 (Mun. 20), and the contract with Peter Streete for its erection was signed on 8 Jan., 1599-1600 (Mun. 22). Although the house itself was built for Henslowe and Alleyn together, all the deeds relative to the site, &c., down to the acquisition of the freehold in 1610 (Mun. 38), are in Alleyn's name only, and the same is the case with the two warrants in furtherance of the project (pp. 17, 18). Ultimately the whole property came into his possession, and it formed part of the endowment of Dulwich College. The date of the completion of the building is unknown, but it was probably open for performance before the end of the year 1600, and Alleyn's own acting no doubt from the first formed one of its principal attractions.

But before this he had begun to provide the public with entertainment of a grosser kind. His interest in the baiting-house at Paris Garden, on the Bankside, dated as far back as Dec., 1594 (p. 67, n. 4), and we have his own word for it that on an outlay of 450*l.* it brought him in 60*l.* a year. It was this success probably, with the desire to get rid of vexatious restrictions, which prompted Henslowe and himself on the death of Ralph Bowes in 1598 to exert all their interest to secure his office of Master of the so-called Royal Game of Bears, Bulls, and Mastiff Dogs. In this attempt they were unsuccessful, the Queen having already granted the reversion to John Dorrington (p. 65); and they were compelled instead to pay the latter a yearly commission for license to bait. Sir William Steward, who succeeded Dorrington in July, 1604 (p. 68, n. 1), made profit from the office in a different way; for, by withholding this license and refusing to take over their house and stock on reasonable terms, he obliged them to purchase his patent at a price which they afterwards declared to have been exorbitant. A new patent in their favour as joint-masters was accordingly made out on 24 Nov., 1604 (p. 67), with the usual fees and privileges, as may be seen on pp. 73–78. Some of these privileges for the taking up of dogs for the King's service were not enforced without trouble to themselves and danger to their subordinate officers. This patent was held by Alleyn as the survivor down to his death; and, notwithstanding complaints to the contrary, the profits in various ways, added to the sums charged for admission to the Garden, were probably considerable. Although too the general management of the baiting seems to have been in the hands of Jacob Mead as lessee or deputy, in presence of royalty or on other special occasions the barbarous sport was directed by the Master in person. Instances of this are recorded by Alleyn himself in his Diary as late as 1622, and a sickening description of his baiting of a lion before the King, Queen, and Prince in 1604 is quoted by Mr. Collier (*Memoirs*, p. 65) from Stow's *Chronicle*. The whole of the contents of MS. ii. relating to the subject of the Bear Garden are exceedingly curious, and for graphic illustration of a certain phase of contemporary manners few letters of the time will compare with Sir William Faunt's on p. 82. The only letter here which comes near it in this respect is that containing an account of a trial for murder on p. 105.

Previous to 1605 the investments which Alleyn's growing wealth enabled him to make appear to have been principally leasehold; and, although Mr. Collier speaks as if it were otherwise, his estate in the parsonage of Firle and in the manor of Kennington formed no exception. His negotiations for the purchase of Dulwich probably began in the summer of 1605. This manor was granted by Henry I. in 1127 to Bermondsey Abbey, to which it belonged until the suppression of the house in 1537–8. On 11 Oct., 1544, Henry VIII. granted it (Mun. 331) *in capite*, at a rent of 33*s*. 9*d*., to Thomas Calton, of London, goldsmith, the grant including also the advowson of the vicarage of Camberwell. Besides this, Thomas Calton had already acquired from Sir Thomas Pope, on 18 Sept., 1544 (Mun. 330), some land called Rigate's Green, in Dulwich Wood, which had been granted to Sir Humfrey Browne in 1542 (Mun. 324) and sold by him to Pope the following day. From Thomas Calton the whole estate descended to his son, Nicholas Calton, and his grandson, Sir Francis, the latter of whom succeeded his father at ten years of age in 1575 (p. 123) and received livery of his inheritance in 1587 (Mun. 383). The precise date of Alleyn's first acquisition of property in the manor has hitherto been a matter of doubt. It is now ascertained to have been 1 Oct., 1605 (Mun. 456). This purchase, however, seems to have been merely a preliminary, in order to clear off a mortgage held by Sir Robert Lee since 1602; and it was followed, on 3 Oct., by articles of agreement[1] on the part of Sir F. Calton for the sale of the manor itself and the whole of his estate, excepting the Camberwell advowson. As the price stipulated was 4,900*l*., the undated letter (p. 88), in which he peremptorily refuses 4,500*l*. and demands sixteen years' purchase at 320*l*. a year, must belong to a still earlier stage in the proceedings. This letter, interesting in itself, is made doubly so by Alleyn's notes of his resources and 'means for money' written on the back. In his Memorandum-Book he records that he bought the manor on 25 Oct., 1605, for 5,000*l*. (p. 89); but the formal deed of sale, for the same sum, is dated 8 May,

[1] The original of this document has been lost. It was printed by Mr. Collier, *Memoirs of Edw. Alleyn*, p. 191.

1606 (Mun. 471). It should be noted too that this deed includes the Camberwell advowson, notwithstanding that the terms used by Alleyn in his expostulatory letter to Sir Francis Calton on p. 111, coupled with the fact of its omission from the articles of 3 Oct., seem to imply that this was a separate bargain for 800 marks. Including 1,700*l.* for redemption of mortgages, the amount paid in hand by Alleyn was 2,000*l.*, of which he raised 1,300*l.* by the sale of his lease at Firle. The balance of the 5,000*l.* he engaged to pay at the end of six years, with 213*l.* 6*s.* 8*d.* yearly for its 'forbearance.' Calton's final acquittance was given on 25 Oct., 1613; but, as may be seen in MS. iii., his applications in the interval for advances on various pretexts, of which the least respectable was the want of 5*l.* to give as a bribe, were almost incessant. In one case at least Alleyn's dealings with him were the reverse of unprofitable; for the lease of Kennington manor, which he bought himself in 1604 for 1,065*l.*, he sold to Calton in 1609 for 2,000*l.* (p. 94, n. 1).

Meanwhile, although Alleyn had become lord of the manor of Dulwich, some part of the soil, freehold and copyhold, still remained in other hands. The successive steps by which he gradually bought up this from Sir Edmond Bowyer, Thomas Calton, and others between the years 1606 and 1614 may be traced in the series of muniments, as well as in his own summary in MS. viii. (*Alleyn Papers*, p. xiv.); and altogether the estate must have cost him not much less that 10,000*l.* In 1606 he was already styled 'Edward Alleyn, of Dulwich, esquire,' but it is doubtful when he removed his residence thither from Southwark. As he was churchwarden of the Clink Liberty in 1610 and letters continued to be addressed to him there as late as 1612, the probability is that he did not settle at Dulwich until 1613, the same year in which he began the building of the College. Only three transactions before this date need be here specified. One of these, which escaped Mr. Collier's notice, is especially interesting, since, excluding forgeries, it associates Alleyn's name for the first and only time in the collection with that of the greatest of his contemporaries. This was his purchase in 1609, the year of publication, of Shakespeare's Sonnets, recorded by himself on the back of a letter (p. 72) and entered, strangely enough to modern ideas, under 'Howshowld stuff.' The sum of 5*d.* which he gave for the book no doubt represents its published price and is in striking contrast with its present market value.[1] The other transactions referred to are his purchase from the heirs of W. Gill, on 30 May, 1610 (Mun. 38), of the freehold of the Fortune and the adjoining tenements, before held only on lease; and his sale to Henslowe, in Feb., 1610–11, of his interest in the Bear Garden. The only evidence of this sale is his note in MS. viii. (p. 67, n. 4). It clearly had nothing to do with the Mastership of the Royal Game, but applied only to the fabric and profits of the baiting-house. In 1606, during their joint occupancy, the woodwork of the structure had been renewed (p. 68), and the whole house was rebuilt and adapted both for baiting and dramatic representations in 1613 (Mun. 49), at which date Henslowe had Jacob Mead for a partner. At Henslowe's death it came again to Alleyn, acting at first perhaps for his mother-in-law, with the result that he was involved in disputes with Mead which were not composed until 1619 (p. 80). On another question of interest, as to the time when Alleyn finally quitted the stage, no positive information can be given. He bore the formal title of 'servant to the Prince of Wales' as late as April, 1612 (p. 75); but this is certainly no proof that he was still an active member of the Prince's company, and, as a

[1] Mr. Huth's copy was bought in 1858 for 154*l.* 7*s.*

matter of fact, his name is neither in the list of 1607 nor in the probably earlier list in Harley MS. 252. From the way too in which Heywood speaks of him in his *Apology for Actors*, 1612,[1] he had evidently ceased to perform for some time previously. His last recorded appearance seems to have been on 15 Mar., 1603-4 (Collier, *Hist. Dram. Poetry*, 1879, vol. i. p. 339), when, in the guise of Genius, he delivered, 'with excellent action and a well-tun'de, audible voyce,' a congratulatory address to James I. at his entertainment in the City; and it may reasonably be concluded that his retirement preceded, rather than followed, his purchase of Dulwich. At the same time it is highly probable that he continued for a while to take part in the management of the Fortune. From Rob. Browne's letter on p. 35 it may perhaps be inferred that this was the case as late as 1612, after which Henslowe's name, until his death, largely predominates.

Alleyn, in fact, at this period, though still pecuniarily interested in theatrical affairs, had assumed the new character of a landed proprietor living on his estate, and, while Henslowe was bargaining with Daborne for plays, he was busied with the work which, more than his fame as an actor, has preserved his memory. If, as above suggested, he removed to Dulwich in 1613, he must have set about it immediately, since the contract for the erection of a chapel, schoolhouse and twelve almshouses is dated 17 May (Mun. 558). It has been thought that he took the idea of his College from the Charterhouse, founded by Thomas Sutton only two years before; but at the most this is only a plausible conjecture strengthened by a certain likeness between the two charities, each of which combined the care of the old with the education of the young. On the other hand, it is interesting to

[1] 'Among so many dead, let me not forget one yet alive, *in his time* the most worthy, famous Maister Edward Allen' (*Shakespeare Soc. Reprint*, 1841, p. 43).

find among his papers, besides references to Eton and Winchester, the statutes of a somewhat similar institution as far off as Amsterdam (p. 145). These statutes are taken from Pontanus's *History of Amsterdam*, 1611; and, although they differ widely from his own, the outward resemblance between the Gerontocomium, of which a view is there given, and the building at Dulwich is perhaps not wholly accidental. While the latter was in course of erection Alleyn was deprived by death of the partner and friend whom for more than twenty years he had familiarly called his father. Philip Henslowe died on or about 9 Jan., 1615–6, and the validity of his will was at once disputed by John Henslowe, his nephew and heir-at-law. Both the bill of complaint and the answer of Alleyn and his co-defendants have been preserved (p. 140); but, in the absence of full particulars, the merits of the case are somewhat obscure, nor does it appear how much of the estate ultimately devolved upon Alleyn at or before the death of his mother-in-law, Agnes Henslowe, in 1617. His agreement, however, with the company at the Hope and their subsequent letter to him (pp. 50, 51) show that he immediately assumed the direction of Henslowe's theatrical concerns. The first of these documents is dated 20 Mar., 1615–6; and to a later period in the same year belongs one, if not both, of the interesting letters of Thomas Dekker (p. 51).

By the end of the summer of 1616 the College was so far ready that the chapel was consecrated by Archbishop Abbot on 1 Sept., the first Fellow, Cornelius Lymar, having been appointed the day before. Between 30 Sept. and 17 Oct. the full number of twelve poor brothers and sisters was made up; but the twelve poor scholars, with their master and usher, were not admitted until the latter half of 1617.[1]

[1] It is of some interest to notice that the admission of paying scholars began at least as early as 1620 (pp. 185, 186).

In order, however, that the College might not collapse at his death under the statute of Mortmain, it was still imperative for the Founder to procure letters-patent for its incorporation and endowment. There were difficulties in the way, which perhaps he never anticipated; and his own Diary, which now comes into use, shows plainly what zeal and pertinacity were required to remove them. Naturally the five years, beginning at Michaelmas, 1617, which this volume covers, are the best known period of Alleyn's life; but the extracts given in the body of the Catalogue make it unnecessary to particularise. The chief, if not the only, direct opposition to his charitable scheme seems to have proceeded from Lord Chancellor Bacon, partly on account of the detriment to the Crown and partly on the ground that 'hospitals abound and beggars abound never a whit the less.' These reasons Bacon explained in a letter to Buckingham (p. 172), whose powerful interest was enlisted on the other side; and he proposed that at the least the endowment should be reduced from 800*l.* to 500*l.* a year. In thus acting he only maintained the position which he had taken up several years before in connexion with the Charterhouse; and the arguments which he then employed in his letter to the King (Spedding, *Life*, vol. iv., 1868, p. 247) to show that foundations such as that of Sutton were productive of more harm than good to the community had equal force against Alleyn's design. The difference was that he was now in a position which made his antagonism far more formidable; but, notwithstanding this, he only succeeded in delaying the patent for a few months. From one cause and another it did not pass the Great Seal until 21 June, 1619, and the corporate existence of the College dates from 13 Sept. following. On this memorable day Alleyn publicly read and subscribed the Deed of Foundation in the chapel before a distinguished company, whom he afterwards entertained at dinner. The first name in the list of guests is that of Bacon, whose presence on the occasion did equal honour to himself and his host.

By the terms of the deed, Thomas and Matthias Alleyn were named Master and Warden respectively; but, for some time at least, the Founder personally administered the affairs of the College, with the aid of the four Fellows in their several capacities of preacher, schoolmaster, usher, and organist. Possibly he continued to do so until his death, but the entries in the Register cease to be made in his own hand after 1622. In this way, besides his own household and personal expenses, his Diary includes payments of every kind on the College account, which show his minute and unceasing care of its inmates. Unfortunately there is equal proof that his benevolence did not always meet with a fitting return. Almost from the first there was drunkenness among the men and 'incharity' and 'unquietness' among the women, while the Fellows neglected their duties and one of them (p. 109) secretly married Anne Alleyn, the Founder's cousin. Although the entries are as brief as they could well be, the MS. generally is of the highest value for the light it throws upon Alleyn's character and the position in the world which he latterly occupied. Except that he was vexed with lawsuits, which provoked the complaint that, of all his expenses, law was the worst, his life was one of dignified ease and comfort. At various times he was the guest of, or dined in company with, the Archbishop of Canterbury, the Bishops of London and Winchester, Lord Treasurer Montague, Sir Julius Cæsar, Master of the Rolls, the Countess of Kildare, the Ambassadors Count Gondomar and Sir Noel Caron, Sir Edward Sackville, Dr. John Donne, and many more. Not the least significant of the names mentioned is that of Lady Kildare, who was daughter of the

Lord Admiral Nottingham, whose theatrical servant he had formerly been. Among his friends too he numbered the art-loving Earl of Arundel and Sir William Alexander, the poet, afterwards Earl of Stirling, the latter of whom, like Ben Jonson, made his merits the theme of eulogistic verse (p. 60).

Of Alleyn's own hospitality at Dulwich there is abundant evidence, and among those who dined at his table was the famous physician, William Harvey. Members of the Fortune company and other actors were constant guests; but, as Mr. Collier remarks, the names of the dramatic poets which might have been expected do not occur. Under different circumstances, however, mention is made of Thomas Lodge, whom he imprisoned, and John Taylor, the water-poet, whom he aided with a liberal subscription for one of his works. The identity of Thomas Middleton, Anthony Munday and Matthew Roydon is less certainly made out. On special occasions Alleyn also entertained the poor people of the College; and in 1621 and 1622 the festivities of Twelfth-night were enlivened by a show and a play performed by the boys. Besides the almshouses which he built in Finsbury or Cripplegate in 1620 (p. 185), many small donations in charity are recorded; and it is curious to find among the recipients a seminary priest (p. 169) and 'a pore knight' (p. 185). On business, or for such purposes as to see the tilting at Whitehall, the Lord Mayor's show, and the funeral of Queen Anne, Alleyn's visits to London were extremely frequent. He then often dined at the house of his friend Lady Clarke, where he seems to have paid for his own drink, or resorted to a tavern. The names of the taverns which he patronised are not without interest. Besides Young's and Hart's ordinaries, they include the Bear, Horn, St. Paul's Head, Cardinal's Hat, Red Cross, Feathers, Plough, Bell in Westminster, Nag's Head, Mermaid, George, Bull's Head, King's Cross, Three Tuns.

Dancing Bears, Golden Tun, Larder, and Devil and St Dunstan.[1] On several occasions he rode to Greenwich to bait before the King, and he also went to the Court at Windsor and to Wanstead for an interview with the Marquis of Buckingham. The longest journey which he made was to Winchester in August, 1618, with the object no doubt of seeing the College. Of the London theatres he names the Red Bull and the Rose, as well as the Fortune, the last being repeatedly mentioned. On 31 Oct., 1618, he let it for thirty-one years on lease; and on 9 Dec., 1621, he records its destruction by fire in a matter-of-fact way which is eminently characteristic. Before 16 Apr., 1622, he had begun the erection of a new house to replace it, and on 20 May he signed leases of some of the shares on terms which bound the lessees to contribute towards the building expenses. Though the contract has not been preserved, it is known from Wright's *Historia Histrionica*, 1699, that it was a 'large round brick building,' in this respect differing from the original theatre, which was square and chiefly of wood. As there is no note of its opening, it was probably not finished until after Michaelmas, 1622,[2] when the Diary breaks off. From the summary with which the volume concludes, Alleyn's expenditure for the five years ending at that date amounted to 8,504*l.*, of which 1,315*l.* was spent on the College generally and 802*l.* on its

[1] A curious sign to be found while James I. was reigning is the 'James' or the 'Fool's Head' (Mun. 53).

[2] To the details of its history, which will be found in the Catalogue, may be added the following memorial from a parish-return in the Lambeth Library, dated 1650:—'The people of that part of the parish of St. Giles, Cripplegate, which is in the county of Middlesex represent that they are poor and unable to build a place of worship for themselves, but think it would be convenient if that large building commonly known by the name of the Fortune Play House might be allotted and set apart for that purpose, which, as we humbly conceive, might be effected at a reasonable charge if the inhabitants were enabled thereunto' (Brit. Mus., Add. MS. 24461, f. 116). The result of the application does not appear.

building and repairs. Unfortunately no record showing the exact sources and amount of his receipts has been preserved.

In the following year Alleyn lost his wife Joan, with whom he had lived, evidently on most affectionate terms, since 1592. Among her husband's papers there is not a word about her illness and death; but, according to the College Register, she died on 28 June, 1623, and was buried on 1 July. A memorial tablet formerly in the chapel added the information that she was fifty-one years of age and died without issue. Just before her death we get some interesting notices of Alleyn outside the Dulwich collection, which, so far as I am aware, have not been quoted in any account of him. The first of these is in connexion with the abortive preparations for the arrival in England of the Infanta Maria as the bride of Prince Charles and forms part of a letter from Dr. Meddus to Joseph Mead, dated 5 June, 1623 (Harley MS. 389, f. 337). Among his items of news Meddus writes that, in addition to the Duke of Richmond, a number of earls and others, 'Allein, sometime player, now squire of the Beares, [and] Inigo Jones, surveyor of the King's works, rode hence on Tuesday towards Winchester and Southampton to take order for his Majestie's entertainment, with the Prince's and the Ladie Marie's.' This is repeated by John Chamberlain in a letter to Sir D. Carleton, 14 June (*Cal. of State Papers*, 1619–1623, p. 608), and it is added that the object of the journey was 'for mending the highways and for shows' and that Alleyn and Inigo Jones alone would have done just as well without so many Privy Councillors. The same writer makes another allusion to Alleyn in a letter[1] dated 20 Dec. (*Cal. of State Papers*, 1623–1625, p. 132): 'But the strangest match in mine opinion is that Allen the player

[1] All three letters are printed in *The Court and Times of James I.*, 1849, vol. i. pp. 402, 441.

hath lately married a young daughter of the Dean of Paul's, which, I doubt, will diminish his charity and devotion towards his two hospitals.' Although it did not have the effect anticipated, the marriage was certainly calculated to excite surprise. It took place on 3 Dec., 1623, only five months after the death of Joan Alleyn, having been arranged, it appears, as early as 21 Oct.; and, while the bridegroom was fifty-seven years of age, the bride, Constance, daughter of the celebrated Dr. John Donne, must have been about twenty at most. On her mother's side she was niece to the wife of Alleyn's friend and neighbour Sir Thomas Grymes, in whose company she had dined at Dulwich College before Alleyn became a widower (p. 193). The whole history of the match is detailed by Alleyn himself in his very curious letter to Donne written early in 1625 (p. 115), which Mr. Collier has printed at length. It is satisfactory to find that his difference with his father-in-law did not diminish his fondness for his wife. He speaks of her most affectionately in his will and, in addition to a settlement of 1,500*l.*, he left her all her jewels and 100*l.* for present use.[1] The larger sum was secured on his property in Southwark; but in his letter to Dr. Donne he refers also to two leases, worth together 250*l.* a year, which he held besides the estate settled upon the College. One of these was a lease of the manor and rectory of Lewisham, the purchase of which for 1,000*l.* is recorded in his Diary, 15 Dec., 1620 (p. 187); the nature of the other, which comprised tenements in the Blackfriars, will be discussed later. Both these properties seem to have involved him in suits at law (Munn. 183, 184), and, as

[1] On 24 June, 1630, she married Samuel Harvey, of Abury Hatch, co. Essex. Dr. Donne died in her house, and in his will, dated 13 Dec., 1630, and proved 5 Apr., 1631, he mentions her as his 'eldest daughter, Constance Harvey, who received from me at her first marriage 500*l.*'

neither is named in his will, it may be inferred that they passed out of his hands some time before his death. The materials generally for the history of the three years which he survived his last marriage are extremely meagre, nor is the meaning of the few documents preserved always intelligible. It has, however, been reasonably conjectured from a letter of H. Gibb (p. 112) that Alleyn was making interest in 1624 to obtain knighthood. The title was one to which, if only as Master of the Royal Game, he might fairly pretend; but it was never conferred, and the wonder is that he cared to have it. Both his own letter to Dr. Donne and a letter to him from Sir T. Grymes (p. 115) show that in the beginning of 1625 he was in need of money. Whatever its cause, the difficulty could only have been temporary, since in the following year he was able to purchase an estate of some kind in Yorkshire. The locality of this property has been until now undetermined; but there can be no doubt that it was situated at Simondstone, in Aysgarth (p. 116, n. 1). There is evidence (p. 117) that Alleyn paid it a visit in July, 1626, and it is not improbable that the journey brought on the illness which ultimately proved fatal. The last extant letter addressed to him is dated 14 Oct., 1626 (p. 117). He was then, as was thought, 'towards a recovery,' but he died on Saturday, 25 Nov. This date rests on the unexceptionable authority of Matthias Alleyn, his executor and the first Warden (Collier, *Memoirs*, p. 182); and, according to the Register (below, p. 196), he was buried on the Monday following. So far as appears, he never had any children; and at the time of his death he had passed his sixtieth year by nearly three months. His will, dated 13 Nov., 1626, is preserved in the Registry of the Prerogative Court of Canterbury and has been printed by Mr. Collier (*Alleyn Papers*, p. xxi.). Its opening sentences are characterised by the same deep religious feeling which found expression in the hymn on p. 120 and in such pious entries in his Diary as may be seen on pp. 173, 185, 194; and his desire was 'without any vain funeral pomp or show to be interred in the quire of that chapel which God of his goodness hath caused me to erect and dedicate to the honor of my Saviour by the name of Christs Chappell in Gods Gift College,' &c. Besides the provision for his widow, before mentioned, bequests were made to several of his relations and dependents; and even Sir F. Calton, with whom latterly he had been on unsatisfactory terms, received 100*l.* and the remission of a long-standing debt of 20*l.* His executors were also required to build within two years ten almshouses in each of the parishes of St. Botolph, Bishopsgate, and St. Saviour, Southwark, the inmates of which, as well as of the ten which he had already built in Cripplegate (p. 185), were to be regarded as members of the Dulwich foundation. To his native parish of St. Botolph for the good of the poor was further given the 'Blew House' in Dulwich (Mun. 521), which it still retains. The estates which formed the endowment of the College had already been settled; but, in addition, he bequeathed to it 'as an augmentation' the residue, after the payment of legacies, of two leases of the Unicorn Inn and of tenements called the Barge, the Bell, and the Cock, in Southwark, together with a quantity of furniture, goods and farm implements. Finally, he left his lands in Yorkshire, also subject to the payment of legacies, to Thomas and Matthias Alleyn, his executors, apparently in their private capacity and not as Master and Warden. On 29 Sept. preceding he had signed the Statutes and Ordinances of his College of God's Gift, which had no doubt been prepared long before; and the last recorded act of his life was to add two clauses on 20 Nov. (Mun. 594). In the first of these he reserved to himself the right of making additions or alterations and of nominating or displacing the members, 'at any time or times during my life'; in the other he confirmed the destination of the leases above, with an injunction upon the College to use their utmost endeavours to get them renewed. Upon the subject of the Statutes in general it is impossible to enter within available limits, and it is beyond the scope of this Introduction to attempt anything like a history of Dulwich College. With the exception of the two clauses above mentioned, they are printed at length in Blanch's *Dulwich College*, 1877. Not the least noteworthy feature in them is the extent to which they modify the constitution of the College as originally laid down in the Patent and Deed of Foundation, the effect, in one direction, being to establish a public school of the ordinary type, with no restriction on admission beyond a preference given to residents at Dulwich.

It will have been observed that more than one allusion is made in the preceding pages to the presence among the Dulwich manuscripts of modern fabrications. Attention has of course been directed to all such cases, as they occur, in the Catalogue, but the subject is too important not to be referred to here. Besides the letter of Joan Alleyn (p. 26), the treatment of which is peculiar, there are in the collection no less than twenty-two actual forgeries, which, however, by counting under one head those which relate to the same subject, may be reduced to eighteen. The general motive which underlies them all is identical—namely, a desire on the part of the forger to palm off upon the world supposititious facts in connexion with Shakespeare and the other early dramatists. Six of the most glaring of the number have long since been thoroughly exposed. I shall have but little therefore to say about these, beyond expressing my unhesitating agreement in the verdict passed upon them; indeed, it is difficult to believe that any one at all familiar with the handwriting of the period to which they profess to belong could fail to recognise at once their imitative character. As is well known, the question of their genuineness was the subject of vehement debate during the so-called 'Shakspere Controversy' which raged twenty years ago. For my own part, however, I entered upon my present task entirely unaffected by the heat of a conflict which I can barely remember; or, if I had a bias either way, it was a natural disinclination to depreciate the value and authenticity of materials which I had undertaken to catalogue. But the evidence supplied by a systematic examination of every volume and paper in the collection is irresistible; and, so far from being able to defend any one of the documents already impugned, I am compelled to add to them other forgeries which appear to have hitherto remained unnoticed or at least have not been publicly stigmatised. At the same time I take the opportunity of stating that my own opinion in every case is confirmed by that of Mr. E. M. Thompson, Keeper of MSS. in the British Museum, whose exceptionally high authority as an acute and experienced palæographer will be universally admitted.

The credit of being the first to detect the handiwork of a modern impostor among the Alleyn Papers belongs to Mr. N. E. S. A. Hamilton. In the course of his researches in connexion with the Perkins *Folio Shakespeare* Mr. Hamilton was led to examine other documents, which, like the alleged seventeenth century annotations in that notorious volume, had been published at various times by Mr. John Payne Collier. The result of his investigations appeared in 1860 in a volume the title of which will be found below (p. 4). Among the documents there ably criticised are four belonging to the Dulwich collection, which were first printed in Mr. Collier's *Memoirs of Edw. Alleyn.* Two of these were rightly condemned by Mr. Hamilton as forgeries from beginning to end, viz. the verses 'Sweete Nedde, nowe wynne an other wager,' mentioning 'Willes newe playe' (p. 4), and the letter of Marston the dramatist to Henslowe (p. 49); the third is a genuine document, to which a spurious list of players, including Shakespeare, has been added (p. 27); and the fourth is Mrs. Alleyn's letter to her husband, referred to above (p. 26). In this instance the letter itself has not been tampered with—in fact, from the rotten condition of the paper it would have been impossible to write upon it—but the printed version included a passage concerning Shakespeare, which is not in the original and can hardly be accounted for on any theory assuming the editor's honesty of purpose. In addition to the above, two more forgeries were exposed by Mr. H. Staunton in the same year in his *Life of Shakespeare*, and again, in more scathing style, by Dr. C. M. Ingleby in his *Complete View of the Shakspere Controversy*, 1861. These are a list of certain inhabitants of Southwark in 1596 (p. 13) and a poor's rate assessment for the Clink Liberty in 1609 (p. 30). Both documents contain the name of Shakespeare, and both were first printed by Mr. Collier. With regard to the assessment list, it is somewhat strange that neither Mr. Staunton nor Dr. Ingleby mentions the first and more remarkable of the two copies. I need not, however, repeat what I have said on this subject in the Catalogue, and I will only call attention to the characteristic subtlety shown by the forger in altering the sums opposite the names which follow his interpolation of 'Mr Shakespeare—vi^d^.' The object of this apparently gratuitous falsification was to remove any ground for suspicion which might have arisen from the amount of Shakespeare's assessment, when those immediately above and below him paid respectively twopence and a penny. In 1868 Dr. Ingleby again came forward with evidence of an interpolation in Mr. Collier's printed version of a paper relating to Thomas Lodge. In this case also two copies of the same document are extant. This fact, which appears to have been unknown both to Mr. Collier and his critic, led to some confusion, as may be seen in the remarks on p. 15. But, although the copy used by Mr. Collier does contain the passage as he published it, there are particular words which are undoubtedly spurious; and Dr. Ingleby's con clusion, in so far as he denied that the original stated that Lodge was an actor, was perfectly correct.

As I have already stated, some of the papers which, before the collection was arranged, were thought to be lost have again come to light. Among them is the letter purporting to be written by R. Veale (p. 13), which Mr. Collier first printed in 1844 and again as recently as 1879.[1] Referring to it, Mr. Staunton (*Life of Shakespeare*, 1860, p. 31) wrote: 'The third of these papers has been sought for in vain, and I fear, like nine-tenths of the so-called "New Facts" relative to the life of Shakespeare, is not entitled to the smallest credence.' That this fear was amply justified will be evident to any impartial person who examines the actual document now recovered and observes particularly the laboriously careful manner in which the forger has copied a genuine signature lying before him.

All the forgeries above enumerated have already been openly denounced or marked as strongly suspicious, but the responsibility of condemning the remainder rests with myself. If, however, they have hitherto escaped notice, it is not so much because they are more skilfully executed as because they have probably never before been subjected to a rigorous

[1] In the second edition of his *History of Dramatic Poetry*. No hint is there given that its genuineness has ever been called in question; nor has any of the spurious matter printed in the earlier edition been withdrawn.

scrutiny. All of them, in fact, belong to the same most insidious class, and no doubt owe their immunity in a great measure to the genuine character of their surroundings, a mere interpolation, it may be of a single word, being easily passed over where a document wholly spurious would at once challenge attention. A typical example of the forger's ingenuity and method will be found on p. 18. The introduction here and there of such names as 'Lear,' 'Romeo,' 'Pericles,' &c., has had the effect, which was of course intended, of making an inventory of theatrical costumes 'much more important and interesting than a mere list of dresses would be supposed to be.' The words quoted are Mr. Collier's (*Memoirs of Edw. Allcyn*, p. 17); and the gravity with which he dilates on the significance of these names will excite different feelings in the mind of the reader, according to the opinion he is inclined to hold with regard to Mr. Collier's own share in the imposture.

The interpolations in Henslowe's Diary (pp. 158–162) are characterised by still greater audacity; and we can only be thankful that the hand, which did not scruple to tamper with the names of Nash, Marlow, Dekker, and Webster, stopped short of Shakespeare. Reverence, we may be sure, had nothing to do with the omission, which was more probably the result of a deliberate calculation of the chances of discovery. The risk in this case was of course proportionately greater. Although Malone in his extracts from the Diary might possibly have omitted the entries relating to less noted dramatists, he must infallibly have mentioned the occurrence of Shakespeare's name; and its alleged discovery therefore by a later writer was too likely to provoke troublesome enquiries. But, as it is, when we are asked to believe that all the eight fabricated entries formed part of the manuscript in the time of Malone, the assumption does violence to all probability, since it involves the remarkable coincidence that, from some unaccountable fatality, he missed every one of them, and that too although four at least are anything but inconspicuous. On the other hand, it may be suggested that if any one inserted them, it was Malone himself, in which case it must have been after the appearance of his Historical Account of the English Stage, with a view to future use for a second edition or on some other fitting opportunity. To this it is almost enough to reply that there is nothing in all Malone's published writings to justify the least suspicion that he was capable of forgery; but such an argument may be met by a still stronger objection. If these and the other Dulwich forgeries stood alone it might perhaps be admissible. It is, however, notorious that they belong to a connected series which culminates in the Perkins Folio, and the ramifications of which are found in places and documents to which it cannot be pretended that Malone ever had access. There is, indeed, the strongest reason for believing that one at least of the entries in Henslowe's Diary was not written until shortly before 1845, when it was first printed in Mr. Collier's edition of the MS. This is the forgery of the name of the pretended play 'Galfrido and Bernardo.' Thanks to Mr. Collier's instructive note, quoted on p. 158, the approximate date of the entry, as well as its particular object, which would otherwise have been obscure, may be easily divined; for it could only have been foisted in for the purpose of giving additional interest to the poem by John Drout on the same subject, an unique copy of which had been only *recently discovered.* And this being so, a pertinent question at once suggests itself, whether we have not here an important clue to the authorship of the forgery—whether, in short, any one was likely to have been at the pains to concoct an allusion to Drout's poem who was not more or less immediately concerned in its discovery or re-publication. Unfortunately the mystery, itself a little suspicious, which is observed in the preface to the re-print prevents this clue from being easily followed up. Excepting the two 'remarkable entries' about Robin Goodfellow (p. 162), which were also first printed in 1845, the rest of the forgeries in Henslowe's Diary must be of somewhat older date, since they all figure prominently in Mr. Collier's *History of Dramatic Poetry*, published in 1831. As I have treated each separately in its place, I will only observe that, on lately examining once again the entry quoted on p. 161, I found additional evidence of trickery, if any were wanted. The forgery of Webster's name, which is written above the word 'gwisse' or 'Guise,' was not a success; and even Mr. Collier remarked that it was 'perhaps' in a different hand. But, badly executed as it is, it seems to have been the result of a second attempt, for below the line are unmistakable traces of an erasure, so carefully made and smoothed over as scarcely to be detected except from the thinness of the paper. In this case luckily there was no possibility of destroying a failure by the simple process, which has too probably been elsewhere adopted, of cutting it bodily out of the volume.[1]

I now pass on to the interpolations, six in number, which are to be found in Alleyn's own Diary. Between these and the other Dulwich forgeries there is one very remarkable difference. The latter, as we have seen, have all been printed, and, as a simple statement of fact, it is necessary to add, printed first in every instance by Mr. Collier. With the forgeries in Alleyn's Diary it is otherwise, for I cannot find that they have been published or referred to either by Mr.

[1] In the sale-catalogue of J. Boswell's library, 1825, no. 3141, was included an exact transcript of Henslowe's Diary. If this could only be traced, it would furnish most valuable evidence.

Collier or any one else. Of the two spurious notices of Shakespeare's *As you like it* (p. 170) and *Romeo* (p. 175) there is nothing more to be said except that the forgery is gross and palpable; nor, in the latter case, has the forger weakened the effect of the evidence against him by a desperate attempt to erase the words. He was equally unsuccessful with his entry about 'poor Tom Dekker' (p. 183), which was so clearly suggested by the imprisoned poet's letters on p. 51. Here too he has tried hard to destroy what he had written, but was again prevented by the absorbent nature of the paper. The inserted 'B. Jonson' (p. 179) is noteworthy, not only as the single instance in which this name has been fraudulently introduced into the collection, but from the fact that Mr. Collier, writing in 1841 (*Memoirs*, p. 154), stated that Jonson was *not* mentioned in the Diary. For the dexterity with which advantage has been taken of an entry originally left incomplete, this forgery may be profitably compared with that of 'Robin Goodfellow' in Henslowe's Diary. But of all the interpolations in this MS. the most curious and instructive are the two on pp. 172, 174. The motive for the insertion of the words 'of the playhouse' and 'theatre' cannot possibly be mistaken, and the subject must be considered in connexion with Mr. Collier's 'facts tending to prove that Alleyn became the purchaser of Shakespeare's property in the Blackfriars Theatre' (*Memoirs of Edw. Alleyn*, pp. 103 *seqq.*). The date Mr. Collier fixes for Shakespeare's final departure from London is the spring of 1612; and he goes on to say that 'it seems very likely, from evidence now for the first time to be adduced,' that his (alleged) interest in the theatre passed to Alleyn as above. The 'facts' upon which he relies are two. The first is thus introduced: 'Among the miscellaneous scraps of paper at Dulwich College is one which appears to be a rough memorandum, in Alleyn's handwriting, of various sums paid by him in April, 1612, for the Blackfriars; and though the theatre is not there expressly named, it will be rendered evident hereafter that it was the "play-house." The paper is precisely in this form :—

'"April 1612

Money paid by me E. A. for the Blackfryers.	160*li*
More for the Blackfryers	126*li*
More againe for the Leasse	310*li*
The writingesf or the same and other small charges	3*li.* 6*s.* 8*d.*"'

Although this paper is nowhere to be found, it cannot of course be assumed that it never existed; but at the same time, as I shall presently show, it is in the highest degree improbable that the date was as Mr. Collier has given it. Be this, however, as it may, the most that the paper can be taken to prove is that Alleyn held property of some kind in the Blackfriars; and of this there was never any doubt. Mr. Collier's second 'fact' would, on the contrary, be conclusive enough, if it were only authentic. Such as it is, it will be found on p. 115, in the four words 'as the plaiehowse theare,' craftily interlined, where a fraud of this nature would be least suspected, in Alleyn's letter to Dr. Donne. That this forgery and the two in Alleyn's Diary above were written by the same hand and for the purpose of affording one another a mutual support, is self-evident; the strange thing is that, although Mr. Collier printed the first he did not print the others, but actually quoted at length the genuine entry in which one of them occurs without the interpolation. Whatever the explanation of this, his theory that Alleyn's Blackfriars property comprised the theatre has absolutely no foundation to rest upon. It might be enough to have pointed out that the only evidence in its favour is undeniably of modern manufacture; but it is possible to go still further. On Mr. Collier's own showing the property referred to in the paper above is identical with that constantly mentioned by Alleyn in his Diary, for which he paid 160*l.* a year rent to Edm. Traves. But, so far from having been acquired, as Mr. Collier makes out, in or before April, 1612, it did not come into his hands until Shakespeare had been dead for nearly a year. The real date of his lease, as we now know from Mun. 184 (p. 271), was 26 Mar., 1617; and it cannot therefore be too rash to conjecture that Mr. Collier's date is a misreading of the later year. In this way too we get an easy solution of what is otherwise a singular fact; for, if the date 1612 were correct, the transaction ought to be found recorded in Alleyn's Memorandum-Book (MS. viii.), where similar purchases are entered down to 1614. But there can be no stronger proof that the building which Alleyn was anxious to save from demolition in August, 1618, was not the Blackfriars Theatre than the sheriff's return in the Record Office quoted on p. 173. The language of this document is sufficiently precise; and, apart from the fact that the theatre was not a new building and so did not come under the statute, its situation, if at all represented by Playhouse Yard, makes its identity with Alleyn's houses in Swan Alley, which was at the other end of the parish, simply impossible.

All the cases of forgery detected have now been briefly touched upon,[1] but the very serious question of their authorship has yet to be decided. Here, however, the reader must be left to draw his own conclusions. This is not a controversial work, and the subject cannot be adequately discussed without going beyond the Dulwich collection and bringing into evidence the entire system of closely analogous im-

[1] See, however, MS. v. art. 52 (p. 146) for an instance of extreme minuteness in fraudulent manipulation.

postures which found their way into print in the second quarter of the present century. Although it is impossible to ignore the fact that Mr. Collier, who gave them to the world as genuine matter, has been distinctly charged with their fabrication, it is no part of my duty either to arraign or defend him. Having stated the facts, just as they stand, with regard to the Dulwich series, with which alone I am concerned, and having, as I hope, secured the collection from the risk of being similarly tampered with in the future, I have done all that is necessary; and if Mr. Collier's name has been specially prominent, the blame rests with himself. Even on the most charitable supposition, the ease with which he allowed himself to be imposed upon argues the most extraordinary carelessness and incapacity. On one point I think no doubt need be entertained. Although the style of handwriting adopted varies considerably and exhibits different degrees of imitative skill, my own decided opinion is that all the forgeries here were executed by one and the same person, whoever he may have been; and, looking both to their appearance and character, I certainly see no cause for making an exception of those in Alleyn's Diary. As the latter were doubtless meant for use and not inserted in mere wantonness, it would be interesting to learn whether an edition of the MS. was ever contemplated and, if so, by whom. It may be laid down as a general rule that literary frauds of the kind found at Dulwich are not concocted by one person in order that the benefit of them may be reaped by another; but there may conceivably be exceptions. After Malone's death there is nothing to show whether any one used the MSS. before Mr. Collier; but, while the earlier forgeries need not be anterior in date to 1831, the most recent may be as late as 1845 or, in the case of Alleyn's Diary, later still. At the most, there could only have been a very few persons who had access to the collection, and who, at the same time, were keenly enough interested in dramatic history not to shrink from actual fabrication in order to support particular theories or to have the credit of discovering new facts of professed importance.

Of the Alleyn collection in general nothing more need here be said; but the Court-Rolls of Dulwich manor, which have been very briefly catalogued, claim some notice. Independently of their genealogical and topographical value, it is superfluous to point out the interest of this particular class of record for the history of English nomenclature. There is no deficiency in this respect in the series at Dulwich, and in the earlier rolls especially a variety of surnames may be traced back to their primitive forms. Thus, to take a few examples only, there are, from nationality, le Freynsshe[1] and le Welsche, Inglysshe, Pycard, and Scot; from residence, By the Wode and Atte Wode, Atte Styghele and Atte Style, Atte Dene and Adene, In the Lane and Adlane, Atte Naysshe, Atte Welle, and the like, besides of course the many local names of the kind represented by Shrowesbury, de Waldene, and de Boloyne. Equally prominent are the names denoting occupation or office. Among others, they include le Cartere, le Webbe, le Mareschal, le Meleward, le Sephurde, le Taburer —whence Tabor—la Kembestre, a female comber or wool-carder—whence Kempster—and Spyndelman, a maker of spindles. Mental and moral qualities account for Margaret la Wyse and for Godeman; bodily characteristics for le White, Baldhevd, and Alice Whiteleg, though the last has been also derived from the Saxon Wihtlæg. In addition to these are

[1] Hence Frenchfield, in Dulwich (p. 282). In the same way nearly all the names of lands mentioned in the terrier on p. 135 and elsewhere, such as Annesfield, Browninges, Napps, Rigates, Spilmans, &c., date back from the earliest Rolls.

to be found le Brand, Courteour, and Hordappel; together with Juliana Kacheuache and Alice Wrekedod or Wrekedoddys, neither of which is easy to explain. Kachevache, indeed, is strongly suggestive of Kekewich, but the family who bear this name are supposed to have obtained it from a place called Kekewick in Cheshire. The jingle again recalls the term kicky-wicky or kicksy-wicksy, disdainfully applied by Parolles to a wife.[1] As to the other name, 'duds' being a well-known cant-word for clothes, Alice Wreck-duds may possibly represent a fourteenth-century equivalent for Shakespeare's Doll Tear-sheet. The common use of the prefix le or la, by which our ancestors supplied the want of a definite article in Latin, will be remarked, and it leads to the inference that some, if not most, of the above names were as yet merely indicative of the individual. And, even after they became, so to speak, stereotyped patronymics, new surnames were no doubt continually being formed. One variety of the process is exhibited here in the case of Robert Aylmer, *alias* Goodsone, where an alternative personal epithet—whether at first applied in compliment or irony, or merely meaning 'godson'—appears afterwards to have supplanted altogether the original surname, itself turning into Goosone and ultimately perhaps into Gosson. Gradual changes of the same kind, by which family names took their existing shapes, are elsewhere also seen actively at work, and in the succession of rolls we get such transitions as those of Spyndelman into Spyleman and Spilman, In the Lane into Lane, and Atte Bregge into Brigges. As curiosities of the fifteenth century I may instance Pottesblode, Goldman, the romantic Gawayn, Pyebaker, Drynk-

[1] He wears his honour in a box unseen,
That hugs his kicky-wicky here at home.
All's well that ends well, act. ii. sc. 3.

water, Longswete, Laweman, Ida Inquirour and Thomas Deville. The last, which is probably the same as Dybbyll (p. 276), is perhaps not so bad a name as it looks. The sixteenth century yields Cownsellor, Sharparowe, and, worst of all, Bugbeard.[1] Another historically interesting name makes its appearance, *temp.* Elizabeth, in Becket, of the same origin probably as 'Thomas Becke, son of Giles a Becke,' who was steward of the manor.

With regard to the subject-matter of the Rolls, I can only refer briefly to a few of the more remarkable presentments at the court of the manor. The earliest specially worth quoting is in 1399, when complaint was made that 'quidam malefactores qui dicuntur Lumbardes' came with ferrets and traps into the Lord's warren for the purpose of catching rabbits. The term Lumbardes[2] is very curious. It appears to be employed generically to denote a particular class of evil-doers, but how they came to be so designated it is difficult to understand. Although the Lombard merchants of London were open to charges of usurious dealings, poaching was about the last offence to which they were likely to be addicted. It is just possible, however, that a contemptuous abuse of their name was one result of their general unpopularity at this period. Evidence that they were in ill-favour at the beginning of the reign of Henry IV. is found in the Chronicle of Adam of Usk (ed. E. M. Thompson, p. 53), who speaks of severe restrictions being placed upon them in 1400.

The Roll for 1402 contains the first of a long series of entries relating to Romseluer. Under this head 1*d.* was then claimed for the Lord from every tenant owning beasts to the

[1] The most curious name in the Catalogue comes, however, from Cheshire. This is John Godsendhimus (p. 78), who was perhaps what is euphemistically termed a love-child.

[2] 'Lumbardes,' perhaps for 'Lubbardes,' lubbers or loafers.

value of 30*d.*, the authority of an old Custumary being adduced in support of the contention. The tenants, however, denied all knowledge of such a custom, and it was therefore resolved to examine the Rolls to discover when it was last presented and how it fell into disuse. Although the result of this enquiry is not stated, it was evidently in favour of the Lord, the payment being regularly made from 1403 onwards. It is entered under a multiplicity of forms, such as Romseluer, Rompans, Rompeny, Romppeny, Rumpepeny, Rumppenys, Romppenes, and Rome pence. Notwithstanding the similarity of name, it can hardly have had anything to do with the so-called Peter's pence, paid yearly to the Pope. It continued to be paid after this impost was suppressed by Henry VIII. in 1534, and latterly it is represented as a customary payment for the right of common pasture.

Besides the ordinary business relating to the descent and transfer of land, which was held 'per virgam,' the court, as usual, took cognisance of various offences and breaches of manorial rights. Cases of assault, the use of false measures, the breaking of the assise of bread and beer, neglect to clear watercourses, and such like, are of constant occurrence. Fines too were imposed for digging turf 'in solo domini,' for cutting down a tree to take a swarm of bees, for tearing wool off a sheep's back, and for milking other people's cows; and in 1440 several persons were amerced for not coming 'ad le Bedrepe in autumpno, ut debuerunt, quum summoniti fuerunt,' the so-called Bid-reap being a day's service at harvest due to the Lord. The reign of Henry VII. seems to have been a quarrelsome period in the manor. Assailants were no longer content with drawing blood 'cum i baculo,' but had recourse to the more formidable 'hokebill,' 'pychfork,' and 'hanger'; and the fines had to be raised from 4*d.* to 1*s.* and 1*s.* 8*d.* One Richard Lane showed himself especially unmanageable, and in 1487 he shared with John Lane and two women the distinction of being presented as 'communes garulatores et pacem [pacis] domini regis perturbatores.' The effect upon him, however, was but slight, for he was in trouble again the next year, and he was fined for assault with a 'hokyd byll' as late as 1523. Another class of bad character appears in 1522 in the person of John Wylkokes, who had to pay 10*s*. 'quia custodit hospicium vocatum a blynde ostery et supportat homines et mulieres malæ gubernacionis.' Later in the same reign, in 1533, we get an ordinance forbidding the collection of 'les crabbes' before St. Bartholomew's Day, 24 Aug.; and in 1564 the whole homage were commanded under penalty to look to the proper placing of the 'meare stones,' or boundary marks. At the same court—to select one such instance out of many—John Bagger was fined 1*s*. for selling beer 'per le pottes vocatos stone cruses et non per le pottes sigillatos cum sigillo.'

Several other entries in Elizabeth's reign attest the enforcement of the well-known statute 33 Hen. VIII. cap. ix. for the encouragement of archery and the restraint of unlawful games. Thus in 1574 a number of persons were presented 'quia luserunt apud quoddam certamen illicitum vocatum Loggettes.' Logget is a diminutive form of log, and the game was played by throwing small staves or billets of wood at a stake fixed in the ground.[1] It answered therefore to the modern 'Aunt Sally' more closely than to nine-pins, with which it has sometimes been identified. Again, in 1578 Christopher Curson was fined 6*s*. 8*d*. for playing 'apud cartas lusorias vocatas cardes,' and in 1587 John Lewes and others had each to pay 4*d*. for playing 'ad globos,' or bowls. The same game is apparently referred to in a presentment made in 1597, that Thos.

[1] 'Did these bones cost no more the breeding, but to play at loggats with 'em?'—*Hamlet*, act. v. sc. 1.

Calton and eleven more 'gobulaverunt in aperto loco contra formam statuti.' The party in this case got off cheaply with a penalty of *2d.* a head. In 1576 there are two entries of a man being fined *3s. 4d.* 'quia usus est galliro in die dominica'; where 'galliro' doubtless stands for 'galero,' a hat. The penalty was incurred under the statute 13 Eliz., cap. xix., 1570, by which every person above seven years of age, excepting the nobility and others, was compelled to wear upon Sundays and holy-days 'a cap of wool knit, thicked and dressed in England,' &c.[1] This was for the benefit of the English cappers, multitudes of whom, according to the preamble of the statute 8 Eliz., cap. xi., 1565, were 'impoverished and decayed by the excessive use of hats and felts.'

Walter Boane, fined *1s.* 'for a drounkard' in 1611, is only worth mentioning as a melancholy example of confirmed evil habits. The man became a poor-brother of Dulwich College in 1619, and his bibulous propensities are more than once referred to in the Founder's Diary. The last entry which I shall quote from the Rolls is dated April, 1622. It records that Theodore Owle was fined *40s.* because his 'penny wheaten bredd' weighed but 7¾ ounces, whereas, wheat being sold at the last market for *40s.* the quarter, it ought to have weighed 12 ounces or more.

It still remains that I should say a few words on the subject of the manuscripts which are not included in the Alleyn collection proper. The only volumes in the body of the Catalogue which call for remark are those relating to the two collections of pictures bequeathed to the College by William Cartwright and Sir Peter Francis Bourgeois. In dealing with Cartwright's

[1] There is an allusion to this statute in Shakespeare :—

'Well, better wits have worn plain statute caps.'

Love's Labour's Lost, act. v. sc. 2.

autograph catalogue (MS. xiv.) I have contented myself with extracting the titles of the portraits, which alone possess any interest; and I have added such brief explanatory notes as seemed necessary. The contents of MS. xvi. are more important, and have been more fully treated. Among them, the letters addressed by Le Brun, the picture-dealer, to Noel Desenfans, the original collector of what is now known as the Dulwich College Gallery, are sufficiently curious and interesting to be printed at length, although it is unfortunately not possible to trace many of the pictures to which the writer refers. I have also reproduced in full the list of the collection of Desenfans drawn up by himself for the purpose of insurance in 1804. As an authentic record of its extent at that date, with the owner's opinion as to the authorship and money's worth of each picture, the list is of considerable value; and it is a pity that its existence was not made known in time enough for notice to be taken of it in the Catalogue of the Dulwich Gallery recently published.

The manuscripts included in the Appendix are of a more miscellaneous character and range over a longer period. Two of the earliest, MSS. xxii. and xxiv., deserve particular notice. The former is made up of fragments of several manuscripts connected together probably not later than the fifteenth century, but the most important article is the English poem on the Life of Christ. Though it would be rash to assert that the copy is unique, I know of no other, and it has no small philological interest. MS. xxiv. contains part of Robert Mannyng's well-known poem *Handlyng Synne*, copies of which, however, are so rare that the discovery of another, even in a mutilated condition, is welcome. Among the later volumes, the most interesting are the political tracts, MSS. xxviii., xxix., xxxi., and xxxv. The first of these has the distinction of being the original copy presented by the author to Sir Christopher Hatton; and, addressed as it is by the Clerk of the Privy

Council to the Lord Chancellor, the doctrine laid down in it is somewhat startling. Osborne's translation of a speech of Æschines (MS. xxvii.) is also the original, dedicated to Sir C. Hatton; and the fact that the letters in MS. xxxv. are addressed to one of Hatton's descendants makes it probable that some of the other volumes belonged to the same family. They must have come to Dulwich at some time after 1689, when the above letters were written, but how they found their way thither is a mystery.

In conclusion, I desire to express my obligations to the Governors of the College for the readiness with which they agreed to my suggestions with regard to the plan of the Catalogue, and for the general freedom and indulgence accorded me during its preparation. I have further to thank the Rev. William Rogers, the Chairman, for giving me facilities for the inspection of the register of Alleyn's native parish of St. Botolph, Bishopsgate, of which he is Rector; and to Mr. William Young, another member of the Court, I am indebted for the loan of some highly interesting and useful notes, which I venture to hope he will hereafter expand into a history of the College. From the Rev. Alfred Carver, D.D., the Master, I have throughout received cordial assistance, though I have too often been compelled to trespass upon his valuable time. Dr. Carver's interest in the collection is of long standing. A proposal that the manuscripts should be arranged and catalogued was made by him, as I am informed, twenty years ago; but, although it was at once sanctioned by the Governors, various circumstances made it advisable to defer the execution of the design till a more favourable opportunity. Lastly, I must record my sense of the kindness of my friend and official chief, Mr. E. M. Thompson, who has not only given me the benefit of his constant advice, but has read all the sheets in their passage through the press.

Errata.

Page 3, note 2, *for* Mun. 75 *read* Mun. 84.
,, 8, line 1, *for* his Maist. Chamber *read* hir Maist. Chamber.
,, 21, note 1, *for* Rich. Drayton *read* Mich. Drayton.
,, 67, note 4, *for* for 160li *read* 60l.
,, 128, line 5, *for* father-in-law *read* step-father.
,, 134, line 1, *for* [1609–10?] *read* 29 May, 1610.
,, 255, line 3, *after* commissioners *omit the comma.*
,, 328, Mun. 558, *for* 19 June, 1612, *read* 19 June, 1613.
,, 329, last line, *for* and *read* land.

MANUSCRIPTS AND MUNIMENTS

OF

ALLEYN'S COLLEGE OF GOD'S GIFT

AT

DULWICH.

MS. No. I.

ALLEYN PAPERS. Vol. I. Letters and Papers relating to the English Drama and Stage during the life of Edward Alleyn and to the subsequent History of the Fortune Theatre; 1559–1662.

1. LETTER from Thomas Phillipson to Francis ——ton, merchant, in London, chiefly on matters connected with the recovery of debts, mentioning 'your brother Phillips' and 'cozen Thomas Bacon,' John Welcheman, George Gybson, and others, and including the passages, 'I founde none so vnresonabell as Wm Kempte,[1] for I was not so few tymes

[1] Possibly Will. Kemp, the famous comedian, whose name is spelt Kempt in the list of actors prefixed to the folio Shakespeare of 1623. If so, Kemp was an older contemporary of Shakespeare than has hitherto been supposed. According to Mr. J. P. Collier (*Hist. of Dram. Poetry*, &c., ed. 1879, vol. iii. p. 332), the earliest mention of him is in 1589, when T. Nash dedicated to him his *Almond for a Parrot*; and he appears to have been alive so late as 1605. The terms, however, in which he is addressed by Nash show that his reputation was then fully established, and he may have been quite a young man when this letter was

as twenty to speke with him, and in the ende, when I met him, his awnser was otherwise then I thoughte it woulde have bin, but nowe I parceve he hathe not his name for noughte. Yet, if I were as youe, I woulde not so take it at his hande; for, if I mighte be so bolde as to wrighte it, it was playne k[na]very and a harde shiftinge awnser, for to say, when I cam to him for to have him firme the bille, that he had lefte a sh[irte?] at my howse worthe bothe them, which I have lefte with my brother Marke for youe, promysinge youe of my faythe that sence your goinge it was never worne of no man, nor I dare saye shall not be. Wherefore youe maye doe as youe thincke good, but in my judgement I promis youe he were worthey to pay dobell for them. . . . As for Anthony Babington, he is as blynde as youe lefte him, and yet he wente downe into the contrey for money, but, as he sayethe, he coulde not get his charges of his brother'; Gravesend, 3 Aug., 1559. f. 1.

Formerly used as a cover for art. 2 in MS. v., below; owing to this the address has been so much worn as to be hardly legible.

2. DEED OF SALE by Richard Jones,[1] of London, yeoman,

---

written. The name was a common one, as Mr. Collier shows; but he does not mention Will. Kempe, son of Steph. Kempe, of Broxbourne, apprenticed to Will. Cooke, 1 Nov., 1566 (*Stationers' Register*, ed. Arber, vol. i. p. 146*b*), or Will. Kemp, whose marriage to Cole Holwyn is entered in the register of St. Botolph's, Bishopsgate, 13 June, 1568. Mr. Jos. Hunter (*Chorus Vatum Anglicanorum*, Brit. Mus., Add. MS. 24487, f. 128) gives some reasons in favour of a not very probable theory that the actor was identical with Will. Kemp, of Spain's Hall, Essex, who imposed on himself a vow of silence for seven years on account of idle words he had spoken. In that case he was born in 1555, and died in 1628. The occurrence of the name of Anthony Babington in the same letter is curious, for a Will. Kempe was the author of *A Dutifull Invective against the most Haynous Treasons of Ballard and Babington*, 1587. The Anthony Babington here mentioned was probably an older member of the same family as the conspirator, perhaps Anth. Babington, of Tymmore, buried at Lichfield, 16 Mar., 1579 (Nichols, *Topographer and Genealogist*, vol. i. p. 335).

[1] A member, with Edw. Alleyn and Robert Browne, of the Earl of Worcester's company in 1586 (*Shakespeare Soc. Papers*, vol. iv. p. 145); after-

to Edward Allen, of London, gent., for 37*l.* 10*s.*, of all his 'share, parte and porcion of playinge apparelles, playe Bookes, Instrumentes and other commodities' held by him 'joyntelye with the same Edwarde Allen, John Allen,[1] citizen and Inholder of London, and Roberte Browne,[2] yoman'; 3 Jan., 31 Eliz., 1588[9]. Signed; with seal, 'R.I.' f. 3.

Printed in the *Memoirs of Edward Alleyn*, by J. P. Collier, Shakespeare Society, 1841, p. 198.

On the back, in the hand of Edward Alleyn, is a list of thirteen documents relating to the family of Calton and their property at Dulwich, dated from 1542 to 1611. They are among the muniments catalogued below.

3. DEED OF SALE by William Wardelo, of London, yeoman, to John Alleyn, of London, 'inholder,' for 5*l.*, of 'one longe clocke [cloak] of black velvett and lyned with taffatye'; 8 Aug., 31 Eliz. [1589]. Signed; with seal. f. 4.

4. DEED OF SALE by Isaacke Burges, of Clifford's Inn, London, gent., to John Allene, of London, innholder, for 16*l.*, of 'one cloke of velvett, with a cape imbrothered with gold, pearles and redd stones, and one roabe of cloth of golde'; 23 Nov., 33 Eliz., 1590. Signed; with seal. Witnesses, John Deane, scrivener, and James Tonstall.[3] f. 5.

---

wards one of the Lord Admiral's players (Henslowe's *Diary*, pp. 6, 257). Possibly the Rich. Jones who was baptised at St. Botolph's, Bishopsgate, 16 Mar., 1561–2. See also below, art. 8.

[1] Elder brother of Edw. Alleyn, described in 1580 as servant to 'the Lord Sheffeilde,' and in 1589 as 'servaunte to me, the Lo. Admyrall' (see below, MS. iii. art. 3, MS. iv. art. 11). He died before 5 May, 1596 (see below, Mun. 110).

[2] See art. 8. Mr. Collier is wrong in assuming Rob. Browne to be Alleyn's stepfather (*Memoirs*, p. 4). The name of the latter was John Browne (Mun. 75).

[3] Member of the Earl of Worcester's company in 1586, afterwards of the Lord Admiral's. In Henslowe's *Diary*, pp. 6, 69, 76, 78, he is called Donstall and Donstone. The baptism of a Dunstone Tunstall is entered in the register of St. Botolph's, Bishopsgate, 20 Aug., 1572.

Printed, *Alleyn Papers*, ed. J. P. Collier, Shakespeare Society, 1843, p. 11.

5. DEED OF SALE by John Clyffe, of Ingstone [Ingatestone], co. Essex, gent., to John Allen, of London, innholder, and Edw. Allen, of London, gent., for 20*l.* 10*s.*, of 'one blacke velvet cloake with sleves ymbrodered all with silver and golde, lyned with blacke satten stryped with golde'; 6 May, 33 Eliz., 1591. Signed; with seal. Witnesses, Godfrey Reyner, scrivener, and James Tonstall. f. 6.

Printed, *Alleyn Papers*, p. 12.

6. W. P. TO EDWARD ALLEN, urging him to accept a theatrical wager against 'the partie affected to Bently,' with 'libertie to make choice of any one playe that either Bently or Knell[1] plaide,' and assuring him that his 'meaninge was not to preiudice Peeles credit': accompanied by six lines of verse, beginning, 'Deny me not, sweete Nedd, the wager's downe'; *circ.* 1590. Finely written, with the words 'Ned Allen,' 'sweete Nedd,' and 'English crowne,' in gilt letters. f. 7.

Printed by Malone, *Shakespeare*, ed. Boswell, 1821, vol. iii. p. 335, and in Collier's *Memoirs of Edw. Alleyn*, p. 12. See also Dyce, *Works of George Peele*, 1828, p. x.

7. SEVENTEEN LINES OF VERSE beginning, 'Sweete Nedde, nowe wynne an other wager,' purporting to be written on an occasion similar to the above. f. 8.

First printed by Mr. J. P. Collier, *Memoirs of Edw. Alleyn*, p. 13; but condemned with reason as spurious by Mr. N. E. S. A. Hamilton, *An Enquiry into the Genuineness of the MS. Corrections in*

---

[1] Bently and Knell are mentioned prominently by Thomas Heywood among the actors before his own time (*Apology for Actors*, 1612), and associated with Tarlton and Ned Allen by T. Nash (*Pierce Pennilesse*, 1592). Bently's name figures in an account of a fray at Norwich in 1583 (Halliwell, *Illustrations of the Life of Shakespeare*, 1874, p. 118).

Mr. J. Payne Collier's Annotated Shakspere, folio, 1632, &c., 1860, pp. 95, 118, and Dr. C. M. Ingleby, *A Complete View of the Shakspere Controversy*, 1861, p. 267, with lithographed facsimile.

8. RICHARD JONES[1] to Edward Alleyn: thanks him for his great bounty during his sickness; is 'to go over beyond the seeas with Mr. Browne and the company,' and prays for a loan of 3*l.*, with which to release from pawn a suit of clothes and a cloak; will send over the first money he gets, for in England he gets nothing, or only a shilling a day; prays to God for his health and 'mistris Allenes'; [Feb., 1591–2?]. Endorsed by Alleyn, 'Mr. Jones his letter wheron I lent hym 3^{l}'; and in the margin, partially torn away, is an acquittance to 'Master Allen,' dat. . . . Feb. f. 9.

Printed, Malone, vol. xxi. p. 396; *Mem. of Edw. Alleyn*, p. 96; *Alleyn Papers*, p. 19.

9. EDWARD ALLEYN[2] to his wife, addressed as 'my good sweett harte and loving mouse': sends her a thousand

---

[1] See Cohn, *Shakespeare in Germany*, 1865, p. xxxviii., where is a passport from Lord Howard in favour of Robert Browne, John Bradstriet, Thomas Saxfield [Sackville], and Richard Jones, going to Germany 'avec intention . . . . d'exercer leurs qualitez en faict de musique agilitez et joeuz de commedies, tragedies et histoires,' dat. 10 Feb., 1591 [1–2?]. If this letter, as is almost certain, refers to the same expedition, the mention of Mrs. Alleyn is curious, since Alleyn was not yet married to Joan Woodward. It is some slight evidence, therefore, in favour of the tradition that he was three times married. See *Memoirs*, p. 180.

Rich. Jones, as appears from Henslowe's *Diary*, was back in England between the years 1594 and 1601, but he seems to have been again abroad before Henslowe's death in Jan., 1615–6 (see below, artt. 111, 112). Rob. Browne was at Leyden with a company in Oct., 1590. Cohn wrongly supposes that he was Alleyn's stepfather (see above, art. 2); but he is right, perhaps, in identifying him with Rob. Browne, who accompanied the Earl of Lincoln on an embassy to Cassel in 1596. The latter, however, may have been a messenger of the Privy Chamber of the same name (*Cal. State Papers*, 1598–1601, pp. 191, 192, &c.). A Rob. Browne, of Shoreditch, occurs below (art. 12), and another, of Clerkenwell (art. 66). See also art. 38 and Collier, *Hist. of Dram. Poetry*, &c., vol. iii. p. 386.

[2] Written when Alleyn was playing in the provinces, owing to the prevalence of the plague in London. A license to play out of London 'in anie other cities,

commendations, hoping that she[1] and his father, mother, and sister are in health; has no news except that all are well, but is sorry to hear that she has been 'by my lorde maiors officer mad to rid in a cart' with all her fellows, for which he will be revenged on his return; Chelmsford, 2 May, 1593. Addressed, as if to himself, 'To E. Alline on the banck side.' f. 10.

Printed, Lysons, *Environs of London*, vol. i. p. 88; *Mem. of Edw. Alleyn*, p. 24.

10. PHILIP HENSLOWE to his 'sonne Edward Allen': sends hearty commendations from himself, his [Alleyn's] mother [-in-law] and sister Elizabeth, and last, not least, from his 'mowse,' who prays night and day for his health and quick return; writes in order to certify him that the joiner has been with them, and has had the money which was promised him, and that all other matters are well; John Gryges[2] and his wife send their commendations, and he himself does the same to all the company; London, 5 July, 1593. Signed, in the same hand, 'Your power mowse for euer and your asured frendes tell death Phillipe Henslow and Ag[nes Henslow]'; and addressed, 'This be delyvered vnto my welbeloued husband Mr Edward Allen with speade.' f. 11*b*.

11. EDWARD ALLEYN to his 'good sweett mouse':

townes and corporacions where the infection is not' was granted, 6 May, 1593, to 'Edward Allen, servaunt to the right honorable the L. Highe Admiral, William Kemp, Thomas Pope, John Heminges, Augustine Philipes, and George Brian, being al one companie, servantes to our verie good the lord the lord Strainge' (Halliwell, *Illustrations*, p. 33).

[1] 'Edward Alen wasse maryed vnto Jone Woodward the 22 of [*sic*] daye of October, 1592' (Henslowe's *Diary*, p. 3). Her mother, Agnes Woodward, had married as her second husband Philip Henslowe, and he and Alleyn habitually called each other father and son.

[2] Probably John Gryges, carpenter, the builder of the Rose Theatre in 1587. See below, Mun. 16.

commends himself heartily to her, and to his father, mother, and sister Bess; hopes the sickness will escape their house, and advises her to keep it fair and clean, to throw water every evening before the door and in the back premises, and to have in the windows 'good store of rwe and herbe of grace, and with all the grace of god which must be obtaynd by prayers'; thanks her for her letter, which he received at Bristol by Richard Cowley,[1] and sends by the bearer, Thomas Pope's kinsman, his 'whit wascote' to keep till his return; any further letters must be sent 'by the cariers of Shrowsbery[2] or to Westchester[3] or to York, to be keptt till my Lord Stranges[4] players com'; writes from Bristol 'this Wensday after saynt Jams his day, being redy to begin the playe of hary of Cornwall'[5]; sends his commendations to Mr. Grigs, his wife and household, and to his [Alleyn's] sister Phillyps; [24 July, 1593?]. In a postscript:—complains that she sends no news of her 'domestycall matters,' as how her 'distilled watter proves or this or that or anything'; prays her to let his 'orayng tawny stokins of wolen be dyed a very good blak' for the winter, and to remember to sow the bed which was parsley with 'spinage' in September, since he will not be home till All Hallows. Addressed 'to Mr Hinslo, on of

[1] Both Cowley and Pope were afterwards in the Lord Chamberlain's company. See memoirs of them in Collier's *Hist. of Dram. Poetry*, vol. iii. pp. 356, 387. Cowley seems to have joined Lord Strange's company after the license quoted above, art. 9.

[2] A payment of 40*s.* to 'my L. Strange and my L. Admyralls players' is recorded in the Shrewsbury corporation MSS., 1593 (Halliwell, *Illustrations*, p. 33).

[3] Chester. See Camden's *Britannia*, ed. 1772, vol. i. p. 481.

[4] Ferdinando Stanley, Lord Strange, succeeded his father as fifth Earl of Derby in Dec., 1593, and died 16 Apr., 1594. At his death his company appears to have passed to Lord Hunsdon, Lord Chamberlain.

[5] Acted by 'Lord Stranges mene' in London, 25 Feb., 1591-2, and subsequently, but not marked as a new play (Henslowe's *Diary*, p. 21).

the gromes of his Maist. Chamber,[1] dwelling on the banksid right over against the clink.'[2] f. 13.

Printed, Malone, vol. xxi. p. 389; *Mem. of Edw. Alleyn*, p. 25.

12. PHILIP HENSLOWE to his 'welbeloved sonne Edward Allen': all send him hearty commendations, and his 'mowse' prays day and night for his health; they have been 'flytted with feare of the sycknes,' but are all well, though it has been in almost every house round, and whole households have died; the 'baylle[3] doth scape but he smealles monstrusly for feare,' for out of 1,603 deaths in all during the last week 113-0-5 [*sic*] were from the plague,[4] which is as yet the highest number; of other news there is none, 'but that Robart Brownes[5] wife in Shordech and all her cheldren and howshowld be dead and heare dores shent vpe'; the joiner has brought a 'corte coberd'[6] and set up a 'portowle' in the chamber, and promises a good bedstead;[7] the garden is well and the 'spenege bead' not forgotten; his 'orenge colord stockenes' are dyed, but there is no market at Smithfield either to buy his cloth or sell his horse, which, as no one would offer more than 4*l.* for it, has been sent into the country till his return; [Aug., 1593]. Signed, in the same

[1] His appointment to this office must have been recent, for his name is not in the list attached to a warrant, dat. 7 Apr., 1592 (Brit. Mus., Add. MS. 5750, f. 114). It is last but two in a similar list, 26 Jan., 1599 (*ibid.* f. 117).

[2] 'Then next is the Clinke, a gaol or prison for the trespassers in those parts [of Southwark]—namely, in old time, for such as should brabble, frey, or break the peace on the said bank,' &c. (Stow, *Survey*, ed. Thoms, 1876, p. 151).

[3] Matthew Woodward, bailiff to Lord Montague (art. 38, below, and MS. iv. art. 45).

[4] 'For all this yeere London was most grievously afflicted with the Pestilence . . insomuch as there dyed this yeere of the pestilence and other diseases within the city and the suburbs 17,890' (Camden, *Annals*, ed. 1635, p. 423).

[5] See artt. 2, 8.

[6] Court cupboard, a moveable sideboard for plate, without drawers (Halliwell, *Archaic Dict.*).

[7] 'Item pd. vnto the Joyner for the beadstead, xv[s]' (Henslowe's *Diary*, p. 2).

hand, 'Your poore and asured frend tell death Phillipe Hensley', and 'Your lovinge wiffe tylle deathe Jone Allen'; and addressed, 'To my wealbeloved sonne Edward Allen, one of my lorde Stranges players,' &c. f. 15.

Printed, *Memoirs of Edw. Alleyn*, p. 27.

13. PHIL. HENSLOWE to Edw. Alleyn: all send hearty commendations and are glad to hear of his good health, for they heard that he had been very sick at Bath and that another had played his part; they feared much because they had no letter when the other wives had, and his 'mowse' wept not a little, thinking he had conceived some unkindness of her; prays him to continue to write, as they themselves would do oftener if they knew where to send; they received a letter written at 'Seant James tide,'[1] mentioning his 'whitte wascote' and his 'lvte bockes,' and another which Peter[2] brought with his horse; his wife prays night and day for his health, and that God may 'seace his hand' in order that she may have him home again; the garden is doing very well, and the 'beanes are growen to hey headge and well coded,' but his tenants 'weax very power' and can pay no rent; the joiner says he will make 'such good stufe and suche good peneworthes' as he hopes will content him; as for his counsel to keep the house clean, &c., they do this and more, for they 'strowe yt withe hartie prayers vnto the lorde'; prays him to commend him to his fellows, for lack of whom he grows poor, so that he can send no gifts but a good and faithful heart; thanks them all for their tokens, and as for the plague, can send no exact account, as it is forbidden, but 1,700 or

[1] Apparently art. 11, above, but there is no mention there of any lute books. In a deed, dat. 26 Apr., 1595 (Mun. 106, below), Alleyn is formally described as a 'musicion.'

[2] The same probably whom in 1595 Henslowe calls 'my soger peter'—i.e. the soldier furnished and armed by him (*Diary*, p. 72).

1,800 die in a week of all sicknesses; London, 14 Aug., 1593. f. 17. Signed, in the same hand, 'Your lovinge ffather and mother to owr powers P H. A[gnes]' and 'Your lovinge wiffe Johne Allen.' f. 17.

Printed, *Mem. of Edw. Alleyn*, p. 29.

14. PHIL. HENSLOWE to Edward Alleyn: complains that they do not hear from him as they would wish; if they themselves could send as certainly, they would write often; almost all his [Henslowe's] neighbours are dead of the plague, and his two 'wenches' have had it, but have recovered, and he, his wife, and two daughters are very well; the market at Smith field was very bad, and as no one offered more than 4*l.* for his [Alleyn's] horse, it has been sent into the country till his return; as for his cloak, there was no cloth sold by retail, but all was bought up wholesale in two days, 'so the fayre lasted but iii dayes'; his stockings are dyed, the joiner has set up the 'portolle' and brought a 'corte cobert,' and the garden is very well, the 'spenege bead and all sowed'; Lord Pembroke's[1] players 'ar all at home and hauffe bene thes v or sixe weackes, for they cane not saue ther carges with trauell, as I heare, and weare fayne to pane [pawn] ther parell for ther carge'; .... 'ther hath abated this last two weacke of the sycknes' 435, and between 1,100 and 1,200 have died in all during the last week; London, 28 Sept., 1593. In a postscript:—his wife prays him to send word what 'goodman Hudson'[2] pays for rent; as for his tenants, nothing can be got from them; Greges [Griggs] and his wife send commendations, and also 'your sister Phillipes' and her husband,[3]

[1] Henry Herbert, second Earl of Pembroke, succ. 17 Mar., 1569–70, died 19 Jan., 1600–1. His company was acting at the Rose in Oct., 1597 and 1600 (Henslowe's *Diary*, pp. 102, 181). It was ultimately merged into that of the Lord Chamberlain.

[2] Ralph Hudson, one of Alleyn's tenants in Bishopsgate (Mun. 97, below).

[3] Mr. Collier suggests that this was Augustine Phillips, the actor (*Hist. of*

who have lost two or three out of their house.' Signed, in the same hand, by Henslowe and 'Jonne Allen comendinge to her mvnshen.' *Imperfect*, wanting about eight lines at the bottom of the first page. f. 19.

Printed, *Mem. of Edw. Alleyn*, p. 31.

15. LETTER to 'Mysteris Alline on the bancksyd' from her 'honest, ancyent and loving servant pige,'[1] written in jocular terms and ending:—'I swear to you by the fayth of a fustyan kinge never to retorne till fortune vs bryng with a joyfull metyng to lovly London. I sesse [cease], your petty prety pratlyng parlyng pyg; by me John Pyk. Mystiris, I praye you kepe this that my mayster may se it, for I gott on to wright it, Mr Doutone,[2] and my M^r knowes nott of it.' f. 21.

16. PETITION to the Privy Council from 'the Lord Straunge his servantes and plaiers' for license to return to their 'plaie-howse on the Banckside,' both on account of the heavy expense of travelling in the country and the loss suffered in their absence by the watermen plying on the river; [1593]. *Contemporary copy.* f. 23.

Printed, *Mem. of Edw. Alleyn*, p. 33.

17. PETITION to 'my Lorde Hayward,[3] Lorde highe Ad-

Dram. Poetry, vol. iii. p. 322), but the supposition is the less probable since Aug. Phillips appears to have been at the time with Alleyn in the country (art. 9, above, n. 2).

[1] 'Pigg' occurs as an actor in the plot of *Frederick and Basilea* (Malone, vol. iii. p. 356), and as 'Pyge' and 'Pygge' in inventories of theatrical properties (*ibid.*, pp. 310, 313, 315). In the latter case Malone suggests that Psyche is meant, and Mr. Collier (*Hist. of Dram. Poetry*, vol. iii. p. 164) that for 'Pyge' should be read 'Page,' the hero of the play *Page of Plymouth*. See also Henslowe's *Diary*, pp. 150, 274, 276. The letter has no date, but Pyk was doubtless at this time with Alleyn in the provinces.

[2] Tho. Dowton or Downton, of the Ld. Admiral's company, and named at the head of Prince Henry's players in the Privy Seal, 30 Apr., 1607. In Linc. Inn MS. clviii. he is called Doubton, servant to the Elector Palatine, 10 Jas. I. (Brit. Mus., Add. MS. 24502, f. 60*b*).

[3] Charles Howard, succ. as Lord Howard of Effingham 1573, cr. Earl of

mirall of Englande and one of her Ma[ties] moste honnorable previe Counsayle,' from 'Phillipp Henslo and others, the poore watermen on the bancke side,' praying him to withdraw his warrant 'for the restraynte of a playe howse belonginge vnto the saide Phillipp Henslo, one of the groomes of her Ma[ties] Chamber,' and to give him license 'to have playinge in his saide howse duringe suche tyme as others have'; [1593]. With signatures or marks of William Dorret, M[r] of her Maiestes barge, Gilbart Rockett, on of her M[ties] wattermen, Wylliam Hodgyes, Thomas Jarmonger, on of her M[ties] wattermen, William Tuchenner, on of her M[ties] mean, Isack Towell, Edward Robartes, on of her M[ties] wattermen, Thomas Cox, Thomas Edmanson, James Russell, Henry Draper, Edward Adysson, on of her M[ties] wattermen, Christopher Topen, Jeames Granger, Fardinando Blacke, and Parker Playne. f. 25.

Printed, *Mem. of Edw. Alleyn*, p. 34.

18. WARRANT from the Privy Council, rescinding an order whereby they 'did restraine the Lorde Straunge his servauntes from playinge at the rose[1] on the banckside and enioyned them to plaie three daies at newington Butts,'[2] and permitting that 'the Rose maie be at libertie without anye restrainte, so longe as yt shalbe free from infection of sicknes'; [*circ.* April, 1594]. *Contemporary copy.* f. 27.

Printed, *Mem. of Edw. Alleyn*, p. 36.

Nottingham 1596, d. 1624. His company became in 1603 the servants of Henry, Prince of Wales.

[1] Erected about the year 1587 (see below, Mun. 16). It stood to the S.W. of London Bridge, and is depicted, as a circular building, in a plan of London in 1593 by P. van den Keere from a drawing by J. Norden, a facsimile of which is given by Mr. Halliwell, *Illustrations*, p. 4. See also Collier, *Hist. of Dram. Poetry*, vol. i. p. 328, vol. iii. p. 126.

[2] Both the Lord Chamberlain's and the Lord Admiral's companies were acting here in 1594 (Henslowe's *Diary*, p. 35).

19. RICHARD VEALE to Philip Henslowe:—

'Mr. Hinslowe, This is to enfourme you that my Mr the Maister of the reuelles hath rec. from the ll. of the Counsell order that the L. Chamberlens seruauntes shall not be dis tourbed at the Blackefryars acording with there petition in that behalfe, but leaue shall be giuen vnto theym to make good the decaye of the saide House, butt not to make the same larger then in former tyme hath bene; ffrom thoffice of the Reuelles this 3 of maie 1596. p me Ric. Veale. Rich. Veale.' f. 28.

First printed by Mr. Collier, *Shakespeare*, 1844, vol. i. p. clvi. See also his *Hist. of Dram. Poetry*, ed. 1879, vol. i. p. 290.

This letter, which is on a slip of paper measuring 8 × 2 inches, is an obvious forgery. It is closely connected in subject with the petition in the Public Record Office, printed, as genuine, by Mr. Collier, *Hist. of Dram. Poetry*, ed. 1831, vol. i. p. 298 (ed. 1879, i. 288), but officially condemned as a forgery. See Hamilton, *Enquiry*, p. 96; Ingleby, *Shakspere Controversy*, p. 289. The body of the letter appears to be in the same hand as the spurious certificate, of which a facsimile is given by Dr. Ingleby, p. 248, sheet x., no. iii.; and the signature is a careful imitation of the signatures to receipts of Rich. Veale on behalf of Edmund Tylney, Master of the Revels, contained in Henslowe's *Diary*, f. 81*b*, ed. Collier, p. 179. The signature first written, 'p me Rich. Veale,' is scored through with the pen.

20. 'INHABITANTES of Southerk as haue complaned this [blank in MS.] Jully 1596': including the name of 'Mr Shaksper'. f. 29.

First printed by Mr. Collier, *Shakespeare*, 1844, vol. i. p. clviii. It has since been justly condemned as a forgery. See Ingleby, *Shakspere Controversy*, p. 274, facsimile sheet xvi.

21. PETITION to Lord Hunsdon,[1] Lord Chamberlain, from Richard Topping, of the Strand, tailor, praying for leave to arrest 'Phillip Inclow [Henslowe], one of the gromes

[1] Henry Cary, first Lord Hunsdon, died 23 July, 1596. He was succeeded in the office of Lord Chamberlain by William Brooke, Lord Cobham, who died in Feb., 1596–7, and was succeeded in his turn by George Cary, second Lord Hunsdon.

of her Ma[tes] chamber,' who had become bail for 'a debte of seaven poundes odd monny for this viii yeares dew vnto him by one Thomas Lodge'[1]: followed, on the same page, but in another hand, by the answer of 'Phillipp Hensley,' pleading a legal discharge from his bail and asserting that Topping's complaint is 'in all pointes most vntrue,' and that it is grounded in malice, as he 'knoweth wheare Lodge the principall ys and howe he maie easelie come by him'; [1596?]. *Contemporary copies.* f. 30.

Printed, *Mem. of Edw. Alleyn*, p. 42.

22. PETITION to [George Cary, second] Lord Hunsdon, Lord Chamberlain, from Richard Toppin, praying for relief in the same suit against Thomas Lodge and Philip Henslowe, the latter having disregarded a warrant of Lord Cobham, late Lord Chamberlain; [Jan., 1597–8]. With the endorsement:—'Henchley, you are to satisfie this Petitioner in what shalbe due vnto him, or otherwise he is to take his remedie by course of lawe against you; Courte, this 29th of Januarie, 1597[8]. G. Hunsdon.' *Contemporary copies.* f. 31.

Printed, *Mem. of Edw. Alleyn*, p. 44.

23. ANSWER of Philip Henslowe to the preceding petition, repeating his former defence, and asserting that Lord Cobham's warrant, issued in the mistaken belief that he 'was priuie to the place of Lodg his biding,' merely ordered him to attach the latter, which he was unable to do, 'for that he is (as I heare) passed byond the seas'; [1598]. *Two copies,* one a draft with corrections, the other a fair copy. ff. 32, 33.

The second sentence in this document as printed for the first

---

[1] The author and dramatist. See the notice of him prefixed to the Shakesp. Society's reprint of his *Defence of Poetry*, 1579–80, and *Alarum against Usurers*, 1584, ed. D. Laing, 1853. His romance of *Rosalynde*, from which Shakespeare took the plot of *As you like it*, had been dedicated to the first Lord Hunsdon in 1590.

time in the *Memoirs of Edw. Alleyn*, p. 45, runs as follows :—'The truth is, right honorable, that one *Thos.* Lodge beinge aboute a yeare nowe paste arrested within the Libertie of the Clinck (wheare I am a dweller) att the suite of the said Toppin, uppon an action of debte, and haveinge some knowledge and acquaintaunce *of him as a player*, requested me to be his baile'; and Mr. Collier adduces this as a proof that Lodge was an actor as well as a dramatist. In the original draft, however, the sentence ends, 'and haveinge *of me* some knowledge and acquaintaunce requested me to be his baile'; but the words 'of me' have been cancelled, and 'of him as a player,' together with 'Tho.' before 'Lodge' higher up, have been inserted between the lines in a hand different from that in which all the rest of the corrections are made. As these latter corrections alone, and that too without exception, are found in the fair copy, it is obvious that the alterations quoted above are of later date; and they have all the appearance of a modern forgery. Mr. Collier makes no reference to the fair copy, and was probably unaware of its existence; while, on the other hand, Dr. Ingleby had certainly not seen the draft, when he printed the document from the fair copy, with a facsimile, in his tract *Was Thomas Lodge an Actor?*, 1868, and argued upon the assumption that it was the identical paper described and printed by Mr. Collier.

24. PHIL. HENSLOWE to Edw. Alleyn: has received his letter, and prays God to continue his good health and that of his wife; understands that he has considered the words between them as to the bear-garden,[1] and thinks it fit that they should both be in London to do what they can; as for their last talk about Mr. Pascalle,[2] does not forget to send news, but will tell him some 'harde and heavey,' for one of his company, 'that is gabrell,'[3] has been 'slayen in Hogesden fylldes by the hands of bengemen Jonson bricklayer';

[1] See below, MS. ii. art. 1.

[2] William Paschall, gentleman sewer to the Queen and an officer of the Lord Chamberlain (Henslowe's *Diary*, p. 192).

[3] As Mr. Collier shows (*Mem. of Edw. Alleyn*, p. 50), this was Gabriel Spencer or Spenser, killed by Ben Jonson. In the introduction to his *Memoirs of Actors*, 1846, p. xxii., he gives the confirmatory extract from the register of St. Leonard's, Shoreditch: '1598. Gabriell Spencer, being slayne, was buryed the xxiiiith of Septemb.'

London, 26 Sept., 1598. Addressed to 'Mr Edward Alleyne at Mr Arthure Langworthes[1] at the Brille in Susex.' f. 35.

Printed, *Mem. of Edw. Alleyn*, p. 50.

25. BOND from Richard Bradshawe,[2] yeoman, and Byrcot Byrde and Robert Archer, gentlemen, all of the par. of St. Saviour's, Southwark, to William Byrde,[3] gent., in 5*l.* for the payment of 50 shillings, on the 2 March, 1599; 10 Oct., 40 Eliz. [1598]. Signed. f. 37.

On the inner sheet, f. 38, is a note by [the same?] William Bird, of Hogsdon, of a debt to Edw. Alleyn of 10 sh., with power to recover the same from Rich. Bradshawe upon the above bond; 8 Jan., 1604[5].

26. ROBERT SHAA[4] to Philip Henslowe:—

'We haue heard their booke[5] and lyke yt; their pryce is eight poundes, which I pray pay now to Mr Wilson,[6] according to our promysse. I would haue come myselfe, but that I ame trobled with a scytation'; [8 Nov., 1599]. f. 39.

On the back is the note:—

'1 sce:[7] Wm Wor: & Ansell & to them ye plowghmen.

'2 sce: Richard Q[ueen] & Eliza: Catesbie, Louell, Rice ap Tho: Blunt, Banester.

---

[1] See below, MS. ii. art. 2.

[2] Described as a player (Henslowe's *Diary*, pp. 182, 183).

[3] Called also Will. Borne, a member of the Lord Admiral's company and included in the list of the Prince's players in 1607. See his engagement in 1597 (Henslowe's *Diary*, p. 258, and artt. 104, 105, below).

[4] Rob. Shaw, the actor, frequently mentioned in Henslowe's *Diary*. He played in the *Shoemaker's Holiday* in 1600.

[5] An acquittance from R. Wilson for 8*l.*, 'in full payment for the second pt. of Henrye Richmond,' 8 Nov., 1599, is in Henslowe's *Diary*, p. 159.

[6] Robert Wilson, the dramatist. According to Mr. Collier (*Memoirs of Actors*, 1846, p. xviii.), he was a son of Rob. Wilson, the actor, who was buried at Cripplegate, 20 Nov., 1600. The younger Wilson died 22 Oct., 1610.

[7] Doubtless scenes from *Henry Richmond*, not, as Mr. Collier suggests, from Ben Jonson's *Richard Crookback*.

'3 sce: Ansell Dauye Denys Hen: Oxf: Courtney Bourchier & Grace to them Rice ap Tho: & his soldiers.
'4 sce: Mitton Ban: his wyfe & children.
'5 sce: K. Rich: Catesb: Louell: Norf: Northumb: Percye.'

Printed, Malone, vol. xxi. p. 392; *Alleyn Papers*, p. 24. See also *Mem. of Edw. Alleyn*, p. 122.

27. WARRANT from [Charles Howard,] Earl of Nottingham, [Lord High Admiral,] to the justices and other officers of Middlesex, requiring them to permit his servant Edward Allen, 'in respect of the dangerous decaye of that Howse,[1] which he and his Companye haue nowe on the Banck and for that the same standeth verie noysome for resorte of people in the wynter tyme,' to build a new theatre[2] 'neare Redcrosse streete, London,' the place being 'verie convenient for the ease of people,' and the Queen having a 'speciall regarde of fauor in their proceedinges'; Richmond, 12 Jan., 1599 [1600]. Signed; with seal. f. 40.

Printed, *Mem. of Edw. Alleyn*, p. 55.

28. ADDRESS of the 'Inhabitantes of ye Lordshipp of Fynisburye' to the Privy Council, certifying their willingness that the building of a new playhouse by the Earl of Nottingham's servants within the lordship 'might proceede and be tollerated'; [*circ.* Jan., 1600]. Signed by Hary Stapelforde, Thomas Reade, Anthonie Marlowe, William Browne, con-

---

[1] The Rose. See above, art. 18. In a letter from the Privy Council to the Lord Mayor, 22 June, 1600, it is the Curtain Theatre, in Shoreditch, not the Rose, on the Bankside, which Alleyn's new house is said to be intended to replace (*Index to the Remembrancia*, 1878, p. 354).

[2] The Fortune Theatre, between Whitecross Street and Golden Lane, which is a continuation of Redcross Street. The original contract for building it will be found below (Mun. 22), dat. 5 Jan., 1599–1600. It was burnt on the night of 9 Dec., 1621, but was rebuilt the next year. Having fallen into decay during the civil war, it was finally demolished in 1661, as will be seen below.

stable, William Hewett, Roger Webe, Richard Goode, George Garland, overseer, John Webbe, John Hitchens, overseer, Austen Garland, and sixteen others. f. 41.

Printed, *Mem. of Edw. Alleyn*, p. 58.

29. WARRANT from the Privy Council to the justices of Middlesex, 'espetially of St Gyles without Creplegate,' requiring them, by order of the Queen, to permit Edward Allen 'to proceede in theffectinge and finishinge' of a new playhouse 'in a verie remote and exempt place neere Goulding Lane,' certified as convenient by the inhabitants of Finsbury, the said house being intended to take the place of that 'wherein his Companye latelie plaied, scituate vppon the Bancke, verie noysome for the resorte of people in the wynter tyme'; Richmond, 8 April, 1600. Signed by [Charles Howard, Earl of] Nottingham, G[eorge Cary, Lord] Hunsdon, and [Sir] Ro. Cecyll. f. 43.

Printed, *Mem. of Edw. Alleyn*, p. 57.

30. AN INVENTORY of theatrical costumes, apparently in the handwriting of Edw. Alleyn; [*circ.* 1590–1600]. f. 44.

CLOKES.

1. A scarlett cloke with ij brode gould laces: with gould buttens of the sam downe the sids [*for Leir*].
2. A black velvett cloke.
3. A scarlett cloke layd downe with silver lace and silver buttens.
4. A short velvett cap clok embroydered with gould and gould spangles.
5. A watshod sattin clok with v gould laces.
6. A purpell sattin welted with velvett and silver twist [*Romeos*].
7. A black tufted cloke cloke [*sic*].
8. A damask cloke garded cloke garded [*sic*] with velvett.
9. A longe blak tafata cloke.
10. A colored bugell for a boye.
11. A scarlett with buttens of gould fact with blew velvett.

12. A scarlett fact with blak velvett.
13. A stamell[1] cloke with gould lace.
14. Blak bugell cloke.

GOWNES.

1. Hary ye viii gowne.
2. The blak velvett gowne with wight fure.
3. A crimosin Robe strypt with gould fact with ermin.
4. On of wrought cloth of gould.
5. On of red silk with gould butens.
6. A cardinalls gowne.
7. Wemens gowns.
8, 9. i blak velvett embroydered with gould.
10. i cloth of gould candish his stuf.
11. i blak velvett lact and drawne out with wight sarsnett.
12. A black silk with red flush.
13. A cloth of silver for par [?].
14. A yelow silk gowne.
15. A red silk gowne.
16. Angels silk.
17. ij blew calico gowns.

ANTIK SUTES.

A cote of crimosen velvett cutt in payns[2] and embroyderd with gould.
2. i cloth of gould cote with grene bases.
3. i cloth of gould cote with oraing tawny bases.
4. i cloth of silver cott with blewe silk and tinsell bases.
5. i blew damask cote the *more* [*in Venus*].
6. A red velvett horsmans cote.
7. A yelow tafata pes [? i.e. piece].
8. Cloth of gould horsmans cote.
9. Cloth of bodkin hor[s]mans cote.
10. Orayng tany horsmans cot of cloth lact.
11. Daniels gowne.
12. Blew embroyderd bases.

[1] Stamell, a kind of fine worsted (Halliwell, *Archaic Dict.*).

[2] Paned hose, breeches formed of stripes, with small panes or squares of silk or velvet (Halliwell, *Archaic Dict.*).

13. Will Somers cote.
14. Wight embroyd[erd] bases.
15. Gilt lether cot.
16. ii hedtirs [head-tires] sett with stons.

Jerkings and Dublets.

1. A crymosin velvett pes [?] with gould buttens and lace.
2. A crymosin sattin case lact with gould lace all over.
3. A velvett dublett cut dimond lact with gould lace and spang[les].
4. A dublett of blak velvett cut on sillver tinsell.
5. A ginger colored dublett.
6. i wight sattin cute on wight.
7. Blak velvett with gould lace.
8. Green velvett.
9. Blak tafata cut on blak velvett lacte with bugell.
10. Blak velvett playne.
11. Ould wight sattin.
12. Red velvett for a boy.
13. A carnation velvett lacte with silver.
14. A yelow spangled case.
15. Red velvett with blew sattin sleves and case.
16. Cloth of silver Jerkin.
17. Faustus Jerkin, his clok.

French Hose.

1. Blew velvett embr[oyderd] with gould paynes, blew sattin scalin.
2. Silver payns lact with carnation s[c]alins lact over with silver.
3. The guises.
4. Rich payns with long stokins.
5. Gould payns with blak stript scalings of canish [?]
6. Gould payns with velvett scalings.
7. Gould payns with red strypt scaling.
8. Black bugell.
9. Red payns for a boy with yelo scalins.
10. Pryams hoes [*in Dido*].
11. Spangled hoes [*for Pericles*].

Venetians.

1. A purpell velvett cut in dimonds lact and spangels.

2. Red velved lact with gould Spanish.
3. A purpell vellvett emproydered with silver cut on tinsell.
4. Green velvett lact with gould Spanish.
5. Blake vellvett.
6. Cloth of silver.
7. Gren strypt sattin.
8. Cloth of gould for a boye.

Printed, with many inaccuracies, *Mem. of Edw. Alleyn*, p. 19.

The words 'for Leir,' 'Romeos,' 'in Dido,' and 'for Pericles' have been introduced by another hand, with an evident attempt to imitate the original. The same hand has tampered with the entry '5. i blew damask cote the moro [?],' changing it into 'the more in Venus,' i.e. the Moor in Venice. Mr. Collier (*loc. cit.*) calls special attention to all these spurious items, as proving that 'Alleyn acted parts, if not in Shakespeare's plays, in plays upon the same stories as those employed by our greatest dramatist'; but he is silent about the difference of hand.

31. ROBERT SHAA to Phil. Henshlowe:—'I pray you, Mr Henshlowe, deliuer vnto the bringer hereof the some of fyue and fifty shillinges to make the 3^li^ fyue shillinges, which they receaued before, full six poundes in full payment of their booke called the fayre Constance of Roome.[1] Whereof I pray you reserue for me Mr Willsons whole share, which is xi^s^, which I to supply his neede deliuered him yesternight'; no date. f. 45.

Printed, Malone, vol. xxi. p. 394; *Alleyn Papers*, p. 26.

32. SAMUELL ROWLYE[2] to Phil. Hinchloe:—'I haue harde fyue shetes of a playe of the Conqueste of the Indes[3] and I

[1] Payments of 3*l.* 5*s.* and 2*l.* 4*s.* (reserving Wilson's 11*s.*) for the *Fair Constance of Rome* were made to Rich. Drayton, Rich. Hathway, Anthony Munday, and Thomas Dekker, 3 and 14 June, 1600 (*Diary*, pp. 171, 172).

[2] The dramatist and actor, author of two extant plays, *When you see me, you know me*, 1605, and the *Noble Souldier*, 1634. His engagement by Henslowe as a 'covenente servante,' 16 Nov., 1598 (not 1599, as printed), is recorded in the *Diary*, p. 260.

[3] The *Conquest of the West Indies*, by Will. Haughton, John Day, and Went-

dow not doute but it wylle be a verye good playe; tharefore, I praye ye delyuer them fortye shyllynges in earneste of it and take the papers into your one [own] hands and on easter eue thaye promyse to make an ende of all the reste'; no date. With the note below:—'Lent the 4 of Aprell, 1601—xxxxs.' f. 46.

Printed, Malone, vol. xxi. p. 391; *Alleyn Papers*, p. 23.

33. SAM. ROWLYE to Phil. Hynchlo:—'I praye ye let Mr Hathwaye[1] haue his papars agayne of the playe of John a gante and for the repayemente of the monye back agayne he is contente to gyue ye a bylle of his hande to be payde at some cartayne tyme as in your dyscressyon yow shall thinke good; which done, ye maye crose it oute of your boouke and keepe the byll, or else wele stande so muche indetted to yow and kepe the byll our selues'; no date. f. 47.

Printed, Malone, vol. xxi. p. 393; *Alleyn Papers*, p. 25.

34. SAM. ROWLYE to Phil. Hynchlye:—'I praye ye dow so muche for vs, if Jhon Daye[2] and Wyll Houghton haue reseved but thre pounde ten shyllynges, as to delyver them thurtye shyllynges more and take thare papers'; no date. f. 48.

Printed, Malone, vol. xxi. p. 392; *Alleyn Papers*, p. 23.

---

worth Smith. It appears that 6*l.* 15*s.* in all was paid for the play, 4 Apr.–1 Sept., 1601 (*Diary*, pp. 185 *seqq.*).

[1] Payments on account of the *Conquest of Spain by John of Gaunt*, amounting in all to 1*l.* 19*s.*, were made to Rich. Hathway and Will. Rankins, 24 Mar.–16 Apr., 1601 (*Diary*, pp. 185, 186). Hathway is named by Meres (*Wit's Treasury*, 1598) among the best writers of comedy; but none of his plays have come down to us in print. Some verses by him are prefixed to Bodenham's *Belvedere*, 1600.

[2] A payment of 1*l.* 10*s.* was made to Will. Haughton for the *Six Yeomen of the West*, 8 June, 1601, in addition to 3*l.* 10*s.* paid 20 May, 4, 6 June (*Diary*, pp. 188, 189). Printed editions of several of Day's works have been preserved, beginning with the *Ile of Guls*, 1606, and the *Travailes of the Three English Brothers*, 1607. The only extant play by Haughton is *Englishmen for my Money*, or *A Woman will have her Way*, 1616.

35. SAM. ROWLYE to Phil. Henchloe:—'I praye ye delyver the reste of the monye to John Daye and Wyll Hawton dew to them of the syx yemen of the weste'; no date. On the same paper:—'I have occasion to be absent about the plott of the Indyes, therfore pray delyver it to Will Hamton[1] [?], sadler. By me John Daye.' f. 49.

On the back are the following lines[2] written by John Day, in a minute and almost illegible scrawl:—

'Brother, they were too nebers of our state,
Yet both infected with a strong disease
And mortall sicknes, proud ambytion;
W^ch^, being ranck and villanously [?] neare,
Had they not been prevented, might have proved
scornfull
Fatall and dangerouse. Then since ~~proud~~ death
Hath, like a skillfull artist, cured that feare,
W^ch^ might have proved so hurtefull to our selves,
vs commit
Lets ~~bear them hence~~, in sad and mournfull sound,
There worthes to fame, there bodyes to the ground;
dead
For the ~~brave~~ Percy bore a gallant mynd.
Ingland has my prayers left behind.'

Printed, Malone, vol. xxi. p. 392; *Alleyn Papers*, p. 23. Malone does not notice the verses. They are printed by Mr. Collier, but with great freedom in some of the readings.

36. ROB. SHAA to Phil. Henshlowe:—'I pray you, Mr Henshlowe, deliuer in behalfe of the Company vnto the

[1] Mr. Collier misreads this name, 'Will Hunt, the Pedler,' and finds fault with Malone for reading it 'Will Haughton.'

[2] Spoken apparently by Henry, Prince of Wales, to his brother, John of Lancaster, over the dead body of Hotspur: compare Shakespeare's *I. Hen. IV.*, act v. sc. 4. There is a difficulty, however, with regard to the second of the 'two neighbours of our state,' since the Earl of Worcester, who would seem to be intended, was not killed in the battle of Shrewsbury, but was executed afterwards.

fifty shillinges which they receaud the other day three poundes and tenn shillinges more in full payment of six poundes the pryce of their play called to good to be true'[1]; no date. f. 55.

Printed, Malone, vol. xxi. p. 393; *Alleyn Papers*, p. 25.

37. ACQUITTANCE from William Playstowe[2] to Phil. Henslowe for 3*l.* for 'one months pay due vnto my Mr Mr Edmund Tylney,'[3] Master of the Revels; 4 Aug., 1602. Below is the note, 'Bookes owinge for |5| Baxsters tragedy,[4] Tobias Comedy, Jepha Judg of Israel, Loue parts frendshipp, The Cardinall.' f. 51.

Printed, Malone, vol. xxi. p. 395.

38. JOANE ALLEYNE[5] to Edw. Alleyn, her husband: rejoices at his good health, and thanks God that she, her mother, and whole house are well, and that the sickness[6] about them is ceasing; all the companies, his own included, are at home and well, but 'Browne of the Boares head[7] is dead,

---

[1] Payments of 5*s.*, 2*l.* 10*s.*, and 3*l.* 10*s.* for the play *Too Good to be True* were made to Hen. Chettle, Rich. Hathway, and Wentworth Smith, 14 Nov., 1601, 6 and 7 Jan., 1601–2 (*Diary*, pp. 204, 206, 207).

[2] Similar monthly acquittances from him are contained in Henslowe's *Diary*, pp. 179, 180, 182, 215.

[3] Appointed Master of the Revels, 24 July, 1579 (Malone, vol. iii. p. 57). He held the office till his death in Oct., 1610.

[4] Payments to the authors for all these plays, made in 1602, are entered in the *Diary*, p. 220, viz. the *Bristol Tragedy*, by J. Day; *Tobias*, by Hen. Chettle; *Jephthah*, by Anth. Munday and Thos. Dekker; *Love parts Friendship*, by H. Chettle and W. Smith; and *Cardinal Wolsey*, by H. Chettle. A fee of 7*s.* was paid to the Master of the Revels on the license for a new play (*Diary*, p. 118).

[5] The hand is probably not her own, since in witnessing a deed (Mun. 496, below) she signs with a mark only.

[6] 'A 23 Dec., 1602, ad 22 Dec., 1603, perierunt Londini 36244, ex quo numero 30578 ex peste' (Camden, *Annales*).

[7] Perhaps the famous Boar's Head tavern in Eastcheap. The companies of the Earl of Oxford and the Earl of Worcester were playing there in 1602 (*Index to the Remembrancia*, 1878, p. 355). Henslowe, however, had an interest

and dyed very pore'; her father [Henslowe] is at the Court, but she is of his own mind that he need not meet him at Basing; will not advise him as to his coming home, but longs to see him and thinks he may safely come; is glad to hear of his delight in hawking, and, although his clothes are worn to rags, he will be as welcome thus as in a cloth of gold or velvet; has paid 50*s.* rent for the wharf to the deputy of 'M[r] Woodward my Lordes bayly,' with a groat for the quittance claimed as the bailiff's fee,—if wrongly, they made her a simple woman; he shall receive a letter from the joiner himself and a printed bill; and so she ends, with commendations to himself, Mr. Chaloner[1] and his wife, praying God still to bless them both; 21 Oct., 1603. f. 52.

With the postscript, partly lost owing to the decay of the paper at the bottom of the sheet:—

'Abovte a weeke agoe ther[e cam]e a youthe who said he was
M[r] Frauncis Chalo[ner]s man [and wou]ld have borrow[e]d x[s] to
have *bought* things for [hi]s M[ri][s] . . . . t hym
Cominge w[th]out . . . . [to]ken . . . . d
I would have . . . .
[i]f I bene sue . . . .
and inquire after the fellow and said he had lent hym a horse. I
feare me he gulled hym, thoughe he gulled not *vs.* The youthe
was a prety youthe & hansom in appayrell; we know not *what* became
of hym. M[r] Bromffeild commendes hym; he was heare yesterdaye. Nicke
and Jeames be well and commend them; so dothe M[r] Cooke and his weife
in the kyndest sorte, and so once more in the hartiest manner
farwelle.'

The words in italic are written between the lines in the MS.

---

in another Boar's Head on the Bankside (*Diary*, p. 265, and Mun. 182, below).

[1] Probably Francis or Thomas Chaloner, of Kenwardes, in Lindfield, co. Sussex (Berry's *Sussex Genealogies*, p. 345).

This letter was first printed by Mr. Collier (*Memoirs of Edw. Alleyn*, p. 62). Besides minor inaccuracies, however, the postscript, as there given, begins as follows:—' Aboute a weeke agoe there came a youthe who said he was Mr Frauncis Chaloner who would have borrowed x^li^ to have bought things for * * * and said he was known unto you and Mr Shakespeare of the globe, who came * * * said he knewe hym not, onely he herde of hym that he was a roge * * * so he was glade we did not lend him the monney * * * Richard Johnes [went] to seeke and inquire after the fellow,' &c. This passage relating to Shakespeare is not to be found in the original, and could not possibly have formed part of it even in its perfect state, as is evident from the words and letters still legible. An exact copy of the whole letter, line for line, is given by Mr. Hamilton (*Enquiry*, p. 90), and the question is fully discussed by Dr. Ingleby (*Shakspere Controversy*, p. 279). Facsimiles of the defective part of the postscript are given in both these works, and also by Mr. J. O. Halliwell (*Curiosities of Modern Shaksperian Criticism*, 1853, p. 27).

39. LETTER from the Privy Council to the Lord Mayor and the justices of Middlesex and Surrey, requiring them to permit 'the three Companies of Plaiers to the King, Queene and Prince publicklie to exercise ther Plaies in ther several and vsuall howses for that purpose and noe other, vz. The Globe[1] scituate in Maiden Lane on the Banckside in the Cowntie of Surrey, the Fortune in Goldinge Lane, and the Curtaine[2] in Hollywelle in the Cowntie of Midlesex' . . . 'except ther shall happen weeklie to die of the Plague aboue the number of thirtie'; Whitehall, 9 Apr., 1604. *Contemporary copy*, the original being signed by the Earls of Notting-

[1] Built in 1599 with materials brought from the theatre in Shoreditch (Halliwell, *Illustrations*, p. 25). It was burnt on 29 June, 1613, but was rebuilt the next year, and was used by the King's company, till the theatres were closed during the civil war.

[2] On the south side of Holywell Lane (Halliwell, *op. cit.*, p. 29). It is first mentioned by name in 1577, and by Stow in his *Survey*, ed. 1598, p. 349, as one of 'two publique houses for the acting and shewe of comedies, tragedies, and histories,'

ham, Suffolk, Shrewsbury, and Worcester, Sir W. Knowles, and Sir J. Stanhoppe. f. 54.

Printed, *Mem. of Edw. Alleyn*, p. 66; and from another copy, Halliwell, *Illustrations*, p. 115.

Mr. Collier also prints (p. 68) what professes to be a list of the King's company of players. This list, which includes the name 'Shaksp[re],' is written, with different ink and in a different hand, along the bottom edge of the sheet containing the above letter. It is not mentioned by Malone, who quotes the letter in his *Enquiry into the Authenticity of Certain Papers*, &c., 1796, p. 215; and it has been justly condemned as a modern forgery (Hamilton, *Enquiry*, p. 95; Ingleby, *Shakspere Controversy*, p. 269, facsimile ii. sheet xvi.).

40. LETTER from the Duke of Lennox[1] to 'all maiors, justeses of peas, shreefes,' &c., praying them not to hinder his company of players' in the 'vse of their playes,' for which they have his license; Hampton Court, 13 Oct., 1604. Signed 'Lenox'; with seal of arms. Addressed 'To my loving freend M[r] Dale Esq. and all other Justeses whatsoeuer.' f. 55.

Printed, *Mem. of Edw. Alleyn*, p. 69.

41. POWER OF ATTORNEY from Abraham Sauere, of Westminster, gent., to Francis Hinchle,[2] of Southwark, gent., to recover 40*l.* from John Garland, of 'the ould forde,' forfeited on a bond 'for the deliuere of a warrant, which was mayd vnto me frome the gratious the duke of Linox'; 1 Mar., 1604[5]. f. 57.

---

situated near Holywell Priory, the other being the Theatre. It was at this time used by the Queen's company, the Prince's company playing at the Fortune.

[1] Ludovic Stuart, succ. as second Duke of Lennox in 1583, cr. Earl of Richmond in 1613 and Duke of Richmond in 1623; died 16 Feb., 1623-4.

[2] A loan of 7*l.* from Phil. Henslowe to his nephew Francis, 'to goyne with owld Garlland and Symcockes and Savery, when they played in the Duckes

42. BOND from Francis Henslowe,[1] of London, gent., to Philip Henslowe, of St. Saviour's, Southwark, esq., in 60*l.* to observe articles of agreement 'betweene the said Frauncis Henslowe and John Garland and Abraham Saverie his ffellowes, servantes to the most noble Prince the duke of Lennox'; 16 Mar., 2 Jas. I. [1605]. f. 58.

On the back of this bond is the draft of a letter from Edw. Alleyn to Alexander Nairne. See below, MS. iii. art. 89.

43. BOND[2] from Daniel, William, and Edmond Gill, of the Isle of Man, yeomen, to Katherine Moore, *al.* Gill [wife of Philip Moore], and Elizabeth, Jane, and Margaret Gill, daughters of Daniel Gill, clerk, of the Isle of Man, deceased, in 600*l.* to abide by an award of William Norres, clerk, and others [Mun. 27, below]; 19 Dec., 3 Jas. I., 1605. f. 60.

44. SIMILAR BOND, the parties reversed; 19 Dec., 3 Jas. I., 1605. f. 62.

---

name,' is recorded in his *Diary*, p. 214. A John Garland was a member of the Duke of York's company in 1610.

[1] Son of Rich. Henslowe, eldest son of Edm. Henslowe, of Lindfield, co. Sussex (Harl. MS. 1562, f. 114*b*). He appears to have belonged to the Queen's company in 1593 (Henslowe's *Diary*, p. 5). See also below, MS. iii. art. 5, MS. iv. artt. 56, 57.

[2] This and following articles connected with the family of Gill relate to the site of the Fortune Theatre. See below, MSS. iii. iv. and Munn. 1–42 *passim.* Alleyn's own account of his purchase of the property is in MS. viii. f. 6*b*.

'What the Fortune cost me.

First for ye leas [from the Gills] to Brew [Mun. 20] . . . . . 240*l.*
Then for ye building ye playhow[s]e [Mun. 22] . . . . . . 520*l.*
For other pr[i]uat buildings of myn owne . . . . 120*l.*
So in all itt hathe cost me for ye leasse . . . . . 880*l.*
Bought the inheritance of the land of the Gills of ye Ile of Man, wch is ye Fortune & all the howses in Whightcrosstrett & Gowlding Lane, in June 1610 [Mun. 38] for the some of . . . . 340*l.*
Bought in [Mun. 36] John Garretts Lease in reuertion from the Gills for 21 years for . . . . 100*l.*
So in all itt cost me . . . . 1320*l.*
'Bleased be ye Lord god euerlasting:'.

45. NOTE by Abraham Sauere, of Westminster, gent., of a debt to 'Phillip Hinchle, of the Banck Syde, gent.,' of 20*s.*, payable on demand ; 11 Mar., 1605[6]. f. 64.

46. WILLIAM NOREIS, vicar-general of the Isle of Man, and Elizabeth,[1] his wife, to Edw. Alleyn, requesting him to pay to their cousin, Patrick Brew, the rent for the land in London which he held of them on lease, and promising him the refusal of the same, if their children should be willing to sell ; Douglas, 1 June, 1608. f. 65.

Printed, *Alleyn Papers*, p. 34.

47. 'SURREY. The state of the Clincke Libertye at this assesment for the first payment of the third Subsidy.

'Consisteth of fiue C: and lx: howsehould[e]rs: two hundred and l: of them being watermen: one hundred and more of handye trades; besides one hundred and l: verie poore people, widdows and others, all being readye to take and not one of them fitt to geue. Of which number manye doe now receave relief of weekely pencion in a farre larger measure then ever heartofore, which charge is cheiflie borne by the Subsidie men, with the helpe of some fewe others of the Libertye, as a burden growing everye day more heauye then other. Notwithstandinge all which, together with the decease of three Subsidye men assessed at Nyne poundes, the taxacion for this payment is improoued, the roome of the dead supplyed, with an encrease to his maiestye of——————xv^li^.' f. 67.

48. 'SURREY, the Clinck Liberty. The booke of the first payment of the third Subsidy graunted to the kinges ma^ty^ for the Clincke Liberty of the parishe of St Sauiours, made in Marche, Anno 1608[9].' f. 68.

---

[1] Widow of Daniel Gill, the younger. She is called Isabel in Mun. 27.

The list includes fifty-one names in all, the highest assessment being that of Christopher Levenes, vi[li]. Phil. Henslowe and Edw. Alleyn appear among the 'Seasors' (assessors), to whose names no amounts are attached. Among the names is 'Mr. Gowghe, iiii[l]'—probably Rob. Gough, the actor, who is known to have lived in Southwark.

49. 'A BREIF NOAT taken out of the poores booke contayning the names of all thenhabitantes of this Liberty [of the Clink], which arre rated and assesed to a weekely paiment towardes the relief of the poore, as it standes now encreased this 6° day of Aprill, 1609. Deliuered vp to Phillip Henslowe Esquio[r], churchwarden, by Francis Carter, one of the late ouerseers of the same Liberty.' Two copies. ff. 70, 71.

First printed by Mr. Collier, *Mem. of Edw. Alleyn*, p. 91.

The first of the two copies is a genuine document, but the line 'Mr. Shakespeare———vi[d]', at the head of the second division of the list of names, is undoubtedly a later insertion, the ink[1] being of a different colour and the letters betraying the forger by their studied, tremulous imitation of the original hand. Besides this, the sums opposite the next five names have apparently been altered by the prefix of a figure in each case, and the name 'Leuens' (the same, doubtless, as 'Christofer Levenes' in art. 48) has been changed into 'Louens,' in order to identify him with John Lowin, the actor. The second copy, which is written on what appears to be a fly leaf torn from a book having red edges, is an unquestionable forgery from beginning to end, perpetrated probably in order to support the falsification made in the genuine document. Mr. Collier prints the list from the first copy, as is proved by his quotation of its endorsement; but it is worthy of notice that his misreadings of names, such as Benfield for Binfeild,[2] Cevis for Cruis, Burkett for Buckett, and

[1] This line and the next, which has been retraced to match it, are the only two which show through on the other side of the page.

[2] This is Will. Benfield, one of the assessors in the preceding list, not Rob. Benfield, the actor, as Mr. Collier assumes in the *Memoirs of Edw. Alleyn*. He corrected the error from the token-books of St. Saviour's in his *Mem. of Actors*, p. 262.

Nasam for Nusam, show a tendency to agree with the second copy. It is apparently upon the evidence of the latter alone that the list has been hitherto condemned as a forgery. This opinion was first publicly expressed by Mr. Staunton (*Shakespeare*, 1858, vol. i. pp. xxxvii. lviii.), and subsequently, among others, by Dr. Ingleby (*Shakspere Controversy*, 1861, p. 276); but neither of these writers seems to have known of the partly genuine document, which so strikingly exhibits the process of manipulation. Mr. Halliwell, on the other hand, does mention 'two contemporary copies,' not detecting the forgery, but his facsimile of the Shakespeare entry is taken only from the second (*Folio Shakespeare*, 1853, vol. i. p. 193). A complete facsimile of the same copy is given by Dr. Ingleby, sheet xvii.

50. '14 OF OCTOBER, 1609. An Accompt taken out of the poores booke for so much receyued and paid for the vse of the poore of this Liberty [of the Clink] in 27 weekes ended the day abouesaid. And also what mony hath been receyued and paid within the same time for the relief of sundry poore famelyes visited with the sicknes.' f. 72.

Under the first account the receipts amount to 31*l.* 13*s.* 9*d.*, and the payments to 30*l.* 1*s.* 3*d.*; and, under the other account 'for relief of the sicke,' the amounts are respectively 7*l.* 0*s.* 10*d.* and 10*l.* 6*s.* 4*d.* 'Mr Henslowe' and 'M^r^ [Roger] Cole' are mentioned apparently as churchwardens, and Thomas Toune (the actor) and Richard Watford as overseers, and the accounts are certified by Francis Carter.

51. 'THINGES necessary to be considered of, and which may tend much to the orderly and peaceable gouernment of this Libertye, being carefully looked vnto,' endorsed (by Francis Carter) 'For Mr Alleyn, touching the Liberty'; *circ.* 1609. f. 73.

'First, there being xxiiii^or^ Inhabitantes allowed as victualers within this Libertye, that no one of them may be suffred to keep a tapster, as a thing by the antyent orders and custome of this place forbidden and found hurtfull. Nor that eny other Inhabitant whatsoeuer keep victualing without being licenced therevnto.

'To haue a prouident care to prevent the taking in of Inmates, as much as may be possible, especiallye of Strangers from other places, which for the most parte arre lodged in suche howses as arre not of suffycyent receipt for thenhabitantes themselues to liue in.

'To represse Drunckennes, strife, and other disorders in the poorer sorte of people, which arre most prone thervnto, and to keep them to their labours.

'To prevent the lodging of single people, both men and maydes, which woorke at their owne handes. As also the harbouring of eny other sorte of people of what qualetye soeuer, without the consent of the forman of the Jurye and Officers first had thervnto.

'To admitt of no new Commers into this Libertye of meane and private sorte without the privitye and consent of the forman of the Jurye and Officers first had and without good securitye to be taken according to the qualetye of the persons, with a certificatt from wheare they came, the better to prevent the coming of lewd and ill disposed people to the slaunder and discreditt of this Libertye.

'To take order that no women Inhabitantes of this Libertye, which liue by washing abroad or keeping women in childbed, or such as keep howses visited [i.e. by the plague] in other places, be suffred to bring home eny manner of person visited, eny cloathes bedding or other thinges to thendangering of their neighbours.'

With four more paragraphs, providing for the fortnightly 'view of the Libertye,' the meeting of the jury, fines, &c.

52. 'A REMEMBRAUNCE of a guifte from the Company of the Lethersellers to the poore of the parishe of St Saviours of vi^s viii^d paid quarterlye to one of the Churchwardens of the same parishe, of which guifte there is due to the poore of the Clincke Libertye every yeare vi^s'; *circ.* 1609. f. 74.

53. PATRICKE BREWE to Edw. Alleyn, 'nere vnto pallace [Paris] garden': wrote to him in December, but is uncertain whether the letter came to hand; the 'Gylles and the daughters of Gill deseased' are willing to sell, but 'strayne curtesye who shall begynn'; cannot yet meet with a trusty messenger by whom to send the promised papers and other matters which he dare not write, since their letters are opened, but he may depend upon having them; 6 Apr., 1609. f. 75.

Printed, *Alleyn Papers*, p. 36.

54. PATRICKE BREWE to Edw. Alleyn: Mrs. Norris is dead, and was buried 25 July; prays him to pay the 6*l.* rent due to her husband for the last year to John More, the bearer, who has advanced the money; has sent what he promised and his [Brew's] wife will tell him other things which he spares from writing; Douglas, 3 Aug., 1609. f. 76.

Printed, *Alleyn Papers*, p. 37.

55. PATRICKE BREWE to Edw. Alleyn, informing him of reports that he or Mr Garrett has paid the rent of Gill's land into the Exchequer, and that the latter has offered 300*l.* for the land, and also of the willingness of the 'yong women and the reste' to sell, now that their mother is dead; Douglas, 9 Dec. [1609]. f. 78.

Printed, *Alleyn Papers*, p. 36.

56. 'DIRECCIONS for Sr Jeremy Turnour[1] touching the busines to be donne in the Isle of Man,' relative to the execution of deeds for the conveyance of the Fortune by the Gill family to Edw. Alleyn; [Mar., 1609–10]. On the back, in the hand of Edw. Alleyn, is a list of deeds, &c., to be 'brought back agayne.' f. 79.

57. 'DIRECTIONS to the Commissioners for takinge the knowledgement of the ffine for Mr Alleyn,' endorsed by Edw.

[1] Styled by Alleyn in his *Diary* 'muster master'; captain of the Surrey trained bands, and knighted by James I. at Chatham in 1604.

Alleyn, 'Directions for Sr Jeremy Turner,' &c.; [Mar., 1609–10]. f. 80.

58. BARGAIN and sale by Phillipp Moore, of Kirk Lonan, Isle of Man, yeoman, and Katherine, his wife, daughter of Daniel Gill, clerk, deceased, to their uncles William and Edmond Gill, of Kirk Christ of the Aire, yeomen, for 37*l.* 10*s.*, of their eighth part of lands, tenements, &c., in the parish of St. Giles without Cripplegate, London, known by the name of the 'Fortune' and in the tenure of Edward Allen; 7 Mar., 7 Jas. I., 1609[10]. Certified by the signatures of John Ireland, Lieutenant and Captain of the Isle of Man, and Thomas Sansburie and Evan Christian, deemsters. f. 81.

59. BARGAIN and sale by William Clarke, of Jurbie, Isle of Man, yeoman, and Elizabeth, his wife, daughter of Dan. Gill, clerk, deceased, to the same William and Edmond Gill, for 30*l.*, of their eighth part of the same lands, &c.; 7 Mar., 7 Jas. I., 1609[10]. Certified as above. f. 83.

60. BARGAIN and sale by Hugh Cannell, vicar of Kirk Michael, Isle of Man, and Jane, his wife, daughter of Dan. Gill, clerk, deceased, to the same William and Edmond Gill, for 40*l.*, of their eighth part of the same lands, &c.; 7 Mar., 7 Jas. I., 1609[10]. Certified as above. f. 85.

61. BARGAIN and sale by Donald Qualtroughe, of Kirk Lonan, I. of Man, yeoman, and Margaret, his wife, daughter of Dan. Gill, clerk, deceased, to the same William and Edm. Gill, for 30*l.*, of their eighth part of the same lands, &c.; 7 Mar., 7 Jas. I., 1609[10]. Certified as above. f. 87.

62. POWER OF ATTORNEY from Daniel Gill, the elder, and Katherine, his wife, and William Gill, his son, and Essable, his wife, to Edmond Gill to sell or lease their title and interest in 'the liveinge neer London commonlye called the Fortune, beinge lyeinge and cituated without Creeplegate in Whitecrosse streete and parte theareoff in goulden layn'; 14 Mar., 1609[10]. f. 89.

63. ACQUITTANCE from Sir William Norris, vicar of Kirk Lonan, Isle of Man, to Edward Allen for 6*l.*, for the moiety of a year's rent due to him in May, 1609, by right of Elizabeth Clearke, his wife, deceased, for lands in 'Whyt crosse' Street, co. Middlesex; 17 Mar., 1609[10]. f. 90.

64. ACQUITTANCE from Edmond Gill, of Kirk Christ of the Ayre, Isle of Man, to Edward Alleyn for 6*l.*, paid to the use of Sir William Norris for the second moiety of the rent due as above; 18 May, 8 Jas. I., 1610. f. 91.

65. AFFIDAVITS of Edmond Gill and of Daniel Gill, the elder, respecting the ages of Katherine, Elizabeth, Jane, and Margaret, daughters of Daniel Gill, the younger, to the effect that the youngest is above the age of 21 years; Castle Rushen, Isle of Man, 29 June, 1610. Certified by John Ireland, Sir Jeremy Turnor, and others. f. 92.

66. ROBERT BROWNE [1] to 'his assured frend Mr Edward Alleyn': understands that Mr Rose [2] is entertayned amongst the princes men and meanes to stay and settell himself in that company'; has been requested by him to solicit Alleyn to 'procure him but a gathering place for his wife,' and trusts he will do so, since Rose has been an old servant of his, 'allwayes honest trusty and trew'; Clerkenwell, 11 April, 1612. f. 93.

Printed, *Alleyn Papers*, p. 51.

---

[1] See above, artt. 2, 8. The writer may have belonged to the Red Bull Theatre, in St. John Street, Clerkenwell.

[2] No actor of this name is included in any of the lists of the Prince's players. The duties of a 'gatherer' may be inferred from art. 104, below.

67. CHARLES MASSYE[1] to 'Mr Edward Allen, at his house at Dvlledg':—

'Ser, I beseche your pardon in that I make boulde to wryte to you wordes consernynge my selfe, and it may be distastfvll to you, but nessessete hath no lawe and therfore I h[op]e the contrarye. Ser, diverse ocasions before the prynses[2] deathe and manye crosses sense hath brovght me intow det, and I [se]e danger, which if you woulde please to helpe me .... shovld .. notwithstandinge I ever shall reste ever to be c[omman]ded by [you]. Never wovld I desire you shovld hassard the [losse of] one [penny] by me; for, Ser, I know you vnderstande th[at ther] is .... composisions betwene ovre [com]penye, that, if [any] one gi[ve] over with consent of his fellowes, he is to r[ecea]ve thr[ee] score and ten povndes, (Antony Jefes[3] hath had so mvch) and, if any on dye, his widow or frendes, whome he appoyntes it, tow reseve fyfte povndes (Mistres Pavie[4] and Mistres Tovne[5] hath had the lyke); besides that lytt[ell] moete I have in the play hovsses, which I wovld willing[ly] pas over vnto you by dede of gifte or any covrse you [w]ovld set dovne for your secvrete. And that you shovld be shvre I dow it not withovte my wiffes consente, she wilbe willinge

---

[1] Member of the Lord Admiral's company in 1599 (Henslowe's *Diary*, pp. 73, 260, &c.), in the Prince's list of 1607, and still attached to the Fortune in 1622 (see below, Munn. 56 *seqq.*). He was dead before 6 Dec., 1635 (art. 115, below).

[2] Henry, Prince of Wales; died 6 Nov., 1612.

[3] Anthony Jeffes, member of the Lord Admiral's company and in the Prince's list of 1607.

[4] There was a player of the name of Salathiel Pavy, one of the company of Chapel Children who acted Ben Jonson's *Cynthia's Revels* in 1600; but Jonson has an elegy upon him, which proves that he died at the age of thirteen. This was, perhaps, his mother.

[5] Agnes, widow of Thomas Towne, of the Lord Admiral's company and in the Prince's list of 1607. He was dead before 5 Nov., 1612 (MS. v., below, art. 8).

[to] set her hand to any thinge that myght secvre it to you. Ser, fifte povndes wovld pay my detes, which for on hole twelve month I wovld take vp and pay the intreste; and, that I myght the better pay it in at the yeares ende, I wovld get Mr Jvbe[1] to reseve my gallery mony and my quarter of the howse mony for a yeare to pay it in with all, and, if in six monthes I sawe the gallerye mony wovld not dow, [then in] the other six monthes he shovld reseve [all my] share, only reservinge a marke a weke . . . . my howse withall. The eyghtenth of this m[onth I have to] pay to Mr Bankes thvrte povndes and other . other dettes I owe. If ether you, ser, wov[ld advance] the monye, or any other whome you shall appoynt, for I knowe wher you will you may, I shall ever reste your pore servant to parforme any offyse you shall comand me. Ther is one Mr Mathvs at the bell in newgat market that six wekes agoe did offer me fifte povndes for a twelfmonth gratis, bvt he desird good secvrete. Ser, I besech howsoeuer pardon me, in that bovldly I have presvmed to wryt vnto you; thvs, not daryinge to troble you any longer, I comyt you to god, to home I will ever pray to blesse you'; [1613?]. f. 94.

The letter covers one side of the first leaf, which is much decayed at the outer edge. On the back of the second leaf are acquittances to Edw. Alleyn, in his own hand, for payments on account of sea coal and bricks, dat. 9 Aug., 1613, 30 July, 1614.

Printed, but with many inaccuracies, *Mem. of Edw. Alleyn*, p. 109.

68. NAT. FIELD[2] to Phil. Hinchlow, asking, on behalf

[1] Edw. Juby, of the Lord Admiral's company, and in the Prince's list, 1607.

[2] See a memoir of him, Collier, *Hist. of Dram. Poetry*, &c., ed. 1879, vol. iii. p. 425, and *Shakesp. Soc. Papers*, vol. iv., 1849, p. 38. Some of the inferences drawn by Mr. Collier are doubted by Mr. Jos. Hunter (*Chorus Vatum Angli-*

of himself, Robert Daborne,[1] and Philip Massinger, for a loan of 5*l.* out of 10*l.* still to be received 'for the play,' and protesting that without it they cannot be bailed, nor he himself play any more, which will be a loss of 20*l.* 'ere the end of the next weeke, beside the hinderance of the new play'; no date. With postscripts by Robt. Daborne and Phil. Massinger, the former stating that 'the mony shall be abated out of the mony remayns for the play of Mr Fletcher and owrs.' On the back is the note:—'Rec. by mee Robert Dauison of Mr Hinsloe for the vse of Mr Dauboern, Mr Feeld, Mr Messenger the some of vl. Robert Dauison.' f. 96.

Printed, Malone, vol. iii. p. 337; *Mem. of Edw. Alleyn*, p. 120. See also Gifford, *Plays of Phil. Massinger*, 1805, vol. i. p. xv.

69. NAT. FIELD to his 'Father Hinchlow,' informing him that he is 'vnluckily taken on an execution of 30l,' and begging for a loan of 10*l.*, which, with 10*l.* lent by a friend, will be enough to procure his discharge; no date. f 97.

Printed, *Alleyn Papers*, p. 65.

70. AGREEMENT between Phillip Hinchlow, esq., and Robert Daborn, gent., for the delivery by the latter, before

canorum, Brit. Mus., Add. MS. 24490, f. 56). Nathaniel, or more probably Nathan, Field was at the head of the Chapel Children in 1600, and finally became a member of the King's company. He was author of *A Woman is a Weathercock*, 1612, and *Amends for Ladies*, 1618. There is a portrait of him at the Master's house at Dulwich in the collection bequeathed to the College by Will. Cartwright.

[1] Author of two extant plays, *Christian Turn'd Turk*, 1612, and the *Poor Man's Comfort*, 1655. In the preface to the former he states that his descent was 'not obscure, but generous,' and he probably belonged to the family of Daborne of Guildford, Surrey, a meagre pedigree of which is given in the *Visitation of Surrey* in 1621 (Harl. MS. 5830, f. 58*b*). At some time in his life he took orders, and became Chancellor of Waterford in 1619, Prebendary of Lismore in 1620, and Dean of Lismore in 1621, and died 23 Mar., 1627-8 (Cotton, *Fasti Eccl. Hibern.*, 1851, vol. i. pp. 146, 167, 190). A sermon is extant, preached by him at Waterford in 1618.

the end of Easter term, of 'his Tragoedy cald Matchavill [1] and ye divill,' for 20*l.* in all, 6*l.* being already received, 'and must hav other four pound vpon delivery in of 3 acts and other ten povnd vpon delivery in of ye last scean perfited'; 17 April, 1613. f. 98.

Printed, Malone, vol. xxi. p. 396; *Alleyn Papers*, p. 56.

71. BOND from Rob. Daborne, of the parish of St. Saviour, Southwark, gent., to Phil. Henslowe, of the same parish, in 20*l.*, to deliver 'one playe called Machivell and the divell vppon or before the last daie of Easter terme'; 17 April, 1613. Signed; with seal. *Vellum.* f. 99.

72. ROB. DABORNE to 'good Mr Hinchlow,' asking for a loan of 20*s.* towards bailing his man 'committed to new-gate vpon taking a possession' for him; 25 April, 1613. With the note below:—'Lente Mr Daborne this money, witt-nes Hugh Attwell.' [2] f. 100.

Printed, Malone, vol. xxi. p. 397; *Alleyn Papers*, p. 57.

73. ROB. DABORNE to Phil. Hinchlaw, asking for 'one 20^s^ more of ye x^l^,' and promising to deliver on Friday night the '3 acts fayr written,' and after to 'intend it speedyly,' if he will let him 'have pervsall of any other book'; 3 May, 1613. With acquittance below for 20*s.*, signed by Thomas More, 3 May, 1613. f. 101.

Printed, Malone, vol. xxi. p. 398; *Alleyn Papers*, p. 59.

---

[1] A play called *Matchavell*, or *Machiavel*, is mentioned in Henslowe's *Diary* as acted in 1592 (pp. 22, 24, 27). This may have been a recasting of it; but, as Mr. Collier remarks, the price was a large one even for a new play.

[2] See below, artt. 107, 110. He was one of the Children of the Revels in 1609, and belonged to Prince Charles's company at the time of his death on 25 Sept., 1621. Will. Rowley wrote an elegy on him, which is printed from a broadside by Mr. Collier (*Hist. of Dram. Poetry*, vol. i. p. 406).

74. ROB. DABORNE to Phil. Hinchlow: has sent some papers, though not so fairly written as he could wish, and intends to fulfil his promise, 'which, though it come not within compass of this term, shall come vpon ye neck of this new play they ar now studijnge'; requests that the 10*l.*, of which he has had 9*l.*, may be made up, and will not fail, if he will 'appoynt any howr to read to Mr Allin'; 8 May, 1613. With acquittance below for 20*s.*, signed by Thomas More, 8 May, 1613. f. 102.

Printed, Malone, vol. xxi. p. 399; *Alleyn Papers*, p. 60.

75. ROB. DABORNE to Phil. Hinchlow: most of his troubles being ended, has taken his wife home again; after Monday will 'intend ye busines carefully,' and on Tuesday night will meet him and 'Mr Allin' and read part, but is unwilling to 'read to ye generall company till all be finisht'; is ashamed to press so much, but prays that 20*s.* more may be added to the 10*l.* he has already received; 16 May, 1613. With acquittance below from Garrett Leniaghe for 20*s.* f. 103.

Printed, Malone, vol. xxi. p. 399; *Alleyn Papers*, p. 60.

76. ROB. DABORNE to [Phil. Henslowe]: did think he 'deservd as much mony as Mr Messenger,' though he forbore to urge it; but, now that occasions press so nearly, beseeches him to make their money even by letting him have 10*s.* more; [1613?]. With postscript:—'I pray, S^{r}, let ye boy giv order this night to the stage keeper to set vp bills against Munday for Eastward Hoe[1] and one wendsday the new play.' f. 104.

Printed, Malone, vol. xxi. p. 401; *Alleyn Papers*, p. 61.

---

[1] Comedy by G. Chapman, Ben Jonson, and J. Marston, 1605, acted by the Children of the Revels in Blackfriars. It was for reflecting upon the Scots in this piece that the authors were imprisoned; but it was afterwards so altered as to be acted at Court with approval (Collier, *Hist. of Dram. Poetry*, vol. iii. p. 463).

77. ACQUITTANCE from Rob. Daborne to Phil. Hinchlaw for 16*l.* in part payment of 20*l.* for his 'Tragoedy of Match-avill and y[e] divill'; 19 May, 1613. With the note :—'This play is to be delivered in to M[r] Hinchlaw with all speed. John Alleyn.'[1] f. 105.

Printed, Malone, vol. xxi. p. 400; *Alleyn Papers*, p. 57.

78. ROB. DABORNE to Phil. Hinchlow: heard from the company he was expected yesterday 'to conclude about thear comming over or goinge to Oxford'; has not only laboured his own play, 'which shall be ready before they come over, but givn Cyrill Tourneur[2] an act of y[e] Arreignment[3] of London to write,' so as to have that also ready; has sent 'y[e] 2 sheets more fayr written,' and prays for 40*s.* to send to his counsel in a matter concerning his whole estate; 5 June, 1613. With acquittance below from Garred Leniaghe for 20*s.* f. 106.

Printed, Malone, vol. xxi. p. 397; *Alleyn Papers*, p. 58.

79. ROB. DABORNE to [Phil. Henslowe]: expected him on Monday; can 'this week deliver in y[e] last word and will y[e] night they play thear new play read this'; has sent a sheet and more, fairly written, and he may know there is not much behind; prays him, on account of the 'necessity of term busines,' to let him have 'y[e] other 20[s]' which he desired, and

[1] Not Edw. Alleyn's brother, who died in 1596; but possibly the John Alleyn, son of the latter, whose name Alleyn entered in his pedigree in 1623. His name is frequently attached as a witness to the muniments below. See also MS. iii. art. 10.

[2] Author of the *Revenger's Tragedy*, 1607, and the *Atheist's Tragedie, or the Honest Man's Revenge*, 1611, both acted by the King's company at the Globe. He also wrote elegies on Prince Henry and Sir Fran. Vere. Another play by him, *The Nobleman*, was entered in the Stationers' Register, 15 Feb., 1611, and was one of the plays burnt by Warburton's servant. See Hunter, *Chor. Vat. Angl.*, vol. v., Brit. Mus., Add. MS. 24491, f. 56*b*.

[3] Nothing is known of this piece, the title of which is not included in Halliwell's *Dict. of Old Plays*.

he will then take the remaining 40*s*. when the play is read; 10 June, 1613. Endorsed:—'Lent vpon this notte xx^{s},' &c. f. 107.

Printed, Malone, vol. xxi. p. 398; *Alleyn Papers*, p. 58.

80. ROB. DABORNE to [Phil. Henslowe]: sat up last night till past twelve to write out the sheet sent, and would have delivered all, but had to go to the Common Pleas to acknowledge a fine; prays for '40^{s} in earnest of ye Arreighnment,' and will meet him on Monday night 'at ye new play and conclud farther'; 18 June, 1613. f. 108.

Printed, Malone, vol. xxi. p. 403; *Alleyn Papers*, p. 64.

81. ROB. DABORNE to Phil. Hinchlow: perceives that he thinks his tragedy will be behind, but has taken 'extra ordynary payns with the end and alterd one other scean in the third act, which they have now in parts'; if he will be paymaster, they shall have the 'Arreighnment'; if not, let them try the tragedy first, and 'as y^{t} proves' so deal with him, but he can get 25*l.* for it elsewhere; prays him, if he 'resolv to do this curtesy for ye company,' to let him have 40*s*. more 'till we seale'; 25 June, 1613. With the note below:—'pade to Mr Daborne xx^{s}.' f. 109.

Printed, Malone, vol. xxi. p. 404; *Alleyn Papers*, p. 64.

82. ROB. DABORNE to Phil. Hinchlow: asks, 'of all ffryndship,' for 20*s*., the last he 'will request till the play be fully by vs ended'; 16 July, 1613. With the note below:—'dd. this xx^{s} the 16 of July, 1613.' f. 110.

Printed, Malone, vol. xxi. p. 402; *Alleyn Papers*, p. 62.

83. ROB. DABORNE to Phil. Hinchlow: wrote to [Edward] Griffyn [the scrivener] requesting his [Henslowe's] answer and end to 'those businesses and debts' between them; wishes him either to be paymaster for another play or to take back 10*l.* of what they have had and security for the rest; his necessities are so urgent, till he has sold his estate, that he must resort to other means if Henslowe will not lend him 20*s.* until Thursday, when they deliver in the play; the receipt sent 'by the waterman at the cardinall's hatt' or the present letter shall be security; 30 July, 1613. With the note below:—'witnes Moyses Bowler.' f. 111.

Printed, Malone, vol. xxi. p. 403; *Alleyn Papers*, p. 63.

84. ROB. DABORNE to Phil. Hinchlow: ever since seeing him has kept his bed from lameness; prays him to 'goe forward with that reasonable bargayn for the Bellman,' for which they ask but 12*l.* and 'the overplus of the second day'; has had 10*s.* of this, and desires but 20*s.* more until the delivery of three sheets; prays him not to forsake him, since, on his account, he has put himself 'out of the assured way to get mony' and has come down from 20*l.* a play to 12*l.*; 23 Aug., 1613. With a note below of a loan of 20*s.* 'in earneste of a playe called the bellman of London.'[1] f. 112.

Printed, Malone, vol. xxi. p. 405; *Alleyn Papers*, p. 66.

85. ROB. DABORNE to Phil. Hinchlow: knows the company will give him [Henslowe] his own terms; if not, will bring back his money for the papers with many thanks, and will not fail to bring in the whole play next week; prays, therefore, for 40*s.*, the present note acknowledging a debt, including his quarter's rent, of 8*l.*, for which he shall either have the whole company's bond to pay the first day the play

[1] Not known, except from this mention of it. A tract by T. Dekker, with the same title, 'bringing to light the most notorious villanies that are now practised in the kingdome,' was printed in 1608.

is acted, or the 'King's[1] men' shall pay it and take the papers; 14 Oct., 1613. With the note below:—'Witnes, Moyses Bowler.' f. 114.

Printed, Malone, vol. xxi. p. 408; *Alleyn Papers*, p. 69.

86. ROB. DABORNE to [Phil. Henslowe]: has been to see him twice about the sheet they spoke of, and to know if he means the company to have the play or not; hears they rail at him [Daborne] because the 'Kingsmen hav givn out they shall hav it'; has sent two more sheets, making ten, and desires 30*s.*, which will make 8*l.*, besides the rent, and he shall be satisfied 'cather by them or the kings men'; no date. With the note below:—'Lent Mrs Dabborne vpon this bille more the 29 of October 1613—xx^s.' f. 115.

Printed, Malone, vol. xxi. p. 406; *Alleyn Papers*, p. 67.

87. ROB. DABORNE to [Phil. Henslowe]: requests him, for his 'great occation and present necessety which with less mony will be vnsupplied,' to send him 20*s.*, together with the book which he promised; 5 Nov., 1613. With the note below:—'Witnes, Moyses Bowler.' f. 116.

Printed, Malone, vol. xxi. p. 410; *Alleyn Papers*, p. 71.

88. ROB. DABORNE to [Phil. Henslowe]: his man has called, and found him writing the last scene; thought to have brought it to-night, but it will be late, and, as it is Saturday, requests him to spare 10*s.* more; as for his money, if he will not 'stay till Johnson's[2] play be playd,' the King's men

[1] The King's company, then under the leadership of John Heminge. Their theatre, the Globe, had been burnt 29 June preceding.

[2] Perhaps, as Malone suggests, Ben Jonson's *Bartholomew Fair*, first acted at the Hope Theatre, 31 Oct., 1614.

'hav bin very earnest' to pay it, with 30*s.* profit; purposes to-morrow night, unless he calls first, to come and show him *finis*; 13 Nov., 1613. f. 117.

Printed, Malone, vol. xxi. p. 407; *Alleyn Papers*, p. 67.

89. ROB. DABORNE to Phil. Hinchlow: as an answer to his charge of breach of promise, sends him the 'foule sheet' of the last scene, and his man can testify that he was writing the fair copy; is not to be judged by 'y[e] common measuer of poets,' and would give over writing if he 'could not liv by it and be honest'; will be obliged if he will perform his request, but, in any case, will not 'fayle to write this fayr and perfit the book'; no date. With the note below:—'Lent at this tyme v[s], the 13 of November, 1613.' f. 118.

Printed, Malone, vol. xxi. p. 409; *Alleyn Papers*, p. 69.

90. ROB. DABORNE to [Phil. Henslowe]: requests him to send the 20*s.*, which he so earnestly desired him to lend last night, promising to give 'honnest and iust satisfaction' for it, and for all the rest of his money, on Tuesday next; 27 Nov., 1613. With the note below:—'dd. xx[s]. Wittnes, Moyses Bowler.' f. 119.

Printed, Malone, vol. xxi. p. 409; *Alleyn Papers*, p. 70.

91. ROB. DABORNE to [Phil. Henslowe]: hoped that, on receipt of all his papers, he would have pleasured him with 20*s.*, if not upon the play he [Henslowe] has, yet upon the other out of his book [see above, art. 87], which will make as good a play for his 'publique howse'[1] as was ever played; wants but 10*l.* for it, and undertakes that the company will give 20*l.* rather than lose it; will shortly be out of his want

[1] For the distinction between public and private theatres see Collier, *Hist. of Dram. Poetry*, vol. iii. p. 140.

and able to 'forbear a play' until he can make the best; 9 Dec., 1613. f. 120.

Printed, Malone, vol. xxi. p. 411; *Alleyn Papers*, p. 72.

92. BOND from Rob. Daborne, of St. Saviour's, Southwark, gent., to Phil. Henslowe, of co. Surrey, esq., in 40*l.*, to deliver on 10 Febr. 'one plaie fullie perfected and ended called by the name of the Oule'[1]; 10 Dec., 11 Jas. I., 1613. Signed; with seal of arms.[2] Witnesses, Edw. Griffin, Walt. Hopkinss, Geo. Hales. f. 121.

Printed, Malone, vol. xxi. p. 412; *Alleyn Papers*, p. 73.

93. ACQUITTANCE from Rob. Daborne to Phil. Henchlowe for 7*l.*, in part payment of 10*l.* for a 'plaie called the Oule'; 24 Dec., 1613. f. 123.

Printed, Malone, vol. xxi. p. 412; *Alleyn Papers*, p. 73.

94. ROB. DABORNE to [Phil. Henslowe]: thanks him for his last kindness, and requests 'only the other tenn shillings'; will come on Monday and 'appoynt for the reading the old book and bringing in the new'; 31 Dec., 1613. With the note below:—'paid vpon this bille toward the Owle x^s^.' f. 124.

Printed, Malone, vol. xxi. p. 413; *Alleyn Papers*, p. 74.

95. ROB. DABORNE to Phil. Hinchlow: is 'vtterly disgract' if he does not help him with 10*s.*; on Friday night will bring him 'papers to the valew of three acts'; no date. With the note below:—'Lent vpon this bille x^s^, delivered to the fencer vpon the Owle.' f. 125.

Printed, Malone, vol. xxi. p. 410; *Alleyn Papers*, p. 71.

[1] Only known from the mention of it here and below.

[2] Apparently a chevron between three fleurs de lis; above the coat are the initials W.H. (Walter Hopkins?). The arms of Daborne of Guildford, as drawn in Harl. MS. 5830, f. 85*b*, are *azure*, a chevron between three crosses patonce *or*.

96. ROB. DABORNE to [Phil. Henslowe]: if he likes not this play when read, he shall 'hav the other, which shall be finished with all expedition, for befor god this is a good one'; prays him to send 10*s*. and 'take these papers, which wants but one short scean of the whole play'.; no date. With the note below:—'paid vnto your dawghter the 11 of Marche, 1613[4]—x^{s}.' f. 126.

Printed, Malone, vol. xxi. p. 401; *Alleyn Papers*, p. 62.

97. ROB. DABORNE to Phil. Hinchlow: has now sent a full play, and desires he 'should disburse but 12^{l} a play till they be playd'; means to urge him no farther, for, if he likes not this play, he shall have another to his content; until he has finished one, desires but 20*s*., the refusal of which will force him to 'ingage a play,' which he [Henslowe] will miss; wishes he knew his mind, to give an answer to Mr Palla[n]t,[1] who is much discontented at his neglect of him; 28 Mar., 1613 [an error for 1614]. With the notes below:—'Lent of this bille the 29 of Marche in fulle payment of his new playe laste written the some of x^{s}'; and 'Delivered vnto Mr Daborne the 2 of Aprell 1614 in earneste of the Shee saynte[2] at his owne howsse the some of viii^{s}.' f. 127.

Printed, Malone, vol. xxi. p. 402; *Alleyn Papers*, p. 82.

98. ROB. DABORNE to [Phil. Henslowe]: prays for the courtesy of 10*s*.; would not for twice as much have written, had it not been Sunday, but has been sent for to go to Lord

---

[1] Rob. Pallant, the actor (see below, artt. 107, 110). The same, no doubt, who is called Richard Pallant in the list of Queen's players in 1609 (*Shakesp. Soc. Papers*, vol. iv. p. 44). It appears from art. 104, below (*Alleyn Papers*, p. 79), that he was taken into Henslowe's company in June, 1614. Some verses by him 'to his good friend and fellow' were prefixed to Heywood's *Apology for Actors*, 1612.

[2] Only known from this mention of it.

Willoughby[1] by six o'clock to-morrow morning, and knows not 'how proffitable it may be'; no date. With the note below:—'Lent vpon this bille the 2 of Aguste, 1614.' f. 128.

Printed, Malone, vol. xxi. p. 408; *Alleyn Papers*, p. 68.

99. ROB. DABORNE to [Edward] Griffin, offering a pawn worth 100*l.*, if he cannot otherwise prevail upon Henslowe to let him have the 40*s.*; no date. With the note below:—'Lent vppon a pattent to Mr Dawborne xls.' f. 129.

Printed, Malone, vol. xxi. p. 411; *Alleyn Papers*, p. 72.

100. NAT. FIELD to Phil. Hinchlow: Mr. Dawborne and himself 'haue spent a great deale of time in conference about this plott, which will make as beneficiall a play as hath come these seauen yeares'; they want 10*l.* only in hand, for which they will deliver the play finished on 1 August; having such hope of it, they are unwilling to lose it, and, of his own knowledge, 'Mr Dawborne may haue his request of another companie'; no date [*circ.* 1613]. f. 130.

Printed, Malone, vol. xxi. p. 395; *Alleyn Papers*, p. 48.

101. A SMALL MEMORANDUM-BOOK, chiefly in the hand of Edw. Alleyn, containing accompts of brick-making, building, &c., in 1614 and 1615. ff. 131–145.

On the second leaf, f. 132, is the entry·

'14 day the noble grandchild[2]

hole	0	16	9
half	0	1	6
re [*sic*]	0	1	2
cresset	0	0	3'

[1] Rob. Bertie, Lord Willoughby of Eresby, cr. Earl of Lindsey in 1626. Mr. Collier conjectures that it was by his means that Daborne obtained preferment in the Church.

[2] This title does not occur in Mr. Halliwell's *Dict. of Old Plays.*

102. BOND from Rob. Daborne, of St. Saviour's, Southwark, gent., and Phil. Massinger, of London, gent., to Phil. Henchlow, of St. Saviour's, esq., in 6*l.*, for the payment of 3*l.* on 1 Aug.; 4 July, 13 Jas. I., 1615. Signed; with seals, that of Daborne bearing the arms as above, art. 92. Witness, Walter Hopkinss. f. 146.

Printed, *Memoirs of Edw. Alleyn*, p. 121.

103. JOHN MARSTON to 'M[r] Hensloe, at the rose on the Bankside'; no date. f. 148.

First printed by Mr. Collier, *Memoirs of Edw. Alleyn*, p. 154, note. See also J. O. Halliwell, *Works of J. Marston*, 1856, vol. i. p. x. The whole letter is manifestly a forgery, having been first traced in pencil, the marks of which are in places still visible. This was first pointed out by Mr. Hamilton (*Enquiry*, p. 94), and may be seen in the facsimile given by Dr. Ingleby (*Shakspere Controversy*, p. 273). See also H. Staunton, *Shakespeare*, 1858, vol. i. p. lvii.

104. W[ILLIAM] BIRDE[1] to Edw. Alleyn: 'one Jhon Russell,' whom he appointed a 'gatherer,' has proved so false that the company have 'many tymes warnd him from taking the box,' and have now 'resolud he shall never more come to the doore'; but for his [Alleyn's] sake he 'shall haue his wages to be a nessessary atendaunt on the stage,' and, if he will mend their garments, they will pay him for that also; no date. f. 149.

Printed, *Alleyn Papers*, p. 32.

105. WILL. BIRDE to Phil. Hinchlowe, entreating a loan of 40*s.* for a week; [*ante* 1616]. With the note below:—'Feched by William Felle his man.' f. 150.

Printed, Malone, vol. xxi. p. 392; *Alleyn Papers*, p. 33.

[1] See above, art. 25. He was one of the lessees of the Fortune in 1618: see below, Mun. 56, in which John Russell is also mentioned as a tenant of two rooms adjoining the theatre.

106. 'ARTICLES OF [GRIE]UAUNCE against M[r] Hinchlowe' on the part of his company, followed on the other side of the same leaf by 'Articles of oppression against M[r] Hinchlowe'; [1615?]. f. 151.

Printed, Malone, vol. xxi. p. 416; *Alleyn Papers*, p. 78. Mr. Collier, the editor of the latter work, takes his copy from Malone, stating that the original is 'not now found at Dulwich,' an error which he repeats in his *Hist. of Dram. Poetry*, ed. 1879, vol. i. p. 375. The printed version contains a number of slight inaccuracies in spelling, &c., together with the more serious misreadings '50[li]' and '40[li]' for '50[s]' and '40[s]' (paragr. 7), 'likewise M[r] Field' for 'because M[r] Feild' (paragr. 8), and 'enter and' for 'enter bond' (paragr. 15).

107. ARTICLES OF AGREEMENT between Edw. Alleyn, esq., and Jacob Meade, on the one part, and William Rowley,[1] Robert Pallant, Joseph Taylor, Robert Hamlett [Hamlen?], John Newton, Hugh Ottewell, William Backsted, Thomas Hobbes, Antony Smyth, and William Penn,[2] on the other part, whereby, in discharge of a debt of 400*l.* due by the latter parties to Philip Henshlowe,[3] deceased, the said Edward Alleyn covenants to accept the sum of 200*l.*, the same to be paid by daily instalments of a fourth part of the receipts of the 'whole galleryes of the playehowse comonly called the Hope[4] . . . or in anye other howse private or publique wherein they shall playe,' with the proviso that the said William

[1] Partner with Henslowe in Paris Garden as well as in the Hope Theatre (see Malone, vol. xxi. p. 413, and below, MS. ii. artt. 32, 34, and Munn. 19, 49.

[2] All these names appear in one or another of the lists of players given in Fleay's *Shakespeare Manual*, p. 114, except Rob. Hamlen and Ant. Smyth. Hamlen's name occurs below, Mun. 47. In the body of the present indenture it is written 'Hamlett,' but both here and in art. 110 the signature appears to be Hamlen, and the name is written 'Hamlyn' in the other document. Ant. Smyth played in Massinger's *Roman Actor*, 1626, and in Ford's *Lover's Melancholy*, 1628.

[3] Died about 9 Jan., 1615-6 (MS. v., below, art. 22).

[4] The Hope Theatre, on the Bankside, used also as a bear garden (Collier, *History of Dram. Poetry*, vol. iii. p. 128). The company playing there were called

Rowley and the rest shall be bound to observe all their former articles of agreement with Philip Henshlowe and Jacob Meade; 20 Mar., 1615[6]. Signed by William Rowley, Robert Pallant, &c., the names 'Ottewell' and 'Backsted' in the body of the document being written 'Attwell' and 'Barksted.' Witnesses, Rob. Daborne, Thos. Foster, Edw. Knight. f. 152.

Printed, *Mem. of Edw. Alleyn*, p. 127.

108. THOMAS DEKKER[1] to his 'worthy and worshipfull freind Edw. Allin,' enclosing some verses (now lost) as 'poore testimonies of a more rich affection,' adding 'and it best becomes mee to sing any thing in praise of charity, be cause, albeit I haue felt few handes warme thorowgh that complexion, yett imprisonment may make mee long for them'; King's Bench, 12 Sept., 1616. f. 154.

Printed, *Mem. of Edw. Alleyn*, p. 131, and, with the following, in the *Dramatic Works of Thos. Dekker*, 1873, vol. i. p. xxxi.

109. THO. DEKKER to [Edw. Alleyn], thanking him for the 'last remembrance' of his love, and saying that he writes now, 'not poetically but as an orrator,' to beg him to take as a servant a young man of his own name of Alleyn, 'sonn to a worthie yeoman of Kent here prisoner'; [1616 ?]. The signature only *autograph.* f. 156.

Printed, *Mem. of Edw. Alleyn*, p. 186.

110. THE PLAYERS of Phil. Henslowe's company to their 'worthy and much respected ffrend Mr Allen,' explaining

---

the servants of the Princess Elizabeth, and, according to Taylor, the water-poet, writing in 1614, were

'Such a company, I'll boldly say,
That better (nor the like) e'er play'd a play.'

[1] According to a note by Oldys in Langbaine's *English Dramatic Poets*, Dekker was in the King's Bench from 1613 to 1616, 'and how much longer I know not' (Brit. Mus., Add. MS. 22592, f. 136*b*).

that they have been driven away from [the Hope on] 'the bankes side' by [Joseph] Meade, and requesting an advance of 40*l.* on the security of 'a great summe of monie,' which they are to receive from the Court; [1616?]. Signed by William Rowley, Robert Pallant, Joseph Taylor, John Newton, Robert Hamlen, Hugh Attwell, and Anthony Smyth, the signatures being in this order, except that Pallant's name is on a level with that of Rowley, to the left. f. 157.

Printed, *Alleyn Papers*, p. 86, with facsimiles of the signatures. Mr. Collier, however, reads 'Hamlen' as 'Hampton.'

111. FRAGMENT OF A LETTER to Edw. Alleyn[1]:—

'Mr Allene, I most hartilly commend me to you and to your good bedffelow mistres Allen, to Mr Hinsslow and Mistres Hinslowe, trustinge in god you ar all in good health, and I geve you great thankes for your kyndnes in sending me the reseait, yff god geve me lif I will not be vnthankfull to you for it. My wif and I have a request vnto you and this it is; she have reseaved a letter that her father is dead, to her great greeff and sorowe and myn, and she knowes not what will he hath made; but for the libardes head in shordich, that is nowe my wifes so longe as she leves, my father had a lease of Mr Vahan dwelinge in the Spitell for three lives, which lease she have hear with her. Good Mr Alen, let me

[1] The writer was evidently husband of 'Haris Joones,' the writer of the letter following. Probably, therefore, he was Richard Jones, the actor, whose name has already occurred; the more so as the handwriting has a resemblance to that of art. 8 and the signature of art. 2. Henslowe being still alive, or his death not yet known to the writer, the date can hardly be later than 1616; and it is not unlikely that Richard Jones, who had already acted in Germany, was a member of the English company which is known to have been at Danzig in that year (Cohn, *Shakespeare in Germany*, 1865, p. xci.). His name occurs in none of the lists of actors in Fleay's *Shakespeare Manual* later than 1600, and in Henslowe's *Diary*, p. 219, is an entry of a loan of 50*l.* 'unto the company to geve unto Mr Jonnes and Mr Shaw at ther goinge a waye' in Feb., 1601–2.

intrat so muche frendshipe at your bandes as to take vpe the rent of the howese for me and my wif, and to keepe it for vs tell our returne into Ingland, for I have no frend nowe but your seilf whom I acownt as my dearest frend. The rent of the libardes head is x poundes a year, out of which iii poundes a year is to be payd to Mr Vahan, the land lord, dwelinge in the spitell. It . . . .' f. 159.

112. 'HARIS JOONES' to 'Mr Edward Allinn':—

'Ladro [?] from Dansicke the firste of Apriell, 1620. My aproved good ffrinde Mr Allin, your helleth wished in the lord witith your good wife, trvsting in God you ar both in good hellth, as I was at the wryting her of. Thes few lines is to intreate your worshype to stand owr good frinde as you hath bin before. I sente you a leeter of atorny by Mr Babties [Baptist?] abowte the lebickes hed [Leopard's Head]; I cnowe not whither you hath reseafed it or no. I woulld intreate your worship to sende me word how Mr Rowly hath delte with me for my rente by this baer [bearer] her of. My husband is with the prince,[1] and as yt I am here in Dansicke lockinge evry daye [to] gooe to him. Thvs desierin God to bles you with your good wife, I commyt you to the almyty God. Your pore frinde to command, Haris Joones. H. I.' f. 160.

113. ACQUITTANCE from William Gore to Mathias Alleyn, Master of Dulwich College, for 11*s*., for his pains in perusing a license in mortmain, whereby it appeared that Edw. Alleyn 'was in his liefe tyme seized of a messuage called the Fortune,' and that he 'disposed of the same to charitable vses'; 8 Nov., 1632. f. 162.

[1] Probably George William, Elector of Brandenburg, succ. 23 Dec., 1619, died 21 Nov., 1640. His wife, Elizabeth Charlotte, was sister of Frederic, Elector Palatine and King of Bohemia.

114. 'A CIRTIFFICATE vnder ye hands of the courte of assistants [of Dulwich College] to ye Lord Keeper for rente due by the Fortune tennauntes,' stating that at Michaelmas the arrears of rent for the theatre will amount to 164*l.* 14*s.* 3¾*d.*, and that, in consequence, the College is compelled to 'take moneys vp at interest to supplie their wantes and relief of the poore of the said colledge'; 4 Sept., 1637. Signed by Mathias Alleyn, master, Thomas Alleyn, warden, and ten others. f. 163.

Printed, *Alleyn Papers*, p. 95.

115. BILL IN CHANCERY preferred by Dulwich College against Margaret Gray, Edward Marrant, and John Roods for the non-payment of rent upon leases of the Fortune Theatre, with the answers of the defendants; Nov., 1637. f. 165.

It appears from their answers that Marrant and Roods were assignees of leases (see below, Munn. 56–58, 63, 66–70) originally granted by Edw. Alleyn to Charles Masseye, the actor, John Fisher, Thomas Wiggett, and Richard Gannill. Masseye is mentioned as dead before 6 Dec., 1635, leaving a widow, Elianor. The answer of the defendants concludes:—

'And they paid their rents vntill Christmas which was 12 monthe, which was Christmas 1635, and then the kinge to hinder the increase of the Plague did forbid Theaters in and about London, for to hinder concurse of people. And soe, acteing of playes being the way to rayse the rent (and forbiden), the defendants haue not euer since bene able, nor are chargeable as they conceiue, to pay rents, they being alsoe inhibited for imployeing the premises to any other vse then for playes.'

116. LICENSE from the master, warden, &c., of Dulwich College for the assignment to Tobyas Lisley of leases of the

'Fortune Playhowse' granted by Edw. Alleyn and lately held by Mary Bryant, Thomas Robinson, Edward Jackson, Thomas Blomfeild, and Margaret Gray; 15 July, 1639. Signed by Mathias Alleyn, master, Thomas Alleyn, warden, and four others. f. 171.

117. ACQUITTANCE from the master, warden, &c., of Dulwich College to Tobias Lisle, grocer, for 50*l.*, in full dis charge of 55*l.* 6*s.* 10*d.* due for arrears of rent [see below, Munn. 66, 67] on a lease of 'a parte and an half parte in twelue partes to be devided of the Fortune playhowse'; 22 July, 1639. Signed by Mathias Alleyn, Thomas Alleyn, and three others. f. 173.

118. PETITION from Dulwich College to Sir Edward Littleton, Lord Keeper, against John Beale [assignee of a lease from Edw. Alleyn to Edw. Jacson] and other tenants of the Fortune play-house, who are in arrear with their rent to the amount of 104*l.* 14*s.* 4*d.*; with an order by the Lord Keeper for a hearing, dat. 9 Feb., 1640[1]. *Copies.* f. 175.

From this petition it appears that the cause above (art. 115) was heard 26 Jan., 1639, and order made 'that the said tennauntes should pay all their rent in arreare without any abatement, which accordingly they did either compound for and pay for a certaine tyme,' but had again fallen in arrear.

Printed, *Alleyn Papers*, p. 96.

119. BILL IN CHANCERY by Dulwich College against John Beale, assignee of a lease of a twelfth part of the Fortune play-house, to compel him to pay arrears of rent, to keep the premises in repair, and to surrender the counterpart of the lease, followed by the defendant's answer and proofs for the plaintiffs; Hilary term, 15 Chas. I. [1640]. *Copies*, as brief for counsel. f. 177.

Beale in his answer alleges that he had paid all rent due up to a certain date, but that the master and warden would not sign the acquittances; also that by the terms of the lease he was bound to pay rent to the heirs of Edw. Alleyn, no mention being made of the plaintiffs.

120. ORDER OF COURT in a suit between Margaret Grey, plaintiff, and Matthias Allen, Thomas Allen, and Tobias Lisle, defendants, to the effect that, in accordance with a former decree, the plaintiff shall pay the rents [on a lease of shares in the Fortune play-house] and receive the profits; 9 July, 17 Chas. I. [1641]. f. 181.

121. ORDERS OF COURT and other papers in a suit between Tobias Lisle and Dulwich College [see below, Mun. 66], ending in the dismissal of the plaintiff's bill for relief 'against accions brought by the defendants for *66l.* 15*s.* 9*d.* arrerages of rent reserved vpon leases of certaine shares of the Fortune playehowse'; 28 Nov., 21 Chas. I. [1645]–26 Nov., 22 Chas. I. [1646]. f. 183.

122. ORDERS OF COURT, &c., in a suit between Dulwich College and Tobias Lisle, Thomas Grimes, John Rhodes, and others [see below, Munn. 67–69] relative to arrears of rent on leases of the 'Fortune,' ending with an order that 'the matters be refferred to one or more tryalles at lawe'; 16 Oct., 23 Chas. I. [1647]–24 Nov., 1649. f. 206.

123. ORDER OF COURT, allowing the plea and demurrer of Thomas Allen and Ralph Allen, master and warden of Dulwich College, defendants in a suit with John Rhodes; 1 Feb., 1649[50]. f. 223.

124. REPORT of Edward Jerman and John Tanner, 'being desired by ye M^r^ and Warden of Dulwich Colledg to vew ye ground and building of the late playhouse called ye Fortune': to the effect that 'by reason ye lead hath bin taken from ye sayd building, ye tyling not secured and ye foundation of ye sayd playhouse not keept in good repaire, great part of ye sayd playhouse is fallen to ye ground, the tymber therof much decayed and rotten, and the brickwalls soe rent and torne y^t ye whole structure is in noe condition capable of repaire, but in greate danger of falling, to ye hazzard of passengers liues'; and recommending that a street be cut from Whitecross Street to Golden Lane, and twenty-three tenements be built on the ground'; 18 July, 1656. f. 225.

Printed, *Alleyn Papers*, p. 98.

125. ORDER of the Court of Assistants of Dulwich College for the lease of 'the Fortune playhouse and ground therevnto belonging,' the same having 'for diuers yeares last past laine void and yeilded noe rent but bene a great losse to ye Colledge,' and being 'at present soe ruinous y^t parte thereof is already fallen downe and ye rest will suddainly follow'; 5 Mar., 1659[60]. Signed by Thomas Alleyn, Ralph Alleyn, and ten others. f. 227.

126. ORDER of the same for the sale of the materials of the Fortune play-house, in consequence of their inability to find a tenant under the order of 5 Mar., 1659–60, notwithstanding their 'vtmost endeauours .... by posting of bills in the Citie of London and putting it into the newes bookes,'[1] &c.; 4 Mar., 1660[1]. Signed by Thomas Alleyn, Ralph Alleyn, and ten others. f. 229.

---

1 An advertisement that 'the Fortune play-house .... with the ground thereto belonging, is to be let to be built upon, where twenty-three tenements may be erected, with gardens, and a street may be cut through for the better accommodation of the building,' was inserted in the *Mercurius Politicus* of 14–21 Feb., 1661 (Lyson's *Environs*, vol. i. p. 104; Collier, *Hist. of Dram. Poetry*, vol. iii. p. 122).

127. MEMORANDUM of a contract for the purchase by William Beaven from Dulwich College of the materials of the Fortune play-house for 75*l.*, and of the ground both on the north and south side at the rate of 2*s.* 6*d.* for 'each foote running measure'; 16 Mar., 1660[1]. f. 231.

128. ACQUITTANCE from Dulwich College to William Beaven, of London, tiler and bricklayer, for 50*l.*, 'in full payment for the materialls of the late demolished Fortune playhowse'; 8 July, 1661. *Copy.* f. 232.

129. MEMORANDUM for a lease from Dulwich College to William Beaven, for 45 years, at a rent of 34*l.* 10*s.*, of the ground 'whereon the late demolished playhowse called the Fortune was erected,' together with tenements, &c., built or to be built by him upon the same and in Golden Lane; 24 July, 1661. f. 234.

130. ACQUITTANCE from Dulwich College to Will. Beaven for 10*l.* for the materials of two tenements in Golden Lane, the one being 'over the gateway leading to y[e] late Fortune playhowse' and the other 'knowne by the name of the Kings head'; 26 July, 1661. *Copy.* f. 236.

131. BILL IN CHANCERY of Will. Beaven against Dulwich College [see below, Mun. 71] for non-fulfilment of an agreement to grant him a building lease for 45 years of the site of 'y[e] Fortune .... heretofore vsed for a playhouse for actinge of publique enterludes and stage playes,' with the answer of the College, alleging an ordinance of the Founder forbidding a lease to be made for more than 21 years; [Nov., 1661]. *Drafts.* f. 238.

132. DECREE IN CHANCERY empowering Dulwich

College to grant to Will. Beaven a lease as below; 21 Nov., 13 Chas. II. [1661]. *Copy.* f. 252.

133. ORDER of the Court of Assistants of Dulwich College for a lease to Will. Beaven, for 21 years, with renewals for 21 years and for 3 years, at the rent of 34*l.* 10*s.*, of all messuages, &c., erected by him on ground which was in part the site of the Fortune play-house, now 'totally demolished'; 4 Mar., 1661[2]. *Copy.* f. 256. For a draft of the lease see below, Mun. 72.

134. ACQUITTANCE from Dulwich College to Will. Beaven for 34*l.* 10*s.* for a year's rent of tenements on ground in part the site of 'the late demollished Fortune playehouse,' and 3*l.* 7*s.* 6*d.* for other tenements in 'Goulding Lane'; 28 July, 1662. *Copy.* f. 257.

135. A TRANSLATION in verse, in the hand of Ben Jonson, of Martial's epigram[1] 'Vitam quæ faciunt beatiorem,' lib. x. 47, beginning, 'The things that make the happier life are these.' f. 259.

Printed, for the first time, from this copy by Mr. Collier, *Mem. of Edw. Alleyn*, p. 54, and reprinted, Gifford, *Works of Ben Jonson*, ed. 1875, vol. ix. p. 345.

136. A COPY, in the hand of Ben Jonson, of Sir Henry Wotton's poem[2] 'How happy is he born and taught.' On the same sheet as the preceding. f. 259.

Printed from this copy, *Mem. of Edw. Alleyn*, p. 53. Mr. Collier, however, does not print the lines, as he says, 'exactly in the form in which they stand in the manuscript,' but with the following misread-

[1] See Jonson's 'Conversations with Drummond of Hawthornden,' *Works*, ed. 1875, vol. ix. p. 366, 'He [Jonson] recommended to my reading . . . . Martiall, whose epigram *Vitam quæ faciunt beatiorem*, &c., he hath translated.'

[2] See 'Conversations,' &c., as above, p. 375, 'Sir Edward [Henry] Wotton's verses of a happie lyfe he [Jonson] hath by heart.'

ings: 'and' for 'or,' st. i. l. 1; 'to' for 'unto,' st. ii. l. 3; 'humors' for 'rumors,' st. iii. l. 1; 'than' for 'then,' st. iv. l. 3. His faulty copy was used for collation by Dyce, *Poems of Sir H. Wotton*, Percy Soc., 1843, p. 5, and Hannah, *Poems by Sir H. Wotton*, &c., 1845, p. 29.

137. POEM, in four six-line stanzas, addressed 'to his deservedlie honored frend Mr Edward Allane, the first founder and Master of the Colledge of God's gift,' in the hand of, and signed by, 'W. Alexander.'[1] f. 260.

Printed, for the first time, from this copy, *Mem. of Edw. Alleyn*, p. 178.

138. COPY of the part of Orlando in Robert Greene's *Historie of Orlando Furioso*,[2] probably played by Edw. Alleyn. *Imperfect*, the paper being in places much decayed and worm-eaten; written on slips, originally pasted together so as to form a long roll, six inches wide. f. 261.

Printed, *Mem. of Edw. Alleyn*, p. 198. See also Dyce, *Works of R. Greene*, 1861, p. 31.

139. A DRAMATIC DIALOGUE, probably played as an interlude, with stage directions. This and the following articles are written in different hands of the end of the 16th and beginning of the 17th centt. f. 272.

Printed, with great freedom, *Alleyn Papers*, p. 8.

The text, which forms Mr. Collier's first four stanzas, is in the original as follows:—

'Seest thou not yon farmers sonn? He hath stolne my love

[1] Sir Will. Alexander, of Menstrie, author of the *Monarchicke Tragedies*, 1603–1607, *Doomesday*, 1614, and other poems. He was made Secretary of State for Scotland 1626, Viscount Stirling 1630, and Earl of Stirling 1633, and died 12 Feb., 1640.

[2] Entered in Henslowe's *Diary*, p. 21, as acted by Lord Strange's company on 21 Feb., 1591–2; but it is not marked as a new play. It was first printed in 1594 (see Collier, *Hist. of Dram. Poetry*, vol. ii. p. 529).

frome me, alas! What shall I doe? I am vndonn; my hart will neer be as it was. Oh, but he gives her gay gold rings, and tufted gloves to were vppon a holly day, and many other goodly things, that hath stolne my love away.

'*Frend.* Lett him give her gaie gold rings, or stufted gloves: were they nere so sweete, my boy, or were her lovers lords or kings, they should not cary the wench away. Oh, but a daunces wondrers well, and with his daunce stolne away her love from me; yett she was wont to say I bore away the bell for daunsing and for courtisie [daunsing].

'*Jack.* Fie, lusty yonker, what doe you heer, that you are not all a daunsing on the greene to day? We feare perce the farmer's sonn is lik to carry your wench away. Good dick, bid them all com hether, and tell perce from me beside, that if he think to haue the wench, heer he stands shall lie with the bride.

'*W*[*ench*] *Fre*[*nd*]. Fy, nan, fie, willt then forsake thee olde lover for any other newcom guest? Thou long time his love did know and whie shouldst thou now vse him soe? Whie, bony Dicky, I will not forsake my bony rowland for any gold; if he can daunce as well as perce, he shall have my hart in hold.'

On the back is written 'Kitt Marlowe,' in a later, and perhaps modern, hand.

140. Seven Stanzas in praise of tailors. f. 273.

The first stanza is:—

'You peu[i]sh foolles of poeitrey,
That seakes for to desgrace
The tayler and the tayleres lades
That weare within this place.'

Printed, *Alleyn Papers*, p. 13, with considerable changes in the spelling.

141. Dialogue on Love between a man and a boy, in eleven stanzas. f. 274.

The first stanza is:—

'*Man.* It fell vpon a sollem holledaye
Boye. Woe me that the daye should be termed holey

Man. When idell wittes had gotten leaue to play
Boye. Such play ill please the mind thates weand from folley.'

Printed, *Alleyn Papers*, p. 29, with corrections in the spelling; but st. 3, for 'state' read 'pompe'; st. 6, for 'in curls' read 'icimt,' i.e. 'ikempt'; and st. 11, for 'ones yerely' read 'one yerth,' i.e. 'on earth.'

142. BALLAD, without title, of the 'Bonny Wench of Adlington.'[1] At the top is partially legible the name 'Thomas My....' f. 275.

'[Farye well the c]hurch of Adlingtunne,
[The windowes] be of glass;
[Full often times] have I gon that way,
[When Ch]rist hath binn at mass;
[And all w]as for that bonny wenches sake,
[That now is] dead, allas;
[For allake] shall I never se hir no more.

'[Farye well] the clark of Adlinge[tunne],
For he will mak ady;
[Who bui]lded the chirch of lime and stonne,
[Upon t]he hill so high;
[And all] was for that bon[n]y wenches sake,
[That] now she lies therby;
For allake, &c.

'Farye well the streates of Adlingtunne,
That be so many fold;
Full often times hav I gon that way,
To chaung vhyt mony for gould;
And all was for that bon[n]y wenches sake,
That now she lyes full could;
For allake, &c.

'Farye well the water of Adlingtunn,
That runs so dark and dime;
Full often times hav I gon therby,

[1] Probably Adlington in Cheshire, known in ballad literature as the home of Sir Urian Leigh, the hero of the *Spanish Lady's Love*.

To se the whitt swann swime;
And all was for that bon[n]y wenches sake,
That now she lies therin;
For allake, &c.

'Farye well the buttes of Adlyngetunne,
That standes vnder the hill;
And often times hav I gonn therby,
And with so good a will;
And all was for that bon[n]y wenches sake,
That now she lyes full still;
For allake, &c.

'Now will [I] sell my shotting glove,
My braser and my bowe;
And wend unto som far cuntrey,
Wher no man shall me knowe;
And all was for that bon[n]y wenches sake,
[That now she lyes full lowe];
For allake, &c.

'Now will I sell my dager,
So will I do my k[n]yfe;
And all was for that bon[n]y wenches sake,
That shold have ben my wife.'

Before the third verse is what appears to be an alternative version:—

'Farye well the streates of Adlingtunn,
That be so many and steppe;
Full often times hav I gonne therby,
In dry wether and wett;
And all was for that bon[n]y wenches sake,
Which now is dead allake;
For allas, &c.'

143. POEM of a jealous husband outwitted, in about twenty-one six-line stanzas. Very *imperfect*, owing to the decay of the paper. f. 276.

The first stanza is :—

> 'A neighbour mine not long ago there was,
> But namelesse he for blamelesse he shalle bee,
> That maried had a tricke and bonny lasse
> As in a sommer day a man might see;
> But he himselfe a fovle vnhandsome groome,
> And farre vnfit to hould so good a roome.'

144. LOOSE AND HUMOROUS VERSES, nearly covering the two sides of a sheet much decayed and mutilated. f. 278.

The first lines are severally as follows :—

> 'When golden dayes be [past]'
> 'Kiss my cheek and chine, boy, but presume no nieyr'
> 'An owld man a woing made bragge off his doinge'
> 'Zounds I ame ye roring boy thats newly come to towne'
> 'Com hobling Gobling grisly ghoast.'

On the back is a fragmentary note in the hand of Edw. Alleyn, apparently the beginning of a clause in a will.

MS. No. II.

Alleyn Papers. Vol. II. Letters and Papers of Philip Henslowe and Edward Alleyn, as Joint Masters of the Royal Game of Bears, Bulls and Mastiff Dogs; 1598–1626.

1. Philip Henslowe to Edward Alleyn, 'at Mr Arthure Langworthes, at the Brille in Sussex': writes to tell him that 'Mr Bowes [1] liesse very sycke and every bodey thinckes he will not escape'; fears, therefore, he shall lose all, for Dr. Seasser [2] has done nothing, while, as for the other matter,[3] the Lord Admiral promised to move the Queen, but the next day rode away to Windsor; spoke himself to Lady Edmonds,[4] who at once went to her Majesty, but 'Mr Darsey[5] of the previ chamber crossed her and made yt knowne to her that the quene had geuen yt all readey in reversyon to one Mr Dorington,[6] a pensenor,' and this is confessed by the latter to

[1] Ralph Bowes, Master of the Queen's Game, by patent dated 2 June, 1573 (see below, Mun. 7). He was dead within a few days after Henslowe wrote, as appears from a letter to Sir Rob. Cecil from Hen. Lok (*Calendar of State Papers*, 1598–1601, p. 60).

[2] Dr., afterwards Sir, Julius Cæsar, judge of the Court of Admiralty and Master of Requests. He was appointed Chancellor of the Exchequer in 1606, and Master of the Rolls in 1614, and died in 1636.

[3] Possibly the building of the Fortune, which, however, was not begun till Jan., 1600.

[4] Probably the wife of Sir Tho. Edmonds, Comptroller of the Household, and the Dorothy Edmonds mentioned as gentlewoman of the Privy Chamber in 1580 (Lansdowne MS. 29, f. 161). Annuities given her by the Queen were still paid in 1614 (Lansd. MS. 165, f. 247).

[5] Edward Darcy, groom of the Privy Chamber.

[6] John Dorrington, gentleman pensioner, knighted 23 July, 1603. The grant to him of the office, with a fee of 10*d.* a day and 4*d.* for his deputy, was made on

be true; Mr. Langworth will report what 'paynes and travell' he [Henslowe] has taken, 'for we haue moved other great parsonages for yt, but as yeat I knowe not howe yt shall pleasse godd wee shall spead, for I ame sure my lord admerall will do nothinge'; London, 4 June, 1598.[1] f. 1.

Printed, *Memoirs of Edw. Alleyn*, p. 48.

2. ARTHUR LANGWORTH[2] to Edw. Alleyn: defends himself against the charge 'out of sight out of mynde,' and proceeds:—'If it please god to take awey Mr Bowes, I cannot helpe it but be sorry. You knowe I suddenly devised a wey to helpe, if your Lord wold do it: therfor, I forshowd it not. I was not acqueinted howe my L. of Nottingham wold geve over the staffe. My lord told you what to do, therfore blame yourself. Suddenly you may do it still, as I said before. I told you I wold gett you a place, if the partie and you could agree, so do I tell you still. I told you the derest price and the lowest or neere theraboutes. I assure you, if I had not lovid you, I wold not haue taken so much paynes and made such a vile jorney, not for the thing. But to finish, if otherwise you can better helpe yourself, do it, I will loose my labore. But if you cannot, I will performe this. You shall haue the place, agreing and paieing for it, and I wilbe reddy as a frend to helpe the best I can, and I will hast to

7 Aug., 1598 (*Cal. State Papers*, 1598–1601, p. 79). His patent was dated 11 Aug., and was renewed by James I. 14 July, 1603 (see below, Mun. 25).

[1] For another letter from Henslowe on the same subject, 26 Sept., 1598, see above, MS. i. art. 24.

[2] Of the Brill or Broyle, in the par. of Ringmere, co. Sussex (*Visitation of Sussex*, 1634, Harl. MS. 1562, f. 118). He married Rose, daughter of Will. Durant of Cottesmore, co. Rutland, and died in 1606, the probate of his will being dated 6 Nov. (see below, MS. iv. art. 54). John Langworth, the only one of his children not mentioned in his will, died in 1612. He married Mary, daughter of Tho. Chaloner, belonging, no doubt, to the family of that name with which Alleyn was on intimate terms.

you as much as I knowe will serve the torne,' &c.; [June, 1598]. f. 2.

3. JOHN DORRINGTON to Phil. Henslowe: is ordered to have 'hir Maiesties games' at the Court on Monday,[1] and begs him and 'Jackcobe'[2] to do their best to help him, the warning being so short and himself not well, having had an ague fit on Friday; has written to his sister Hide[3] to let the Queen know the loss they have had in the winter of their best bears, and to signify the same to 'them that executes my Lord Chamberlins place'; Wigell, . . May, 1600. f. 3.

Printed, *Memoirs of Edw. Alleyn*, p. 60.

4. ACQUITTANCE from Richard Lefwicke[4] to Phil. Henslowe and Edw. Alleyn for 10*l*., for 'i quarters rent dewe vnto my M^r^, Mr Doryngton, for the commisyon for the Beargarden'; 1 Jan., 1601[2]. f. 4.

Printed, *Alleyn Papers*, p. 26.

5. PATENT from James I. to Philip Henslowe and Edw.

---

[1] The occasion was perhaps the same as that referred to in a letter from Rowland White to Sir R. Sidney, 12 May, 1600, 'tomorrow she hath commanded the beares, the bull and the ape to be baited in the Tiltyard' (*Sidney Papers*, 1746, vol. ii. p. 194).

[2] Jacob Meade, joint lessee with Henslowe of Paris Garden.

[3] See Nichols, *Progresses of Queen Elizabeth*, vol. iii., where Mrs. Luce Hyde, gentlewoman, is included among the ladies of the Court who gave presents to the Queen on New Year's Day, 1599–1600.

[4] A similar acquittance for the next quarter is in Henslowe's *Diary*, p. 267. The commission of 40*l*. a year was paid to Dorrington, as Master of the Queen's Game, for license to bait, &c., at Paris Garden; an account of which is given by Mr. Collier, *History of Dram. Poetry*, ed. 1879, vol. iii. p. 93. Alleyn's connexion with the Garden, as lessee, appears to have begun in 1594; for in MS. viii., below, f. 5*b* (*Alleyn Papers*, pp. xiii. xvii.), is the note:—

'What the Bear Garden cost me for my owne part in December 1594
First to Mr Burnabie . . . . 200^l^
Then for the pattent[t] 250
Some is . 450
I held itt 16 year and R. 160^l^ per an[n]um which is . . . . . 960^l^
Sowld itt to my father Hinchloe in Februarie 1610 for . 580^l^'

Alleyn, of the 'office of Cheefe Master, overseer and ruler of our beares, bulls and mastiffe dogges,' in as full and ample manner as Sir William Steward,[1] Sir John Darrington [Dorrington] and Raphe Bowes, with power, for reasonable prices, 'to take up and kepe for our service, pastyme and sporte any mastife dogge or dogges and mastife bitches, beares, bulls and other meete and convenient for cur said service and pastymes,' to stay all mastiff dogs and bitches going beyond the seas without special warrant, and to bait in any place at their discretion, no other being permitted to do the same without their license and appointment, the fee for the said office to be 10*d.* a day and 4*d.* for their deputy; Westminster, 24 Nov., a° 2 [1604]. Endorsed by Edw. Alleyn, 'A draft off ye pattent.' *Imperfect*, wanting the first sheet of the four. f. 5*b.*

Printed, *Mem. of Edw. Alleyn*, p. 72.

6. ACQUITTANCE from Sir William Steward, knt., to Phil. Henslowe and Edw. Alleyn, esquires, for 450*l.*, for the assignment of a patent of 'the Mastership of his Maiesties games of Beeres, Bulls and Dogges and the ffees, proffittes and appurtenaunces whatsoeuer to the same place or office belonginge'; 28 Nov., 2 Jas. I. [1604]. Signed 'Williame Steuarte.' f. 11.

Printed, *Mem. of Edw. Alleyn*, p. 71.

7. CONTRACT of Peter Streete, of London, carpenter, with Phil. Henslowe and Edw. Alleyn, of the parish of St. Saviour, Southwark, esquires, for 65*l.*, to pull down 'so much of the tymber or carpenters worke of the foreside of the messuage

[1] The grant to him was made on 20 July, 1604 (*Cal. State Papers*, 1603–1610, p. 134); and the docket of the grant to Henslowe and Alleyn on his surrender bears date 14 Nov., 1604 (*ibid.* p. 167).

or tenemente called the beare garden, next the river of Thames, in the parishe of St. Saviors aforesaide, as conteyneth in lengthe from outside to outside fyftye and sixe foote of assize and in bredth from outside to outside sixeteene foote of assize,' and to rebuild the same with 'good new sufficient and sounde tymber of oke'; 2 June, 4 Jas. I., 1606. Signed, by a mark. On the back is an acquittance for 10*l.*, dat. 3 June, 1606; and notes of subsequent payments amounting to 40*l.* 11*s.* 8*d.*, dat. 17 Sept., 1606–9 Jan., 1606[7]. f. 13*b*.

Printed, *Mem. of Edw. Alleyn*, p. 78.

8. PHIL. HENSLOWE and Edw. Alleyn to Christopher Goffe, their deputy:—

'Your sodayne departur out of the towne att your last being with vs and our then ocassion of busines made that to be neclected, which otherwise showld haue been performed, we mean your deputation. Yett nott withstanding wee haue thought good to diricht theys our letters vnto you, which shalbe a sufitien warant for you to deale in our busines, by which we do not only will and requier you as our sufitient seruant and deputie, but also doe authorise you, to proseed in the busines, acording to theys directions folowing, videlicet that, whear as, by reson of our great seruis this year both befor the K: Maiestie, the French prine,[1] and with ye hous, our whole store of doggs are wasted and spent, as yourself can testifie, so that we ar forced to sent downe his ma^tie^ comission into theys cuntries to tak and bring vp such and so many suffitient doggs (wherof we vnderstand you haue great store) as shall sufies to performe any servis, when his Matie

[1] Charles de Lorraine, Prince de Joinville, eldest son of Henry, third Duke of Guise. He came to England 8 May, 1607, and was present at Jonson's masque before the King at Theobalds, 22 May (Gifford, *Works of B. Jonson*, ed. 1875, vol. vi. p. 474; Nichols, *Progresses*, vol. ii. pp. 126, 128). Camden in his *Annales* describes him as the brother of the Duke of Guise.

shall comand, nevertheless, considering our speches wee had with you, for ye good of ye gamsters of your Cuntrie and his Maties seruis, that they shall haue no ocasion of dislik nor our offic [be] vnfurnished, nether at this tym nor heer after, we do by you make this offer vnto them, that, iff they will call themselues together in eueri town and vilage, wher such doggs ar kept, and sett down among themselues how many eueri plac yearly will alow for the sayd servis, and them to send vp to our offie att pallass garden between easter and whitsvntid, that in so doing the Comission shall never com downe to take any doggs from them, but theyr wholl store shalbe left to them selues; and for more securitie wher of we will, at euerie reseat of such doggs yerly, giue vnder our hands and sealls a sufitient dischard for ye sayd year. This shall you promiss in our names, which they performing, we will keep, but otherwise we must be forsed to send ye comission oftner among them, and espetially to those places which shall refuse this kind offer. Send vs word of this busines as sone as you can, and the names of those places that do acept of itt, sertified vnder theyr own hands, that we may vse them kindly, and those that do refuce vnder your hand, that we maye know them. Thus with our hartie salutations we comitt you to god; London, this .... of June, 1607.' Draft, in the hand of Edw. Alleyn. On the back are accounts of charges 'for the Beares meate' at various places in Kent, including Canterbury, Maidstone, Dover, &c. f. 15.

9. PETITION to James I. from Phil. Henslowe and Edw. Alleyn, complaining of the high rate at which they were forced to buy their office from Sir William Steward, of the withdrawal of the license to bait 'one the sondayes in the afternone after devine service, which was the cheffest meanes and benyfite to the place,' and of their loss of bears in baiting before himself and the King of Denmark,[1] and praying for full liberty of baiting, as in the time of Queen Elizabeth, with an addition of *2s. 8d.* to their daily fee of *1s. 4d.* and license to apprehend all vagrants travelling, contrary to the laws, with bulls and bears; [*circ.* 1607]. Three copies; the first being a draft in the hand of Phil. Henslowe, the second a fair copy of the same, and the third a fair copy somewhat differently worded. ff. 17, 19, 20.

Printed, *Mem. of Edw. Alleyn*, p. 75, from the first copy; and by Lysons, *Environs of London*, vol. i. p. 92, from the second copy.

10. ROUGH MEMORANDUM-BOOK,[2] containing the receipts and payments of a travelling bear-ward, employed by Phil. Henslowe and Edw. Alleyn, when on a provincial tour in Berks, Wilts, and Gloucestershire; 13 Aug.–20 Sept., 1608. f. 21.

Part of the book, ff. 34–37, is occupied by acquittances from Thomas Towne, the actor, to Edw. Alleyn for quarterly payments of an annuity[3] of 12*l.* 'out of ye manor off Dullwich'; 28 Oct., 1608–15 Jan., 1611[2].

11. HENRY MIDDLETON to Edw. Alleyn, praying him to restore a bear taken from Henry Ashmore, 'till yow be further satisfied from Sr Tho: Midleton,[4] who is now in Wales'; 9 Mar., 1608[9]. f. 42.

Printed, *Alleyn Papers*, p. 34.

12. THOMAS BOWKER to Edw. Alleyn, entreating him

---

[1] Christian IV., brother of Anne, Queen of James I., visited England 17 July–14 Aug., 1606 (Stow's *Chronicle*, continued by Howes, 1631, p. 885). See also Nichols, *Progresses of James I.*, 1828, vol. ii. p. 54.

[2] See *Mem. of Edw. Alleyn*, p. 84.

[3] See above, MS. i. art. 67, and, for the original grant of the annuity, 28 Oct., 1608, Mun. 32, below.

[4] Sir Tho. Middleton, of Chirk, knighted 26 July, 1603, Lord Mayor of London in 1613; elder brother of Sir Hugh Middleton, projector of the New River.

to send by the bearer a 'mastife whelpe'; Rowhampton, 19 June [1609]. f. 44.

On the back are notes of payments by Edw. Alleyn, under the headings 'purchase,' 'rent,' 'lawe,' 'aparell,' and 'Howshowld stuff.' The entries under the first head are 'Sr Baptist Hickes,[1] 42^{l}' (Mun. 153); 'to Stret for a part (?), 01^{l}'; 'S^{r} Ed. Bower, 300^{l}' (Mun. 527). The second head includes 'T. Towne's an[nuity] 3^{l}' (Mun. 32); 'Sr Fra. Calto[n] 48^{l}'; 'Tiethes in Whitcrostret, o^{l} 5^{s}'; 'of ye fortun rent, 6^{l}.' Under 'Howshowld stuff' the only entry is 'a book. Shaksper sonetts[2] 5^{d}.'

13. EDWARD BARRETT to Edw. Alleyn :—

'Good Sir, my bounden deutie remembred, these maie be to certifie vnto you that, since my comminge downe into the contrie, I haue seene as good doges bothe for the bere and bull as euer I saue fighte, especially in Warrickesheere, Worcestorsheere and Glocestorsheere; yet I woolde wishe you to forbeare to sende vntill I speake with you myselfe. I prie youe remember my humbell dewtie vnto my lovinge M^{r}, your father in lawe, not forgettinge my kinde remembrance vnto my wiffe, as alsoe all my frendes and fellowes in generall. The beares haue with greatt victorie perforemed all their M^{rs} matches, especially Littell Besse of Bromly, whoe foute in one daie xx^{ti} duble and single coorsses with the beste doges in all the cuntrie, whose M^{rs} brought euerie duble coorse a beare dogg and a bull dogg, thincking therby to beate hir owtt, but the beare soe bestirde her, that some she killed out righte and the moste parte shee sent haltting awaie. The

[1] A mercer in Cheapside, created a Bart. in 1620 and Lord Hickes and Viscount Campden in 1629. Hickes Hall, mentioned below (MS. v. art. 20), was built by him for a Sessions-house in 1613.

[2] The Sonnets were entered in the *Stationers' Register*, 20 May, 1609. As the payments here noted by Alleyn were made in the early part of the same year, he probably procured his copy immediately after the book was published. Unfortunately it is no longer to be found in the College library.

M[r] of the beares, nowe he bathe performed his matches, woolde for some resonable consideracion putt them of againe. This leving to trouble you any further at this time, beseechinge the almighty euer to protecte you, expectinge your aunswer by this berer, I end; Evesham, this xi[th] of June, 1610. Good sir, if you haue any need of doges before my comminge vp, that you wovlde directe your commission with all thinges appertaining with all the haste you thinke best, while I am here remaining in Evesham.' f. 45.

14. JOHN ITHELL to Edw. Alleyn, entreating his favour, on behalf of Sir Edward Dimoke,[1] 'in letting his people trye 3 or 4 dogges at bull and beare'; Lymehouse, 30 Oct., 1610. With seal of arms.[2] f. 46.

15. DEPOSITIONS of Bryan Bradley and Richard Tyler, servants of Phil. Henslowe and Edw. Alleyn, respecting their ill-treatment by Dr. Steward, a magistrate, near Alton, in Hampshire, when they were travelling with 'ther Comission vnder the great sealle to tacke vpp dogges for his Ma[ties] service,' alleging that the said Dr. Steward had accused them of carrying 'a cownterfet comission vp and downe the contrey to connetache[3] pore men of ther dogges,' and of having, under colour of it, 'tacken maney a purse by the highwaye,' and that, after keeping them in custody for two days and threatening to commit them as rogues to Winchester gaol, he had dismissed them 'to goo the redey waye to London,' but had refused to give them back the commission; [1611]. The preamble runs:—'Wheare as abowt July laste paste 1611

[1] Sir Edw. Dymoke, of Scrivelsby, champion at the coronation of James I.

[2] *Argent*, a cross flory between four Cornish choughs *sable*, the arms of Ithell, of co. Cambridge (Harl. MS. 6774, ff. 8*b*, 90*b*).

[3] For 'conycatch,' to deceive a simple person, to cheat (Halliwell, *Archaic Dict.*).

comandement was geuen vs [Phil. Henslowe and Edw. Alleyn] by my Lord of Walden[1] to showe what sporte we cold to the Landgrave of Hesse his sone[2] and his company, both Engleshe and strangers, at his Ma[ties] beargarden, which was pereformed accordingley to ther greate contente and lickinge, in doinge wherof wee kelled many of our beaste dogges, which to repaier agayne we weare enforced with all convenient speed to seand owt our commission,' &c. In the hand of Phil. Henslowe. f. 47.

16. STATEMENT of the circumstances in the case against Dr. Steward as above, endorsed 'Henslowe, concerning y[e] commission'; [1611]. f. 48.

17. 'E BEDFORD'[3] to Edw. Alleyn, requesting him to restore a mastiff which had been taken from his servant Edward Parkines, of Woburn, by officers sent into the country 'for the takinge of certaine mastife dogges in his maiesties name for Parrish garden'; Cathol-house, 13 April, 1612. f. 48.

18. BARGAIN and sale by Thomas Morris, of London, gent., and William Grove, of London, fustian dresser, to William Peadle, of London, armourer, for 12*l*., of 'one male lyon'[4]; 13 April, 1612. Signed; with seals. f. 50.

Printed, *Mem. of Edw. Alleyn*, p. 193.

---

[1] Theophilus Howard, Lord Howard of Walden, succeeded as second Earl of Suffolk in 1626, and died in 1640.

[2] Otto, son of Moritz, Landgrave of Hesse, came to England 23 June, 1611 (Camden, *Annales*). A MS. account of his journey is in the library of Cassel, extracts from which are given by Rommell (*Geschichte von Hessen*, Cassel, 1837, vol. vi. p. 327). See also W. B. Rye, *England as seen by Foreigners*, 1865, p. 141.

[3] Edward Russell, third Earl of Bedford, succeeded 28 June, 1585, died 1 May, 1627.

[4] The same, perhaps, which is mentioned in the *Calendar of State Papers*,

19. COMMISSION from Phil. Henslowe, 'one of the sewers of his highnes chamber,' and Edw. Alleyn, 'servant to the highe and mightie prince of Wales,' as masters of the King's game, empowering John Morgan and Richard Tyler, in conjunction with Bryan Bradley, to 'take vpp and provide for his highnes beares bulles and dogges, whersoeuer the same shall or maye be found'; 18 April, 1612. Signed; with seals of arms. f. 51.

Printed, *Mem. of Edw. Alleyn*, p. 99.

20. PETITION to James I. from Phil. Henslowe and Edw. Alleyn, to the same effect as art. 9, above, but referring to the losses of bulls and bears to the value of 200*l.* at least, 'nowe this yeare when the Duke of Bullyn[1] was at White-hall'; [1612]. f. 53.

21. WARRANT from Thomas Dutton,[2] Thomas Brooke,[3] and Thomas Marburie,[4] justices of Cheshire, charging all constables, &c., to assist Thomas Radford,[5] deputed by Phil. Henslowe and Edw. Alleyn to 'take vpp provide and keepe anie mastiffe dogges or mastiffe bitches, beares and bulls, which he shall thinke meet for his maiesties service'; 3 May, 1613. Signed. f. 54.

1603–1610, p. 631, where is a license by Sir Geo. Buck, Master of the Revels, to the same Tho. Morris and Will. Grove to 'shew a strange lion, brought to do strange things, as turning an ox to be roasted, &c.,' 6 Sept., 1610.

[1] Henri de la Tour, Duc de Bouillon, visited England in April and May, 1612 (*Cal. State Papers*, 1611–1618, pp. 127–129; *Court and Times of James I.*, vol. i. p. 166). He came to treat for a marriage between Henry, Prince of Wales, and Christina, sister of Louis XIII. (Nichols, *Progresses*, vol. ii. p. 442).

[2] Of Dutton, sheriff of Cheshire in 1611, died 1614 (Ormerod, *Cheshire*, vol. i. p. 481).

[3] Of Norton, sheriff of Cheshire in 1578 and 1592, d. 1622 (*ibid.* p. 501).

[4] Of Marbury or the Mere, b. 1578–9, d. 1634 (*ibid.* p. 470).

[5] For his warrant see below, Mun. 46.

22. WARRANT from John Ireland,[1] Edward Stanley,[2] and John Ashton,[3] justices of Lancashire, to the same effect; 19 May, 1613. Signed; with seals. f. 55.

23. GEORGE BRAKE to Phil. Henshlawe:—

'Vnknowne I commend me vnto you; and in respect of my good cossin M[r] James Starkey, of whos carefull endeuour in your commission and towards your office I assure it you in extraordinary diligence he performed it, I thought it fitt to acquainte you with the abuses offred in this county of Chester, whereof I think you should to your greate right acquaint y[e] Lord Chamberlaine, and procure his warrante by a purseuante to answer thes theyr contempts. Your commission was first at a Bearebeatinge in Swinhead questiond to be counterfayt by one Lathome,[4] a petty gentleman and son in lawe to Richard Leigh of Swinhead, gentleman, who, if your peaple had not bin better aduised, hazarded theyr lyves. Afterward they were riotously assaulted by one Richard Penkith,[5] of Penkith in comit. Lancast., gentleman, Richard Massy, his servante, and Ralph Barnes, of Warrington, a drvnkarde, with many more whos names are vnknowne. My cossen Starkey skapt lyfe narrowly, M[r] Radford sore wounded as you may behold, and one John Pots, hyred for y[t] seruice, in danger of death, of all which they can fully assure you. If letters were directed to Thomas Brooke of Norton, esquire, Thomas Marbury of the Meyre, and Thomas Dutton, of Dutton, esquires, for y[e] examinacion of thes

[1] Of the Hut, co. Lanc. (*Visitations of Lancashire*, 1613, Chetham Soc., vol. lxxxii. p. 105).

[2] Of Bickersteth (*ibid.* p. 111).

[3] Of Ashton (*ibid.* p. 14).

[4] John Latham, of Congleton, married Priscilla, daughter of Rich. Leigh, of Swinehead, 2 Feb., 1607 (Ormerod, *Cheshire*, vol. iii. p. 66).

[5] See his pedigree in the visitation of Lancashire in 1613 (Chetham Soc., vol. lxxxii. p. 132).

iniuryes, I think you did not amisse; and for ye principalls, if they tast imprisonement in ye Fleete for such contempts, truly you would be much better regarded. Neyther were it vnfitt if you scourd the contry onct again ouer with your authority by warranty from ye Lords of ye councell. Thus in hast and commending my true respects I bid you farewell. Warrington, Maye 19th, 1613. S^r, they haue but taken 8 dogs in Cheshire and y^t with greate hazard of theyr lyves.' f. 56.

24. DEPOSITIONS of Richard Barrowe and Anne Hall, of Warrington, Richard Whitlowe, of Gropnall, and John Pott, of Macclesfield, relative to an assault by Richard Penketh and others upon James Starkey, Thomas Radford, and the said John Pott; 29, 30 May, 1613. f. 58.

25. BOND from Thomas Radford, of the par. of St. Bartholomew the Great, near Smithfield, yeoman, to Phil. Henslowe in 10*l.*, for the due performance of a commission to 'take vpp for his Maties vse bulls, beares and dogges'; 7 June, 1613. Signed, by a mark. Witnesses, James Starkye, Jacob Mede, Edward Griffin. f. 60.

26. PETITION to the Earl of Suffolk,[1] Lord Chamberlain, from Phil. Henslowe and Edw. Alleyn, Masters of the King's Game, complaining of the ill-treatment of their servants in 'the weste contry' by Sir Moryes Bartlet,[2] a justice of the peace, and of assaults committed upon them in Cheshire and Lancashire by 'a swagering gentelman, whom they calle Mr Pancketh,' and others, and praying him to send

[1] Thomas Howard, cr. Lord Howard of Walden, 1597, and Earl of Suffolk, 1603; Lord Chamberlain, 1603–1613; Lord Treasurer, 1613–1618; died 28 May, 1626.

[2] Probably Sir Maurice Berkeley or Barkley, M.P. for co. Somerset, knighted at Cadiz in 1596, father of Sir Charles Berkeley, Viscount Fitzhardinge, and Sir John Berkeley, Lord Berkeley of Stratton.

a warrant for the principal offenders or a letter to the justices; [June or July, 1613]. Draft and fair copy, the latter somewhat differently worded. ff. 62, 64.

27. THE EARL OF SUFFOLK, Lord Chamberlain, to Thomas Dutton, John Ireland, Thomas Brooke, Edward Stanley, Thomas Marbery, and John Ashton, justices of the peace in cos. Chester and Lancaster, requesting them to examine and punish 'one Lathome,' Rich. Penkith of Penkith, Rich. Massy, his servant, Ralph Barnes of Warrington, and others, charged with having abused and beaten the deputies of Phil. Henslowe, one of the masters of the game of bears, &c., in 'the execucion of his comission for taking vp of dogges'; Whitehall, 13 July, 1613. Signed, 'T. Suffolke.' f. 65.

Printed, *Mem. of Edw. Alleyn*, p. 100.

28. THOMAS DUTTON and Thomas Brooke to the Earl of Suffolk, in answer to the above, explaining that as yet they have been unable to act because all the offenders named in his letter dwell in Lancashire, and that they have also 'been hindered by accydent of taking a dog from Mr John Venables[1] of Agdon,' who means to prosecute Brian Bradley and Thomas Bradford [Radford], Phil. Henslowe's deputies, at the next assizes for felony; Dutton, 17 Aug., 1613. Signed. Enclosed are depositions of John Sproston, John Godsend-himvs, and Francis Kniveton relative to the taking of Mr. Venables' dog, dat. Dutton, 16 Aug., 1613. ff. 67, 69.

Printed, the letter only, *Mem. of Edw. Alleyn*, p. 101.

29. THOMAS DUTTON and Thomas Brooke to Phil. Henslowe, informing him of the charge of felony made against his deputies by John Venables and of the failure of

[1] Second son of Rich. Venables, of Horton (Ormerod, *Cheshire*, vol. i. p. 409)

their attempt to bring about a compromise ; Dutton, 17 Aug., 1613. Signed. f. 70.

30. DECLARATION by Thomas Radford :—

'September 4, anno dni. 1613. Bee it knowne to all men by thesse presentes that I Thomas Readffourd, seruant to Mr Philipe Hinckley [Henslowe], maister of the kinges maistye his beare game, ffor diuers ffauours and good considerations receiued of the townsmen of Manchester, and espetially for a masty doge which the said townsmen haue ffreely beestowed one mee for the kinges maisty his vse, and alsoe thos whose names are vnder written haue vndertooke to send vpp every yeare (of their owne proper coste and charges) a masty dog or bytche to the beare garden ; for the which I the said Thomas doe assume and promisse in my maister his name to ffree the said towne of Manchester in Lancasheire from hencefourth from the takeinge of any doge or bytche by vertue of my commition from the garden, and the said townsmen do vndertake the doge which the haue yearely promysed to bee sent vp euery yeare beetweene Mydsomer and Mickelemas and that thee sendinge vp euery yeare a doge according to this agreement shall still bee ffreed from tim to time, and the said townesmen haue herevnto put their hands.' Signed by Franches Wousencrofe, senior, Rodger Barlow, William Ellor, Thomas Heawoode, Thomas Peele, Robert Hilton and nine others. Some of the signatures appear to be written by the same hand. f. 71.

31. ANTHONY COOKE[1] to the Earl of Suffolk, Lord Chamberlain, acknowledging his letter sent by 'one John

---

1 Probably Sir Anthony Cooke, of Giddy Hall, co. Essex, grandson of Sir Anthony, tutor to Edward VI., and cousin to Francis Bacon and Robert Cecil. The younger Sir Anthony died in 1604 (Wright, *Hist. of Essex*, vol. ii. p. 440).

Skales, keeper of the beere garden,' and defending himself against charges of opposing the officers of the garden, not having 'made staye of the dogges in generall taken by them elles where, but onelye of one dogge taken by them in this place of pryvyledge, wherein noe dogge can be taken'; [*ante* 1614]. The writer styles himself 'your honours poor kynseman and servaunte.' f. 72.

Printed, *Mem. of Edw. Alleyn*, p. 102.

32. MEREDITH MORGAN[1] to Phil. Henslowe, 'or in his absence to Jacob [Meade], at the beare garden,' asking him, on the part of 'my lord,' to receive a wolf; [*ante* 1616]. f. 74.

33. THOMAS YONGE to Edw. Alleyn, or 'in his absence to his father in law, at Paris garden,' respecting his commission [to procure dogs or bulls], promising 'you shalbe so well provided as ever you were in your lyffe'; Sturmester [Stourminster], 24 Aug. [*ante* 1616]. f. 75.

Printed, *Alleyn Papers*, p. 50.

34. PETITION to the Earl of Pembroke,[2] Lord Chamberlain, from Edw. Alleyn, in answer to a petition preferred to him at Edinburgh on behalf of Jacob Meade 'touchinge somme interruptions by him pretended to be made by the petitioner touchinge the baytinge of bears and bulls and the

---

[1] Mentioned as Examiner in the Court of the Marches of Wales (*Cal. State Papers*, 1625–1626, pp. 154, 524).

[2] William Herbert, third Earl of Pembroke, succeeded 19 Jan., 1600–1; Lord Chamberlain, 1615–1625; died 10 Apr., 1630. Meade's petition was probably presented to him when he was at Edinburgh in attendance on the King in May–August, 1617 (Nichols, *Progresses*, vol. iii. pp. 37, 390).

keepinge of that game'[1]; [*circ.* 1617–1619]. Draft, but not in Alleyn's hand. f. 76*b.*

Printed, *Mem. of Edw. Alleyn*, p. 160.

35. STATEMENT in the hand of Edw. Alleyn of matters in dispute between himself and Jacob Meade,[2] relative to leases of the Bear Garden and 'ye stock of bears, bulls, doggs and other things apertayning to ye personall estate of Phillip Henslowe nott by hym bequeathed,' &c.; [*circ.* 1617–1619]. f. 78.

Printed, *Mem. of Edw. Alleyn*, p. 161.

36. JOHN NURSE to Edw. Alleyn, his 'kind landlord,' excusing himself from coming, on the ground that he is to 'attend my lord Chamberleine this morninge aboute procuringe his letter towchinge my baytinge,' and sending 10*l.* by Mr Facye; 23 June, 1625. With notes below by Edw. Alleyn of receipts from Mr. Facie and Mr. Nurse, the last dated 14 July, 1626. f. 80.

37. PETITION[3] to the Privy Council and the Commissioners of the Treasury from Edw. Alleyn, 'Master of his Maiestie game of beares and bull and mastiffe dogges,' praying for the payment of 438*l.*, due 'by way of disbursement for prouision . . . beinge 4 yeares'; of 80*l.* for 'the rente of an house yeard wharfe and docke for the stowedge of her Maties barges'; and of 50*l.* for services 'done thes fower yeares past as baytinge before his Matie seuerall times,' &c.; no date. f. 82.

---

[1] For another letter relating apparently to the same dispute see below, MS. iii. art. 82.

[2] Their differences were finally settled 22 Sept., 1619 (see Alleyn's *Diary*, MS. ix., below, f. 38*b*).

[3] Perhaps the petition referred to by Alleyn in his *Diary* (MS. ix., below), 7 Jan., 1617–18.

38. WILLIAM FAWNTE[1] to Edw. Alleyn:—

'I vnderstoode bey a man, which came with too beares from the gardeyne, that you haue a deseyre to beyh one of mey boles. I haue three westerne boles at this teyme, but I haue had verey ell loock with them, for one of them hath lost his horne to the queyck, that I think that hee will neuer bee to feyght agayne, that is mey ould Star of the West, hee was a verey esey bol. And mey bol Bevis hee hath lost one of his eyes, but I think if you had him hee would do you more hurt then good, for I protest I think hee would ether throo vp your dodges [dogs] in to the loftes or eles ding out theare braynes agenst the grates, so that I think hee is not for your turne. Beseydes I esteme him verey hey, for my Lord of Rutlandes man bad mee for him xx marckes. I haue a bol which came out of the west which standes mee in twentey nobles; if you so did leyck him, you shall haue him. Of mey faith, hee is a marvilous good boole and coning, and well shapte and but fore eyre ould feine com leine[2] and shuch a on as I think you haue had but few shuch; for I aseure you that I hould him as good a doble bole as that which you had on mee last a singlle, and one that I haue played therty or fortey coursses before he hath bene tacken from the stacke with the best dodges which halfe a dosen kneyghtes had. If you send a man vnto mee, hee shall see aney of mey boles playe, and you shall haue aney of them of reson, if the will pleseure you'; no date. f. 83.

Printed, with inaccuracies and omissions, *Alleyn Papers*, p. 31.

---

[1] Sir William Faunt, of Foston, knighted at Belvoir Castle, 20 Apr., 1603, died 1639 (Nichols, *Leicestershire*, vol. iv. p. 175).

[2] This seems to be a proverbial expression. Something of the same kind appears in the *Pennilesse Pilgrimage* of John Taylor, the water-poet, 1618, p. 4:—

'I found a host, that might lead a host of men,
Exceeding fat, yet named *Lean* and *Fen*.'

39. WILL. FAWNTE to Edw. Alleyn, entreating him to send 'a cople of hee beare cobes,' the same to be 'black ones and shuch as you think will macke greate beares'; no date. f. 84.

40. WILL. FAWNTE to Edw. Alleyn, desiring him to send 'by this carier a hee cob and shuch a one as you think will macke a great beare'; Foston, 9 Nov. f. 85.

41. ADVERTISEMENT for the Bear Garden:—

'Tomorrowe beinge Thursdaie shalbe seen at the Beargardin on the banckside a greate mach plaid by the gamstirs of Essex, who hath chalenged all comers whatsoeuer to plaie v dogges at the single beare for v pounds and also to wearie a bull dead at the stake and for your better content shall haue plasent sport with the horse and ape[1] and whiping of the blind beare. Viuat Rex'; *temp.* Jas. I. Written in a large, coarse hand, being probably the original placard exhibited at the entrance to the Bear Garden. f. 86.

Printed, Lysons, *Environs*, vol. i. p. 91; Collier, *Hist. of Dram. Poetry*, ed. 1879, vol. iii. p. 98.

42. ADVERTISEMENT of 'A generall Prize, for all those that desire to approue their skill, either with Musket or Long

[1] This sport is described in a Spanish account of travels in England in 1544 (quoted by Mr. Collier):—'At the same place [the Bear Garden] a pony is baited, with a monkey on his back, defending itself against the dogs by kicking them; and the shrieks of the monkey, when he sees the dogs hanging from the ears and neck of the pony, render the scene very laughable.' Whipping the blind bear 'is performed by five or six men, standing circularly with whips, which they exercise upon him without any mercy, as he cannot escape from them because of his chain; he defends himself with all his force and skill, throwing down all who come within his reach and are not active enough to get out of it, and tearing the whips out of their hands and breaking them' (Paul Hentzner's *Journey into England in* 1598, ed. H. Walpole, 1757, p. 42). See also a quotation by Mr. Collier from Dekker's *Work for Armourers*, 1609.

Bow'; the marks to be set up in St. George's Fields on the 21st August, 'as well for Muskets with cock-matches, as for Long-bow and arrowes,' and the prizes ranging from 'a faire peece of Plate valuable xx crownes' to 'a seale Ring valuable v crownes,' the entries for which, from *2s. 6d.* to *1s.*, are to be paid to 'M[r] Euan Floyd gentleman, dwelling in Winchester house neare S. Mary Oueries in Southwarke'; *temp.* Jas. I. or Chas. I. *Printed.* f. 87.

MS. No. III.

ALLEYN PAPERS. Vol. III. General Correspondence of Edward Alleyn and Philip Henslowe, his wife's step-father; 1577–1626.

1. ALEXANDER WHITE to 'Mr Phyllype Henslowe, in the Clincke,' begging him to assist Isbell Keys, who is about to be arrested at the suit of FRauncis Chambres; 21 Feb., 1576[7]. f. 1.

2. THOMAS KEYS to Alex. Whyt, complaining that he is compelled to sell the parsonages of Hesell and Hacthorne, and that his wife will not grant him a life-interest in her tenements in Westminster and on the Bankside [see below, Mun. 112]; Lincoln's Inn, 7 April [*circ.* 1580–1600]. f. 3.

3. THE PRIVY COUNCIL to Aldermen [John] Harte and [Henry] Billingsley, Thomas Hunte and Humfrey Huntley, requiring them to take order for the relief of John Allen, 'servaunte to me the Lo. Admyrall,' against 'one doctor [Thomas] Martin, who seeketh by indirecte meanes to make frustrate a lease of a certein tenement and a garden demised by one John Roise to the suppliant's father, mother and himselfe, ... clayminge certaine right and tytle thereunto as executor vnto the said Roise'; Nonsuch, 14 July, 1589. Signed by C[harles Howard, Lord] Howard [of Effingham, cr. Earl of Nottingham, 1596], A[mbrose Dudley, Earl of] Warwick, H[enry Cary, Lord] Hunsdon, T[homas Sackville, Lord] Buckhurst [cr. Earl of Dorset, 1603], W[illiam Brooke, Lord] Cobham, [Sir] Francis Walsingham, and [Sir] James Croft. f. 5.

Printed, *Alleyn Papers*, p. 5. See also below, MS. iv. art. 25.

4. [CHARLES HOWARD, Lord Howard of Effingham] to [William Drewry, D.C.L.], umpire in the above dispute, asking his 'frendship and fauour' in behalf of his servant, John Allen; Richmond, ... Dec., 1589. Draft, without signature or address. f. 7.

Printed, *Alleyn Papers*, p. 4.

5. FRAUNCYS HENSLOWE[1] to his 'vncle Mr Phillip Henslow, or his brother Edmond Henslow,' begging for assistance to obtain his release from 'ye counter in Woodstret'; [*circ.* 1590]. Below is a note by Phil. Henslowe of 'carges for Frances Henslow,' amounting to 16*s.* 4*d.* f. 8.

6. WILLIAM HENSLOWE[2] to his brother Philip, on business connected with an action at law on a copyhold title of their sister Margery; Buxted, 7 Dec., 1592. f. 10.

7. WILLIAM CROWE [of the Isle of Man], parson, to Patrick Brewe, of London, goldsmith, his cousin, relative to the affairs of the Gill[3] family; 12 Jan., 1592[3]. f. 11.

Printed, *Alleyn Papers*, p. 17.

8. LOVE VERSES, beginning, 'Can she excuse my wronges

[1] See above, MS. i. artt. 40–42. He was again a prisoner in the White Lion, Southwark, apparently in 1601 (Henslowe's *Diary*, p. 192), and was dead before 6 Oct., 1606 (MS. iv. artt. 57, 58). Edmond Henslowe, who was the third son of Edm. Henslowe, of Lindfield, died in 1592 (*Diary*, p. 112).

[2] Fifth son of Edm. Henslowe, of Lindfield (Harl. MS. 1562, f. 114*b*). Margery, his sister, appears in the same pedigree as Margaret, wife of Ralph Hogge.

[3] See above, MS. i. art. 43.

with vertious cloke?', transcribed by an illiterate copyist; 'Finis, 1596.' f. 12.

Printed, *Alleyn Papers*, p. 21.

9. JOHN LANGWORTH[1] to Edw. Alleyn, informing him that the land, about which he had enquired, was worth 80*l.* a year, 'yf corne beare any good price,' and asking whether he would 'be willinge to take a yearely annvetie of me for the money I haue of yours or not'; the Broyle, 6 Feb., 1598[9]. f. 13.

Printed, *Alleyn Papers*, p. 22.

10. JOHN ALLEYN[2] to Mr. 'Brune,' or 'Burne,'[3] asking for his 'datter in marrige'; no date. f. 14.

Printed, *Alleyn Papers*, p. 15.

11. EDW. ALLEYN to [John] Page, of Croxted, asking for information as to land for which he is in treaty; London, 15 July, 1602. f. 15.

Printed, *Alleyn Papers*, p. 27.

12. JOHN PAGE to Edw. Alleyn, answering that he has 'delt with Mr Sherley,'[4] and has the 'fforsakynge of the land for xiiii dayes for 1300l,' and it will be worth 80*l.* a year; Croxted, 17 July [1602]. On the same sheet as art. 11. f. 15.

Printed, *Alleyn Papers*, p. 27.

13. MERC[URY] PATTEN[5] to Phil. Henslowe, referring to

---

[1] Son of Arthur Langworth, of Broyle, co. Sussex (see above, MS. ii. art. 2).

[2] The writing and signature are not those of Edw. Alleyn's brother, who died in 1596, but of the other John Alleyn, mentioned above (MS. i. art. 77).

[3] Possibly Will. Borne, or Birde, the actor (MS. i. art. 25).

[4] John Sherley, of Ifield, co. Sussex, knighted at the Charterhouse, 11 May, 1603; died 1632–3 (*Visitation of Sussex*, 1634, Harl. MS. 1562, f. 47).

[5] Blue Mantle pursuivant, 1597 (Noble, *College of Arms*, pp. 185, 217). He

his decision the matters in dispute between himself and Mrs. Keyes; Westminster, 26 Sept., 1603. f. 16.

14. JOHN PAGE to Edw. Alleyn, giving particulars of the extent and value of the manor of Riches, about the purchase of which he has talked with Sir John Sherley on his behalf; Croxted, 28 Jan., 1640 [*sic.*, 1604–5 ?]. f. 17.

Printed, *Alleyn Papers*, p. 28; but after 'have it not' read 'I woolle gladly you shovlle deale ffor it becavse it lyeth,' &c., and for 'would *have* it' read 'woolle *survaie* it.'

15. SIR FRANCIS CALTON to 'Mr Harres'[1] :—

' I knowe not almoste any lande in England but is worthe xv yeares purchase and yet I am offered but xii yeares purchase for myne. It shoulde seeme the partie knowethe not how to valew and proportion thinges, or els he is obstinatelye resolved, thoughe it weare worthe 500li the yeare, to gyve but 4500li for it, as not meaninge, whatsoever the purchace be, to exceed that some. I have not rated or sette downe any thinge vnto him that shall not be made good; then I doe wonder how he can offer 4500li for 330 and odd poundes, which yf he caste but at xv yeares purchase comethe verye neare to 5000li, besydes the woodes vpon the waste, which he shall either take or leave at 300li. To be shorte, yf he like the thinge, so as he will gyve xvi yeares purchase for it at 320li by the yeare, I will once againe have conference with him, otherwise I pray you send me the perticuler againe without more doinges . . . .' [1605 ?]. f. 18.

This is the earliest document connecting Edw. Alleyn with Dulwich. The actual terms of his purchase of the manor are stated by himself in his memorandum-book (MS. viii., below, f. 8*b*) :—'In

sold the office to Hen. St. George in 1611, for reasons which Noble could not discover, but which may have been connected with his difficulties, referred to below, MS. v. art. 52.

[1] William Harris, a scrivener.

no : do : Amen. Anno 1605. Bought the Lordshipp of Dullwich of Sr Francis Calton, knight, this 20th of October for 5000^{l}. Wherof 2000^{l} is payd in hand, ye other 3000^{l} att ye end of 6 years, with consideration yearly for forberaunc of ye 3000^{l} ye some of 213^{l} 6^{s} 8^{d} per annum.' To this is added:—'pd. S^{r} Fr: ye said some of 3000^{l} att seuerall paymentes and ye last on ye 25 of October 1613.' The actual deed of sale is dated 8 May, 1606 (see below, Mun. 471).

On the back of Sir Fran. Calton's letter are notes by Edw. Alleyn of his resources, including 'my share of [theatrical] aparell, 100^{l},' and a list of names headed 'means for money,' viz. 'S^{r} Jo. Swinerton,[1] a procuror Smith, Mr Moyce, Woodward of ye Bear, Homden[2] y^{t} would buy Firles in Gratius strett, he y^{t} bought ye great coppiehowld att Lambeth, Fulk, the owld gamster att Howndsditch.'

16. SIR FRAN. CALTON to Edw. Alleyn : 'the devill is dead and all those monstrous horrible terrible coseninge knaveries turned to apparante directe and honeste matter'; understands where both the indentures 'which weare such daungerous beastes be'; protests his freedom from all taint of 'arte, cunninge or dishonestye'; and begs for a last advance of 10*l.*; no date. With an acquittance below from Thos. Stephans, on behalf of Sir F. Calton, for 10*l.*; 24 Dec., 1605. f. 20.

On the back is a draft of a letter from Edw. Alleyn to Dr. Coxe and Mr. Blackston, informing them that he has sold the parsonage of Firle to Robert Homden, 'being forced ther vnto by reson of some great somes I haue to paye for a purchase I haue entred vpon neer London.'

17. JOHN POYNTZ to Edw. Alleyn, asking him to send his lute by the bearer, and he will pay for its mending on his return to London ; Woodhatch, 6 Mar., 1605[6]. f. 21.

Printed, *Mem. of Edw. Alleyn*, p. 77.

---

[1] A merchant-tailor and alderman of London; knighted 26 July, 1603; Lord Mayor, 1612; died in Dec., 1616.

[2] Robert Holmden, leather-seller (Mun. 144, below). See also *Alleyn Papers*, p. xiii.

18. SIR FRAN. CALTON to Edw. Alleyn, praying him to send the 30*l.* 3*s.* left in his hands at their last parting; Greenwich, 7 July, 1607. With acquittance below. f. 22.

19. THE SAME to the same, requesting him to send the 'odd xx markes' of the amount due at Michaelmas, his 'long and grieuous sickness' making him bold; 'from ye spittle in my bedd, this Saterday morning.' With acquittance below for 13*l.* 6*s.* 8*d.*; 3 Oct., 1607. f. 23.

20. THE SAME to the same, praying him to send 'such monies as weare due' at Christmas: is glad to hear from 'my cosine Staple' that 'the defeasances vpoñ ye statutes were now perfected'; Cheam, 22 Jan., 1607[8]. With acquittance for 53*l.* 6*s.* 8*d.*, due at Christmas 'for the vse of of three thowsand poundes.' ff. 24, 25.

21. THE SAME to the same: is to ride into Kent to-morrow to the burial of his wife's father,[1] and, being disappointed of a payment, requests a loan of 4*l.*, which shall be repaid on Good Friday with the 13*l.* borrowed a fortnight since; hears that he spoke of a convenient house for him, but cannot learn whether it is to be let or sold; means never to live in another man's house, but will gladly buy one for himself; Rutland House, Tuesday [1608?]. f. 26.

22. THE SAME to the same: has at length found a fit house at Greenwich[2] on a lease from the Crown for 27 years at 40*s.* rent; must pay 240*l.* for it to 'one Myles Whitakers, a gentleman attendinge on my l. of Salisburie in his chamber,' and requests Alleyn to provide the money, the lease to be

---

[1] Sir Fran. Calton married Dorothy, daughter of Tho. Duke, of Cossington, co. Kent, and sister of Sir Edw. Duke (Harl. MS. 1548, f. 186*b*).

[2] See below, Mun. 169.

taken in his name and assigned to himself upon conditions; 12 April, 1608. f. 27.

23. THE SAME to the same: requests him to 'paye vnto Mr Whitakers the fortye poundes, whiche he desirethe,' at once, as he hears the bargain 'is iudged a very good peniworth' and 'ye ladye Stanhope paiethe fortie poundes by ye yeare for a howse and a guarden nothing so good as this'; Greenwich, 19 April, 1608. f. 28.

24. THE SAME to the same, requesting 'the monye due for ye laste quarter'; 25 April, 1608. With acquittance below for 53*l*. 6*s*. 8*d*. f. 29.

25. THE SAME to the same, asking for an advance of 11*l*.; will make 'reasonable alowance for it, but not so large as heretofore, for y^t^ as you knowe ye worlde is altered'; no date. With acquittance below; 15 June, 1608. f. 30.

26. THE SAME to 'Mr Boulton at ye bridg foote' [Tho. Bolton, the scrivener], praying him to 'steppe ouer or send to Mr Allen' for 4*l*., to be given to the bearer on a bond for repayment at Christmas; 8 July, 1608. With acquittance below. f. 31.

27. THE SAME to Edw. Alleyn: prays for an advance of 30*l*. towards the charges of the 'alteringe of my or your howse [at Greenwich] I cannot certainely tell which to call it'; if he will give 15*l*. to the bearer, will call himself for the rest next week and 'dispatch such busines as is yet vnperfecte' between them; no date. With acquittance below for 15*l*.; 3 Sept., 1608. f. 33.

28. THE SAME to the same: prays him to send 'the xxvii^li^ residew of ye three score,' and 'then these my presente letters shall testifie with you, y[t] togither with y[e] iicii and twentie poundes for my howse at Greenewiche I haue receaued of you 300[li] of the 3000[li]'; 14 Oct., 1608. With acquittance below for *27l.* f. 34.

29. THE SAME to the same, praying him to send *30l.* of what was due at Michaelmas; 26 Oct., 1608. With acquittance below. f. 35.

30. THE SAME to the same, praying him to pay *18l.*, due at Michaelmas for the use of *2,700l.*; 8 Nov., 1608. f. 36.

31. THE SAME to the same, praying him to send *10l.*, being forced to have recourse to him by 'the euill dealinge of others'; 30 Dec., 1608. With acquittance below. f. 37.

32. MATHIAS ALLEN [1] to Edw. Alleyn: thanks him for his kindness, and assures him that himself and his wife are in health; no date. f. 38.

On the back are acquittances from Thomas Garland to Phil. Henslowe and Edw. Alleyn for rent of land called 'y[e] Long Slipp'; 10 Jan., 1608[9]–14 Oct., 1610. See below, Mun. 31.

33. JOHN LANGWORTH [2] to Phil. Henslowe: explains his efforts to arrange a dispute between his brother, [William] Henslowe, and [Richard] Heath concerning the payment of tithes [3]; Canterbury, 15 Jan., 6 Feb., 12 Mar., 1608[9]. Three letters. ff. 40, 41, 42.

---

[1] According to the *Visitation of Bucks*, 1634 (Harl. MS. 1234, f. 13), son of Anthony, first cousin of Edw. Alleyn. He was warden of Dulwich College, 1619–1631, and master, 1631–1642.

[2] Canon of Canterbury, Archdeacon of Wells, and rector of Buxted, co. Sussex; a cousin probably of the John Langworth mentioned above (art. 9). He was buried in Canterbury Cathedral, 13 Jan., 1613–4 (*Register of Christ Church*, Harleian Society, 1878, p. 114).

[3] See MS. iv, artt. 47, 71.

34. R. REDMER[1] to Edw. Alleyn :—

'I would gladly know what answer my Lord gaue touching your last motion, that accordingly I might worke. For the other matter, as I thinke you are provided now, so if it please you twixt this and Thursday night to put into my hands that which I lately propounded to you, I am in very good likelyhood to effect your desire vpon the forementioned termes. Only this, that I may not loose time, I pray resolue sometimes to day by your letters whether I shall relye on you or no. So with my hartyest wishes for your happynes I rest Yours in loue to comand R. Redmer. July, 1609.' With seal of arms.[2] f. 44.

35. THE SAME to the same: entreats him 'of all loves to respitt sending to Mr Walgrave,'[3] and hopes to-morrow to give 'that satisfaction which my friend at Court is to giue me'; Lambeth, 24 Jan. f. 46.

36. THE SAME to the same: if he will lay down 30*l.*, his 'desire shalbe effected or the mony restored within a month or two,' a bond being taken for security, either his own or 'a citizens of good worth'; if he knows where to 'find Mynsheu[4] or any other Italian or Spanish teacher' it will be a favour to signify it; Lambeth, 27 May. f. 48.

Printed, *Alleyn Papers*, p. 84.

37. THE SAME to the same: has 'appointed a payment of xxli to be made as to morow,' and entreats him to send

[1] A Richard Redmer took up his freedom of the Stationers' Company, 16 Jan., 1610 (*Stationers' Register*, ed. Arber, vol. iii. p. 30).

[2] [*Sable*] a bend [*argent*] between 6 fleurs-de-lis [*or*], impaling another coat.

[3] Rob. Walgrave, a printer, is mentioned in the *Stationers' Register* in 1586 (ed. Arber, vol. ii. f. 55). Chamberlain also speaks of a 'Walgrave, the Palsgrave's agent here,' 7 Dec., 1616 (*Court and Times of James I.*, vol. i. p. 446).

[4] John Minshew, author of the *Ductor in Linguas*, &c. (see below, MS. ix., 22 Jan., 1618–9).

'that x[li]' to-night or by six or seven o'clock in the morning; Sunday. f. 50.

Printed, *Alleyn Papers*, p. 85.

38. SIR FRAN. CALTON to Edw. Alleyn, on business connected with a 'bargaine in Hamshyre,' a lease of Kensington [Kennington manor?], &c., and asking for a loan of 50*l.*; no date [1609?]. f. 51.

39. THE SAME to the same: prays him to send 5*l.*, to be repaid 'vpon Bartho: daye nexte or y[e] daye after at y[e] furtheste'; no date. With acquittance below; 18 Aug., 1609. f. 52.

40. THE SAME to the same: prays him to send 'the letters patentes of Kenington' with 'the odde monye which is behinde for the vse of 2700[li]'; no date. With note of payment by Edw. Alleyn of 3*l.* 11*s.*; 29 Sept. [1609]. f. 53.

41. THE SAME to the same: prays him to send all 'wrytinges, evidences and notes' concerning Kennington manor,[1] and all the notes 'had from M[r] Skeuington touching inchrochers vpon the Kinges lande,' also to lend him 5*l.* and to remember to pay 35*l.* to 'father Symons'; 22 Oct., 1609. f. 54.

42. WILLIAM SPENDER to Phil. Henslowe and Roger Cole and the rest of the churchwardens [of St. Saviour's,

---

[1] See below, Mun. 156. In MS. viii. f. 7 is the note:—

'What the manore of Keningtone cost mee Novemb. 1604

First to M[r] Skeuingtonn for the lease in posession . . . . . . 660[l]

Then to Tho. Webber for his lease being in reuertion . . 405[l]

So in all 1065[l]

Sowld this mannor of Kennington to S[r] Fr. Calton knight y[e] 7th of Septemb. 1609 for 2000[l].'

Southwark], praying, on behalf of himself and Alsebeth, his wife, for 'that charitable fauiour from the Church, which many poore people haue had beinge in the like extremety of want'; [1609?]. f. 55.

43. SIR FRAN. CALTON to Edw. Alleyn, on business with Sir Edw. Duke [his brother-in-law] and Mr. Knight; requests also a loan of 16*l.*, and sends 8*l.* 5*s.* 5*d.* for 'the Kinge rente' [for half a year on a lease of Kennington manor]; 30 April, 1610. f. 56.

44. THE SAME to the same: purposes to match his second daughter with 'one Doctor Mollyers, a phisition,' and requests, therefore, an advance of 250*l.* before the 24th; 'the cause bothe of this my shorte warninge to yow and his sodaine agreemente with mee is for that hee bathe a very good confidence to haue his countriman Doctor Martin's place, who died sodainlye the last Sondaye nighte, hee was phisition to the Queene. Wherefore nowe presentlye to furnishe him convenientlye as wilbe befittinge, and happelye to bestowe some gratuities (for both yow and I knowe that places in Courte fale not into mens mouthes for gapinge) he is contente to abate 100[li] of what he bathe hitherto insisted vpon'; .... 9 May, 1611. f. 57.

Printed, *Mem. of Edw. Alleyn*, p. 94.

45. THE SAME to the same: begs him not to refuse his request of Thursday, since his daughter will miss a better match than he 'may well hope for hereafter, for besydes his [Dr. Mollyer's] presente meanes, which inablethe him to liue in more then an ordinarie fashion, the place he is to obtaine thereby will be worthe twelue score poundes more by the yeare'; 12 May [1611]. f. 59.

46. EDW. ALLEYN to Sir Fran. Calton: has moved

friends for the money, but it will not be ready until 12 June; if it must be had sooner and can be procured by other means, will give his security for it; prays him to send the two letters they spoke of to Mr. Harris and Mr. Thos. Martin, and also to 'send to S^r Ed. Duke, getting his promise'; [May, 1611]. f. 60.

47. SIR FRAN. CALTON to Edw. Alleyn: has promised to deposit 200*l.* 'till the place be procured for ye Doctor, and that ye marriage be consummated'; will use his best means to obtain it, and prays that Alleyn will not fail him on 12 June, till when the 50*l.* will be forborne; [May, 1611]. f. 60.

48. —— to Thomas Calton,[1] his son: advises him as to his sale to Edw. Alleyn of 'Hethersalls howses,'[2] &c., and prays him to send by the carrier 2½ yards of 'blackest fustyan' at 2*s.* 10*d.* a yard 'and a rondlett of secke abowt vi or vii gallons'; 19 May [1611]. f. 61.

49. RICHARD FORKENCH to Edw. Alleyn: has received his letter and believes it all, but there is now no need for giving bonds for the money; Lord Montagu[3] comes to London in a fortnight, 'and as he commeth to loge at my howse (nowe the countys of Dosset is com to London, he lyeth not at Horsly) so, with Godes helpe, I will atend him

---

[1] Younger brother of Sir Francis. The letter is unsigned, but may be supposed to be from his father-in-law.

[2] In MS. viii. f. 36*b* is the note:—'Bought of Tho: Calton and his wyfe Anne ther dwelling Howse and Hethersalls Howse,' &c. . . . . 'theys parcells for 510^li the 28 off November, 1611.' On f. 12, however, 'Hethersalls howse and land,' 32 acres in all, are said to have been bought for 300*l.*, 3 July, 1606. See below, Munn. 483, 548, and *Alleyn Papers*, pp. xv. xvi.

[3] Anthony Browne, second Viscount Montagu. The letter probably refers to property rented of him by Edw. Alleyn in the parish of St. Mary Overy (see MS. iv. artt. 43, 45, and Mun. 122). He married Jane, daughter of Tho. Sackville, Earl of Dorset, and the 'Countys of Dosset' is probably her mother.

to London and that day you shall haue word wher you shall find his logginge the morro and then wil I tell you the party that told me the newes I did writ you and I pray kepe secekertes about the matter' .... 1 Nov., 1611. f. 63.

Printed, *Alleyn Papers*, p. 47.

50. JOHN HEBBORNE to Edw. Alleyn: proposes to deal with him for a 'little habitation' at Dulwich, and requests him to come to his lodging at Whitehall before Tuesday, when he has to attend the King to Royston; 3 Jan., 1611[2]. f. 65.

Printed, *Alleyn Papers*, p. 48.

51. SIR FRAN. CALTON to Edw. Alleyn: prays him to send 5*l.* for 'the moytie of a brybe .... to bestowe vpon one this daye, yf matters succeede accordinglye'; no date. With acquittance below; 18 Mar., 1611[2]. f. 67.

Printed, *Alleyn Papers*, p. 55.

52. THE SAME to the same: has completed the purchase for which 'Sr Francis Clarke of Clapham would haue giuen aboue xx^li^ more,' and deals 'in the waye of honestye with a widowe even for all that shee hathe'; requests him to send 20*l.* to pay a half-year's rent to Sir Peter Fretswell [Frescheville]; 31 Mar., 1612. With acquittance below; 2 Apr., 1612. f. 68.

53. THE SAME to the same: prays him to pay the bearer 'the reste of the monye, which is 70 pound'; no date. With acquittance below; 8 Apr., 1612. f. 69.

54. THE SAME to the same: 'The Doctor hath dealte with Sr Thomas Challiner[1] to vndertake my busines with y^e^

[1] Sir Tho. Chaloner, chamberlain to Henry, Prince of Wales (Harley MS. 252, f. 8). The name of Sir David Foulis appears in the same list (f. 10*b*) as cofferer.

Prince, but he disclaimethe to deale therein, and his reason is, bycause he alwayes opposed his opinion to the avoydinge of the sayd leases,[1] averrynge still that it was more agreeable to æquitie and iustyce, and more for the dignitye and honor of the Prince, to suffer the tenantes to inioye their tymes withoute impeachmente then to call their estates in question. Howebeit Sr Davye Fowle, the Princes Cofferer and a neare intimate to ye sayd Sr Thomas Challiner, who also maye happilye share in the consideration, hath at the instance of the Doctor vndertaken for the some of one c^li^ to haue either my tyme confirmed or els a terme for three lyves, yealdinge his highnes onlye 400^li^ more and not above and to have all the vnder tennants to stand at my courtesye'; begs Alleyn, therefore, to let him have 20*l.* on Monday, Sir D. Fowle only desiring so much in hand; [15 Aug., 1612?]. f. 70.

55. THE SAME to the same: begs he will satisfy his request of Saturday last; no date. With acquittance below for 20*l.*; 17 Aug., 1612. f. 72.

56. ELIZABETH SOCKLEN to her 'lovinge cozen' Edw. Alleyn: sends him a 'littell cheise,' and entreats him to write word whether his tenant John Clemente delivered a letter from her three or four years ago; has never seen him, though she has seen his brother, John Alleyn, who, when he dwelt with Lord Howard and came into the country, lay at her father's house, 'Goorde Everytt in Tuddington parishe'; Wardon, 22 Sept., 1612. f. 73.

Printed, *Alleyn Papers*, p. 54.

[1] In the manor of Kennington, held on lease by Sir Fran. Calton; vested in the Crown, 11 Edw. III., and made part of the Duchy of Cornwall (Lyson's *Environs*, vol. i. p. 326).

57. J[OHN] TOWNLEY[1] to his 'gentle landlord,' Edw. Alleyn: entreats him to help him with 'a little timber or poles' for the repair of his house, &c.; 10 Nov., 1612. f. 75.

Printed, *Alleyn Papers*, p. 52.

58. SIR FRAN. CALTON to Edw. Alleyn: prays him to deliver to the bearer the 'meane conveiancies' concerning Kennington manor to take to Sir Noel Caron,[2] and authorises him to pay 20*l.* to Mr. Harris [the scrivener], if he deserves it; no date. With acquittance below from John Cockin for six deeds; 3 Mar., 1612[3]. f. 76.

59. THE SAME to the same, on business concerning a proposed purchase from Sir Edw. Duke[3]; requests him also to help him with 20*l.* and to send 5*l.* by the bearer; [1613?]. f. 77.

60. EDW. ALLEYN to Sir Fran. Calton: complains of his not keeping an appointment at 'Sr Tho: Bedles[4] loging,' and prays him to 'send ye letter for S^r^ E: Duke[5] by ye boye and wright his whole money shalbe paid in Micaellmass terme'; [1613?]. With answer below, fixing another meeting 'in the Rounde Churche.' f. 78.

61. JOHN BENSON to Edw. Alleyn: offers to glaze 'a

---

[1] See below, Munn. 553, 566.

[2] Noël de Caron, Heer van Schonewal, Dutch agent and ambassador in England for more than thirty years; died in London, 1 Dec., 1624. He lived in a house 'at Stockwell by Lambeth,' in Kennington manor (*Court and Times of Jas. I.*, vol. ii. p. 281).

[3] 'Bought of Sr E. Duke, knight, ye 2 of Nouember 1613, 17 acres off land, lyeing betwene blanch downes and ye highe waye towardes ye north, for ye some off 160^l^' (MS. viii. f. 39*b*). See below, Munn. 560–562, and *Alleyn Papers*, p. xvii.

[4] Grandson of Silvester Bedell, of Hamerton, co. Hunts, whose daughter, Joan, married Nicholas Calton, of Nedingworth, father of Sir Francis (Harl. MS. 1075, f. 17).

[5] See above, art. 21.

peece of billding at Dwllige,' if he will provide 'stufe, as glase and lead and soder,' but prays him to keep it close for fear of the glaziers; no date. With acquittance below for 10*l.*; 14 May, 1614. f. 79.

62. THE SAME to the same: desires him to give the bearer 7*l.*; 22 April, 1614. With acquittance below. f. 80.

63. A. P. to —— Henslowe: complains of the credit he gives to malicious reports against his wife and himself; no date. f. 81.

64. SAMUEL JEYNENS to 'ye worshipfull and well affected to all good purposes Mr Allen': urges him to 'a worke of charity toward Chelsey Colledge[1] neere London, which was founded, though not yet finished, to this intent y^t^ learned men might there haue maintenance to aunswere all ye aduersaries of religion'; or else to 'build some half a score lodging roomes, more or lesse, neere vnto you, yf it be no more but to giue lodging to diuers schollers y^t^ come from ye university'; [*circ.* 1615–1620]. f. 82.

Printed, *Mem. of Edw. Alleyn*, p. 115.

65. THE SAME to the Recorder and Lord Mayor of London, Sir Thos. Middleton,[2] and 'ye Lady Weild,'[3] com-

---

[1] Chelsea College, founded by Dr. Matthew Sutcliffe, Dean of Exeter, and incorporated by charter, 8 May, 1610, under the name of 'King James's College at Chelsey.' It was never completed, and after Dr. Sutcliffe's death in 1629 it fell into decay. The site was finally granted by the Crown, in 1669, to the Royal Society, and bought back in 1682 for the erection of the present Chelsea Hospital for soldiers. See Lysons, *Environs of London*, vol. ii. p. 149.

[2] Lord Mayor in 1613 (see above, MS. ii. art. 11).

[3] Probably the widow of Sir Humphrey Weld, Lord Mayor in 1608, died 29 Nov., 1610. According to his pedigree in Clutterbuck's *Hertfordshire*, vol. ii. p. 358, he married Anne, daughter of Nich. Whelar; but a Dame Margaret, wife of Sir Humphrey Weld, is mentioned as founding the Lady Weld lectureship at St. Olave's Jury, by will dated 22 Feb., 1622 (Heath, *Hist. of the Grocers' Company*, 1854, p. 254).

mending to them the 'furthering and finishing of Chelsy Colledge'; [*circ.* 1615–1620]. Referred to, and enclosed in, the preceding. f. 83.

66. CORNELIUS LYMER[1] to Edw. Alleyn: accepts an invitation to 'read prayers and to p[reach in the after]noone' at the consecration of his chapel on 1 Sept., and proceeds:—'I conclude with thancksgiuing vnto God, who moued your heart to begin so good and charitable a worke, and hath granted you leaue to finish it; and I pray God you may long liue to see the blessed fruite of your costs and chardges to your owne contentment and encouragement of others by your good example to doe ye like, y^t^ so in ye end of your dayes you may receiue ye end of your hope, an immarcessible crowne of immortall glory'; Christ Church, Oxford, 22 July, 1616. f. 87.

67. THE PARISHIONERS of St. Giles, Cripplegate, to Edw. Alleyn: thank him for his 'so bounteous graunt to this half parishe,' and recommend John Jones,[2] Alice Foster and Margarett Chapman, aged poor people, to be taken into his 'proteccion and charge'; 14 Sept., 1616. Signed by —— Michell, John Brocke, churchwarden, William Hewett, and three others. *Mutilated.* f. 88.

68. T[HOMAS HOWARD, Earl of] Arundell, to his 'louing frend' Edw. Alleyn: understands he is 'in hand with an hospitall for the succouring of poore old people and the mainteynance and education of yong,' and desires he will 'accept

1 'Cornelyus Lymar off Christchirch in Oxeford fellow,' the first name in the College *Register* (MS. x. f. 4*b*). He entered 31 Aug., 1616, but was 'gon' on 30 Sept., 1617.

2 All admitted, 1 Oct., 1616 (MS. x. f. 4*b*).

of a poore fatherles boy'; Arundell House, 17 Sept., 1616. f. 90.

Printed, *Mem. of Edw. Alleyn*, p. 132.

69. THE RECTOR and parishioners of St. Botolph's, Bishopsgate, to Edw. Alleyn, presenting for his almshouses Mawde Lee,[1] Henry Phillipes, and John Muggleton; 29 Sept., 1616. Signed by Stephen Gosson,[2] rector, Clement Buck, 'depute,' and three others. f. 92.

70. STEPHEN GOSSON, rector of St. Botolph's, to Edw. Alleyn, sending him 'a personale view' of the three candidates for his 'hospitale of poore folkes' mentioned above; 2 Oct., 1616. f. 94.

Printed, *Mem. of Edw. Alleyn*, p. 133.

71. THE CHURCHWARDENS and others of the liberty of the Clink, in the parish of St. Saviour, Southwark, to Edw. Alleyn, presenting James Saunders[3] as a 'poore elected beadesman'; no date. Signed by Roger Cole, Edw. Griffine, Will. Corden, and five others. The letter contains eight lines of complimentary doggerel, beginning, 'As god did move your mynd to build.' f. 96.

72. THOMAS CHARD,[4] 'prisoner in Ludgate,' to Edw. Alleyn:—

---

[1] All admitted, 7 Oct., 1616 (MS. x. f. 4*b*). Muggleton, 'after many admonishions for dronkeness and contrackt of mariag wase expeld,' 20 Sept., 1617 (*ibid.* f. 6*b*). The contract was doubtless with Sarah Shepperd, one of the poor sisters, who 'went away to be maryed to Muggleton' in Sept., 1618.

[2] Author of *Catiline's Conspiracies* and other plays, and subsequently of the *School of Abuse*, 1579, and other tracts directed against the stage. In the title-page of his sermon, *The Trumpet of Warre*, preached at Paul's Cross, 7 May, 1598, he is designated as parson of Great Wigborow, in Essex. According to the register of St. Botolph's he had been rector for more than twenty years at his death, 17 Feb., 1623-4 (Malcolm, *Londinium Redivivum*, vol. i. p. 346).

[3] Admitted, 10 Oct., 1616 (MS. x. f. 4*b*).

[4] Thomas Chard, son of Tho. Chard of Dartford, apprenticed as a printer in

'My humble duetie and kind commendacions remembred to your worship from an vnkind place, etc. I happened to be at Dulledge the first of Septembre last, when as my L. Archbisshoppe of Canterbury his Grace, in the presence of many worthie and worshipfull jentlemen of the countrie and els where were assembled to so worthie a woorke and place, did consecrat your ffounded Chappell, hospitall, schole and churcheyard, and likewise preached at the same tyme, where you gave honorable entertaynment: I was shortlie after at the vniversitie of Cambridge, where I did relate the same in my simple manner, as neere as I could, to the heades of the Colleadges there, who did mutche applaude the same, with great commendation and liking and praising God for the performance and endowing of so good a woorcke and memorable a monument. I did at the same tyme present vnto his Grace a woorke then newly printed by me of the Archbisshoppe of Yorkes[1] Sermons, which his Grace accepted very gratefullie. I did embolden my selfe to present your worship at the same tyme with the like, which it pleased your worship to accept of very kindlie. My adversaries have laid sutche heavie burthens and actions vpon me for molestation, by reason that I have them in suit in the highe Court of Chauncerie, for my house and state wherein I have been a dweller theise 50 yeares, out of the which they have eiected me now allmost theise thre yeares, as is not vnknowen, whearby they doe empeache me in my suit and other my affaires and busines, and therby allso have stollen a verdict and execution agaynst me by sinister meanes of 50^{li} to my vtter overthrowe, I beyng in durance theise eyght monthes, vntill I can gett redresse in

---

1565 (Ames, *Typographical Antiquities*, ed. Herbert, 1786, vol. ii. p. 1194). His first registered publication was on 3 Nov., 1578 (*Stationers' Register*, ed. Arber, vol. iii. p. 29).

[1] Tobias Matthew, Archbishop of York, 1606–1628.

that honorable Court. Wherfore my humble request vnto your good worship is, that you would be pleased in this my extremitie agaynst this good tyme to remembre me with your comfortable remembrance and charitable contribution to be aiding to release me out of prison, with what it shall please God to put in your minde. And I shall be bound,' &c. . . . Ludgate, 14 April, 1617. f. 97.

73. RICHARD BARLOW to Edw. Alleyn, giving his reasons for declining the offer of the ushership of Dulwich College:—

'The first is the present occasion now offered me wheare I am; the seconde is the condicions which weare betwixt you, Mr Lymer and myselfe. For the first, I finde such means stirred vp for my maintenaunce amonghste those my worthie freinds with whome I liue, that certes (in my opinion) it weare great follie in me toe refuse, and much inhumanitie not in some sorte to congratulate, which I can doe noe otherways then by bestowinge my painfull and industriouse labor vpon those little ones, whome they haue soe willingly committed vnto my charge. As touchinge the seconde, I meane condicions, what man is he that will loose a competente maintenance for twentie marks and his diet for one yeare, and afterwards (peradventure) be forced to seeke vntoe his olde freinds for anciant fauour? Againe, this yearly pencion (and I feare me more) must be laide out in a goune, a bed and such like commodities, and at the yeares end (it may be) we must be constrained to packe them to London vnto a broker and loose halfe in halfe. Well, these are noe such greate matters but Mr Lymer might easily haue contained them within the compasse of a letter, if it had pleased him, allthoughe he say nay, and haue saved me xx^s in my purce. Againe, good sir, pardon me if I bee to bolde (for I speake for myselfe), whoe knoweth not but this your memorable act will be published farre and neare, and beinge once knowne that you afforde such maintenaunce and that there is one in place of a yeares triall, howe manie sutors shall you haue in the behalfe of manie (more woorthie then myselfe) whoe shall vse such perswasive retorique vnto you, that I feare me will be little for my good. These things considered, good sir, haue hindered my cominge vnto you; and I humble desire you not to take them in anie sinister respect, for I meane nothinge but trueth and plaine sinceritie of hart. Thus, with my humble duty remembred vnto you and good Mris Allen, with my kindest salut: vnto Mr Lymer, I committ you to God: Newport Pagnell, May the 12, Anno 1617.' f. 98.

74. ROBERT EARLE[1] [?] to Edw. Alleyn, complaining of his dealings with 'that apysshe Jacke Stanton' in connexion with a lease; London, 24 June, 1617. f. 100.

75. ROBERT NEWMAN[2] to Edw. Alleyn:—

'.... This is to sertifi your worshipe conserning the biusnes at our sies [assizes], that my Lorde Cheife Gestis[3] sat on the Geayle deliuerri and, thankes be to God, wee had good suckces in our besnes as wee coulde wishe or desier, wee giue God thankes. And to sertifi your worshipe more at large, our beysnes was the first that was called vpon thare; and when the charge was giuen, before the grante Juri went; our Conceler moued our case and desiered that my lord and

[1] Apparently a scrivener, Mun. 573, below, being written and witnessed by him.

[2] Married Elizabeth, daughter of Edw. Alleyn, of Newport Pagnell, cousin to the Founder (see below, art. 109).

[3] Sir Henry Montagu, Chief Justice of the King's Bench, or Sir Henry Hobart, Chief Justice of the Common Pleas.

the Juri choulde heare our witnes excamened before the wente, and so the ware. Then my lorde sayd vnto the Juri, "The case is playne. Goo forth." So the went and stayed away a grete whill, and my lord sente for them; and, when the cam in, the sayde the could not agree. Then my lord was anggry with them, and sayd, "What corrupt felloues are yee! Is not the mater playne in nought? I will finde [fine] yee all and mack you anser it in the Ster Chamber." Then on of the contrari side sayd, "My lorde, wee are alenne [eleven] of vs finde it and tene stand out." Then my lorde sayde, "Call them ouer, that I may tacke thare names that are so corrupt." Then sayd the forman, "This Cock was euer hellen to be a honist man vntill this myshap befell, and that my brother was a hout quarellsom fello." Then my lord rise vp and sayde, "Thou art a paltri, corrupt fello thy selfe; get thee of of the Juri, and let the next be forman." So the wente forth and brought in willfull murther; and then olde Cock and his other sones cried forth for marci vnto vs, and set all thare frendes and ours vnto vs to desier vs by all meanes that wee wolde be pleased and the wolde thinck and ackknollig thare selles euer beholding vnto vs for his life, if wee wolde cese theare and not proceequit the lawe ani further; and so vpon som considderration wee dide yellde. And for the constabell he was commited at the exeamennation of the witnes and lay at the Jeler house vntill the marro, and then hee was finde at twenti nobles. Thus had wee comfort in our heui bisnes, thankes be to god and to you for youre furtherance in all our prosedinge.... Newporte, the 27 of July 1617. My father Allyen and my mother and my brother Archbould and my br[o]ther Edward Allyen with all vmbell thanckes vnto your worship.' f. 101.

76. THE RECTOR and parishioners of St. Botolph's to

Edw. Alleyn, presenting three children for his school—Richard Merrydall,[1] aged 10, Simon Waddup, aged 8, and Thomas Shippey, aged 8; 7 Aug., 1617. Signed by Stephen Gosson, rector, Raphe Pinder, 'depewte,' and three others. f. 103.

77. RICHARD MERIDALL to Mrs. Alleyn, with laudatory verses beginning, 'Loe heare shee dwells, whome virtue doeth imbrace'; no date. f. 105.

Printed, *Alleyn Papers*, p. 83.

78. THE RECTOR and parishioners of St. Botolph's, Bishopsgate, to Edw. Alleyn, presenting Edw. Cullen to be one of his 'Beadsmen,' in consequence of the removal of [John] Mugleston and the rejection of John Woodhouse, 'for that hee hath a wife'; 1 Sept., 1617. Signed by Stephen Gosson, rector, Raphe Pinder, deputy, Will. Whittwell and Dominick Comesyg, churchwardens, Richard Cowlay,[2] and three others. f. 106.

Printed, *Mem. of Edw. Alleyn*, p. 135.

79. JOHN WARNER[3] to Edw. Alleyn:—

'Accordinge to your request, tendered vnto me by Mr Younge, I haue desired this gentleman, the bearer herof, Mr Streatinge, in his iourney from Oxon to Canterbury to turne vnto you, who is a master of Artes and a minister, and accordingly by his good life and painefull studyes hath pur-

[1] All admitted, 7 Sept., 1617 (*Register*, MS. x. f. 6*b*). Meridall, the writer of the verses following, left the college, 16 Mar., 1621–2 (*ibid.* p. 13*b*).

[2] The same signature occurs below, art. 91, dat. 17 Mar., 1621–2. It cannot, therefore, be that of Rich. Cowley, the actor, who was buried at St. Leonard's, Shoreditch, 12 Mar., 1618–9 (Collier, *Memoirs of Actors*, p. 163).

[3] Rector of St. Dionis, Backchurch, London, afterwards Dean of Lichfield, 1633, and Bishop of Rochester, 1637–1666 (Wood, *Athenæ Oxonienses*, ed. Bliss, vol. iii. p. 731). He was himself the founder of a hospital at Bromley in Kent for clergymen's widows.

chased himselfe a good name in the Vniversity. I haue hearde him preach in London and Canterbury, he hath also preached in Oxon, so that I may speake with the wordes of St. Paul, i. Tim. 4. 12, Let no man despise thy youth. And although his outwarde face and demeanour promise a gentle softlines, yet his inwarde partes shall testify much sufficiency in learninge and his profession. Thus much I thought fitt to write, partly to giue you some foreknowledge of him and partly to witnes a truth on his behalfe. The reste leauinge to your good consideracion, I take leaue and rest, though vnknowen vnto you, yet one ready to doe you any good office'; 17 Jan., 1617[8]. f. 107.

80. JOHN NORTHE to Edw. Alleyn, on matters in dispute concerning the making of tiles; Hampstead, 22 April, 1618. f. 109.

81. THOMAS GRYMES[1] to Edw. Alleyn: has notice that the meeting of the Commissioners for New Buildings is put off until Monday, when he will be ready to do him 'the best frendly office'[2]; Peckham, 25 Aug., 1618. f. 110.

82. EDWARD FERRERS to Edw. Alleyn: will call on Saturday at the house of Will. Parsons[3] to learn when and where they can meet, and will do the best he can to make peace;[4] 'Mr Titchbarns Chamber,' 13 April, 1619. f. 111.

---

[1] Sir Tho. Grymes, knt., of Peckham, M.P. for Surrey in 1623, died 1644. He married Margaret, daughter of Sir Geo. More, of Losely, sister of the wife of Dr. Donne and aunt of Alleyn's second (or third) wife, Constance Donne.

[2] See Alleyn's *Diary* (MS. ix. f. 20), 27 Aug., 1618.

[3] Husband of Anne, niece of Phil. Henslowe (see below, Mun. 182).

[4] See above, MS. ii. artt. 34, 35. In Alleyn's *Diary* (MS. ix. f. 30*b*) are the entries:—'17 Apr., 1619. Water to ye temple to Tichborn, 0 0 4. 19 Apr. I went to London; water to Gryes inn to meet Jacob [Meade], 0 0 6. Dinner with Ferrers, Tichborne and hym, 0 2 6.'

83. THOMAS BOLTON[1] to Edw. Alleyn: has 'bin prisoner in the Marshalsey 28 weekes att the suite of one Low, a scrivener, vpon a bond of x^{li},' and entreats him to send something towards his release and payment of his fees; Marshalsey, 14 April, 1619. f. 113.

84. PETITION to Francis [Bacon], Lord Verulam, Lord Chancellor, from Vrsley Sherbeyrd, widow, daughter of 'Basile Johnson, servante to [Sir Nicholas Bacon] your honours honorable father in the Chancery and kinswoman to Jeremy Becknum,' praying him for a letter to Edw. Alleyn to receive her 'amongst the nomber of his pentioners'; no date. Below is the note, 'Write a letter[2] to the purpose desired, Octob: 7: 1615. Fr. V. Ca.' f. 115.

85. [REV.] JOHN HARRISON[3] to Edw. Alleyn, excusing himself for having secretly married his kinswoman, employed as a servant in the college; [1620]. f. 116.

Printed, *Mem. of Edw. Alleyn*, p. 148.

86. THE SAME to the same, asking him to be godfather to his son:—'In your colledge god sent him a ffather, and my wiues desire with mine is that god might send him also in the same place a Godfather, y^t^ the place of his generation might be seconded with a better help of his regeneration'; [*circ.* 1620]. f. 118.

---

[1] For Alleyn's answer to this appeal see his *Diary* (MS. ix. f. 31), 21 Apr., 1619.

[2] The letter seems to have had no success, as the petitioner's name does not appear in the College *Register* (MS. x., below).

[3] Admitted usher of the College on 20 Dec., 1617, but 'gon' on 28 Sept., 1620 (*Register*, MS. x. ff. 6*b*, 11*b*). His wife was Anne Alleyn, daughter of Edward Alleyn, the Founder's cousin (see below, art. 109). The last payment of wages to her, recorded in the Founder's *Diary*, was on 24 June, 1620; and on 3 Oct. is the entry, 'This daye Nan Allen went away, given her 1*l.* 2*s.*' He left her 20*l.* in his will (*Alleyn Papers*, p. xxiv.).

87. THE SAME to the same, apparently in answer to a refusal of the above request, saying that he 'thought time or grace had eaten out or at least moderated passion'; [*circ.* 1620]. f. 120.

88. THOMAS BURNET to 'Mr Scheargene Owein,'[1] entreating him to procure from Edw. Alleyn, on pain of legal action, the payment of a sum of 35*l.*, being the balance of 220*l.*[2] deposited with him as purchase money for Philip Henslowe's place of Gentleman Sewer, the sale not having taken effect; [1621]. f. 122.

89. ALEXANDER NAIRNE[3] to Edw. Alleyn, on the same subject, suggesting a settlement and giving his own account of the transaction:—'All that I cane say to the perticollar is that to my best remembrenc their wes dellyuirid into your hands in considiration of a plac your lait father of lawe should haue surrandirt to Mr Burnit 220^l^, whitche my lord Chambirlin refoissinge to permit, their wes retornit bak of this mony upon my motione nyn scoir pownd, the rest beinge reseruid wpon sum pryuat consideration as your father said to me From my hoos in tithillstrit this 21 of Jully 1621.' f. 123.

In MS. i. f. 58*b* (see above, p. 28) is the draft of a long answer by Edw. Alleyn to this letter. It is printed at length in the *Memoirs of Edw. Alleyn*, p. 136; but Mr. Collier assigns it to too early a date and misreads many of the words: e.g. for 'trouble,' l. 3, read 'trueth'; for 'consyder of his estat,' p. 137, l. 8, read 'comesserat

---

[1] See Alleyn's *Diary*, MS. ix., below, under the dates 1 May, 20 Dec., 1620.

[2] For a bond for the surrender of the office on payment of this sum see below, Mun. 148. In Alleyn's *Diary*, 7 Aug., 1621, is an entry of a payment to Burnett of 5*l.*, probably in connexion with this claim.

[3] The name appears in a list of the King's surveyors in 1614 (Brit. Mus., Lansdowne MS. 165, f. 252).

his estat'; for 'by his letters,' l. 11, read 'by his behaviour'; for 'do and will,' l. 34, read 'do still'; for 'Sergiant Greene,' p. 138, l. 1, read 'Sargiant Owine;' and for 'matter,' l. 3, read 'iniustice.'

90. PETITION to [John Williams,[1] Bishop of Lincoln] Lord Keeper, from John Jones, of Westminster, praying him to use interest with Edw. Alleyn to procure him the next vacant almsroom at Dulwich; [*circ.* 3 Aug.-10 Nov., 1621]. Below is the note, 'Lett the petitioner present his owne suyt,[2] and therewithall my request, to Mr Allen in this behalfe. Jo: Lincoln. elect., custos sigilli.' f. 125.

91. THE RECTOR and parishioners of St. Botolph's to Edw. Alleyn, presenting four poor children—Randall Sparrow, John Sparkes, Thomas Heyes, and Robert Brounrigg[3]; 17 March, 1621[2]. Signed by Stephen Gosson, Raphe Pinder, Richard Cowlay, and eight others. f. 126.

92. SIR FRAN. CALTON to Edw. Alleyn, alleging reasons that 'yow woulde nowe at the lengthe yealde to make me some proportionable recompence for ye losse which I haue sustained by your Kennington'; 12 May, 1623. f. 127.

93. EDW. ALLEYN to Sir Fran. Calton, in answer to charges of hard dealing with respect to Dulwich and Kennington manors; [1623?]. Draft; written on the back of a sheet of brief paper containing part of a will in the hand of, and signed by, Edw. Alleyn. Of the two clauses that remain, one provides for the building of thirty almshouses in or near London, and the other directs that, in consideration of legacies, the testator's cousin, Thos. Alleyn, barber-surgeon,

1 Lord Keeper, 10 July, 1621–30 Oct., 1625; elected Bishop of Lincoln 3 Aug., consecrated 11 Nov., 1621; Archbishop of York, 1641; died 25 Mar., 1650.

2 The applicant's name does not appear in the College *Register* (MS. x.).

3 Brounrigg only was admitted (*Register*, f. 13*b*).

of London, and his son, Edw. Alleyn, the testator's godson, shall be surgeons to Dulwich College for life. f. 129.

The letter is printed, but with some inaccuracies, in the *Mem. of Edw. Alleyn*, p. 143. Mr. Collier also prints, as belonging to the same letter, a passage in which Alleyn replies to some alleged taunts of Sir Fran. Calton with regard to his having been a player. Mr. Collier says (p. 146) that this passage is written on a loose slip, marked with an asterisk; but the slip (if it ever existed) is no longer to be found.

94. JOHN LUNTLEY to Edw. Alleyn, informing him that he has assigned to John Freebody for two years the rent of tenements 'on the Bancke side' leased of him by Alleyn at 14*l.* a year[1]; 'From the White Lyon in Southwark,' 8 Jan., 1623[4]. f. 131.

Printed, *Alleyn Papers*, p. 90.

95. ROBERT NEWMAN to Edw. Alleyn, thanking him for his good cheer and stating that his father [-in-law, Edw. Alleyn of Newport] and brother will bring up 'all thare euedences of that hows'; Newport, 1 March, 1623[4]. f. 132.

96. HENRY GIBB[2] to Edw. Alleyn: understands he has received the boy about whom he wrote and thanks him for his care of him; will willingly assist his desire to have 'sum further dignetie'[3] conferred upon him, but advises him to wait till the King 'be cuminge homward neie Windsor forrest,' before which time he will 'speik with all these men

[1] See below, MS. v. artt. 36, 38. The White Lion was used as a prison for the county of Surrey (Stow, *Survey*, ed. Thoms, 1876, p. 153).

[2] Groom of the Bedchamber to James I., and previously to Henry, Prince of Wales; created a baronet of Nova Scotia in 1634. A long account of him is given by Sir G. D. Gibb, *Life and Times of Rob. Gib*, 1874, vol. ii. p. 99.

[3] Probably the honour of knighthood, as Mr. Collier suggests.

y[t] M[r] Holliburton speiks of'; Westminster, 23 July, 1624. f. 134.

Printed, *Mem. of Edw. Alleyn*, p. 172.

97. [SIR] JOHN HUNGGERFORD to Edw. Alleyn: has imparted his [Alleyn's] project to Sir Arthur Aston, who, if they can agree, will move the King in it, and wishes for a conference at once, 'that he may macke up his peticion against tomorrow morning'; [1624?]. f. 136.

98. AMBROSE WHEELER, George Lowe, and George Handcoke to Edw. Alleyn: complain of his having broken his promise, and threaten, if he will not 'goe forwardes' with them, that they 'must lett my Lord Keeper knowe tomor row' how they are crossed, since his 'suspending the tyme is cause of all the ruine that is like to fall vpon this busnes'; [1624]. f. 137.

Printed, *Alleyn Papers*, p. 20.

99. AMBROSE WHEELER to Edw. Alleyn: has heard from Sir William Cokine[1] that his solicitor, Henchman, 'told him that, as far as he could perceaue by your consell M[r] Brocks, you were not minded to deale any farther in the busines,' and they entreat him, therefore, to meet them 'at S[r] Richard Moores[2] in the Inward Temple, where will be M[r] Gottes and young M[r] Finch and the Allderman and his consell, wherby you shall not onlye before the m[tes] of the Chancerye manifest your good and charitable integretie in the busines, but also the aboue said oposicion to be mere inuen-

[1] Sir Will. Cockayne, knighted with the City sword at an entertainment which he gave to James I. at his house in Broad Street, 22 June, 1616; Lord Mayor in 1619; died 20 Oct., 1626.

[2] Master in Chancery, 1616–1635; knighted at Greenwich, 29 June, 1619.

tion of the Alldermans and Henchmans. . . . This Thursday, 1624.' f 139.

100. W. HERVY[1] to Edw. Alleyn, asking his consent, 'as Lord of Lewsham,' that his wife may 'inclose a smale parcell of comon grownd before her doore'; London, 27 Aug., 1624. f. 141.

101. E. SKORY[2] to Edw. Alleyn: recommends the bearer, 'father Barnes,' as a 'tru, paynfull, innocent, iust creature,' on whom his [Alleyn's] charity had already been well bestowed; understands that one Talboys, a 'wittless and monnyless foole,' is in prison at his suit, and prays for his authority 'to bidd him paie the duties of the prison and be gon,' promising that the Attorney-General[3] and Sir Thos. Fanshawe[4] will thank him for his charity and that 'the senceless yet paynfull verses that this Talboys will make' in acknowledgment will be worth the money to 'laugh at'; Redcross Street, 12 Jan., 1624[5]. f. 143.

102. WILLIAM BECHER,[5] the elder, to Edw. Alleyn, re-

[1] William Hervey, or Hervy, of Kidbrook, co. Kent, knighted at Cadiz in 1596; created bart., 31 May, 1619; Lord Hervey of Wexford, 5 Aug., 1620; and Lord Hervey of Kidbrooke, 7 Feb., 1627–8; died 1642. He married as his second wife Cordelia, daughter and co-heir of Brian Annesley, of Lewisham.

[2] Probably Edmund Scory, second son of Silvanus Scory and grandson of John Scory, Bishop of Hereford (Harl. MS. 1545, f. 34*b*); author of *An Extract out of the Historie of the Last French King, Henry the Fourth*, &c., Lond., 1610 (Wood, *Athenæ*, ed. 1815, vol. ii. p. 89).

[3] Sir Thomas Coventry, Attorney-General, 1620; Lord Keeper, 1625; cr. Lord Coventry, 1628; died in 1640.

[4] Surveyor-General and Clerk of the Crown, knighted 19 Sept., 1624.

[5] Probably Sir Will. Becher, of Howbery, co. Bedford, knighted at Kirkby 29 July, 1619, died in 1641; son of Henry Becher, alderman of London. There was another Sir Will. Becher (the younger), knighted at Newmarket 16 Sept., 1622; Clerk of the Privy Council Jan., 1623; died 8 April, 1651. He was son of William Becher, younger brother of Alderman Henry. See the pedigree of the family, Brit. Mus., Add. MS. 20774, f. 21.

commending Henry Petty for 'a rome vacant for a poore aged man'; Southwark, 24 Jan., 1624[5]. f. 145.

Below and on the three blank pages at the back is the draft of a long letter from Edw. Alleyn to Dr. John Donne, father of his second (or third) wife, Constance, complaining of his 'manie vnkind passages,' and especially the 'vnkind vnexspeckted and vndeserved deniall of y^{t} comon curtesie afforded to a frend, I mean ye loane of vnvsefull moneys.' This letter has no date or address, but it was written 'allmost 5 quarters sinc our maryag,'[1] which took place on 3 Dec., 1623 (*Alleyn Papers*, p. xx.). It has been printed in full by Mr. Collier (*Mem. of Edw. Alleyn*, p. 173), but with numerous inaccuracies. In his remarks upon it Mr. Collier observes, 'Here also we find it distinctly stated by Alleyn, that a portion of his property was the playhouse in the Blackfriars.' This is not the case. The passage to which he refers runs as follows:—'I then towld you all my landes wear stated [i.e. settled] on ye Coll: 3 leases I had, one off them wase giuen to ye Coll: ye other 2 being ye manor and recktory off Lewsham[2] worth 130^{l} a year, and diuer tenementes in ye black fryars, *as the plaiehowse theare,* worth 120^{l} ye year, boath which cost me 2500^{l}.' The words in italics, however, were certainly not written by Alleyn, but they have been inserted between the lines evidently by the same hand to which are due the forgeries noticed above in MS. i., and below in MSS. vii. ix.

103. SIR THOMAS GRYMES to Edw. Alleyn:—'S^{r}, The last night meeting you vppon the highe waye you tould me you might haue iic^{ll} vppon your bond and myne. I then did let you vnderstand how I had promised vppon my brother John Grymes[3] his death (for whom I now paye a c^{li} that I

[1] Not '3 quarters,' as it is printed by Mr. Collier.

[2] See below, MS. ix., 15 Dec., 1620, and for the tenements in the Blackfriars, *ibid.*, 22 Oct., 1617, note.

[3] Of Bury St. Edmunds; married Susan, daughter of Ambrose Jermyn, of Stanton, co. Suffolk (*Collect. Genealogica et Topographica*, vol. iii. p. 157). In a letter from J. Chamberlain to Sir D. Carlton, 20 April, 1616, is an account of the burial of a Sir John Grimes, a great friend and favourite of Sir Geo. Villiers, afterwards Duke of Buckingham, but he is spoken of as if he were a Scotchman (*Court and Times of Jas. I.*, vol. i. p. 399).

stood bound for, besides many hundreds more I paid before) I wold not enter agayne in bond for anye man, and rashly then wished I might loose my hand when I subscribed to bond as suertye agayne. This I protest vnto you standes my case, the consideration wherof hath trobled my mynd very much since I sawe you, being vnwilling to denye you anye thinge. iic^{li}, as I tould you, I haue lying by me; it shalbe redy for you at a quarter of an howres worning, and all my plate (but that I vse daly), which I am sure will amount to aboue a c^{li}, if you please, you shall haue it to pawne to helpe to furnishe your occasions. So comending my loue to your self and my neece I rest,' &c.; Peckham, 4 Febr., 1624[5]. f. 147.

104. LEONELL TYCHEBOURN to Edw. Alleyn, asking for a loan of 20*s.* till the end of term; 10 Oct., 1625. With acquittance below from Simon Tichborne, his son. f. 149.

105. GEORGE COLE[1] to Edw. Alleyn, respecting debts from the latter to Henry Wright and 'Mr Boyer in the poultry,' and on other legal business; 16 Feb., 1625[6]. f. 150.

Printed, *Mem. of Edw. Alleyn*, p. 181.

106. GEORGE PAULE[2] to Edw. Alleyn, asking, on behalf of a friend 'that hath gott the best right and howlde of Sr Nowell Carons[3] house and lande,' what is the value of the lease of Kennington passed by Alleyn to Sir Fran. Calton; Lambeth, 26 June, 1626. f. 151.

[1] Named in Alleyn's will as the person from whom he purchased his lands in Yorkshire. This estate appears to have been at Simondstone, in the manor of Dale Grange, and to have been bought in July, 1626 (see below, art. 107, MS. v. art. 51, and Munn. 135–143).

[2] Sir Geo. Paul, of Lambeth (Harl. MS. 1046, f. 207), chief clerk for enrolling pleas in the King's Bench (*Cal. State Papers*, 1619–1623, p. 241).

[3] See above, art. 58, n.

On the back is a draft, in the hand of Edw. Alleyn, of clauses 120, 121, 123 in the statutes of Dulwich College.

107. JOHN GOODMAN to Edw. Alleyn: expects him on Monday, and, if he can get a horse, will go with him into Yorkshire; Much Hadham, 11 July, 1626. f. 153.

On the back is a note of a tender by Edw. Alleyn of 188*l.* made in 'the house of Margarett Turnor att the signe of the Vnicorne' at Ripon, 22 July, 1626; together with rough notes in his own hand relating to the Simondstone estate.

108. HENRY UNDERWOOD to Edw. Alleyn: is glad to hear that he is 'towardes a recouery,' and doubts not that in due time he will be restored to his 'woonted ioye'; proposes to hold the Court Leet on the 24th inst. and encloses a warrant for the summoning of it; St. Marget's Hill, in Southwark, 14 Oct., 1626. f. 155.

This is the last dated letter addressed to Edw. Alleyn, who died on 25 Nov. following.

109. NINE LETTERS from Edw. Alleyn, of Newport Pagnell, glover, to his cousin, Edw. Alleyn, of Southwark and Dulwich, chiefly acknowledging acts of kindness and on matters of no interest, some of them referring to his daughter Anne, employed by the Founder as a servant; no dates, but the earliest written before 1616. The last letter is in a different hand, and is perhaps from Edw. Alleyn the younger. ff. 156–165.

On the back of f. 162 is a draft, in the hand of Edw. Alleyn, of clause 120 in the Statutes of Dulwich College.

110. TWO LETTERS from Matthias Alleyn to Edw. Alleyn, 'at the banckside,' in acknowledgment of kindnesses, and the latter asking his goodwill 'concerninge my comminge to London to settell'; 20 April, 10 March, *s. a.* ff. 166, 168.

111. DOROTHY CALTON [wife of Sir Francis] to Edw. Alleyn, entreating a loan of 5*l.*; no dates. Two letters, the second with an acquittance, dated 20 March. ff. 169, 170.

112. PETITION from Frances Davys, widow, to Edw. Alleyn, praying for the grant of one of his almshouses in the parish of St. Giles, Cripplegate; no date. Signed by John Millin, Thomas Cotes, and Nicholas Cooke, churchwardens, and seven others. f. 171.

On the back is a letter from Edw. Alleyn to John Millin, reminding him that it was agreed that the number of men and women should be equal, and desiring him to find out 'sume honeste man' for the vacancy.

113. ISABELL FOUND, widow, to Edw. Alleyn, begging for admittance into the number of his 'poore almsweemen'; no date. f. 173.

114. WILLIAM HULL to Edw. Alleyn, asking for the loan of 40*s.*; no date. f. 175.

115. RICHARD KIPPEIS to Edw. Alleyn, asking for the payment of 6*s.* 8*d.*, paid by himself to 'my ladie of Derbie'; no date. f. 176.

116. I[NNOCENT] LANIER[1] to Edw. Alleyn, praying, on behalf of his sister, for some more of his powder, since taking which 'shee never had fitt'; no date. f. 177.

117. INNOCENT LANIER to Sir Fran. Calton, assuring him that his 'bargen wass not easie' and the security not good, having his knowledge from a gentleman who desires

[1] One of the King's 'musicians for the flute' (see the accounts of Lord Stanhope, Treasurer of the Chamber, for 1613, Brit. Mus., Add. MS. 23090, f. 8).

his name not to appear, as he has business 'which must pass the hands of some of Mr Allens freends'; no date. f. 179.

118. E. PHILIPPES to Edw. Alleyn, thanking him for a gift and a 'most loving letter'; no date. f. 181.

119. ANNE POYNTZ to Edw. Alleyn, asking for a loan of 5*l.* and that he will speak with her concerning her unkind husband;[1] no date. f. 182.

120. JOAN RATCLIFF to Edw. Alleyn, asking for aid to enable her to go into Worcestershire to 'my lady Sandes,'[2] her husband, a minister, having left England on account of his debts and gone to Virginia with Lady Sandes's daughter, the Governor's wife; no date. f. 183.

121. 'JOAN RATCLIFFE *alias* YARNER, widdowe,' to Edw. Allen, praying for assistance, being in extreme want and poverty; no date. f. 184.

122. MARTHA STOCKE AND JOHN STOCKE to their landlord, Edw. Alleyn, complaining of encroachments upon 'this littell comon' by one Cooke of Lambeth; 19 April, 1619. f. 185.

123. WILLIAM STYLE to Edw. Alleyn, concerning a horse in his [Alleyn's] custody which was stolen out of the stable of John Williams, 'inkeper in Hethfielde'; no date. f. 186.

124. JULIAN TYSON, widow of George Tyson, late 'sinker of the mynt' in the Tower, to Edw. Alleyn, praying

1 Perhaps the John Poyntz whose name occurs above, art. 17.

2 Mercy, wife of Sir Sam. Sandes, of Ombersley and Wickhamden, co. Worc. Their daughter Mary married Sir Francis Wyat, Governor of Virginia (Nash, *Worcestershire*, vol. ii. p. 221).

for assistance, her brother, John Armstronge, having once been his tenant without Bishopsgate; no date. f. 187.

125. LETTER, without signature or address, on matters in dispute concerning leases of lands in Dulwich; no date. f. 188.

126. LETTER, beginning, 'My verie good lord,' but with out signature or address, containing proposals with regard to the inspection of weights and measures; no date. f. 189.

127. LETTER, without signature or address, beginning, 'Most fayre and Nonsuch Lady,' and purporting to be written by a 'pore sheppard,' giving information of a stray nag which had been appropriated by his master against the right of 'the Lady of the soyle'; no date. f. 190.

128. HYMN, in the hand of Edw. Alleyn, beginning, 'O prayse y[e] Lord y[e] seruantes all': six verses. f 191.

Printed, *Mem. of Edw. Alleyn*, p. 158.

129. LIST, in the hand of Mr. J. O. Halliwell, now Phillipps, of thirty-six letters and papers, which originally formed part of the Dulwich collection, and were restored by him to the College; Islip, 20 Mar., 1843. They are now bound up with the rest of the collection in their proper chronological order. Most of them are printed by Mr. Collier in the *Alleyn Papers*. f. 194.

MS. No. IV.

Alleyn Papers. Vol. IV. Legal and Miscellaneous Papers of Edward Alleyn and his Family; 1461–1611.

1. 'The Turkes Letter to Scanderbeg,' being a translation of a letter from Mahomet II. to George Castriote, or Scanderbeg, Prince of Epirus; Constantinople, 1 July, 1461. f. 1.

The version differs very little from that printed in *A Commentarie of the Warres of the Turke made against George Scanderbeg*, the second of *Two very Notable Commentaries . . . . translated oute of Italian into Englishe by John Shute*, London, 1562, f. 25*b*, where the date is 2 May, 1461. A Latin version, with considerable differences, is given by Marinus Barletius, *De Vita et Gestis Scanderbegi*, Francoforti, 1578, f. 192.

2. Will of Henry Hunt, of Dulwich, mentioning Emme, his wife, and Thomas, John, Henry, and Agnes, his children, and appointing Walter Dove supervisor; 2 Feb., 1558[9]. With probate, 16 Nov., 1560. *Copies.* f. 2.

3. 'The Acompte of Robart Brokesbe, George E[ten? and] Henry Brygges, chvrche wardens of the paryshe of [Camberwell], from the fest of the byrth of our Lord god, a. 1562, vntyll the same fest, 1563, for one hole yere, made before the hole parishe.' Much decayed at the edges. f. 4.

The receipts include subscriptions for 'bell castynge,' and payments for knells with 'the great bell' at 1*s.* the knell, and with 'the mydell bell' at 8*d.* the knell. Among the payments are:—

'payd for a hondred of bell mettell xxxiiii^{s} and payd for the castyng of the great bell iii^{li} xiii^{s} iiii^{d} } v^{li} vii^{s} iiij^{d}

'Item payd for the caryinge of that bell forth ij^{s} i^{d}, payd for the bryngyng of that bell home i^{s} v^{d}, payde to the bel founder for ernest for a bell castyng xii^{d}	iiij^{s} vi^{d}

. . . .

'payd for a boke of the new Iniuncyons ii^{s} viii^{d}, payd for a boke of the commen prayer iii^{d}, payde for to bokes more ij^{s} iiij^{d}	v^{s} iii^{d}
'payd for glashyng of the windo in the body of the chvrche of the sowth syde and for the wyndo in the bellfre	iij^{s} iiij^{d}
'Item payd for wasshing of the lynnen for the chvrche for ij yeares	ii^{s} viii^{d}
'Item payd for bread and wyne for the chvrche for one hole yeare	xiij^{s} iiij^{d}'

4. COPY of a report addressed to Sir Christopher Draper, Lord Mayor, and the aldermen of London by Thomas Peacock, Walter Cooper, Thomas Wylde, and John Owtyng, 'the fower Masters of the Free Masons, Carpenters, and Tylers, viewers indifferently sworne to the said cittie,' respecting the title to a brick wall in the par. of St. Botolph without Bishopsgate, in dispute between Edward Alleyn, 'one of the Queens Maiesties porters,' and the Corporation of London as governors of Bridewell; 26 May, 1567. Endorsed, 'A veiwe of a Bricke wall at Pye Ally.' f. 7*b*.

5. COPY of the fine by Margaret Calton and William Calton of the manor of Dulwich, &c., as below, Mun. 345; Hilary term, 12 Eliz. [1570]. *Lat.* f. 15*b*.

6. SURRENDER by John Hunt, to the use of Robert Wythe, of land, &c., in the manor of Dulwich, followed by a summons in a plea of Arnold Hunt relative to the same, a statement of the case, and a final release and bond by the said Arnold; 10 July, 1572–21 April, 1574. ff. 25–32, 35.

7. GRANT by Edward, William, Bartholomew, Acton, and Edgar Scott [sons of John Scott, of Camberwell, d. 1558] to

John Lever, fishmonger, of the remaining year of their lease of the manor of Dulwich, after the expiration of a lease for 8 years held of them by Walter and John Dove [see below, Mun. 349]; 22 Jan., 15 Eliz. [1573]. With seal of arms of Edw. Scott. f. 33.

8. COPY of a portion of the will of Will. Gyll, as below, Mun. 9; 21 April, 1575. f. 37*b*.

9. 'A BREIFE NOTE of Sr Frauncis Caltons office founde after the death of Mr Nicholas Calton his father,' containing the descent and title of Dulwich manor, &c., since 1540: endorsed 'Inquisicio indentata capta 20 Maii anno xvii^{o} Regine Eliz.' [1575], Francis Calton being then of the age of 10 years, 3 months, and 9 days. f. 41.

10. 'KENYNGTON RENTALL at Mighelmas, 1577.' f. 43.

11. GENERAL RELEASES to John Allen or Alleyn, variously styled 'of London, yeoman,' servant to 'the Lord Sheffeilde,' and 'inholder,' from—

- *a.* Edw. Dowttye, of London, yeoman; 6 Oct., 1580. f. 45.
- *b.* Rich. Johnson, of London, carter; 18 Nov., 2 Dec., 1580. ff. 46, 47. See *Alleyn Papers*, p. 1.
- *c.* Rob. Cox, of Beaminster, co. Dors., yeoman; 28 Nov., 1586. f. 54. See *Alleyn Papers*, p. 2.
- *d.* Raphe Knighton, of London, baker; 24 July, 1587. f. 56.
- *e.* Nich. Harrison, of London, haberdasher; 5 Feb., 1588[9]. f. 67.
- *f.* Will. Davies, of London, gent.; 10 Nov., 1592. f 76.
- *g.* Nich. Furnyer, of St. Katherine's, felt-maker; 1 Nov., 1593, 8 Jan., 1593[4]. ff. 80, 82.

h. John Allyn, of St. Giles without Cripplegate; 24 Nov., 1593. f. 81.

i. Thos. Iles, of Barkley, co. Som., yeoman; 18 Feb., 1594. f. 84.

k. Geo. Tedder, of London, merchant-tailor; 16 Jan., 1595. f. 88.

12. SURRENDER by Rob. Wyth, of the Inner Temple, esq., of a house and land in Dulwich manor to the use of Ellys Parrye; 29 June, 1584. f. 48.

13. COVENANT by Patrick Brewe, of London, goldsmith, to pay to Daniel Gill, the elder, of the Isle of Man, yeoman, a yearly rent of 12*l.* in the 'Vtter Pentice' at Chester for a lease for 41 years of six messuages, &c. [in the par. of St. Giles, Cripplegate], late in the occupation of Will. Gill [see below, Munn. 12, 13]; 11 July, 26 Eliz. [1584]. Signed; with seal. f. 50.

14. POWER OF ATTORNEY from Daniel Gill, the elder, to Patrick Brewe, to deliver seisin to Daniel Gill, his son, of messuages, &c., in Goldinge Lane and Whytecrosse Street, in the par. of St. Giles, co. Midd., which lately came to him by the will of his uncle, William Gill; 5 Nov., 26 Eliz., 1584. With a letter from Dan. Gill, the younger; 10 Nov., 1584. ff. 51, 52.

15. CERTIFICATE of the Court of Wards and Liveries of the grant to Francis, son and heir of Nicholas Calton, of a continuance of the tender of his livery until 1 Nov., 'without losse of any meane proffittes'; 14 May, 28 Eliz. [1586]. f. 53.

16. WARRANT from the Commissioners of Sewers for co. Surrey to Hen. Brygges, 'balyffe of the sewers in the weste parte of Surrey,' to summon Nich. Adams, of Barnes, yeoman, to appear at the court-house in Southwark; 3 April, 1587. Signed by John Sotherton, Humfrey Smythe, Tho. Taylor, Edm. Bowyer, Fran. Muschamp, and others. f. 55.

17. ACQUITTANCES to John Allen, Alleyn, or Allyn, innholder, from—

a. Raphe Knighton, of London, 'white backer' [baker], for two sums of 20*s.* in part payment of a bond of 5*l.*; 12 Nov., 1587, 8 April, 1588. ff. 57, 60.

b. Alex. Beale, for 20*s.*, in part payment of a debt of John Browne, haberdasher; 20 Oct., 1588. f. 62.

c. Alex. Beale for 20*s.*, to the use of Rob. Beale, of Whitechapel, brewer, in part payment of a bond; 10 Jan., 1588[9]. f 63.

d. Matt. Small, for 5*l.*, a half-year's rent for a tenement without Bishopsgate, London; 27 Jan., 1588[9], 2 Nov., 1589. ff. 64, 69.

e. Julyan Cropwell, widow, for quarterly payments of 10*s.*, for rent of two tenements in the parish of St. Botolph without Bishopsgate; 18 Jan., 1592[3]–28 Jan., 1594[5]. ff. 77, 79, 83, 89. See below, Mun. 111.

f. Nich. Furnyer, of St. Katherine's, felt-maker, for 40*s.*, for a quarter's rent of a house, &c., in St. Katherine's; 4 April, 1594. f. 84.

18. ACKNOWLEDGMENT by Will. Barnes, of London, merchant-tailor, of a debt to John Alleyn, innholder, of 35*s.*; 23 Dec., 30 Eliz. [1587]. f. 58.

19. INVENTORY of the goods, chattels, &c., of Rich. Browne, shipwright, late of the parish of All Hallows, Lombard Street, renounced by Margery, his wife, and appraised by

Phil. Browne, gent., and Jas. Tonstall, yeoman; 8 Jan., 30 Eliz. [1588]. 'Extractum fuit huiusmodi inventarium,' 23 Jan., 1587[8], 'per Johannem Allen, creditorem et administratorem,' &c. f. 59.

Printed, *Alleyn Papers*, p. 3. See also below, Mun. 93.

20. NOTE of the payment by Richard and Robert Northe to Henry Budder of 13*l.* 3*s.*; 22 April, 1588. f. 61.

21. ASSIGNMENT by John Whit, of Southwark, yeoman, to John Malthowes of a lease of a messuage called 'The barg, the bell and the cocke'; 5 Feb., 31 Eliz. [1589]. f. 65.

See Alleyn's will in the *Alleyn Papers*, p. xxii., and Collier, *Hist. of Dram. Poetry*, vol. iii. p. 126.

22. GENERAL RELEASE from Nich. Harrison, of London, haberdasher, to John Allen, innholder, and Edw. Allen, gent., sons of Edw. Allen, late of London, innholder; 5 Feb., 1588[9]. f. 67.

23. CIRCULAR LETTER of Queen Elizabeth, asking for a loan towards the charges of preparation against a Spanish invasion; Nonsuch, 11 July, a° 31 [1589]. *Copy*, with blank spaces for the name and sum. f. 68.

24. BOND from Thomas Martyn, D.C.L., to John Allen, innholder, in 100*l.*, to observe any award respecting their differences which should be made by Will. Salter, grocer, and Hugh Woodcock, salter, as arbitrators, or by Will. Drewry, D.C.L., as umpire; 14 Nov., 1589. f. 70.

Printed, *Alleyn Papers*, p. 7. See also above, MS. iii. artt. 3, 4.

25. ACQUITTANCE from Will. Bedingfeld to Henry Goodgyer [Goodere or Goodyer], of Hertford, esq., for 35*s.* paid through John Allen for rent of a house, &c., 'in More meade, somtyme Doctor Penneyes'; 15 Nov., 32 Eliz. [1590]. f. 71.

26. ACKNOWLEDGMENT by John Allein, innholder, and Edw. Alleyn, gent., of a debt to John Webster, of London, merchant-tailor, of 15*s.*, to be paid on 30 Sept.; 25 July, 1591. f. 72.

Printed, *Alleyn Papers*, p. 14.

27. ACKNOWLEDGMENT by Henry Aske, of Newington, husbandman, of a debt to John Allin, innholder, of 10*s.*; 2 May, 1592. f. 73.

28. ASSIGNMENT on mortgage by John Allin, innholder, to Robert Robinson, of London, white-baker, of a lease from Julian Cropwell, of the parish of St. Botolph without Bishopsgate, widow, of two messuages in the same parish for 9 years [see below, Mun. 111]; 18 July, 1592. f. 74.

29. BOND from John Allen, innholder, Thos. Goodale, of London, mercer, and Rob. Lee, of London, gent., to John Allen, of London, gent., in 38*l.*, for the payment of 19*l.*; 18 May, 35 Eliz. [1593]. f. 78.

30. POWER OF ATTORNEY from Hen. Orrell, of St. John Street, co. Midd., yeoman, to Edw. Allen, of St. Saviour's, Southwark, gent., to recover to his own use sums due on bonds from Arnold Vancullen, *alias* Shepparde, and William Pattenson, of London, yeomen; 17 Aug., 1594. Witness John Pik [Pigge, the actor; see above, MS. i. art. 15]. f. 86.

31. ACKNOWLEDGMENT by Rich. Garrett, of London, merchant-tailor, of debts of 3*l.* and 6*l.* to Thomas Keyes, one of the cooks to the Queen, and Isabell, his wife; 24 Mar., 1594[5]. f. 87.

32. WILL of Anne Rigbie, of the parish of St. Katherine Christchurch within Aldgate, London, widow, containing bequests to Thos. Shorte, her son, Jane and Frances Shorte, her granddaughters, her 'poor cozen Dawes,' and 'old aunte Mills,' John Browne, haberdasher [Edw. Alleyn's father-in-law], and others; 7 Feb. 1595[6]. With probate, 18 Feb., 1595[6]. *Copy.* f. 90.

33. LIST of sixty-four knights made by the Earl of Essex and the Lord Admiral Howard in the expedition to Cadiz; June, 1596. At the end is written, 'Thes gentellmen where knyghted at Challes' [*sic*]. See Stow's *Chronicle*, ed. 1615, p. 1283. f. 92.

34. WILL of Will. Plogg, of Camberwell, yeoman, bequeathing his land, &c., in Kent to Agnes Plogg, Eliz. Glover, and Phillip [*sic*] Netlingham, his three daughters, for their lives, with remainder in tail to Benjamin, son of William and the above Phillip Netlingham, in tail, and in default to John, son of the above Elizabeth Glover; 26 Mar., 1597. *Copy.* f. 93.

35. ACQUITTANCE from Will. Lardge, bailiff of Brixton and Wallington hundred, co. Surr., for 10*s*., for a post fine on a messuage, &c., in Dulwich and Camberwell; 14 Sept., 1598. f. 95.

36. ACQUITTANCE from Will. Chamber, on behalf of Will. Marten, churchwarden of St. Mildred's, Bread Street, to Phil. Ensley [Henslowe] for 35*s*., for a quarter's rent to 'the vse of the parrysh chvrch'; 16 Jan., 1598[9]. f. 96.

37. SURRENDER by Nich. Knight, of Brockholes, of lands, &c., in Dulwich manor, to the use of Edw. Duke, conditional upon the payment of 400*l.* by the said Edw. Duke and Francis Calton; 24 Sept., 41 Eliz. [1599]. f. 97.

38. LICENSE from Richard [Vaughan], Bishop of London, lord of the manor of Patteswicke, co. Essex, to Edw. Nowell, haberdasher, to lease to Will. Frithe, of London, haberdasher, a messuage, &c., called Blamishes; 15 July, 1601. f. 100.

39. ACQUITTANCE from John Middleton, on behalf of Thomas [Bilson], Bishop of Winchester, to Phil. Henslowe, for 9*s.* 7*d.*, for a year's rent of tenements 'one the bankesyde, late one William Paynes'; 23 Oct., 1601. f. 101.

40. 'A NOTE of certayne goods of Henry Briggs, thelder,' and of wearing apparel of Isabel Briggs; 11 Mar., 1601[2]. f. 102.

41. BOND from John Hynde, of the par. of St. Andrew, Holborn, gent., to Edw. Alleyn, of St. Saviour's, Southwark, gent., in 12*l.*, for the payment of 6*l.*; 8 May, 1602. f. 103.

42. COPY of the fine by Fran. Calton, esq., to Rob. Lee, Mayor of London, of messuages in Dulwich, as below, Mun. 437; 3 Feb., 45 Eliz. [1603]. *Lat.* f. 104.

43. ACQUITTANCE from Matt. Woodwarde to Rob. Broomffeild for 50*s.*, due to Anthony [Browne], Viscount Montagu, for a half-year's rent of a wharf, &c., 'within the close of St. Marye Overies'; 22 April, 1603. See below, Mun. 121. f. 108.

44. JUDGMENT of John Notley, M.A., surrogate of Garrett Williamson, Dean of South Malling, &c., in favour of John Langworth, DD., rector of Buxted, co. Sussex, in a tithe suit against William Henslowe; 30 June, 1603. *Lat.* f. 110.

45. ACQUITTANCE from Matt. Woodwarde to Edw. Alleyn for half-yearly payments due as above, art. 43; 6 April, 1604–25 Oct., 1611. See below, Mun. 122. ff. 112–114, 118, 129, 134, 142, 146, 151, 152, 159, 161, 164 170, 171, 237.

46. LETTER from the Privy Council to [Thomas Gerard], Lord Gerard, Governor of the Isle of Man, bidding him permit John Curghye, deemster, and others to come to the Court in order to 'declare and open there gryffes' against Robert Molynaxe [Molyneux], his deputy; Greenwich, 21 April, 1605. *Copy.* f. 115.

47. ACKNOWLEDGMENT by Rob. Stoberte of a debt to Phil. Henslowe of 25*s.* for money lent; 23 Sept., 1605. f. 116.

48. ACQUITTANCE from Sir Fran. Calton, knt., to Edw. Allen, esq., for 35*l.*, in part payment of 5,000*l.* 'for the absolute purchase of the mannor of Dulwich . . . . . and all other the landes of me the saide S[r] Frauncis in Dulwich aforesaide, and of other landes, whereof the said Edward hath a perticular'; 12 Nov., 1605. With notes below of further payments of 5*l.* 'att his first reseat of y[e] bargaine,' and 50*l.* 'att Greenwich, in his owne howse att my ladys chirching'; together with an acquittance for 25*l.*, 28 Nov., 1605. f. 119.

49. BOND from Sir Fran. Calton to Edw. Alleyn in 115*l.*, to make assurance from himself and Sir Rob. Lee, as mortgagee, of the manor of Dulwich, &c.; 5 Dec., 1605. On the back are notes by Edw. Alleyn of various payments to Sir Fran. Calton, Sir Rob. Lee, and others, on account of Dulwich manor; 5 Dec., 1605–9 July, 1606. f. 120.

50. ACQUITTANCE from Sir Fran. Calton to Edw. Alleyn for 736*l.* 5*s.*, to be paid to Sir Hugh Brawne for the redemption of a lease of Dulwich woods; 11 Dec., 1605. With a note below of a further payment of 20*l.* to Sir Fran. Calton; 19 Dec., 1605. f. 122.

51. 'A RENTALL of Kenington of all suche quitt rentes as are dew vnto his maiesti yearlye,' with notes by Edw. Alleyn; 1605. f. 123.

52. ACKNOWLEDGMENT by Sir Fran. Calton of a debt to Edw. Alleyn of 50*l.*; 9 Jan., 1605[6]. f. 125.

53. WARRANT of Sir Edmund Bowyer, knt., J.P. for co. Surrey, admitting Francis Henslowe, of the par. of St. George, Southwark, to bail to appear at the next sessions; Camberwell, 10 Jan., 1605[6]. *Lat.* f. 126.

54. WILL of Arthur Langworthe, gent. [see above, MS. ii. art. 2], mentioning Rose, his wife, Richard, Arthur, Nicholas, and Edward, his sons, and Rose, Jane, and Agnes, his daughters, and lands at Horsted, Pemsey Marsh, Ringmer, and Langton, with a note of a debt from Edw. Alleyn of 100*l.*; 19 Feb., 1605[6]. With probate, 6 Nov., 1606. *Copy.* f. 127.

55. ACQUITTANCES to Edw. Alleyn for payments of 34*s.* 1*d.*, for tenths due yearly to the King for the manor of Dulwich; 7 Mar., 1605[6], 23 Oct., 1611. ff. 128, 236.

56. ACKNOWLEDGMENT by Frauncys Henslye [Henslowe], of the par. of St. George, Southwark, gent., of a debt to Benjamin Harrys, of Newington, gent., of 42*s.*; 30 Mar., 1606. f. 130.

57. 'A NOTE of suche chardges as was laied owte for [the funeral of] M[r] Frauncis Henslowe, gent., and his wife'; [1606]. f. 132.

58. ACQUITTANCE from John Filter, of London, cloth-worker, to Phil. Henslowe, as administrator of Francis Hens lowe, deceased, for 4*l.* 2*s.*, and for goods to the value of 41*s.* 1*d.*; 6 Oct., 1606. f. 133.

59. ASSIGNMENT by John Ewen, of Dulwich, yeoman, to John Berry, of Dulwich, yeoman, of a lease from Thomas Townshend, of Farnham Royal, co. Bucks, Rebecca, his wife, and others to Edward Strange of a messuage, &c., in Dulwich; 16 Oct., 1606. See below, Muniments 421, 440, 447. f. 135.

60. BILLS from Ralph Bovey to Edward Alleyn for law charges, with acquittances; 25 Nov., 1606–21 Feb., 1606[7]. f. 137.

61. GENERAL RELEASE from Edw. Husbandes, of Dul wich, gent., to Edw. Alleyn, esq.; 22 April, 1607. f. 141.

62. ACQUITTANCE from Sir Fran. Calton to Edw. Alleyn for 53*l.* 6*s.* 8*d.*, the fifth payment due for the 'forbearance' of 3,000*l.*; 30 June, 1607. f. 143.

63. STATEMENT of Thos. Kellocke [to Edw. Alleyn] of 'wronges and iniures' done to him and his wife by Alis Dought; 7 Aug., 1607. f. 144.

64. DEED OF SALE by Ellis Parrey, of London, weaver, to Edw. Alleyn, esq., of three tenements in Dulwich for 410*l.* 10*s.*; 24 Aug., 1607. With a surrender of the same by Ellis Parrye and Marrian, his wife; 22 Oct., 1607. See below, Mun. 517. ff. 145, 147.

65. ASSIGNMENT on mortgage by Jacob Maiden [Meade], of the par. of St. Olave, Southwark, waterman, to Phil. Henslowe, of the par. of St. Saviour, esq., of a lease from Katherine Smith, of Westminster, widow, of two messuages, a wharf, &c., in the par. of St. Olave; 8 Dec., 1607. f. 149*b*.

66. 'A RENTALL of Kennington att ye Court held ye 29 of October, 1608'; with the estreats, 30 Nov., 1608. Among the freeholders are Sir John Wild, Jas. Alleyn, the elder, and Tho. Grimes; and among the copyholders Sir Tho. Parrie, Sir Tho. Horsman, John Lannyer [Lanier, one of the King's musicians], and Tho. Towne [the actor]. ff. 153, 155.

67. 'AGREEMENT betwixt widdow [Mary] Wingrave and Mr Belton,' relative to the guardianship of the infant son of John Wingrave, a copyholder in Kennington manor; 30 Nov., 1608. ff. 156, 157.

68. PETITION from Will. Henslowe to the Privy Council for a warrant against Rich. Heath, for 'sinister and wrongfull dealinges' with respect to a claim for tithes assigned to him by Dr. [John] Langworth, parson of Buxted; [1609?]. See above, MS. iii. art. 33. f. 158.

69. 'EVIDENCES for Dullwich': a list in the hand of Edw. Alleyn of eight deeds, 6 Edw. VI.–10 Jas. I. [1552–1612], with notes of the age of Duke Calton, bapt. 14 Nov., 1602, and Henry Calton, bapt. 21 Nov., 1605, sons of Sir Fran. Calton. f. 160.

70. ACQUITTANCE from Edw. Wilson to Edw. Alleyn for 50*s*. for a quarter's rent; 8 Jan., 1609[10]. f. 162.

71. ACQUITTANCE from Sir Fran. Calton to Edw. Alleyn for 33*l*. 15*s*. for two quarters for the 'forbearinge' of 650*l*.; 4 April, 1610. f. 163.

72. LIST of persons presented by 'John Lee being sidman [sidesman] of the Liberty of the Clincke vnto the Church warden M[r] Allein Esquire'; [1609-10?]. On the back are various accounts by Edw. Alleyn. f. 165.

Printed, *Mem. of Edw. Alleyn*, p. 93.

73. 'THE COMPLAYNT of Mawdlyn Foord for wronges offerd her by Ch[r]istopher Horsebrook and his wife,' endorsed 'Clynch,' or Clink; [1610?]. f. 166.

74. ACKNOWLEDGMENT by Magdalen, wife of Hugh Samwayes, of a debt to Phil. Henslowe of 40*s.*; 28 Aug., 1610. f. 169.

75. BILL IN CHANCERY of Edw. Alleyn against Sir Fran. Calton, alleging his concealment and suppression of deeds relating to Dulwich manor; 27 May, 1611. *Copy.* f. 172*b.*

Printed, *Alleyn Papers*, p. 40.

76. ANSWER of Sir Fran. Calton to the bill above, disclaiming any right or title to Dulwich manor, and denying the concealment of any deed relating to the same; 3 June, 1610 [*sic*]. *Copy.* f. 212*b.*

77. NOTE by Sir Fran. Calton that, 'all recknonings made euen,' the sum due to him from Edw. Alleyn amounts to 370*l.*; 6 Dec., 1611. f. 238.

MS. No. V.

Alleyn Papers. Vol. V. Legal and Miscellaneous Papers of Edward Alleyn and his Family; 1612–1626.

1. Note by Edw. Alleyn of 'moneys disbursed to Sr Fran. Calton since his quittaunc of ye 6 of September 1611' to 12 April, 1612, amounting to 160*l.*, leaving 210*l.* still due. f. 1.

2. 'A Particuler of the groundes within the mannor of Dulwich'; [*circ.* 1609]. ff. 2–6.

'*A.*	Inprimis Hunger hill conteyning	xiiij acres
	Item one close called the	vj acres
	Horse croft	iiij
	Hathorne feild	xxv acres
	the two hills.	xxv
	great woodsier	xxx acres
B.	litle woodsier with a close adioyning to yt	xiiij acres
	Addingtons meadowes	x^en acres
	one close called the three acres	iiij acres
	the litle Lordshipp	iij acres
	Blanchdowne	vj acres
	the hill in thoccupacion of Robert Turner	vij acres
	the hill in thoccupacion of Symmes . . .	vij acres
	the ground in thoccupacion of Best . . .	iiij acres
	the fursiefeild that Bassington holdeth . . .	iiij acres
	the hill in thoccupacion of Traughton . . .	iiij acres
	the Butchers feild.	vj acres
	Peryfeild in thoccupacion of Hamond . . .	xij acres
	Ambrose Sheppard to his house	xvj acres

	Thomas Calton about his house	iiij acres
	Mr Parry his litle Browninges	ij acres
C.	Mr Parry adioyning to his house	x^en acres
	great browninges	v acres
	the litle browninges	ij acres
	Henr. Hunters browninges and ground adioyning to his house	iij acres
	Cokmans	vij acres
	Richard Pare	ij acres
	Jn° Cassinghurst	vj
	Jn° Goodenough	xiiij acres
	Annes feild	iiij acres
	Rigaites	v acres
	Savage adioyning to his house	vj acres
	Dickairdinges	iiij
	Robert Bodgerson thelder to his house	j
	Tho. Abeck	j [?]
	Jn° Hall about his house	j
	Howletes	vj
	Jn° Bone adioyning to his house	x^en acres
	Hill croftes	iij acres
	Whites feild	v acres
	New mead	iij acres
	Mr Stoughton about his house	ij acres
D.	Great Spilmans	iiij acres
	Jn° Shott to his house	xj acres
	Jn° Ambler to his house	xij acres
	litle Spilmans	iij acres
	Gilcot land	iiij acres
	Court mead	x^en acres
	the ground in thoccupacion of Hall	xij acres
	Mr Knight to his house	xxx acres
	Jn° Feering adioyning to his house	iiij acres
	Newlandes in thoccupacion of Mr Stoughton	vj acres
	Newlandes in the holding of Staple	iij acres
E.	Henr. Hunters ground lieing betwene Mr Knightes house and Feeringes	ij acres

the close called the xviij acres conteyning .	x acres
Kennoldes	vj acres
Henr. Mathew adioyning to his house . . .	iij acres
Robt. Best adioyning to his house . . .	x acres
Robt. Bogerson the younger about his house	ij acres
Staple adioyning to his house	ij acres
Jn° Mathew to his house	xj acres
Hunters Napps	ij acres
Savages Napps	iiij acres
Bogerson the younger his Napps	ij acres
Jn° Staple his Napps	j acre
Nic. Foster his bornes	viij acres
Mr Knightes Napps	iiij acres
Mr Caltons bornes	vij acres
Feeringes bornes	ij acres
Norcroftes	x^en acres
Carters Hall	iiij acres
the hill in thoccupacion of Nic. Feild . . .	vij acres
Hunters hill.	ij acres
Pynners mead	iij acres
Robt. Bogerson thelder	j acre'

On the inner side of the sheet which served as a cover (f. 6) is an acquittance from Will. Ladds, high constable of Brixton hundred, for 29*s.* 6*d.*, for 'composicion wood and coale' for the royal household, 4 Feb., 1611[2]; and on the outer side (f. 6*b*) is inscribed, 'Edward Foster his booke, 1609.' A letter, which was also used as a cover, is catalogued above (MS. i. art. 1).

3. BOND from Abraham Wall, of St. Saviour's, Southwark, fishmonger, to Phil. Henslowe, in 100*l.*, to observe an award respecting the title to lands, tenements, goods, &c., 'at the vpper pyke garden on the banke syde in Sowthwarke'; 17 Feb., 9 Jas. I. [1612]. f. 7.

Printed, *Alleyn Papers*, p. 49.

4. BOND from John Johnson, of St. Saviour's, Southwark, victualler, to Phil. Henslowe, in 3*l.*, for the payment of

30*s.*; 9 Apr., 1612. Endorsed 'Bores heade' [see below, Mun. 182, and Henslowe's *Diary*, p. 265]. f. 8.

5. ACQUITTANCE from Sir Fran. Calton to Edw. Alleyn for 190*l.* 14*s.*, received since 6 Dec., leaving 200*l.* still due; 12 May, 1612. f. 10.

6. BOND from John Morgan, of St. Saviour's, Southwark, yeoman, and Rich. Luke, of London, bowyer, to Phil. Henslowe in 50*s.*, for the payment of 25*s.*; 17 June, 1612. f. 11.

7. CONTRACT by William Hatton, of Lambeth, brickmaker, with Edw. Alleyn, of Dulwich, esq., to make bricks at 8*s.* and 7*s.* a thousand; 7 Oct., 1612. With acquittances on the back and on f. 36; 15 May, 1613–25 Apr., 1615. f. 13.

8. ACQUITTANCE from Sir Fran. Calton to 'widdow Towne' [see MS. iv. art. 66] for 20*s.*, a year's quit-rent for lands in Kennington manor; 5 Nov., 1612. f. 14.

9. ACQUITTANCES to Edw. Alleyn for yearly payments of 34*s.* 1*d.*, for tenths due to the King for Dulwich manor, &c.; 25 Nov., 1612–30 Oct., 1623. ff. 15, 28, 32, 37, 58, 61, 62, 80, 106, 107, 110.

10. 'A SESSE for the owte parisheners wythin the [*sic*] of Peckham, as foloweth, the 30th of November in the yere a 1612 for the kynges maiestis removes and other services'; followed by 'a sess for the towneshyp of Peckham,' &c. f. 16.

11. BILL IN CHANCERY of Abraham Wall, fishmonger, [against Edw. Romney, scrivener], for the settling of disputes concerning the 'Pike garden . . . neare the bancke syde in Southwarke,' which had been successively held, under a grand lease for 50 years from John Gibons, 27 Eliz. [1584–5], by John Browne, of Layston Abbey, co. Suffolk, Armiger Browne, Arderne Milwarde, Abraham Wall, Edw. Romney, and Abr. Wall again, and had been in the interval [see below, art. 24] purchased by 'one Phillip Henselow'; [*circ.* 1612]. *Copy. Imperfect.* On the back is a rough draft of a bill by the same Abr. Wall respecting a foreclosure on his mortgage to Will. Jobson of a tenement in the par. of St. Saviour, now the property of Phil. Henslowe. f. 20.

12. ACQUITTANCE from Nich. Knight, of Lambeth, to Sir Fran. Calton for all sums due for a surrender of lands, &c., in Dulwich manor; 26 Feb., 1612[3]. f. 24.

13. GENERAL RELEASE from Will. Backer, of St. George's, Southwark, butcher, to Edw. Alleyn; 3 June, 1613. f. 25.

14. ACQUITTANCE from Sir Fran. Calton, 'of Pasloes in the parrishe of Dagnam,' co. Essex, to Edw. Alleyn of all claims, &c., on account of the purchase of Dulwich manor, one statute and defeasance, dat. 11 Dec., 9 Jas. I., excepted; 25 Oct., 1613. f. 26.

15. ACQUITTANCE from Peter Warburton to —— for 40*s.*, to the use of Thos. Brokes, esq.; [1613?]. With the note below, 'sente to Bryane Bradlaye' [see MS. ii. artt. 15, 19]. f. 29.

16. NOTE of the delivery to Edw. Alleyn of 'the letters patentes of the Corporacion of the Colledge or hospitall of the pore of St. Savioures in Southwark' and the copy of the 'booke of orders' for the same college; 9 Mar., 1613[4]. Signed by Edw. Alleyn. f. 30.

Printed, *Mem. of Edw. Alleyn*, p. 114.

17. CONTRACT of Will. Varley and Fran. Willsone with Edw. Alleyn to execute for 48*l.* certain 'bricklayers and plasterers worke,' minutely specified, 'in vpon and neer y[e] building lately erected by y[e] saide Edw. Alleyn in Dullwich'; 12 Oct., 1614. With acquittances on the back for 24*l.* in all; 15 Oct.–19 Dec., 1614. f. 31.

18. POWER OF ATTORNEY from Walter Ethersoll, of Dulwich, husbandman, to Edw. Alleyn to recover from Henry Stane, of Bulf. . . ., co. Essex, yeoman, the sum of 11*l.* due on a bond; 7 Nov., 1614. f. 33.

19. LIST, in the hand of Edw. Alleyn, of eighteen 'evidences' or deeds relating to land, &c., purchased from Thos. Calton. f. 34.

20. NOTES OF FINES imposed upon Edw. Allen, late of Golding Lane and of Goswell Street, for omitting to appear before the King's Commissioners at Hickes Hall 'de quibusdam nocumentis,' &c.; 9 Dec., 13 Jas. I. [1615], 12 Dec., 14 Jas. I. [1616]. *Lat.* With acquittance below for 50*s.* in payment; 27 July, 1619. f. 38.

21. 'THE NAME of Philip Hinslie, gentelman, litterallie set downe in verse [as an acrostic] vppon these three especiall poyntes: his love to god, his prince and contrie,' followed by a prayer in verse 'speakinge in the termes of a gardiner'; signed 'Richarde Williams.' f. 39.

Printed, *Alleyn Papers*, p. 38.

22. 'THE BREVIATE of the cawse dependinge in Chawncery between John Henchlow, plaintiff, [and] Edward Allin, Agnes Henchlow, Roger Cole, deffendants,' relative to the validity of the will of Philip Henslowe, 'about 14 days last past deceased without issue,' containing copies of the bill and answer, with notes of counsel and minutes of evidence. 'The Bill exhibited 23 Januari 1615[6].' Two sheets, the second *imperfect*. John Henslowe is described in the next article as 'sonne and heire of Edmond, the elder brother and heire of the said Phillipp.' f. 40.

Printed, *Mem. of Edw. Alleyn*, p. 123.

23. A SECOND 'BREVIATE' in the same cause, containing somewhat different versions of the bill and answer, together with further particulars, from which it appears that, on 15 Feb., their insufficiency was referred to Dr. James, and that, on 'the 8th of this instante Aprill,' order was made 'that the defendants shall shew cawse whie a sequestration shall not be of the proffitts of the landes and whie the evidences showld not be brought into the Court.' The brief ends with the answer of the defendants to this order. f. 42.

24. 'A NOTE of such evidences as doe concerne the land bought [by Phil. Henslowe, 22 Jan., 1606–7] of James Munsey,' and of 'evidences concerning the Pikegarden' bought by the same of Henry Throgmorton and Sara, his wife, and Eliz. Gibbons, heirs of John Gibbons, 1 June, 1609; 7 May, 1616. Signed by E. Alleyn and Geo. Pitt. f. 44.

25. ACQUITTANCES from Edw. Alleyn to John Griffin and 'widow Mathew,' for 15*s*. respectively, for a quarter's rent due to Anne Henslowe [niece of Phil. Henslowe]; 2 July, 1616. f. 46.

On the back are some accounts, probably relating to an entertainment on the occasion of the consecration of the chapel, together with the note, 'md. to send ye booke for Mr. Daborn.'

26. 'A TRUE COPIE of the Instrument of consecracion

of ye Chappell dedicated to ye honour of Christ in Dullw[i]ch, with the churchyarde therunto belonging'; 13 Sept., 1616. 'Translated out of the originall [Mun. 572, below], being in Latine.' f. 47.

27. ACQUITTANCES from Edm. Traves to Edw. Alleyn for 3*l.* 10*s.*, for 'a quarters rente of a howse in the blacke Fryers late in the ocepasone of Robarte Jones' [Mun. 184, below]; 9 Oct., 1616, 7 Jan., 1616[7]. ff. 57, 60.

The second is printed, *Alleyn Papers*, p. 83.

28. ORDER OF COURT in a suit between John Henslowe and Edw. Allen, referring to 'Mr Wolueridge,' Master in Chancery, 'thexamynacions of the defendant taken touching a supposed contempte'; 18 Oct., 14 Jas. I. [1616]. f. 59.

29. LETTERS PATENT of James I. for the foundation and endowment of the College of God's Gift at Dulwich; Westminster, 21 June, a° 17 [1619]. Endorsed, 'A true copie of the deede of mortmaine,' viz. Mun. 581, below. f. 63.

Printed, Blanch, *Hist. of Camberwell*, 1875, Appendix, p. i.

30. ACQUITTANCE from Thos. Cheynie, bailiff of Kennington manor, to Edw. Alleyn for 1*s.* 8*d.*, for a year's quit-rent 'to the vse of the princes heigh[n]esse'; 30 Sept., 1619. f. 79.

Printed, *Alleyn Papers*, p. 88.

31. 'A COPIE of the deed of foundation of Gods guift Colledge in Dulwich,' viz. Mun. 584, below; 13 Sept., 17 Jas. I. [1619]. f. 81.

Printed, Blanch, *Hist. of Camberwell*, App. p. vi.

32. COVENANT by Edw. Alleyn to levy a fine to William Alleyn and William Austen for the endowment of Dulwich

College; 24 April, 18 Jas. I. [1620]. *Copy* of Mun. 586, below. f. 86.

Printed, Blanch, *Hist. of Camberwell*, App. p. ix.

33. FINE by Edw. Alleyn and Joan, his wife, to Will. Alleyn and Will. Austen in fulfilment of the covenant above; Easter term, 18 Jas. I. [1620]. *Copy* of Mun. 589, below. See Alleyn's *Diary*, MS. ix., below, under the date 26 May, 1620. f. 99.

34. FRAGMENT of the beginning of a will of Edw. Alleyn, written in his own hand; 3 Nov., 1620. f. 104.

35. ACQUITTANCES from Edm. Manninge to Edw. Alleyn for 14*l.* 15*s.* and 2*l.* 0*s.* 6*d.*, for 21 and 3 chaldrons of coals; 23 June, 1621, 22 Oct., 1622. ff. 105, 108.

36. ASSIGNMENT by John Luntley, of St. Saviour's, Southwark, gent., and Rebecca, his wife, to Matthias Alleyn, of Dulwich, yeoman, of 7*l.*, being two quarters' rent for tenements on the Bankside, held of them on lease by Edw. Alleyn; 28 Jan., 20 Jas. I. [1623]. f. 109.

37. LIST OF FINES 'to the vse of Edward Allen, esq., his maiesties farmour of the mannor' of Lewisham; 20 Mar., 1622[3]. Among the defaulters are Lord Harvye [Hervey], Sir John Wildgoose, Sir Tho. Smith, Sir Fran. Lee, Sir Nich. Stoddard, Sir Roger James, and Sir Anth. Mayne. f. 111.

38. ACQUITTANCE from John Freebody to Edw. Allen for 3*l.* 10*s.*, for a quarter's rent for tenements on the Bankside, assigned to him by John Luntley; 15 Jan., 1623[4]. f. 113.

Printed, *Alleyn Papers*, p. 91. See also MS. iii. art. 94.

39. QUIT-RENTS of Lewisham manor, co. Kent, &c.; 1625. f. 114.

40. ACQUITTANCES from L[eonard] Bilson to Edw. Allen for 20*s.*, for a quarter's rent; 3 July, 1625–3 April, 1626. ff. 115–118.

41. APPOINTMENT by Edw. Alleyn of John Wickenden to collect quit-rents in Cowden, in the manor of Lewisham; [1625?]. *Imperfect.* f. 119.

On the back is a prayer, written perhaps by Alleyn's wife, Constance Donne, together with the doxology, the beginning of Ben Jonson's translation of Martial's epigram x. 47 (see above, MS. i. art. 135), and four lines in praise of sack beginning, 'Sake will make the mery mind be sade.' See *Alleyn Papers*, p. 88.

42. PREAMBLE to the statutes of Dulwich College; [29 Sept., 1626]. In duplicate. ff. 120, 126.

On the back of the last sheet of the first copy, f. 125*b*, is a draft, in the hand of Edw. Alleyn, of clause 120 in the Statutes (see Blanch, *Hist. of Camberwell*, App. p. xxxiii., and *Mem. of Edw. Alleyn*, p. 184). The preamble is printed in the *Alleyn Papers*, p. 91.

43. SCHEDULE of 'copihold landes of inheritance in the parishe of Lambith in the county of Surrey, holden [by Sir John Leigh, knt.] of the L. Archbisshop of Canterbury of his mannor of Weeke Courte'; no date. f. 128*b*.

44. PETITION to James I. from [Phil. Henslowe?] 'one of the ordinary groomes of your Maiesties Chamber,' for the office of inspector 'to searche veiw seale and sease [if faulty] all and euerye the woollen clothes to be made within the counties of Kent and Essex'; no date. f. 134.

45. PETITION to James I. for the incorporation of 'a

sartayne Mysterye,' of late years brought over from Germany, for 'the makynge of hayleshot or dropshot,' and for the imposition of a tax of 10*s*. upon every fother of lead taken out of the kingdom; no date. f. 135.

On the back is a list of books in the hand of Edw. Alleyn; printed in the preface to the catalogue of the College library.

46. PAPER entitled by Edw. Alleyn 'note from M[r] docter Love warden of Winchester Colledg' [Nicholas Love, Warden, 1613–1630], containing suggestions for the statutes of Dulwich College, with an offer to revise them, when framed, by comparison with the statutes of Winchester; no date. See below, MS. ix., under date 3 Aug., 1618. f. 136.

47. 'THE ORDER in Eaton Colledge bakehouse and brewhouse'; no date. f. 137.

48. STATUTES of the 'Orphanocomium, or the Hospitall for Orphanes,' and the 'Gerontocomium, or Hospitall for olde Folkes,' at Amsterdam; translated from J. I. Pontanus, *Rerum et Urbis Amstelodamensium Historia*, Amstelodami, 1611, lib. ii. capp. ii. vi. pp. 68, 87. f. 138.

49. 'AN EXTRACT out of y[e] Records of y[e] first fruits office relateing to y[e] Abby of Bermondsey, 26th of Hen. 8th [1535]'; giving particulars of temporalities and spiritualities, including the rents of Dulwich manor, &c. *Lat.* f. 140.

50. ANSWER of John Badger in an action against him by Joan Calton [wife of Nich. Calton] for cutting wood in Dulwich manor; [*ante* 1580]. f. 142.

51. A RENTAL of Simondstone, co. York, amounting to 119*l.* 16*s.* 4*d.*; [*circ.* July, 1626]. See above, MS. iii. artt. 105, 107. f. 146.

52. 'A TRUE NOTE how M[r] Pattent [see above, MS. iii. art. 13] is chardged for rent and other chardges'; no date. f. 148.

Printed *Alleyn Papers*, p. 52. Mr. Collier misreads the name as Pallent and suggests that Rob. Pallant, the actor, is intended. The name occurs twice, and in both cases a recent attempt seems to have been made to erase the cross-strokes of the *tt*.

53. LIST OF DEEDS relating to lands in Dulwich bought by Edw. Alleyn of Thos. Emerson on 1 June, 1606 [Mun. 476, below]. f. 152.

MS. No. VI.

ALLEYN PAPERS. Vol. VI. Legal and Miscellaneous Papers relating to Dulwich College after the death of the Founder; 1627–1744.

1. BILL FOR DRUGS, &c., supplied to [Edward Conway] Lord Conway, probably by Thos. Alleyn, barber-surgeon, Master of Dulwich College [1619–1631]; 10 Jan., 1626[7]–2 April, 1627. f. 1.

2. JAMES JOHNESTONE to [Thomas] Allen, 'Master of the frea school at Dulludge,' asking for a line or two to take to 'Hary' when he goes to Court; Westminster, 2 Nov., 1629. f. 2.

3. PETITION from Dulwich College to Charles I., praying him to stay proceedings in a suit by Roger Kilvert and Geo. Hanger, tenants of Edmond Bowyer, a ward of the Crown and parson of Camberwell, who claim from the College tithes from woods in Dulwich, lately belonging to Bermondsey Abbey; [1631?]. With a note below of reference by the King to the Privy Council; Oatlands, 18 July, 1631. *Copy.* Followed by affidavits of John Casinghurst, John Scrivener, and Sir Francis Calton relating to the same suit; 21 Jan., 1631[2], 23 Nov., 1632. ff. 4–8.

4. CASE as to the right of appointment of a successor to David Fletcher [preacher-fellow, 25 June, 1632–12 Aug., 1634], who had forfeited his fellowship at Dulwich College by staying away 'three times longer then the statutes of the Colledge allowe'; [1634]. f. 9.

On the back is the draft of a letter asking assistance for 'a poore maid, Marie Heathe.'

5. ACCOUNTS of weekly disbursements by the Warden of Dulwich College; 23 April–13 May, 1636. Signed by the Master, Warden, and Fellows. f. 10.

6. PETITION from Dulwich College to [William Laud] Archbishop of Canterbury, praying that their cause with Sir Edmond Bowyer respecting tithes of wood, &c., in Dulwich may be heard and ended in accordance with a reference of the King and a former order of the Council; [1636]. *Copy.* With orders of Court in the same case; 10 July, 1640, 1, 12 Feb., 1641. ff. 12, 17, 19, 21.

7. PETITION from the same to the same, presenting Francis Hooke [preacher-fellow, 11 July, 1639–3 May, 1644], Elkanah Downes, William Dun, and Peter Elliston, Masters of Arts of Cambridge, two of whom should draw lots for a vacant fellowship; [1639]. *Copy.* f. 13.

8. LICENSE for the insertion in a College lease to Nich. Hunt of a covenant for renewal, on condition that he expend 100 marks in rebuilding; 15 April, 1640. ff. 14, 15.

9. BOND from Andrew Hall and Hugh Pember, of London, glaziers, to Dulwich College, in 20*l.*, to make, for the sum of 11*l.*, a 'new glasse windowe of divers coloured glasse' in the College chapel, 'of the same worke and fashion as the east windowes of the Parishe Churches of St. Martin in the feilds and St. Clement Danes'; 5 Oct., 1641. With acquittance for 11*l.*; 21 Oct., 1641. ff. 23, 24.

10. ARTICLES OF AGREEMENT between Sir Edmond Bowyer, knt., and Dulwich College, for the payment by the latter of 5*l.* yearly in lieu of tithes from wood-lands in Dulwich formerly belonging to Bermondsey Abbey; 9 May, 1642. *Copy.* f. 25.

11. NOTE by Ralph Alleyn of the names of his competitors, Elias, Henry, and Peter Allen, when he drew lot for the wardenship; 16 May, 1642. f. 27.

12. AFFIDAVIT of Edw. Allen, son of Thos. Allen, cousin-german of the Founder, denying the validity of a claim of another Edw. Allen to be of kin to the Founder as great-grandson of John, his brother—John Allen, son of the last-named, having died without issue and unmarried; 6 June, 1642. f. 28.

13. DEED OF SALE by Dulwich College to John Hudson, of Lewisham, tanner, of wood and underwood in Dulwich; 9 Jan., 1644. *Imperfect.* f. 30.

14. POWER OF ATTORNEY from Dulwich College to William Jenkins, of Blackfriars, scrivener, to receive their rents, &c.; 4 Mar., 1645[6]. On the back and on f. 35 are notes of demands for rent by the above Will. Jenkins on twenty-seven occasions, 'but there was none paid or tendered'; 25 Mar., 1646–20 Oct., 1653. f. 32.

15. JAMES PARRY to the Master and Warden, respecting a charge on Camberwell parish and liberty of 16*l.* a month by virtue of an ordinance, dat. 23 June, 'for 60000^{li} per month one the kingdome'; 11 Dec., 1647. Endorsed, 'Mr Perrey, the high Constable, his letter.' f. 33.

16. 'DECAYES observed att the Hospitall of Dullwich and meanes prescribed for prevention of damage,' a report by

Edw. Jarman and John Tanner, City surveyors; 30 June, 1656. f. 36.

17. PLAINT of John Cogan against John Warner for ejectment from messuages and lands in Dulwich leased to him by Silvester Calton; Trinity term, 1657. Seven copies, endorsed with notes by John Warner to the Master, Warden, &c., praying them to defend their title; 29, 30 Dec., 1657. ff. 38–44.

18. BRIEF in an action by John Cogan *v.* Thos. Alleyn, Master of Dulwich College, for ejectment, containing an abstract of the title of the College to lands purchased from the Calton family; 22 Mar., 1657[8]. f. 45*b*.

19. ORDER for the payment by Dulwich College of 5*l.* 16*s.* 4*d.*, 'set upon you by the Commissioners for new buildings'; [June, 1658]. f. 49.

20. ORDER by the Commissioners 'for preuenting the multiplicity of Buildinge, &c.,' for the discharge of fines imposed upon Edw. Beavor and Dulwich College 'for their respectiue interests and estates in two howses in the parish of Giles Cripplegate,' both houses being 'proved old foundations'; 30 June, 1658. *Copy.* f. 50.

21. 'INVENTORIE of M^r^ [John] Skingles goods and bookes taken out of his chamber & studdye ye 20 Sept., 1658,' with an acquittance for the same from Rich. and Will. Skingle, his brothers and executors; 21 Oct., 1658. f. 53.

22. [CAPT.] JOHN GREENHILL to the Master and Warden, giving reasons for the renewal of his lease [of a tenement in Pye Alley, Bishopsgate Street]; 19 Feb., 4 Mar., 1658[9]. ff. 57, 59, 60.

23. GENERAL RELEASE by Thos. Woodcock, of London, haberdasher, to Dulwich College; 29 Mar., 1661. f. 62.

24. LICENSES from Dulwich College for the assignment of leases by—

a. Phil. Collins, of Dulwich, gent., to Will. Buckeridge, of London, silkman; 22 Oct., 1661. f. 63.

b. Elizabeth, widow of Phil. Collins, to Leonard Lytcott, of St. George's, Southwark, esq.; 5 May, 1662. f. 65*b.*

c. John Cutter, of Dulwich., gent., to Nich. Thurman, of Sherborne Lane, London, merchant; 26 May, 1662. f. 67*b.*

d. Jane, widow of Rob. Glover, of Dulwich, husbandman, to Edm. Nelham, of Dulwich, husbandman; 18 May, 1664. f. 69*b.*

e. Anth. Handcocke, of London, painter, to Rog. Harsnett, of Westminster, esq.; 11 July, 1664. f. 71*b.*

f. Edm. Nelham to Thos. Cranwell, of Croydon, yeoman; 20 Oct., 1665. f. 73*b.*

g. Faver Barrett, of Dulwich, husbandman, and Joan, his wife, to Thos. Blechynden, of London, merchant; 6 Sept., 1667. 75*b.*

h. Dorothy, widow of William Beaven, of London, tyler and bricklayer, to Richard Wymondesold, of London, bowyer; 24 May, 1673. f. 94*b.*

i. Ann, wife of Will. Kington, administratrix of Rob. West, late of Dulwich, gent., to Edw. Horwood, of Westminster, gent.; 30 Sept., 1684. f. 121*b.*

25. COPIES OF LETTERS, &c., in the hand of John Alleyn, Warden of Dulwich College:—

a. Miles Smith, secretary to [Gilbert Sheldon] Archbishop of Canterbury, conveying an order that 'the

30 poore shall haue their Gownes against this Christmas'; Lambeth, 21 Dec., 1667. f. 77.

b. Will. Cannon and Christ. Marshall, churchwardens of St. Saviour's, Southwark, applying for 10*l.*, 'for gownes for Mr Alleyns poore members in his almeshouses'; 19 Dec., 1667. f. 77.

c. Diploma of John Alleyn as D.C.L. of Oxford; 24 Jan., 1670[1]. *Lat.* f. 77*b.*

d. Letters of Gilbert [Sheldon], Archbishop of Canterbury, appointing Rob. Bond a fellow of Dulwich College in place of Geo. Alleyn; 8 May, 1672. *Lat.* With note of admission, 16 May, 1672. f. 78.

26. ACQUITTANCES from the churchwardens of the parishes of St. Botolph, Bishopsgate, St. Giles, Cripplegate, and St. Saviour, Southwark, to Dulwich College for 10*l.* respectively for ten alms-people, 'outmembers of the said Colledge'; 31 Dec., 1667. ff. 79, 80, 81.

27. COVENANT by [Major] Will. Strode, of London, draper, to supply bricks to Dulwich College in return for a license to break ground for brickmaking; 3 Feb., 1667[8]. f. 82*b.*

28. LICENSE from Dulwich College to Thos. Blechynden, of London, merchant, to break ground in Dulwich for brickmaking; 2 May, 1668. f. 84.

29. 'A TERRIER of the lands tenements and woods belonging to God's Gift College in Dulwich, finished June ye 6th, 1668.' *Mutilated.* f. 86.

30. ACQUITTANCE from Will. Strode and Thos. Blechynden, surveyors of highways in the liberty of Dulwich, for

10*l.* for repairs; 16 Oct., 1668. With similar acquittance from John Redman and John Hamond; 23 June, 1669. ff. 88, 89.

31. M[ILES] SMYTH, secretary to the Archbishop of Canterbury, to the Court of Dulwich College, stating that the Archbishop would not interfere to prevent the admission of the Warden's wife into the College; Lambeth, 2 Sept., 1669. *Mutilated.* Endorsed, 'This letter was read at a Courtt of Assistants, Satterday, 4 Sept., 1669, brought by Mr John Alleyn the warden, to admit his wife into the Colledge, but nil granted.' f. 90.

It appears from the *Register* (MS. x., below, f. 70*b*) that John Alleyn was 'elected [warden] by a mandamus from his Maiestie,' 5 Apr., 1669; that his election was 'made voyd by his Maties letter vnder his privy signet,' 4 Mar., 1669[70]; and that he 'was elected warden againe, he being then a single person according to ye statutes by ye death of his wife,' 21 Mar., 1669[70].

32. PROCEEDINGS at courts-leet, &c., with warrants, notes of impoundings, and other papers relating to Dulwich manor; 1668–1685. ff. 92, 96–106, 108, 112, 123–129, 146.

33. 'A NOTE of all ye boyes yt haue gon to ye vniversity since ye founders death, 1626' to 1677. f. 107.

34. CASE of Anthony Bowyer, esq., *v.* John Starkey, claiming tithes from lands in Dulwich; Easter term, 31 Chas. II. [1679]. f. 109.

35. JOHN ALLEYN, Master, to Richard Alleyn, Warden, enclosing the case of Cotton Ode, respecting an encroachment upon leasehold land in Whitecross Street; 14 Feb., 1680[1]. ff. 114, 115.

36. LICENSE from Dulwich College to John Tillotson, comptroller to the Archbishop of Canterbury, to fell timber for the repair of his house, &c.; 2 May, 1681. *Copy.* f. 116*b*.

37. 'AN ACCOUNT of S[r] [Benjamin] Bines his charge at the vniversity yearely,' amounting to 15*l.* 8*s.* 8*d.* for College charges and 12*l.* 11*s.* 4*d.* for 'clothes and expences'; 3 Jan., 1681–2. f. 118.

B. Bynes went to Cambridge, 1675, and was admitted preacher-fellow 1 June, 1689, 'without lot, once poor schollar of y[e] colledg' (*Register*, f. 90*b*).

38. THO. BRAY to 'M[r] Lewis, at y[e] signe of the Feathers in Dulwich,' threatening legal proceedings if he will not arrange for 'a fayre meethinge'; 6 Nov., 1683. f. 120.

39. 'THE JOINT AND SEVERALL ANSWERS of Francis Johnson and Jane, his wife, defendants, to the bill of complaint' of Dulwich College, relative to the disposal of the property of Will. Cartwright, their master, the said Fran. Johnson being 'employed as his servant to look after his affaires in their Ma[ties] Playhouse .... hee being one of the Players there'; [*circ.* 1690]. *Imperfect.* Followed by a note of pictures, books, and other articles missing, including 'two Shakspares playes, 1647; three Ben Jonsons works, y[e] 1st vellum; one Ben Jonsons works, 2[d] vellum.' f. 130*b*.

Printed in the Shakespeare Society's edition of T. Heywood's *Apology for Actors*, 1841, p. ix. Will. Cartwright, who died in Dec. 1687 and left his books, pictures, &c., to Dulwich College, was probably the son of Will. Cartwright, also an actor and friend of Edw. Alleyn.

40. 'A SPEECH in Parliament' by Rob. Price, member for Weobly [afterwards Baron of the Exchequer and Justice of the Common Pleas], against the grant by the Crown to the Earl of Portland of the lordships of Denbigh, Bromfield, and Yale, &c.; [1695]. Originally ten pages, of which the third and fourth are lost. f. 137.

Printed in the *Somers Tracts*, ed. 1814, vol. xi. p. 387, and in Cobbett's *Parliamentary History*, vol. v. p. 979.

41. LETTERS of Administration of the goods, &c., of John Allen, M.A., archdeacon of Chester, granted to Tho. Allen, his brother; 26 April, 1695. With seal of the Chancellor of Chester. f. 142.

42. INDENTURES of apprenticeship, tradesmen's bills, &c.; 29 May, 1695–5 July, 1744. ff. 144, 147, 160–168.

43. 'INTERROGATORIES . . . . on ye behalfe of Faver Barrett, David Payne, and George Gibbon, defendants, att ye suite of Anthony Bowyer, esq., complainant,' respecting tithes from woodland in Dulwich, with other papers on the same subject; [*circ.* 1690]. ff. 148, 152, 154.

44. 'CATALOGUS [librorum] ex dono Rev^di Job Brockett [died 2 Jan., 1704–5], Coll. Dul. Soc., Jan. 2, 1705.' Reversing the sheet, 'Books lent out of the Library of Dulwich Colledge,' 16 Dec., 1705–14 Apr., 1715. f. 155.

45. PART of a letter of advice grounded on an astrological scheme; James Deeping, co. Linc., 11 Dec., 1722. f. 157.

46. ORDER fixing the fees for interments in the College burial-ground, 'all under 6 years of age 2*s.*, and all above 7*s.* 6*d.*,' the same to be 'for books for ye Publick Library of ye College'; 9 Aug., 1723. With a list of books bought, 23 Nov., 1723–23 Oct., 1740. f. 158.

47. CLAIM by the churchwardens of the parishes of St. Botolph, Bishopsgate, St. Giles, Cripplegate, and St. Saviour, Southwark, to be ex-officio members of the governing body of Dulwich College; 4 Sept., 1725. Signed by Edw. Grafton, Sam. Higgs, Jacob Grant, Jas. Kinder, John Brewer, and Thos. Vinter. f. 159.

48. Brief for Hen. King, plaintiff, in a suit against Hen. Stonestreete for ejectment from two messuages, &c., leased to him by Dulwich College; [*circ.* 1660]. f. 169.

49. 'An Occasional Address' to 'Mr Alleyn, warden of Dulwitch College,' in three stanzas, signed 'R. Bryan, of Peckham, gent'; 18th cent. f. 170.

MS. No. VII.

DIARY and Account-Book of Philip Henslowe; 1592–1609.

The bulk of the contents relate to the Rose, the Fortune, and other theatrical companies in which Henslowe was interested. Among other valuable matter are included lists of pieces acted, noting the daily receipts and first per formances, transactions with and payments to authors and actors, and disbursements for the building of the Fortune Theatre and for repairs, theatrical properties, &c.

The entries are generally made by Henslowe himself; but in various places occur the handwritings, with signatures, of the dramatists George Chapman, Henry Chettle, John Day, Thomas Dekker, Michael Drayton, Richard Hathway, William Haughton, Henry Porter, William Rankins, Samuel Rowley, Anthony Wadeson, and Robert Wilson, together with those of a large number of actors. Mention is also made of Thomas Heywood, Ben Jonson, John Marston, Thomas Middleton, Anthony Munday, Thomas Nash, Wentworth Smith, and John Webster.

Interspersed are various accounts unconnected with the stage, relating to private and family business, advances made on pledges, and the cutting of wood in Ashdown Forest,[1] co.

[1] See a paper on Ashdown Forest by Rev. Edw. Turner in the *Sussex Archæological Society's Collections*, vol. xiv., 1862, pp. 47, 51, where Edmond Hensley, or Henslowe, of Lindfield, father of Philip Henslowe, is named as master of the game in Ashdown Forest and Broil Park in 1539 and 1556–7.

Sussex. The last-named accounts are at the end, reversing the volume, and belong to the years 1577 and 1578.

Extracts are given by Malone, *Shakspeare*, 1790, vol. i. part ii. p. 288 (ed. Boswell, 1821, vol. iii. p. 295); and the whole volume, so far as it relates to the stage, has been edited by Mr. J. Payne Collier, *The Diary of Philip Henslowe*, Shakespeare Society, 1845.

Mr. Collier, however, has accidentally omitted to print a bond (f. 102) from William Paschall, of Maplestead, co. Essex, esq. (cf. ed. Collier, p. 192), to Phil. Henslowe for the payment on 1 Nov. of 10*l*., dat. 28 Sept., 1599. He has also overlooked the following entry (f. 236):—

'Layd owt for my Lorde Admeralle seruantes[1] as̄ foloweth, 1594.

Layd owt for gowinge and cominge to somerset howe [house] for iiij tymes	1^s 4^d
Layd owt for mackinge of our leater twise	xii^d
Layd owt for drinckinge with the jentellmen .	$iiij^s$ 8^d
Layd owt at another time for drinckinge . . .	xii^d
Layd owt goinge vp and downe to corte twise . .	1^s 4^d'

N.B. The following entries may without hesitation be condemned as forgeries:—

I. f. 11*b*. '18 of Maye 1595—℞ at galfrido & Bernardo—xxxi^s.'

This is written at the very bottom of the page in a style of hand which appears nowhere else in the volume. The entry is printed by Mr. Collier (*Diary*, p. 52), with the note:— 'An entry omitted to be noticed by Malone. It relates to a play founded, doubtless, upon the recently-discovered poem by John Drout, entitled "The pityfull Historie of two loving

[1] Probably in connexion with the withdrawal of the injunction against performances in London during the prevalence of the plague (see above, MS. i. art. 18). The Lord Admiral's men began to play again 14 May, 1594 (*Diary*, p. 34).

Italians, Gaulfrido and Bernardo le Vayne," printed in 1570 by Henry Binneman. . . . An impression, limited to twenty-five copies, has been recently made from the original.' The re-print gives neither the name of the possessor of the original nor that of the editor; but from the handwriting of an inscription in the British Museum copy it may be inferred that the editor was Mr. Collier himself.

Mr. Collier does not remark in his note that the 18 May, 1595, was a Sunday. This fact, however, added to the suspicious appearance of the entry, is significant; for, although in other parts of the volume there is some confusion in the dates, the accounts for the season from Easter to the end of June, 1595, are very regularly kept, and there is no other instance of a Sunday performance.

II. f. 19*b*. 'Pd vnto Thomas Dickers the 20 of desembr 1597 for adycyons to ffostus twentie shellings and fyve shellinges more for a prolog to Marloes tambelan, so in all I saye payde twentye fyve shellinges.'

Mr. Collier prints this entry (*Diary*, p. 71) without comment; but in his *Hist. of Dramatic Poetry* (ed. 1831, vol. iii. p. 113; ed. 1879, vol. ii. p. 491) he refers to it in the following terms:—

'There are three pieces of evidence to show that Marlow was the author of *Tamburlaine the Great*, two of which have never yet been noticed. The most conclusive is the subsequent entry in Henslowe's MS. *Diary*, preserved at Dulwich College, which escaped the notice of Malone. . . . Here we see Marlow's *Tamburlaine* mentioned in connection with his *Faustus*, to the latter of which Dekker had made some addi tions, and written a new prologue for the former. . . . This testimony may be considered decisive.'

So far from being decisive the testimony is worthless,

since the whole entry is evidently a forgery, written in clumsy imitation of Henslowe's hand. The forger, however, has shown some skill in his treatment of a narrow blot or smudge which intersects the upper part of the 'll' in the second 'shellinges'; for, in order that the writing may appear to be *under*, and not *over*, the old blot, he has at first carried up the *ll* (as if writing *u*) only as far as the lower edge of the blot, and has then started again from the upper edge to make the loops.

III. f. 29*b*. 'Lent the 14 May 1597 to Jubie vppon a notte from Nashe twentie shellinges more for the Jylle [Isle] of dogges, w^oh^ he is wrytinge for the company.'

f. 33. 'Pd this 23 of aguste 1597 to Harey Porter to carye to T. Nashe nowe at this tyme in the flete for wrytinge of the eylle of dogges ten shellings, to be paid agen to me when he canne, I saye ten shillinges } x^s^'

f. 33*b*. 'Pd vnto Mr Blunsones the M^r^ of the Revelles man this 27 of Aguste 1597 ten shellinges for newes of the restraynte beinge recaled by the lordes of the Queenes counsel } x^s^'

Mr. Collier, in a note to the second of these entries (*Diary*, pp. 94, 98, 99), refers to his *Hist. of Dram. Poetry*, where (ed. 1831, vol. i. p. 306; ed. 1879, vol. i. p. 294) they are thus introduced:—

'We find Nash in May 1597 writing for the Lord Admiral's players, then under Philip Henslowe, and producing for them a play called *The Isle of Dogs*, which is connected with an important circumstance in the history of the stage, viz. the temporary silencing of that company, in consequence of the very piece of which Nash was the author.

The following singular particulars are extracted from the Diary kept by Henslowe. . . . Malone published none of them.'

All three entries are written by the same hand as No. **II.**, the ink being plainly doctored to give it a fictitious appearance of age. Immediately above the first entry a slip of paper, the whole width of the page, has been cut out, upon which the same words had previously been written. This is evident from an examination of the edges above and below the excision, on which may still be seen the top of the *L* in the first line and the bottoms of the long strokes in the last line,[1] corresponding exactly with the letters in the entry below. It may be inferred from this that the first attempt at the forgery was a failure, though it is possible, of course, to argue that the duplicate was cut out to send to Nash. It should be added that four similar excisions have been made (possibly for the same reason) between the first and second entries.

IV. f. 94. 'Lent vnto Wm Jube the 3 of November
1601 to bye stamell cllathe for a clocke for the gwisse iii^ll^'
— *Webster*

Mr. Collier in his note (*Diary*, p. 202) says, 'The name of Webster is interlined, perhaps in a different hand.' He quotes the entry also in his *Hist. of Dram. Poetry* (ed. 1831, vol. iii. p. 101 ; ed. 1879, vol. ii. p. 482), adding that it 'sufficiently connects Webster with the performance, which we may conjecture was a new version of Marlow's tragedy.' There can be no doubt whatever that the name was not

[1] They are now covered by the edges of the slip which the binder has inserted in repairing the leaf, but they are still visible if the leaf be held up to the light.

written by the same hand as the rest of the entry; and it is equally evident that it is a spurious modern addition.

V. f. 116. 'Lent vnto Harey Chettell the 7 of September 1602 at the apoyntment to lend in earenest of a tragedie called *Robin hoodfellowe*[1] some of } x^{s}

. . . .

'Lent vnto Harey Chettell the 9 of September 1602 in part of payment of a tragedie called *Robin goodfellowe* some of } x^{s}'

Mr. Collier in his note (*Diary*, p. 239) observes that 'Malone takes no notice of these remarkable entries.' The probable reason of this omission (which is the more significant as he does notice the other plays mentioned on the same page) is that in Malone's time the entries remained in the state in which Henslowe left them, viz. with a blank space for the title of the projected tragedy, as in another entry on the next page (ed. Collier, p. 241). This space in both instances is now filled in with the title printed above in italics, written with a different ink and in a hand which has all the appearance of forgery. Besides this, the word 'tragedie' in both entries has been blotted out, as unsuited to the title inserted, and in the second entry the word 'playe' has been written over it. Mr. Collier notices this correction; but he does not mention that the title is an insertion.

The volume has been mutilated in various places by the cutting or tearing out of leaves in whole or in part. In some cases the mutilation dates apparently from Henslowe's own

[1] The initial letter is perhaps meant for a 'g,' though, owing apparently to carelessness on the part of the forger, it is more like the 'h' of the genuine hand.

time, but much of it is probably of a later period. All the leaves have now been repaired, and the excisions filled in with blank paper. The original vellum covers, which are partly covered with names and other scribbling, are now bound up at the beginning as fly-leaves.

A narrow slip, evidently cut from this volume, was bought for the British Museum at a public sale in 1878, and is now numbered Additional MS. 30262, f. 66. It contains, on the two sides, the following entries:—

'Receaued by me George Chapman for a Pastorall ending in a Tragedye[1] in part of payment the sum of fortye shillinges, this xviith of July anno 1599.

'By me George Chapman.'

'1 August, 1599. Receaued by mee Thomas Dekker at the hands of Mr Phillip Hynchlow the some of twenty shillings[2] to bee payd the last of this moneth.

'Thomas Dekker.'

Small folio, ff. 238.

---

[1] The same payment is entered by Henslowe in the *Diary*, f. 63*b* (ed. Collier, p. 154), 'in earneste of a pastrall tragedie.'

[2] See the *Diary*, f. 63*b* (p. 155), 'Lent vnto Mr Deckers at that time [1 Aug.] xx^{s}.'

MS. No. VIII.

MEMORANDUM-BOOK of Edward Alleyn; 1594–1616.

The contents, which occupy a small portion only of the volume, consist chiefly of notes of the purchase of the Bear Garden, the Fortune Theatre, Dulwich manor, and other properties, with lists of 'evidences' and particulars of price, subsequent profits, &c. On f. 41*b* is 'a generall note of all my writings, deedes or evidencis, bondes or bills belonging to me E. Alleyn.'

All these notes, the lists of 'evidences' excepted, are printed in Mr. J. Payne Collier's introduction to the *Alleyn Papers*, Shakespeare Society, 1843, p. xiii. The note, 'What the Fortune cost me, Nov. 1599,' &c., f. 6*b*, is also given by Malone, *Shakspeare*, ed. Boswell, 1821, vol. iii. p. 55, and by Collier, *Hist. of Dram. Poetry*, ed. 1879, vol. iii. 119. See also above, MS. i. art. 43*n*, and MS. ii. art. 4*n*. Most of the evidences are included among the muniments catalogued below.

At the beginning of the volume are four acquittances from Edw. Alleyn to Arthur Langworth for payments on a statute-staple bond, 19 May, 1599–20 Nov., 1600; and at the end, reversing the volume, are a number of medical recipes.

Small octavo, ff. 62.

MS. No. IX.

DIARY and Account-Book of Edward Alleyn; 29 Sept., 1617–1 Oct., 1622.

The entries, which are all in Alleyn's own hand, begin as follows:—

'29 Sept.	My wife, Mr Austein, Mr Young and myself went to see Sutton's Hospitall.[1] water		1	
	Dind with La. Clarck:[2] giuen ye sarvauntes	0 0	2	0 6
30 „	I mett Mr Austen on Bristone [Brixton] causwaye and rid w^{t} hym to Croydon. dind w^{t} ye borough men	0	4	0
	pd Mr Gillpine, ye mace berer, for ye Lord of Canterburie for his fee of ye consecration[3]		6	8
1 Oct.	I came to London in ye Coach and went to ye Red Bull[4]	0	0	2

[1] The Charterhouse, founded by Thomas Sutton in 1611.

[2] Joyce, widow of Sir Robert Clarke, Baron of the Exchequer, who died 1 Jan., 1606–7. By a former husband, James Austen or Austin, who died in 1602 (Stow, *Survey of London*, ed. Strype, 1754, vol. i. p. 704), she was mother of William Austin, the same doubtless as the 'Mr Austein' here mentioned and the William Austin, of St. Saviour's, Southwark, in Muniments 586–589. She died, aged 66, in 1626, and was buried in St. Saviour's church, where there is a monument to her memory. From the frequency of Alleyn's visits to her, she appears to have been one of his most intimate friends.

[3] The consecration of the chapel at Dulwich by Archbishop Abbot, 13 Sept., 1616 (see below, Mun. 572).

[4] The Red Bull Theatre, in St. John Street, Clerkenwell (Collier, *Hist. of*

2 Oct.	giuen Okey ye barber for tryming	0	0	6
	pd Mr Young[1] his quarters pencion	3	6	8
3 „	I went to ye Red Bull and rec. for ye younger brother[2] but 3 6 4: water	0	0	4
	supt w^t Tho. Allen att ye 3 tuns	0	1	0'

Among other entries of interest are:—

'1617.

4 Oct.	pd for 2 cathachismes for ye chilldren	0	0	4
7 „	pd Cornelyus Lymare[3] his pencion .	6	13	4
13 „	water, 8*d*: giuen Mr Roydon[4] 1*s*	0	1	8
	Lute strings	0	0	8
18 „	pd ye pore theyr pencion[5] .	8	8	0
19 „	our wedding daye:[6] ther dind w^t vs doc. Natt *etc.*			
22 „	pd ye Kings rent[7] for ye banck . .	13	17	5

Dram. Poetry, vol. iii. p. 132). According to Mr. Collier it was at this time in the occupation of the Queen's company.

[1] Edward Young, schoolmaster-fellow, 20 June, 1617–29 Sept., 1618 (*Register*, MS. x., below, ff. 6*b*, 7*b*).

[2] A play with this title was entered in the *Stationers' Register*, 29 Nov., 1653, but it was not printed (Halliwell, *Dict. of Old Plays*, p. 280).

[3] The first fellow of Dulwich College (see above, MS. iii. art 66), but appointed before the regular foundation was completed.

[4] The same doubtless as the Matthew Roydon to whom Alleyn gave 6*d*. on 15 Aug., 1622 (see below). A poet of this name is mentioned in very good company by Meres (*Wit's Treasury*, 1598, f. 282*b*). He was author of an elegy on Sir Phil. Sidney, printed in the *Phœnix Nest*, 1593, and in Spenser's *Colin Clout*, 1595, and has commendatory verses before Tho. Watson's *Passionate Centurie*, 1582. Chapman dedicated to him his *Shadow of Night*, 1594, and *Ovid's Banquet of Sence*, 1595.

[5] This item is repeated monthly, sometimes with deductions for misconduct, as will be seen further on.

[6] The 25 Oct., 1618, and the 22 Oct., 1620, are also noted by Alleyn as the anniversary of his wedding day. He was married on 22 Oct., 1592 (see above, p. 6, n. 1).

[7] A payment recorded half-yearly; evidently the rent for the Unicorn and other messuages mentioned below in Mun. 174, as well as in the Founder's will (*Alleyn Papers*, p. xxii.).

	pd xths for Dullwich and Rigates .	1	14	1
	pd Mr Travise rent[1] for ye Blackfryars .	40	0	0
31 Oct.	I went to London to ye Lo : tresurers[2]			
	Supper att Youngs ordinarie w^t^ ye Starr chamber men	0	6	0
11 Nov.	pd by Morton ye Fortune quitt rent	0	1	10
15 „	giuen ye boyes of Powles	0	1	0
29 „	Sr Randelle Crwe[3] a fee for a motion to alter W. H.[4] peticion for hauing ye cause referd to Mr More[5] and Mr Woolveridg	4	8	0
	bought a book of ye generall pracktis off phisick[6]	0	6	8
	2 gramars for ye chilldren	0	1	10
3 Dec.	water to York Howse[7] att a seale day for a motion mad by S^r^ Ra : Crwe	0	0	8
8 „	giuen a noyse[8] off trumpeters y^t^ sownded	0	2	6
17 „	water to fetch my euidences from ye Chauncerie	0	1	0

[1] A quarterly payment, the rent of messuages, &c., in the parish of St. Anne, Blackfriars, leased to Alleyn for 50 years, 26 Mar., 1617 (see below, Mun. 184).

[2] Thomas Howard, Earl of Suffolk, Lord Treasurer, 1613–1618. His wife, mentioned below, was Catherine, daughter of Sir Henry Knevet and widow of Richard, son and heir of Lord Rich.

[3] Sir Ranulphe Crewe, serjeant at law and King's Serjeant; Chief Justice of the King's Bench, 26 Jan., 1625–9 Nov., 1626; died 13 Jan., 1646.

[4] William Henslowe, either the brother of Philip Henslowe (MS. iii., above, art. 6) or perhaps a nephew. The cause may have related to the property mentioned below in Mun. 174.

[5] Richard More and John Wolveridge, masters in Chancery.

[6] Probably *The General Practise of Physicke*, &c., translated from the German of Christopher Wirtzung by Jacob Mosan, London, 1605, fol. It is not in the College library.

[7] York House, in the Strand, the birth-place and residence of the Lord Chancellor Bacon; held by him on lease from the Archbishop of York.

[8] A technical term for a company of musicians; e.g. 'in comes a noise of musicians,' quoted from Tho. Deloney's *Jack of Newbury* by Ritson (*Ancient Songs*, &c., ed. 1877, p. xvii.).

19 Dec.	giuen balye Large in gratuitye for keeping me off Juries	0	5	0
25 „	Christmass daye: wee receuid [the Communion] and dind ye pore people.			
29 „	my wife and I dind w^t^ ye bishop off Winchester[1]			
30 „	bought a booke, ye bishop of Spalates[2]	0	0	6
31 „	water to Suffolk Howse . .	0	1	0
	giuen my La: my silver booke.			
	pd for wrighting ye verses .	0	10	0
	to Buckett for lyming itt[3] . . .			
	to Mr Brambeel for ye glass work		2	0
	ye whole valewe wase 15^l^			
1618.				
4 Jan.	this daye wee rec. ye comunion at Camberwell and S^r^ Ed. Bowyar[4] dinde all our pore peopl[e].			
7 „	W[illiam] H[enslowe's] answer to my bill in Chauncerie	0	10	0
	water to ye Court w^t^ my petetion,[5] w^ch^, blessd be God, wass fully graunted .	0	1	2
11 „	giuen trumpeters a twelfe day	0	2	6

[1] James Montague, translated from Bath and Wells, 1616; died 20 July, 1618.

[2] Marc Antonio de Dominis, a Jesuit, Bishop of Segni and Archbishop of Spalatro; turned Protestant and came to England in 1616; made Dean of Windsor 13 May, 1618; returned to Italy and was reconciled to the Church of Rome in 1622; died 1624. The first volume of his *De Republica Ecclesiastica* appeared in this year, but the book bought by Alleyn must have been one of his many controversial pamphlets.

[3] See below, 22 Nov., 1618.

[4] Sir Edmond Bowyer, of Camberwell, sheriff of Surrey and Sussex, 1600; knighted 11 May, 1603; M.P. for Surrey, 1603; buried in Camberwell church 12 March, 1626–7.

[5] See above, MS. ii. art. 37. The petition, however, may have related to his projected foundation at Dulwich.

Date	Item	£	s.	d.
30 Jan.	pd for reparing Graces[1] howse in Gowlding lane	0	12	8
6 Feb.	pd Mr Shepperd for 2 termes ecskusing ye bringing in ye inventorie off my mother[2]	0	2	0
	pd Mr Pye for my bale[3] in ye Counter att Lee sute	0	2	8
11 „	to Doc. Comons for W: Henslow's case: pd for ye copie off my answer in Star chamber, beeing 58 sheets, 12d a sheet	2	18	0
2 Mar.	I dind wt ye vestrye, and gaue a seminarie preest	0	:	0
7 „	giuen Mr Gerratt a fee for coming to ye beargarden this daye	1	2	0
	wine att ye garden wt Jacob	0	0	4
17 „	cullers and gowld for ye chimney pece .	1	7	10
20 „	pd att rec. my fee[4] att Courte, beeing 5 6 4: for ye Mr of ye office . 2 6; giuen ye clarckes . 1 0; ye chamber keeper . 1 0	0	4	6
22 „	Redman and his wife, Cartwright, Gunnell and Parr[5] dind wt vs.			
24 „	giuen ye vergers off Powles	0	0	6
	pd Mr Younge, my chapline and schoolemaster, for his quarters wages .	3	0	0

[1] Probably Francis Grace, the actor, a member of the Fortune company.

[2] Agnes Henslowe, his mother-in-law, who was buried 9 April, 1617.

[3] Mr. Collier (*Mem. of Edw. Alleyn*, p. 156, n.) reads this 'babe,' and finds it difficult to explain; it is of course for 'bail.' For the nature of Lee's suit see below, 15 June.

[4] His fee as Master of the Game, being at the rate of 10*d.* a day for himself and 4*d.* a day for his deputy (see above, MS. ii. art. 5).

[5] William Cartwright, Richard Gunnell, and William Parre, all members of the Fortune company. Redman was one of Alleyn's Dulwich tenants.

Date	Entry	£	s	d
	pd Mr Harrisone, my chapline and vsher, for his quarters wagis	3	6	8
26 Mar.	Jo Hopkins,[1] ye organist, came to me.			
7 Apr.	Easter daye: wee receved ye comunion wt ye pore, dind and suppt them.			
9 „	water and ale att ye Fortune: *as you like itt*[2]	0	0	6
17 „	I wase att Arundell Howse, wher my Lord[3] showed me all his statues and picktures that came from Italy: giuen his man .	0	2	0
25 „	this morning, blessed be God, I sickned att my Ladye Clarckes.			
	sent doc. Lister[4] my water and	0	2	0
26 „	this daye my wife came to me.			
27 „	bought a p: orgaines for ye chapell off Mr Gibbs of Powles	8	2	0
28 „	giuen Mr doc. Lister, that came to me	0	11	0
6 May.	this daye I went abroad, bleased be our good God.			
27 „	giuen Mr Burward for tuning ye orgaines	0	2	6
15 June	pd Luke Lee in full payment off all			

[1] Called Thomas Hopkins further on, and so in the College *Register*. He held the post till Sept., 1622. For Mr. Harrison see above, MS. iii. art. 85.

[2] The words in italics, which are meant, of course, to refer to Shakespeare's *As You Like It*, are interlined, and are evidently a modern forgery.

[3] Thomas Howard, Earl of Arundel (MS. iii., above, art. 68). 'His statues [were] equal in number, value and antiquity to those in the houses of most princes; to gain which he had persons many years employed both in Italy, Greece, and so generally in any part of Europe where rarities were to be had. His paintings likewise were numerous and of the most excellent masters' (Sir Edw. Walker, *Life of Tho. Howard, Earl of Arundel*, 1651, in *Historical Discourses*, 1705, p. 220). The Arundel marbles, now at Oxford, were purchased by him later, in 1622.

[4] Matthew Lister, Fellow of the College of Physicians 5 June, 1607; physician to Qu. Anne and Charles I.; knighted 11 Oct., 1636; died Dec., 1656, æt. 92.

Date	Entry	£	s	d
	acountes and demaundes dwe to hym from P. Henslow	4	0	0
22 June	W. H. and I had a hering this afternone att Docters Comons.			
	pd. Sr Jo: Benett[1] 11s and Mr More 11s		1	2
24 „	pd Mr Younge his quarters wagis . .		5	0
	pd Mr Harrisone his wagis . . .		3	6
	pd Mr. Hopkins his quarters wagis .		2	10 8
3 July	I rod to Tuchborne [the scrivener] in ye morning: water	0	0	4
	we drwe vp ye patten[2] for ye corporacion.			
8 „	I went to Mr Atorneys[3] about my fown dacion.			
11 „	I receved my pattent from Mr Attorney and he would rec. nothing, but Mr Beale had for itt . . . 5l 10s; His 2 men . . . 1 02; ye chamber-keeper I gaue . 0 05 6	6	17	6
14 „	I rode to Wansted, wher ye markques off Buckinghame[4] vndertooke ye Kinges hand for me.			
16 „	Mathias[5] went to Theobaldes to fetch ye patent from my Lord off Buckingam .	0	1	0

[1] Sir John Bennet, Master in Chancery and Judge of the Prerogative Court; convicted of bribery and 'other foule corruptions,' 29 Nov., 1622 (Stow's *Chronicle*, continued by Howes, 1631, p. 1034).

[2] Muniment 581, below.

[3] Sir Henry Yelverton, Attorney-General, 1617–1620; Justice of the Common Pleas, 1625–1630.

[4] George Villiers, Earl of Buckingham, 5 Jan., 1617; Marquis, 1 Jan., 1618; Duke, 18 May, 1623. The manor and house of Wanstead, which had formerly belonged to Robert Dudley, Earl of Leicester, were at this time in his possession; but he sold them in the following year to Sir Henry Mildmay.

[5] Matthias Alleyn, the Founder's cousin (MS. iii., above, art. 32).

18 July.	I rode to London : water to ye Signett office[1] att Whight Hall .	0	:	0
22 „	I rode to London for ye patten[t].			
24 „	to London agayne for ye pattent.			
3 Aug.	I rode towardes Wincester.[2]			
4 „	I came to Winchester.			
5 „	dinner att Winchester		1	5
	wine wt regester and Coale and bond		3	0
	pd for ye sear[c]h		6	8
	wrighting itt and his hand . . .	8	3	4
	I came to Mr Allens back.			
16 „	pd Mr Anthony[3] for my pattent passing ye signett an[d] prive seall . . .	8	0	0
17 „	I went to London to ye Lo : Chancellers[4] about stayeing ye pattent.			
20 „	I went to London about building : water to Whight Hall	0	1	0
27 „	Pole brought me word yt ye building *of the playhouse*[5] would be puld downe, so			

[1] The license for the foundation was given 17 July, 1618 (*Cal. State Papers*, 1611–1618, p. 555).

[2] This journey was probably undertaken for the purpose of seeing the College and examining the statutes. See above, MS. v. art. 46.

[3] Edward Anthony, one of the clerks of the Privy Seal.

[4] Francis Bacon, Lord Verulam. On the next day, 18 Aug., Bacon wrote to Buckingham to explain his reason for staying the patent :—'I like well that Allen playeth the last act of his life so well; but, if his Majesty give way thus to amortize his tenures, his Court of Wards shall decay, which I had well hoped should improve.' He suggested, therefore, that the proposed endowment of 800*l.* should be reduced to 500*l.* See Spedding, *Life*, vol. vi. 1872, p. 324.

[5] The words in italics are interlined, and are evidently a modern forgery. Mr. J. P. Collier prints the entry (*Mem. of Edw. Alleyn*, p. 106), but *without the spurious addition.* The threatened demolition was evidently in connexion with the proclamations issued about this time in restraint of new buildings, in pursuance of the statute 35 Eliz. cap. 6, 1593. This Act prohibited the erection of any new building within three miles of London or Westminster, as well as the conversion of any single existing building into several tenements. It was used in

	I went to London: first water to ye strond to Coronell Cesell[1] . . .	0	0	6
	He being gon I followed to Chellsey · water	0	3	0
	from ye fryars to La: Clarckes: att supper	0	0	2
	after supper to Shreue Johnson[2] wt ye sertificate I had procured: water		0	4
29 Aug.	water to ye Lord Chancellors . . .	8	0	6
1 Sept.	This day ye pore people dind and supt wt vs, itt being my birthdaye[3] and I 52 years owld, blessed be ye Lord God ye giuer off lyfe, amen.			
5 „	I and Mathias went to Windesor about ye Fryars.			
18 „	dinner att ye Marmayd[4] in Bredstreet wt			

the reign of James I. as a means of raising money by fines for compounding, and a commission for this purpose was issued to the Lord Chancellor on 25 July in this year (*Cal. State Papers*, 1611–1618, p. 558). A return of the houses demolished was made by Rob. Johnson, the sheriff, 20 Sept., 1618 (*ibid.* p. 574), and includes the entry, 'In Swan Alley, near the Wardrop, Edward Allen his howses are respited by warrant.'

[1] Sir Edward Cecil, an eminent military commander, third son of Thomas, [illegible]eter; cr. Lord Cecil, 1625, and Viscount Wimbledon, 1626; died 1638. He was Lord-Lieutenant of Surrey.

[2] Robert Johnson, goldsmith, sheriff of London, 1617–18.

[3] According to the register of St. Botolph's, Bishopsgate, he was baptised 2 Sept., 1566.

[4] This was the famous Mermaid tavern, the resort of the most noted wits and literary characters of the time, and celebrated in the often-quoted lines addressed by Francis Beaumont to Ben Jonson—

> 'What things we have seen
> Done at the Mermaid!' &c.

Jonson himself alludes to it in his Epigram 133, telling how a party

> 'At Breadstreet's Mermaid having dined, and merry,
> Proposed to go to Holborne in a wherry.

It is mentioned as early as 1464 in the accounts of the steward of Sir John Howard.

	Mr Edmonds,[1] Mr Bromfeeld, Tho. Allen and 5 of ye Fortune company .	0	5	0
	pd for ingrosing a particuler of ye Capite lands to show my Lord Chanceller .	0	1	0
28 Sept.	ye Comission wase sate one this daye att ye beargarden; dinner att ye Bull Head[2] wt Mr Bromefeeld and Tuchborne: wine first att beargarden 8d, dinner 5s 6d	0	6	2
	water for Watt to fetch stones from Blackfryars *theatre*[3]	0	0	10
	more disbursed for ye building in ye Blackfryars for this yeare and in ano 1617, when itt first begane wt ye 200l first disbursed by my father: buyeing in off leases: chargis in lawe: and ye building itt selfe, wt making meanes to kepe them from being puld down, is 1105l 00s 02d			
29 „	Here endes ye years acount begining att Michellmasse 1617 and ending this Michellmass 1618, in which hath bene disbursed in generall, wth the charge off ye Blackfryars building, 2093l 12s 08d Wheroff in perticulers as followeth:			

[1] Perhaps the John Edmonds who was a member of the Queen's company at the time of her death in 1619 (Collier, *Hist. of Dram. Poetry*, vol. i. p. 397). He was one of three of 'her majesties servants' who obtained from the Privy Council a letter of assistance to act at Bristol in April, 1618 (*ibid.* p. 395; *Cal. State Papers*, 1611–1618, p. 549).

[2] Mentioned again, further on, as the Bull Head in Cheapside.

[3] The word 'theatre' is interlined, and is a forgery. The object of the forger, both in this case and in that above (p. 172, n. 5), is to make it appear that Alleyn's property in the Blackfriars included the Blackfriars Theatre, and, by inference, that he had bought Shakespeare's interest. See also above, MS. iii. art. 102.

In howshowld charge	137[l]	14[s]	08[d]
for y[e] Colledge	184	09	06
for rentes	258	02	07
for debtes, building or r[e]paring .	1254	13	06
for aparell	010	13	06
for lawe y[e] worst of awe [all]	067	05	06
The some off theys partis .	1912	19	03
other exspences in this booke . .	190	13	05

29 Sept.	bought 6 pictures of K J : Q E : Q M : K E : K H y[e] 8[th] and K H y[e] 5[th]	2	0	0
4 Oct.	. Tho. Allen . . . . Jo. Taylore[1] dind w[t] vs.			
8 „	bought 8 pictures off E y[e] 3 : R y[e] 2 : H y[e] 4 : H y[e] 6 : E y[e] 4 : E y[e] 5 : R y[e] 3 : H y[e] 7	02	13	4
13	I rec. rent att ye banksid and Fortune.			
23 „	I dind w[t] y[e] company att y[e] Fortune.			
24	W. He[nslowe] and I mett and seald a bond of a 100[l] to stand to an aword.			
25 „	this daye wase our wedding day.			
30 „	I went to London : water to y[e] Fortune : *saw Romeo.*[2]	0	0	4
31 „	after dinner, w[t] y[e] Fortune men att selling [sealing] the leasse.[3]			
22 Nov.	pd M[r] Buckett . . . . for paynting a			

[1] Probably Joseph Taylor, the actor (MS. i., above, art. 107). John Taylor, the water-poet, who is mentioned below, did not reach London on his return from Scotland till 15 Oct.

[2] The words 'saw Romeo' are interlined, and are a forgery. The imitation of a 17th cent. hand was not successful, and *an attempt has consequently been made to erase the words.*

[3] The original counterpart of this lease is still at the College (Mun. 56, below).

	smalle title to a booke w[ch] I gaue to my Ladye off Suffolk	0	6	0
12 Dec.	giuen Jo: Taylor[1] y[e] poett for his jorney into Scottland	1	0	0
16 „	bought 5 songe bookes for y[e] boyes	0	4	0
19 „	bought off Mathewe all y[e] vpper part off y[e] quenes barge[2].	2	2	6
21 „	I went to London: water: and pd y[e]	0	0	6
	pore of y[e] Clinck Lyberty a legacie anualy to be paid	2	0	0
29 „	pd y[e] Collegiantes ther pencion:			
	M[r] Samuell Wilsone preacher[3]. 6 13 4 M[r] Jo: Harisone scholemaster. 5 00 0 M[r] Martyne Symondes vsher . 3 06 8 M[r] Tho: Hopkins organist . 2 10 0	17	9	10

[1] Mr. Collier (*Mem. of Edw. Alleyn*, p. 155) spoils an interesting entry by misreading the amount as 4*d.*, a sum which applies to the entry preceding. Taylor published an account of this journey, in mixed prose and verse, with the title *The Pennyles Pilgrimage, or the Moneylesse Perambulation of John Taylor alias the Kings Majesties Water-poet. How he travailed on foot from London to Edenborough in Scotland, not carrying any money to or fro, neither begging borrowing or asking meate drinke or lodging*, &c., London, 1618. This was followed by *A Kicksey Winsey or a Lerry Come-twang, wherein John Taylor hath satirically suited* 800 *of his bad debtors that will not pay him for his return of Journey from Scotland*, London, 1619. He here says that he had sixteen hundred and fifty subscribers to the former work:

> ' They took a book worth 12 pence, and were bound
> To give a crown, an angel or a pound,
> A noble, piece or half-piece, what they list;
> They passed their words or freely set their fist.'

Alleyn's subscription seems to have been duly paid; but the book is no longer in the College library.

[2] The panels still form part of the chimneypiece in the library of the new College at Dulwich.

[3] Samuel Wilson, preacher-fellow, 29 Sept., 1618–28 Sept., 1620; Martin Symonds, usher and schoolmaster-fellow, 29 Sept., 1618–28 Sept., 1623.

	after dinner I went to London to ye Lo. of Lester.[1]			
30 Dec.	pd for a peticion drawing to ye Lordes for ye officers of ye game for reçeiuing our fees : pd for itt	0	1	0
'1619.				
2 Jan.	I rec. of Sr W. Vdall[2] 10^{l} for servies att Court last Whittson.			
5 „	giuen 2 dromes and a fyfe y^{t} playd here .	0	2	6
8 „	I went to London to rec. rentes ale w^{t} them att ye Fortune .	0	0	3
12 „	I went to ye Fortune to rec. rent.			
	This daye att 10 of ye clock in ye fore-none Whight Hall[3] wase one fyer.			
22 „	bought between me and Jo. Harrison my chapline Mr Mincshawes[4] dictionarie being ii [11] languagies : ye price wase 22^{s}, wherof I gaue	0	11	0
1 Mar.	this day Will. Hensloe dind w^{t} vs and we scald our wrighting of peac.			
14 „	giuen toward reparing Camberwell Chirch	1	0	0

[1] Sir Robert Sydney, Baron Sydney, 1603; Viscount L'Isle, 1604; Earl of Leicester, 1618; died 1626. He was Chamberlain to Queen Anne; and Alleyn's visit to him, therefore, may have had something to do with the Queen's company.

[2] Sir William Uvedale, Treasurer of the Chamber.

[3] Particulars of the fire are given in letters of J. Chamberlain and T. Lorkin, 16 and 19 Jan., 1618-9 (*Court and Times of James I.* vol. ii. pp. 123, 126); and another account is contained in a news-letter in Cotton MS. Titus, B. viii. f. 374. It was caused by the carelessness of a workman, who was employed in making preparations for a royal masque; and, within two hours, the Banqueting Hall was completely destroyed. The damage extended also to the offices of the Signet and Privy Seal under the Hall, and nearly the whole of the records and papers are said to have been burnt.

[4] John Minsheu, author of *Ductor in Linguas: The Guide into the* [*eleven*] *Tongues*, London, 1617, folio, and *Vocabularium Hispanico-Latinum et Anglicum copiosissimum*, London, 1617, folio.

Date	Entry	s.	d.	£	s.	d.
25 Mar.	Mathyas arested Lodg.[1]					
13 Apr.	pd Mr Burett for a dyapason stop to my organe and other alteracions			5	10	0
21 „	giuen Bowlton ye skrivener, beeing in ye Marshallsey in great povertye as by his letter[2] apereth			0	10	0
25	. this daye Mr Willsone fayld and so no sermone in ye afternoone, and all so euerie Sunday sinc Easter.					
27 „	pd ye apothecaries bill for my last sick nes					
	a dose of pills by doc. Harveys[3] directions . . .		6			
	a pectorall lotion by doc. Gulstons directions	2	0	0	4	0
	a glass off oyle of camomille .	0	6			
	pd Sr Jerimy Turner[4] Muster Mr for 2 years mustering for my light horse	2	0			
	a muskett	1	0			
	a corslett	0	8	0	7	0
	and as much for this yere .	3	8			
6 May.	water wt my wife to Somersett howse to see ye hersse off queen Ann[5]			0	[illegible]	0

[1] The 'doc. Lodge' mentioned below, 4 June; being, doubtless, Thomas Lodge, the dramatist, who was a doctor of medicine. See above, MS. i. artt. 21–23.

[2] See above, MS. iii. art. 83.

[3] William Harvey, the discoverer of the circulation of the blood; at this time Fellow of the College of Physicians, Lumleian lecturer at St. Bartholomew's Hospital, and physician extraordinary to James I.; died 1657.

[4] See above, MS. i. art. 56*n*.

[5] Queen Anne died at Hampton Court 2 Mar., 1618–9. Her body was brought to Denmark House in the Strand 9 Mar., and was buried at Westminster 13 May.

13 May.	md. ye queens funerall wase this day: after dinner my wife and I went to see itt: water 1^{s}, standin 6^{d}	0		6
26 „	I rec. my patten onc more off Mr Attorney: giuen his men, for he would take nothing	5	13	0
27 „	I rode to Grenewich and gott ye K[ing]es hand.			
30 „	Ther came and dind w^{t} vs docter Harvey and doc. Argent[1] and a courtyer and a strang preacher. •			
4 June.	for sueing doc. Lodges bond	0	6	10
7 „	pd onc more for ye signett and privie selle [seal]	5	0	0
8 „	bought a book of witches	0	0	3
20 „	Ther dind w^{t} vs Mr Michell, docter Poell and Mr Hewitt, Mr Austen, Mr Dustome (?), Sam. Calvert and Mr *B. Jonson*,[2] 4 off ye princes men,[3] &c.			
30 „	md. y^{t} this daye cam ye Lord Carone[4] w^{t} 3 of ye generall states off ye Lowe Countrye to see this place.			

[1] John Argent, Fellow of the College of Physicians 1597; President in 1625; died 1643.

[2] After 'M^{r}' a blank space was left by Alleyn, as in other instances when he had forgotten the name of a chance visitor. This space has been filled up with the name 'B. Jonson' by another hand. The addition is certainly spurious, and seems to have been made since the publication of Mr. Collier's *Mem. of Edw. Alleyn*, 1841, in which it is stated (p. 154) that Ben Jonson's name does not appear among Alleyn's guests at Dulwich.

[3] The company of Charles, Prince of Wales. See below, 10 Aug., 1621.

[4] Noël de Caron, the Dutch Ambassador (see above, MS. iii. art. 58). He himself founded some almshouses at Lambeth in 1622 (Lysons, *Environs*, vol. i. p. 307).

Date	Entry		£ s d
11 July.	Ther dind wt vs Will Borne[1] and his wife, Mr Borne, a surgian, &c.		
	pd for 2 tennors and 1 treble vialls		15 0
15	againe to Lor: Chanceller for ye sealle.		
16 „	Mathias fetcht ye great sealle.[2]		
	for joyners work about ye chimney peces of ye barge: for stuff to add to ye barge stuff		2 9 5
	The charge of ye great seale		
	ye seale.	8 13 0	
	ye dockett and rec.	0 03 0	
	ye inrowlment . . .	2 00 0	
	ye devident	2 00 0	
	ye officers fee . . .	2 13 4	
	for drawing, ingrossing and entring ye dockett . .	0 03 4	18 16 10
	vellome and strings .	0 17 6	
	ye clarck	1 00 0	
		17 10 2	
	for vellome and ingrossing of ye first patent . . .	1 06 8	
	pd to Tomsone for a boxe to keep itt in .		0 5 0
19 „	I rode to London to Sr Will. Vdall: water		0 0 6
26 „	I went to ye Fortune wt Mr Scott, wher my mare wase atached.		
30 „	setting vp bills in ye Chainge [Exchange] and wrighting		0 0 6
2 Aug.	I rode to Croydon to ye Lo: of Canterbury.		

[1] Bird or Borne, the actor, one of the lessees of the Fortune (see above, MS. i. art. 25, and Mun. 56).

[2] Attached to the Letters Patent, dat. 21 June, 1619 (Mun. 581, below).

6 Aug. I dind w my Lo: of Canterbury and red to hym ye corporacion and fowndacion.

8 „ pd Jo. Russell[1] his legacie giuen by my mother Hensloe 10 0 0

15 „ Ther dind wt vs Mr Taylore, Mr Gunell, his wife and daughter, Franc: Grace.

5 Sept. I rode to Windsore: pd for horsmete and lodging and what I gaue att ye court 0 2 8

10 „ I rode to London to envit Lordes to ye creacion.

12 „ I rode to ye Lo: of Canterburys, but he wase sick and cowld nott com.

13 „ This daye wase ye fowndacion off ye Colledge finish and ther wear present:[2] ye Lord Chancellore: ye Lo. of Aron dell: Lo. Coronell Ciecell: Sr Jo. Howland, Highe Shreue: Sr Ed. Bowyare: Sr Tho. Grymes: Sr Jo. Bodley: Sr Jo. Tunstall: Inigo Jones, ye Kinges

[1] See above, MS. i. art. 104. He was probably a relation of Agnes Henslowe.

[2] Edmond Howes, who was present, gives an account of the ceremony in his continuation of Stow's *Chronicle*, 1631, p. 1032, recording that the founder 'did very publiquely and audibly in the Chappell of the same Colledge reade and publish one writing quadrupartite in parchment whereby hee did make, create, erect, found and stablish the said colledge . . . . and did subscribe his name and fix his seal,' &c. One of the copies of the deed of foundation, signed by Alleyn and the witnesses named above, as well as by Howes himself, will be found below, Mun. 584. Howes gives the same list of those present, with the addition of his own name, 'gentleman and chronicler,' and 'Lyonell Titchborne of Grayes Inne, gent.' To the names of Sir Edm. Bowyer, of Camberwell, Sir Tho. Grymes, of Peckham, Sir John Bodley, of Streatham, and Sir John Tonstall, of Carshalton, he appends a note: 'These foure knights were justices of the peace for the co. of Surrey'; and he describes Jo. Finch [afterwards Lord Finch, Lord Keeper] as of Gray's Inn, Rich. Jones as Secretary to the Lord Chancellor, and Rich. Talboyes as of the Inner Temple.

Surveyer: Jo. Finch, Counceller: Ric. Tayleboyce: Ric. Jones: Jo. Anthony. They first herd a sermond and after ye instrument of creacion wase by me read and after an anthem they went to dinner.[1]

19 Sept. Md. y^{t} Mr Harisone had leave to goe and prech att Becknam and he stayd all night y^{t} one ye mor[row] ye schoole wase vntaught and no servis red.

22 „ I dind w^{t} Jacob [Meade],[2] Mr. Adye and Mr Foster, and wee concluded our matters both w^{t} hym and Tho. Angell, blessed be ye God off peac.

29 „ The perticuler off ye years expenc:

For the Colledge .	316^{l}	02^{s}	05^{d}
Howshowld .	113	09	05
Rentes . . .	257	02	09
Debtes	433	13	02
Aparell	010	17	09
Lawe	031	12	02
Some of theys perticulers .	1162	17	08
Some off other exspences .	0214	17	04

1 Oct. a noyes of trompeters came and sownded: giuen them 0 2 6

26 „ I rode to Sr Tho. Edmondes[3] and after to ye buriall of Mr Benfeeld.[4]

---

[1] A list of the courses follows, together with 'the charg off ye diner,' which amounted in all to 20*l.* 9*s.* 2*d.* This is printed at length by Lysons, *Environs of London*, vol. i. p. 98.

[2] See above, MS. ii. art. 35.

[3] Treasurer of the Household, 1618–1639.

[4] Not Robert Benfield, the actor; but William Benfield, of St. Saviour's, Southwark (see MS. i. art. 49).

12 Nov.	I went to see poore Tom Dekker.[1]			
2 Dec.	I dind att Mr Scotes, and after ye Lordes Pagett[2] and Wi[n]dsor, S^{r} Ed. Gorge w^{t} diuers ladyes came to ye Colledg.			
'1620.				
26 Jan.	in ye afternoone I went to S^{r} Jo. Jackson.			
27 ,,	in ye morning Jo. Jackson made a motion in ye checker y^{t} ye bishope off Winchester[3] showld answer: I gave hym .	1	0	0
10 Feb.	giuen Mr Bowyar for Mr Attorneys hand to ye replycation to ye bish. off Winchesters answer 1^{l} and to Mr Bower 10^{s}	1	10	0
27 ,,	pd for pills by Do. Harveys direction for my wife	0	3	0
24 Mar.	I rod to se ye tyltyng[4]: pd for a standing	0	1	0
1 Apr.	an oz. of tobacko	0		0
5 ,,	I dind w^{t} Mr Hewitt and ther wase ye princes musitions Mr Ball and Mr Drewe.			
9 ,,	Ther dind w^{t} vs Mr Gunnell, Cartwright,			

[1] This entry is a forgery, the imitative character of the hand being strongly marked, and an attempt having been made at erasure. It is meant, doubtless, to be read in connexion with Dekker's letter to Alleyn in MS. i. art. 108.

[2] William Paget, 4th Lord Paget, restored to the title 1603; died 1629. Thomas Windsor, 6th Lord Windsor, suc. 1605; died 1642. Sir Edward Gorges, Bart.; cr. Lord Gorges of Dundalk, 1620.

[3] Lancelot Andrews, translated from Ely, 9 Feb., 1618–9; died 1626.

[4] 'On Friday, the 24th, Prince Charles, Marquesse Hamelton, Marquesse Buckingham, with diuers earles and others, performed great justing at Whitehall in honour of the anniversary of King James' (Stow's *Chronicle*, by Howes, 1631, p. 1033). Camden adds, 'ubi Princeps Carolus, 12 cursibus decursis, omnem laudem retulit.'

	Parr and Price, ye King of Bohemes[1] men.			
12 Apr.	I dind att ye Dancing Bears w Jacobe: spent	0	3	6
16 „	Easter daye: we receued ye Com[mun]ion w^{t} Mr Robinsone and his wife and all ye pore, excepting Aylec [Alice] Man, whoe for incharitye wase put by by Mr Harrisone: this daye ye chapple wase furnished w^{t} basone and candell sticke, ye chilldren w^{t} 10 surplices and ye fellowes allsoe.			
30 „	Mr Mondaye[2] and his wife dinde w^{t} vs.			
1 May.	This day cam S^{r} Ro. Banister, Sar. Owen[3] and his wife . . . . and dynd w^{t} me.			
10 „	I went to London to seale and acknowledg ye deed off my landes to ye Colledge.			
15 „	pd for inrowlling ye Colledg deed in ye Chauncerie	2	2	0
	water to Westminster, to acknowledg itt in ye Comon pleas	0	0	4
17 „	pd for another tenore viall wch makes 6 in all	0	13	0
23 „	pd my fyne, being rated all ye Landes att			

[1] Down to the election of Frederic, Elector Palatine, as King of Bohemia, in 1619, styled the Palatine's or Palsgrave's servants. This was the company acting at the Fortune (see below, Mun. 56).

[2] Probably Antony Munday, the actor and author. He died at the age of 80 in 1633.

[3] See above, MS. iii. art. 88, and below, 20 Dec., 1620. No serjeant-at-law of this name appears in the lists given by Dugdale and Foss for this reign. Tho. Owen, made serjeant in 1589, became a Justice of the Common Pleas in 1594, and died in 1598.

65^{l}, ye howses in Bushopsgate at 20^{l}, ye Fortune att 20^{l}. I pd ye xth peny, wch came to 10 10 0

26 May. my wife and I acknoweledg ye fine[1] att ye Comon pleas barre off all our landes to ye Colledge, blessed be God y^{t} hathe lent vs lyfe to doe itt.

31 " pd for inrowlling ye Colledg deed in ye Comon pleas 6 8

5 June. I rode to Greenwich to ye king.

6 " ye bayghting wase att Greenwiche this daye and ye king sent a young tyger to ye garden.

15 " Md. y^{t} Mr Rogers sent this daye his 3 sones att board and scholling for 12^{l} per annum a peece.

13 July. This day I layde ye first brick of ye fowndacion of ye almes howses in Finsburie.

13 Aug. John Lowen[2] and his wife dind w^{t} me.

20 " I herd doc. Done[3] att Camberwell, and after dyned w^{t} Sr Tho. Grymes: theye and Mr Angell came to Dullwich in ye afternoone.

A pore knight Sr James Bogg[4] dind here and I gave hym 0 2 6

---

1 See below, Mun. 588.

2 John Lowen, the actor, of the King's Company. According to Mr. Collier (*Hist. of Dram. Poetry*, vol. iii. p. 396), he married Joan Hall, a widow, 29 Oct., 1607.

3 Dr. John Donne, Alleyn's future father-in-law; made Dean of St. Paul's, 27 Nov., 1621; died 31 Mar., 1631. He and Sir Tho. Grimes married sisters (see above, MS. iii. art. 81).

4 Sir James Bogg, of co. Lincoln, knighted at Whitehall, 7 Mar., 1608-9.

21 Aug. I dind att ye Lord Mayors.[1]

24 „ I dined w^{t} ye M^{r} off ye Rowles[2] att ye bishops off Winchester.

8 Sept. my wife gaue to ye queen of Bohemes ayd 3 0 0

12 „ This day Mr Woodwardes sone came to soiorne and be taught here att 20^{l} per annum.

13 „ S^{r} Jo. Wildgoss[3] dind here and captayne Allen and affter I rod to Lewsham.

15 „ I went to Lewesham and survagh ye mannore.

26 „ This day ye Comission wase executed att ye beargarden.

29 „ Some [sum] off theys perticulers [for 1619–20] 779 07 07
other expences in this booke 241 02 01½

2 Oct. this daye att a court held in Kenington I wase admytted tenaunt.

14 „ pd ye pore ther pencion: Boane wase mulkt 12^{d}, for drunken[e]s 6^{d} and for going out 6^{d}, so 8 7 0

22 „ this daye wase our weding daye and ther dind w^{t} vs Mrs Knight, Mr Maund and

---

(Philpott, *Catalogue of Knights*, 1660, p. 46); the same probably as the James Bogg who appears in a pedigree of Bogg, of Sutterton, co. Linc., in Harl. MS. 1550, f. 163, as 15 years of age in 1603. His father, Humphrey Bogg, married Isabel Quarles, aunt to Francis Quarles, the poet.

[1] Sir William Cockayne (MS. iii. art. 99*n*).

[2] Sir Julius Cæsar (MS. ii. art. 1*n*).

[3] Sir John Wildgose, of Salehurst, co. Kent. He held the manor of Lewisham by right of Grace, his wife, daughter and co-heir of Bryan Annesley (Lysons, *Environs*, vol. iv. p. 503).

	his wife, Mr Mylyon, Mr Jeffes[1] and 2 frendes, w^t^ them a precher and his frend, Mr Willson ye singer w^t^ others.			
30 Oct.	I rod to ye king att Theobaldes and gaue hym a peticion for money			
7 Nov.	I went to Westminster and herd ye tryall for ye way betwene ye burowgh and Parish garden.			
10	bought of Mr. Gibkin 14 heads of Christ our Lady and ye 12 apostells att [a] noble a peece	4	13	4
11 "	I dind w^t^ ye M^r^ off ye Rowles, wher ye bishop off Winchester wase.			
18 "	ye Currant off Newes	0	0	2
29 "	I dind att S^t^ Jo. Hed w^t^ ye French musition	0	3	4
11–14 Dec.	I wase att London w^t^ S^r^ Jo: Wildgoss about ye mannor off Lewshame.			
15 "	this daye I pd for ye mannor and par-[so]nage off Lewsham	1000	0	0
20 "	I went to Smithfeeld: dinner w^t^ Sar-giant Owen, &c.	0	1	6
29 "	I dind w^t^ Sr Ric. Smith.			
	This day ye French ambasadore[2] Duk of			

[1] Probably Anthony Jeffes, the actor. Humphrey Jeffes, also an actor, died in 1618 (Collier, *Memoirs of Actors*, p. xxx.). Mr. Collier suggests that 'Mr Willson ye singer' was the 'Jacke Wilson' who performed the part of Balthazar in *Much Ado about Nothing* (*Mem. of Edw. Alleyn*, p. 153).

[2] The ambassador was not the Duke of Lorraine, but Honoré d'Albert, Sieur de Cadenet, Marshal of France, afterwards Duc de Chaulnes. Alleyn perhaps confounded him with his brother, Charles d'Albert, Duc de *Luynes*, favourite of Louis XIII. An account of his reception, taken chiefly from Sir John Finett's *Philoxenis*, is given by Nichols, *Progresses of James I.*, vol. iv. p. 630.

	Lorayne wt 373 persons came to Somersatt Howse.	
'1621.		
4 Jan.	This daye ye French ambasadore wase feasted att Westminster: water . .	0 1 0
7 „	Ther dind wt vs Mr Calton, Withers, Mathew . . . . att night ye 12 pore supt and ye boyes made a shoe [show].	
27 „	Md. this day I took a pore fatherless child, Ed: Alleyn.	
23 Feb.	I went to meet Sr Nic: Stoddard[1] in Powles: spent att ye pole Head[2] wt hym, Mr Borne and Gunell .	0 0 6
	giuen Mr Daniell, a Scotishman	0 0 6
18 Mar.	Charles Massy . . . . dind here.	
15 Apr.	Borne, Massey, Cartwright, Gunnell, Grace, Hunt[3] dind here.	
16 „	Md. this daye I kept ye first court att Lewshame.	
21 „	spent att ye beargarden att ye sealing off ye lease	0 1 0
26 „	I dind att Shreeue Allens:[4] pd to ye shreeue off Surrey[5] for a post fyne of all my landes past to ye colledge . .	15 15 0

[1] Sir Nicholas Stoddard, of Mottingham. A lease for 40 years of Lewisham manor had been granted to him or his father by Queen Elizabeth in 1575.

[2] St. Paul's Head Inn, in Great Carter Lane, Doctors' Commons, mentioned as 'the Polles Hed' by Machyn in his Diary, 25 May, 1562.

[3] Probably a member, like the rest, of the Fortune company; but his name is not in the lease, Mun. 56. A Thomas Hunt was one of the company, who signed the bond to Henslcwe, 29 Aug., 1611, Mun. 47.

[4] Edward Allen, sheriff of London. No relationship can be traced between him and Edw. Alleyn.

[5] Sir Richard Michelborne, knt., of Broadhurst, co. Sussex.

30 Apr.	I went to towne and plact 3 men and 7 weomen in ye howses off Finsbury Lyberty : ye building cost in all .	200	0	0
22 May.	I bayghted before ye kinge at Greenwich.			
25 „	Mr Myddleton[1] browght me a book : giuen hym	0	5	0
	giuen 2 noyes off trompeters att 2 tymes	0	4	0
28 „	I went to my Lord off Arundell[2] in ye tower : water	0	0	6
7 June.	my dinner w^t^ Tuchborne att ye divell and St Dunston[3]	0	3	0
15 „	I dind w^t^ ye Lord Tresorer.[4]			
10 July.	rec. my fee att Courte and ther pd a sub-sydy	3	0	0
21 „	pd ye pore ther pencion all but Aylece man, whoe wase exspulcd [expelled], and Boane, y^t^ wase drounk, so . .	7	0	0
10 Aug.	I agreed w^t^ they princes men for 30^l^ to quitt all.			
	I went to Yeald [Guild] Hall to ye Court off Sewars for ye Fryars.			
12 „	Mr. Edmondes, Charles Massey and on other off ye company dynd here.			

[1] Perhaps Thomas Middleton, the dramatist. The 'book' may have been a play in MS., the term being so used, as above, MS. i. art. 26.

[2] He was sent to the Tower for refusing a proper apology after an altercation with Lord Spencer in the House of Lords, but was released early in June (*Cal. State Papers*, 1619–1623, pp. 254, 257; *Court and Times of James I.*, vol. ii. pp. 254–257).

[3] A famous tavern at Temple Bar, the meeting-place of Ben Jonson's Apollo Club, and frequently alluded to by the dramatists. See an account of it, Larwood and Hotten, *Hist. of Signboards*, 1867, p. 291.

[4] Henry Montague, Viscount Mandeville, afterwards Earl of Manchester; made Lord Treasurer, 3 Dec., 1620, having previously been Chief Justice of the King's Bench.

20 Aug.	we dind att Barbar Surgions Hall, and after went to ye glasse howse: giuen .	0	1	0
21 Sept.	I went to Croydon and dind w^t^ ye Lo. of Canterbury.			
29 "	Here endes this years acount . . . . in wch hath bene disbursed in generall 2485 01 02.			
13 Nov.	I rec. my fee and in y^t^ pd my subsydye	2	0	0
19 "	giuen Charles Massye att his playe . .	0	5	0
23 "	I went and herd St Bees cause in ye Starr Chamber.			
3 Dec.	I rod to Mr Adye: his fee about Jacob .	0	5	0
	Jacobs arest	0	2	6
9 "	Md. this night att 12 of ye clock ye Fortune was burnt.[1]			
24 "	. . . went to ye borowgh cort about Jacobs tryall: Mr Adyes fee . .	0	5	0
'1622.				
6 Jan.	all ye pore, Mr Steele, Mr Fowles, w^t^ ther wifes, and Tho. Allen and his wife supt here: ye boyes playd a playe.			
7 "	Mr Adys fee for this days tryall att ye burowgh court	0	5	0
14 "	this daye my cause wase tryd: giuen Mr Adye a fee	0	5	0
29 "	dinner w^t^ Tuchborne: drawing Jacob and my answers	0	2	0

[1] The fire is mentioned by J. Chamberlain in a letter to Sir D. Carleton, 15 Dec.:—'On Sunday night, here was a great fire at the Fortune in Golding Lane, the fairest playhouse in this town. It was quite burned down in two hours, and all their apparel and playbooks lost, whereby these poor companions are quite undone' (*Court and Times of James I.*, vol. ii. p. 280).

13 Apr.	y^{e} klnges majestie for y^{e} manore of Lewsham	14	14	0
	pd y^{e} klnges majestie for y^{e} bancksid .	13	17	5
16 „	dinner att y^{e} Hart in Smithfeeld w^{t} y^{e} builders off y^{e} Fortune[1]	0	3	0
23 „	I dind w$_{t}$ S^{r} Ed Bowyar and apoynted y^{e} officers for y^{e} parishe.			
26 „	water to London, 6^{d}: wine w$_{t}$ y^{e} Fortune workmen, 12^{d} . . .	0	1	6
	I dind w^{t} y^{e} Spanish embasadore Gondomarr.[2]			
29 „	I went to Westminster to mete y^{e} workmen off y^{e} Fortune: spent	0	01	0
1 May.	I mett y^{e} workmen att Ric. Gunnells · water	0	01	6
3 „	I gaue to y^{e} benevolenc for y^{e} kinge to y^{e} justice in Southwark	3	00	0
	I rec. 23l of Jacob of y$_{e}$ execution, and spent att diner w^{t} hym and y^{e} Fortune builders	0	07	0
6 „	I dind w^{t} y^{e} Fortune workmen att Angells and spent	0	01	6
13 „	pd y^{e} first payment for y^{e} Fortune build ing 25^{l}: spent	0	1	6
	pd Mr Attorney for his hand to my book			

[1] For deeds relative to the rebuilding, see below, Muniments 58 seqq.

[2] Diego Sarmiento d'Acunha, Conde de Gondomar. This was a farewell visit, as he left England in May. Alleyn had probably entertained him at the Bear Garden, as he did the Marquis Inijosa, Spanish Ambassador Extraordinary, in the following year; of whom we read in a letter of 12 July, 1623:—'The Spanish Ambassador is much delighted in bear baiting. He was the last week in Paris Garden, where they showed him all the pleasure they could, both with bull, bear and horse, besides jackanapes, and then turned a white bear into the Thames, where the dogs baited him swimming, which was the best sport of all' (*Court and Times of James I.*, vol. ii. p. 410).

	in Checker [the Exchequer] for clering and pleading my mortmayn 2l, and to his clarck 10s	2	10	0
24 May.	I went to West. Hall and dind wt ye Lo: of London.[1]			
4 June.	I dind wt Mr Hemings.[2]			
11 „	I baighted before ye king, and my men washt my shep and pd 2d a skore	0		0
12 „	I went to ye Lord off Arundle: showed ye Fortune plott.			
17 „	I dind att ye Fortune att Smiths howse: spent	0	1	3
	(in the summary, f. 59*b*) ye tyeth dwe for ye rose[3] 00 01 0			
7 July.	I dind att Detford wt ye Countes of Kildare.[4]			
14 „	. . Dune [Dr. Donne] preched at Camberwell.			
19 „	I seald ye Leases off ye Fortune.			
21 „	Charles Massy and his cosen Ned Collins, 2 shagbuttes and a cornett dind here.			
2 Aug.	I went to Westminster and to Chellsey to ye Lo. Treserer[5] and Sr A. Ingrame[6] .	0	2	6

[1] George Mountaigne, Bishop of London, 1621; translated in 1628 to Durham and York, and died in the same year.

[2] John Heminge or Hemmings, at the head of the King's Company; joint editor of the first folio *Shakespeare* of 1623.

[3] It may be inferred from this entry that Alleyn still retained an interest in the Rose; but there is nothing to show whether it was still used as a theatre.

[4] Frances Howard, daughter of Charles Howard, Earl of Nottingham, to whose company of players Alleyn once belonged. She was widow of Henry Fitzgerald, Earl of Kildare (d. 1597), and of Henry Brooke, Lord Cobham (d. 1618).

[5] Lionel Cranfield, Lord Cranfield, 1621; Earl of Middlesex, 1622; Lord Treasurer, Oct. 1621–May, 1624; died 1645.

[6] Sir Arthur Ingram, Cofferer of the Household, 1615–1620.

15 Aug. I went to ye Fortune to meet w^t^ Mr Thicknis and others. I wase served w^t^ a writt att Dorington's shut ye clarck off ye Counter

giuen Mathew Roydon . . . . . o o 6

18 ,, Mr Doughton,[1] Mr Gwalter, Mr Gunell, Mr Garman and Wigpitt, W. Cartwright [dind here].

1 Sept. wee rec. ye comu[n]ion, feasted ye pore and gaue the 12 ther newe gownes, and this being my birthday I am full 56 year owld, blessed be ye Lord God ye giuer off lyfe, Amen.

3 ,, I dind w^t^ ye Lo. Corone.

4 ,, ye Lo. Carone: S^r^ Ed. Bowyar: his brother: Lady Byne,[2] her brother and frend: Mr Dennis: Sr Tho. Grymes: his lady and his son and ye dean off Pales dahter:[3] ye Lady Clarck: Mr Austen, his wiff and dawghter dind w^t^ vs.

6 ,, I went to doc. Backer att ye Charter Howse, from thenc. to ye Fortune: I dind w^t^ Mr Axell[4] and gaue his wife for Ned Laighton[5] 20^s.^ I gaue his man 6^d^, his mayd 6^d^, so . . . . . . o

---

[1] Thomas Downton, the actor (see above, MS. i. art. 15*n*). All the other guests were lessees of the Fortune.

[2] Wife of Sir John Byne or Bynd, knt., son of John Byne and Elizabeth Bowyer. The latter was sister to Sir Edmond Bowyer, who himself married Katherine Byne.

[3] Constance Donne, whom Alleyn afterwards married, 3 Dec., 1623.

[4] Probably Robert Axel or Axen, a member of the Queen's Company in 1631–3 (Fleay, *Shakespeare Manual*, p. 117).

[5] Mr. Collier (*Mem. of Edw. Alleyn*, p. 166) reads this name 'Mr. Houghton,'

I seald att Vnderwoodes ye Fortune leases and so came home.

21 Sept. I went to Croydon fayre: dind w^t ye Archbishop, wher wase ye deane off Pawles and S^r Ed. Sackvile.[1]

1 Oct. pd Mr Hamden for mending ye orgaines and making 3 or 4 newe pipes for a dyapason 0 15 0

Here end this years acount [Mich., 1621–Mich., 1622] . . . . wherin hath bene disbursed in generall . 1527 06 2

'The generall disbursed for theys 5 years is 8504 04 8½

wheroff in perticuler as followeth

Howshowld charge	0917	11	2
The colledge	1315	04	2
Rentes	1547	19	2
Debtes, building or reparing .	3373	17	7
Lawe	0207	08	1½
Aparell	0078	18	8½
Some off theys perticulers . . .	7440	19	0
Other exspence . .	1063	05	8½

'In theys 5 years hath bene disburssed about building or reparing ye Colledg 0802 07 9

Praysed bee ye name off our good God both now and euer through Christ Jesue our Lord. Amen.'

Extracts from this *Diary* are printed by Lysons, *Environs*

and identifies him with Will. Haughton, the dramatist. Ned Laighton's name occurs often before in the volume as a servant of Alleyn.

[1] Succeeded his brother Richard, as 4th Earl of Dorset, in 1624; died 1652.

of London, 1792, vol. i. pp. 113–117; Collier, *Mem. of Edw. Alleyn*, pp. 138 seqq.; and Blanch, *Hist. of Camberwell*, pp. 429 seqq.

The original vellum cover is bound in at the beginning of the volume. On the inner side of it is a lease from Edward Alleyn to William Penfold, of the par. of St. Olave, Southwark, and William Champion, of the par. of St. Saviour, Southwark, woodmongers, of a wharf, &c., in the par. of St. Mary Overy, for 12 years, at an annual rent of 26*l.*; 8 July, 1 Jas I., 1603.

Narrow folio, ff. 62.

MS. No. X.

REGISTER of Dulwich College; 1616–1757.

At the beginning is the following inscription, in the hand of Edward Alleyn :—

'A Regester Book for this Colledge off God's guift in Dullwich in ye Countye off Surrey, wherin is contayned first all ye names off the Colledgiantes, then all ye Christenings, Burialls, or mariages, which hath bene since the Chapple off ye said Colledge wase consecrated and dedicated to ye honor off Christ by the most Reverent father in God, George Abbot, Archbishopp off Canterbury His Grace, on Sundaye ye first off September and in ye yeare off our Lord, 1616.'

Among the entries are the following :—

9 Apr., 1617. 'Anne [Agnes] Henslowe, widoe, ye late wife off Phillip Henslowe esq. and mother to Joan Alleyn, ye wife off Edw. Alleyn, fownder off this Coll: buried in ye north side off ye chapell quire.' f. 7.

1 July, 1623. 'Joane Alleyn, the wife of Edward Alleyn, esquire and ffounder of this Colledg of Gods gifte, departed this life the eight and twentieth of June, and was buried in the chappell of the same colledge the first day of July following.' f. 19.

27 Nov., 1626. 'Mr Edward Alleyn, esq., and ffounder of this Colledg was buried.' f. 25.

1 June, 1644. 'By vertue of an order from ye comittee for plundered ministers John Crofts and James Mead made preacher and schoolmaster.' f. 43*b*. Steph. Street and Edm. Colby were appointed to the same offices in a similar way, 2, 13 Aug., 1645.

25 Mar., 1658. 'Put in by the Visitors, William Carter, John Harrison, preachers, John Bradford, schoolmaster, Hen. Tilley, Vsher.' f. 57*b*.

24 May, 1659. 'Abell Millar . . . . and Katherine Rickis or Rickisis . . . . were married May 24 in this chappell, having beene cried in the market place in Southwarke . . . . on three severall market daies.' f. 59.

1665–6. Numerous deaths from the plague registered, including Col. Lytcott, his wife, and four sons; Nicholas Weekes, his wife, and four children; Ralph Bonnicke, his wife and child, and John Bonnicke and child. ff. 65–67.

19 Feb., 1727. 'Buried John Egleton, a player.' f. 127.

10 Jan., 1731. 'Buried Mr. Anthony Boheme, ye famous Tragedian.' f. 131.

At the beginning and end are various lists of books, music, &c., 1626–1649:—and on ff. 166*b*–168*b* are orders relative to a fine upon the Warden for a fraud in his accounts, 1 Mar., 1679–80, and n. d. [1693 ?].

On f. 2*b* is the note, 'The Colledge porch with ye Treasury Chamber, &c., tumbled down to ye ground, Friday, May 28, 1703.'

Narrow folio, ff. 173.

MS. No. XI.

'A GENERALL COLLECTION of all the offices in Englande, withe their ffees, in the queenes guifte'; *circa* 1600.

Further described as containing:—

'All the offices and ffees of her Maties Cortes, boothe of Justes and Revennuse at Wustmister.

'All the offices and [ffees] of her Highnes moste Royall Houshoulde, with other rewardes and allowances.

'All the offices and ffees belonginge to captaines, officers, and shouldiers hauinge charge of townes, castles, bullwarkes, and ffortresses.

'And all the offices and ffees ffor the keepinge of her Maties howses, parkes, fforestes, and chaces withein the realme of Englande.'

The copy appears to have been made by William Collins, whose name is written at the end, f. 28*b*. It was probably procured by Philip Henslowe about the time when he was in treaty for the office of Master of the Queen's Game of Bears, Bulls, &c. A copy in the British Museum, Additional MS. 12512, is dated 1597.

Among the items are the following, ff. 15*b*, 25*b*:—

'Players of interludes—fe a peece 66^{s} per annum.'

'Parris garden

Keeper of the queenes beares—fee 12^{li} 8^{s} 1^{d} ob.

Keeper of queenes mastiues—fe 21^{li} 5^{s} 10^{d} ob.'

At ff. *29b*, 30 are the following notes in the hand of Phil. Henslowe :—

'R[eceived] 10[li]

Pd. for my Lo. Worsters mens warant for playinge at the cort vnto the clarke of the cownselles for geatynge the cownselles handes to yt . . . . vii[s]

pd. at the receuinge of the mony owt of the pay-howsse to M[r] Moysse for fese [fees] . . . . x[s] vi[d]'

1603.

'Layd owt as folowethe for sewinge at the cort when the kinge laye at Grenwiche.

Itm. pd. for a peti[ci]on, which M[r] Doryngton hade xij[d]

Itm. pd. for a peti[ci]on, which my Lord Chamberlen hade . . . : . . . . . xii[d]

Itm. pd. for a peticion to deliver to the cownsell table . . . . xii[d]

Itm. pd. for mackinge of ii lycenses in parchment iii[s]

Itm. pd. for our warent for baytynge . . . . vii[s]

Itm. pd. for goinge and comminge by water 4 tymes ii[s]

Itm. pd. for goinge by water ii tymes in a daye xvi[d]'

Small quarto, ff. 31.

MS. No. XII.

'NOTES touchinge the office and authority of the Lorde Chauncellor of Inglond, colected oute of a Readinge made in the Middle Temple in Lente, Anno Domini 1570, vppon the xxviiith Chapter of the greate Chartre of Inglond graunted in the nynthe yeare vnder the greate seale and enacted and made a statute at Marlbridge in the two and fyftye yeare of Kinge Henry the thirde'; with a preface addressed by the author, 'Roberte Snagge, an apprentice of the common lawes,' to Sir Christopher Hatton, Lord Chancellor [1587–1591].

According to Watt (*Bibliotheca Britannica*, 1824) printed by T. L., London, 1654, 8vo. Both in the printed title, as given by Watt, and on the fly-leaf of the present MS., the author is styled Serjeant-at-Law; but the only serjeant of the name in Dugdale's *Origines Juridiciales* is Thomas Snagge, appointed in 1580. R. Snagge appears in a list of counsel in Elizabeth's reign given by Foss, *Judges of England*, 1857, vol. v. p. 423.

Quarto, ff. 21.

MS. No. XIII.

1. 'COLLECTIONES quædam ex libris Christophori Scheibleri in Metaphisicam per me Jo: Hillary, e coll. Wadh. Oxon., 1664': being an abstract of portions of the *Opus Metaphysicum* of Christoph Scheibler, first printed at Giessen in 1617. f. 1*b*.

2. 'A brief and plaine exposicion on ye Catechisme of the Church of England'; with a preface beginning, 'Our holy mother ye Church Catholike desirous to embrace St. Paul's advice in bringing up her children,' &c.; *circa* 1665. f. 84.

Small octavo, ff. 108.

MS. No. XIV

CATALOGUE of a collection of pictures belonging to William Cartwright, actor and bookseller; *temp.* Charles II.

The catalogue is apparently in Cartwright's own hand. It originally contained descriptions of two hundred and thirty-nine pictures, a few prints and drawings being included; but a single leaf, containing nos. 186-209, has been lost. The prices for which the pictures were purchased are generally given in the margin; and, in some cases, the names of the artists are added. The name which most frequently recurs is that of Heemskerk [see below]; and there are examples of Greenhill [see below], William Dobson [b. 1610, d. 1646], Flusshers [Balthazar Flessiers, *temp.* Chas. I.], John Payn [d. *ante* 1648], Breughel, Tintoretto, Johnson [Laurence Johnson?, engraver, *temp.* Jas. I.], Isaac Fuller [d. 1672], Housman [see below], Burbage [see below], and Walton [Parrey Walton, keeper of the King's pictures, d. *circ.* 1700].

William Cartwright died at the end of 1686 or 1687, and bequeathed his pictures to Dulwich College[1]; but many

[1] John Aubrey, in his account of Dulwich College, writes:—'In it [the picture gallery] are several worthless pictures, and some not so bad, viz. the Founder and his first wife, Henry, Prince of Wales, Sir Thomas Gresham, Mary, Queen of Scotland, and several others given by Mr. Cartwright, a comedian, whose picture is at the upper end' (*Natural History and Antiquities of Surrey*, 1719, vol. i. p. 195). To this he adds in the Appendix (vol. v. p. 356):—'Here is a library, in which is a collection of plays given by Mr. Cartwright, a bookseller, who lived at the end of Turnstile Alley. . . . This Cartwright was an excellent player, and besides his plays gave many pictures; one a view of London, taken by Mr. John

of those here enumerated either never came into possession of the College or were afterwards lost, and others were probably destroyed on account of the grossness of the subjects depicted.

The collection in general appears to have been of little value; but many of the portraits are of historical interest, and some, especially those by Greenhill, possess considerable artistic merit. A list of the portraits is given below, the numbers referring to Cartwright's catalogue and the asterisk marking those which are still at the College.[1] The spelling, which in the original is very illiterate, has been modernised.

Norden in 1603, with the representation of the city cavalcade on the Lord Mayor's Day, which is very curious.' The name of Will. Cartwright as an actor frequently occurs in Downe's *Roscius Anglicanus*, 1708. He was a member of the King's company after the Restoration, and among other characters played Falstaff in *Henry IV.* and Brabantio in *Othello.* He was probably a son of Will. Cartwright, the actor, mentioned by Alleyn in his *Diary* (see below, p. 207, n. 4.); and a passage in praise of Alleyn is inserted in his reprint of Heywood's *Apology for Actors*, published in 1658. The circumstances of his bequest are stated in the College Audit Book, 4 Sept., 1688 (Extracts by Rev. E. A. Giraud, Brit. Mus., Add. MS. 29479A, f. 22*b*), as follows:—'William Cartwright, gent., deceased, by his will in writing in or about December, 1686 [*sic*, but 1687 in MS. vi., above, art. 39], not naming any executors, gave unto this College his books and pictures, two silver tankards, damask linen, an Indian quilt, and a Turkey carpet, together with 400*l.* in money, as a legacy for the benefit of the said College, and soon after died, leaving the said legacy and all he had besides in the possession of his servants, Francis Johnson and his wife. On or about the 14th of January following, by commission or direction from the Prærogative Court, all the goods of the said Mr. Cartwright which his said servants would produce, besides 390 pieces of broad old gold, were inventoried, appraised and valued at 94*l.* 15*s.* . . . . About the 1st of February following, the said Warden with great difficulty got into possession of all the goods that were so appraised, except such goods as are mentioned at this latter end of the inventory, exhibited by him into the Prærogative Court, valued by two of the said appraisers at 29*l.* 10*s.*, which the said servants with their confederates have carried away, together with the said 390 pieces of broad old gold.' Of the pictures mentioned by Aubrey only those of the Founder and his wife and Prince Henry are now at the College.

[1] These pictures are in the Master's official residence, and form no part of the Dulwich College Picture Gallery, which was bequeathed by Sir P. F. Bourgeois in 1810. The identification in some cases is merely from tradition. It is possible that a few of the pictures without an asterisk may also be at the College, but they cannot be recognised from the descriptions.

5. Queen Mary's picture, in orange-coloured bodice, after Vandyck, copied by 'oul Reme'[1]; in a gilt frame; a closet piece. 5*l.*

10. The print of Erasmus; in a black frame, 'filited' with gold.

12. The print of Thomas Howard, Duke of Norfolk; a closet piece, in a gilt frame, by 'Hollbaine.'

56.* Bishop Laud's picture, in black and white; in a gilt frame; a small closet piece.

62. 'Hemskirt's'[2] head, done by himself; in a gilt frame; a small closet piece. 10*l.*

68.* The Duke of York; in a gilt frame, on 3 quarters cloth. 'Grinhill.'[3] 2*l.*

72.* A woman in a blue mantle; in a gilt frame, on a 3 quarters cloth; done by 'Housman.'[4] 5*l.*

76.* King Charles the Second, on 3 quarters cloth; in a gilt frame. 2*l.*

77.* Althea's[5] picture, her hair dishevelled; on 3 quarters cloth, in a gilt frame. 2*l.*

78.* My first wife's picture like a shepherdess, on 3 quarters cloth; in a gilt frame. 3*l.*

93.* Queen Mary [Henrietta Maria] in a white satin gown; a large piece, in a gilt frame, to the knees. 5*l.*

94.* King Charles the First, in a slashed doublet and a ruff; a large piece, in a gilt frame, to the knees. 2*l.*

95.* 'Grenhill's' picture to the knees, in red, done by himself. 5*l.*

96.* The Duchess of Suffolk,[6] on a board, in a white gown embroidered with pearl; in an old-fashioned frame, to the knees. 5*l.*

---

[1] Probably Remi van Leemput, a native of Antwerp, who came to England about the middle of the 17th cent., and was well known as a copyist of Vandyck; died 1675. Queen Mary must mean Henrietta Maria.

[2] Egbert van Heemskerk, the younger, born at Haarlem, 1645, died at London, 1704.

[3] John Greenhill, born 1649, died 1676; a pupil of Sir P. Lely and a promising artist. His portrait of himself, no. 95, is engraved in the later editions of Walpole's *Anecdotes of Painting* (ed. Dallaway, 1827, vol. iii. p. 46). The engraving in Walpole's first edition, 1763, is taken from another picture.

[4] Jacob Huysmans, born at Antwerp, 1656, died at London, 1696 or 1699.

[5] The 'divine Althea' of the poem, by Richard Lovelace, 'To Althea from prison,' containing the well-known lines, 'Stone walls do not a prison make,' &c.

This was thought by Lysons (*Environs of London*, 1792, vol. i. p. 109) to be Catherine, Lady Willoughby d'Eresby [d. 1525], fourth wife of Charles Brandon,

98. Sir George Sands[1] in trunk hose to the knee, on a board. 10*s.*

100.* Colonel 'Louliss,'[2] his picture in armour; in a great gilt frame, 3 quarters cloth. 3*l.*

101.* The Earl of Exeter's[3] head, the ground of it gold; in a black frame. 5*l.*

103.* A woman's head, on a board, done by 'Mr Burbige,[4] ye Actor'; in an old gilt frame. 3*l.*

105.* 'Mr Burbig' his head; in a gilt frame; a small closet piece. 5*s.*

106. 'Mr Demetrus' picture; in a gilt frame; done by Gild [Geldorp?] 10*s.*

108.* 'Mickill Darayton,'[5] the poet; in a black frame. 15*s.*

109. Mr. Sly's[6] picture, the actor; in a gilt frame. 1*l.*

Duke of Suffolk. The costume, however, is of a later period; and, if the picture really represents a Duchess of Suffolk, it is more probably Frances Brandon, wife of Henry Grey, the last Duke [created 1551, beheaded 1554], by whom she was mother of Lady Jane Grey. She afterwards married Adrian Stokes, and died at the end of 1559.

[1] Perhaps the Sir George Sands, or Sandys, who was hanged at Wapping for highway robbery, 4 Mar., 1617–8 (Camden, *Annales; Cal. of State Papers*, 1611–1618, p. 527).

[2] Richard Lovelace, the poet, colonel in the Royalist service; born 1618, died 1658. This portrait is engraved in S. and E. Harding's *Biographical Mirrour*, 1795, vol. i. p. 84.

[3] This is a very interesting portrait. It is, however, far too early for any *Earl* of Exeter, the first who bore the title being Thomas Cecil, cr. in 1605. It may, perhaps, be Henry Holland, the last Duke of Exeter, succ. 1446, died 1473. By his wife Anne, sister of Edward IV., he had a daughter, Anne, married to Thomas Grey, first Marquis of Dorset, grandfather of Henry Grey, Duke of Suffolk, mentioned in the note above.

[4] Richard Burbage, the most famous actor of his time and the supporter of the leading characters in Shakespeare's plays at the Blackfriars and Globe Theatres; died 13 Mar., 1618–9 (Collier, *Hist. of Dram. Poetry*, ed. 1879, vol. iii. p. 293). His skill in painting is alluded to in an epigram and elegy quoted by Mr. Collier (*ib.*, pp. 280, 291). The portrait of him, no. 105, is engraved in Harding's *Shakspeare Illustrated*, 1793.

[5] Michael Drayton, author of the *Polyolbion*, born 1563, died 1631. Lysons wrongly reads the price as 15*l.* The portrait, but without the wreath round the head, is engraved in Harding's *Biographical Mirrour*, 1795, vol. i. p. 102.

[6] William Sly, a member of the King's company; died 1608. For a memoir of him see Collier, *Hist. of Dram. Poetry*, ed. 1879, vol. iii. p. 381. This picture is mentioned by Lysons as being still at the College.

112. 'Mis Wessons' picture; in a black frame, 3 quarters cloth, studded with gold. 1*l.*

113. 'Mr Wessons' picture; in a black frame, studded with gold, 3 quarters cloth. 1*l.*

114. 'Mr Brutnalls' picture; in a black frame, 'filited' with gold, 3 quarters cloth. 2*l.*

115. My last wife's sister's husband; in a black frame, 3 quarters cloth.

116.* My last wife's picture, with a black veil on her head; in a gilt frame, 3 quarters cloth. 3*l.*

117.* A man with a bald head; in a gilt frame, in 3 quarters cloth; done by 'Grinhill.' 10*l.*

118.* Queen Mary,[1] in blue; in a gilt frame, 3 quarters cloth. 2*l.*

120.* My last wife's sister[2]; in a black frame, 3 quarters cloth; a book in her hand, and in a hat. 10*s.*

121.* 'My Lord Louless'[3] in a red mantle; in a black frame, 3 quarters cloth. 1*l.*

148.* Tom Bond's[4] picture, an actor, in 'a band rought with imbrodery, bared neck,' on a board; in a black frame, very old. 5*s.*

150. Mr. [or Mrs.] Blundall in an old-fashioned dress; in a black and gilt frame, on a 3 quarters cloth. 8*s.*

155. The Earl of Essex[5] lying dead in his bed, his crown on his bosom; in a black frame. 5*s.*

156.* Mr. Dirge's wife in a hat and ruff; in a black frame, 3 quarters cloth.

---

[1] This is thought to be the Princess Mary, daughter of Charles I. and wife of William, Prince of Orange.

[2] Dated 1644, *ætatis suæ* 65; a very poor work of art.

[3] Probably John Lovelace, second Lord Lovelace of Hurley; succ. 1634, died 1670. He married Lady Anne Wentworth, daughter of Thomas, Earl of Cleveland. Richard Lovelace dedicated to her his *Lucasta*, 1649.

[4] Little is known of this actor. His name is in the cast of Marmion's comedy, *Holland's Leaguer*, played by the company of Prince Charles in 1632.

[5] Probably Robert Devereux, third Earl of Essex, the Parliamentary general. He died 14 Sept., 1646, and was honoured with a public funeral in Westminster Abbey. An account of the mutilation of his effigy and hearse, which is referred to below, no. 184, is quoted by Lysons from *The Perfect Diurnal*, 23–30 Nov., 1646.

165.* 'Sir William Loulass,'[1] on a board, to the knees, with a chain of gold about his neck, in a ruff and trunk hose; in a black frame. 2*l.*

166.* Mr. Pirkines,[2] the actor, in a 3 quarters cloth; in a gilt frame. 2*l.*

167.* 'Master Feild's'[3] picture in his shirt; on a board, in a black frame, 'filited' with gold; an actor. 10*s.*

168.* Old Mr. Cartwright,[4] actor; in a gilt frame. 15*s.*

169. Young Mr. Cartwright, actor; in a gilt frame. 15*s.*

174.* 'Sr Martin Furbusher's'[5] picture, in a white doublet and a great ruff, with a gold chain; in a black frame. 10*s.*

179.* 'Loulass his father'[6] in black armour and a red scarf; on a board, in an old black frame.

180.* 'Thomas Loulass'[7] his picture, with a hare lip; on a board, in a black frame. 10*s.*

181.* 'Serjeant Loulass'[8] in his red robes, on a board, with his coat of arms; in a black frame, 'filted' with gold. 10*s.*

---

[1] Sir William Lovelace, of Bethersden, co. Kent, son of Serjeant Lovelace (no. 181) and grandfather of the poet; born 1561, knighted 1599, died 1629. See the pedigree of the family in a paper on the Kentish Lovelaces by the Rev. A. J. Pearman, in the *Archæologia Cantiana*, vol. x., 1876, p. 208.

[2] Richard Perkins, a member of Queen Anne's company at the time of her death in 1619, and named first among the performers of Shirley's *Wedding* at the Phœnix Theatre in 1629. Wright, in his *Historia Histrionica*, 1699, says that he died some time before the Restoration and was buried at Clerkenwell. Some verses by him are prefixed to T. Heywood's *Apology for Actors*, 1612.

[3] Nathan, or Nathaniel, Field (see above, MS. i. art 68). This portrait is engraved in Harding's *Shakspeare Illustrated*, 1793. Lysons wrongly reads 10*l.* instead of 10*s.*, and makes a similar mistake with regard to the next two pictures.

[4] William Cartwright is mentioned in Henslowe's *Diary* (p. 71) in 1591, and as one of the cast of *Tamar Cam* in 1602. He was one of the lessees of the Fortune Theatre in 1618, and a guest of E. Alleyn at Dulwich (see pp. 183, 188, above, and Mun. 56). 'Young Mr. Cartwright' was probably his son; but, the picture being lost, there are no means of judging whether he was identical with the William Cartwright who owned the collection, and whose portrait is below, no. 234.

[5] Sir Martin Frobisher, the navigator, knighted for his services at the defeat of the Spanish Armada; died 1594.

[6] Sir William Lovelace, of Woolwich, father of the poet; born 1584, knighted 1609, died 1628.

[7] A younger son of Serjeant Lovelace; born 1563, died 1591. The picture is dated 1588, *ætatis suæ* 26.

[8] William Lovelace, of Bethersden, great-grandfather of the poet; M.P. for Canterbury 1563–1577, serjeant-at-law 1567, died 1577.

182. 'My lady Loulass' with a little monkey in her arms, on a cloth, to the knees; in a black frame. 1*l.*

184. The old man that demolished the Earl of Essex in the Abbey of Westminster, with a 'hattich' [hatchet?]: in a black frame.

229. A great picture of 'my lady Blundall,' with a dog by her. 10*s.*

230. A picture from head to foot of 'my Lord of Dorset'; in a black frame. 2*l.*

231. A picture from head to foot, in black, with a counsellor's staff; in a black frame. 2*l.*

234.* My picture in a black dress with a great dog.

Folio, ff. 25.

MS. No. XV.

A COLLECTION of Drawings, apparently students' copies, in various hands, and generally of little merit, together with a few paintings of flowers, coloured coats of arms, &c.; 17th century.

The volume probably came to the College with the pictures bequeathed by William Cartwright.

Small folio, ff. 88.

MS. No. XVI.

LETTERS and Papers relating to purchases of pictures made by Noel Joseph Desenfans,[1] and to that portion of his collection bequeathed by him to Sir Peter Francis Bourgeois,[2] knt., R.A., and by the latter to Dulwich College; 1787–1810.

1. ACCOUNT by N. J. Desenfans of his business transactions with Jean Baptiste Pierre Le Brun,[3] art critic and picture dealer, of Paris; Sept., 1787–Jan., 1788. f. 1.

---

[1] Born at Douai in 1745. He came to England as a teacher of languages, but ultimately devoted himself to the business of a picture dealer. In 1790 he was commissioned to collect pictures for Stanislaus Poniatowski, King of Poland, and was named Polish Consul-General for Great Britain. After the partition of Poland he was compelled to offer the collection for sale, having first made two attempts to dispose of it to the Czar (see below, art. 12). His *Descriptive Catalogue* (London, 1802, 2 vols.) includes 188 pictures. Only thirty-nine of these are now at Dulwich; and there is no evidence that the rest of the 381 pictures in the College gallery ever formed part of the collection made for Stanislaus. Desenfans died 8 July, 1807, having by his will, dated 8 Oct., 1803, left the whole of his pictures, &c., to his friend Sir P. F. Bourgeois.

[2] Born in London in 1756, of a family of Swiss extraction. He studied painting under Loutherbourg, and during his travels abroad was knighted by Stanislaus, King of Poland. He was made A.R.A. in 1788 and R.A. in 1793, and held the appointment of landscape painter to George III. He died 8 Jan., 1811. For his will see below, art. 21.

[3] Born 1748, died 1813. He was husband of Marie Louise Elisabeth Vigée, famous as a portrait painter and for *esprit*. Mad. Le Brun has drawn his character in her *Souvenirs* (Paris, 1835–1837):—'Ce n'est pas que M. Le Brun fût un méchant homme. Son caractère offrait un mélange de douceur et de vivacité: il était d'une grande obligeance pour tout le monde—en un mot, assez aimable—mais sa passion effrénée pour les femmes de mauvaises mœurs, jointe à la passion du jeu, a causé la ruine de sa fortune et de la mienne, dont il disposait entièrement, au point qu'en 1789, lorsque je quittai la France, je ne possédais pas vingt francs de revenu après avoir gagné pour ma part plus d'un million; il avait tout mangé.'

Exclusive of those marked as returned, the number of pictures ent by Le Brun to Desenfans during the above period was forty-six, sixteen of which were for sale on commission with joint profits. The most important works purchased were:—'un tableau représentant Thesée[1] par N. Poussin,' 334*l.*; 'un grand paysage de Cuyp,' 300*l.*; 'un grand paysage de Cuyp,' 254*l.*; 'un paysage[2] de Nicolo Poussin, avec Calisto,' 70*l.*; 'deux Claudes' 75*l.*; 'un boiteux de Teniers,' 65*l.*; 'un petit St Jean par Raphael,'[3] 25*l.*

On f. 3*b* is the note, '1788, dans le courant de Janvier j'ai achetté pour Mr Lebrun Le Vanderwerff de feu Mr Antrobus pour £500 sterlings'; and on f. 5 is a list of six pictures purchased in 1787 of Mr. Donjeu, viz. 'des Anges par Rubens,' 50*l.*; 'le Mariage de Ste Catharine par Cortone,' 75*l.*; 'une Ste famille par Paris Bourdon,' 20*l.*; 'Les Maries au tombeau par S. Rosa,' 40*l.*; 'l'offre des Bergers par A. Sacchi,' 33*l.*; 'une tête de Rembrandt,' 25*l.*

2. LIST, in the hand of J. B. P. Le Brun, of forty-two pictures, with prices attached; [1787]. f. 6.

Besides the works named in art. 1 the list includes: 'La fontaine de Philipe Wowermanse,'[4] 260 louis; 'L'intérieur d'une chambre d'Ostade,' 200 louis; 'Le jeux de Galet par Ostade,' 208½ louis; 'Un grand Vinatse [Wijnants] très capital,' 150 louis; 'Un grand Salvator,' 500 louis.

3. GAVIN INGLIS HAMILTON[5] to N. J. Desenfans: is sorry to hear he is not satisfied with Vanni's picture, which is certainly genuine; wishes he had mentioned his disapproval before it was shown to the public, as it will now be looked

[1] Probably no. 164 in Smith's *Catalogue Raisonné*, 1829–1837.

[2] Described in art. 2, below, as 'Calistau changé [*sic*] en orse'; probably, therefore, no. 325 in Smith's *Catalogue*.

[3] In art. 2 said to be from the 'Collection de Julienne,' which was sold at Paris in 1767.

[4] Perhaps 'La Fontaine des Tritons,' Smith's *Catalogue*, no. 117; in the sale of the Chev. de Clène, 1786, 250*l.*

[5] A painter, but better known as a collector and excavator of classical antiquities; died at Rome in 1797. He was author of *Schola Italica Picturæ*, London, 1773.

upon as his refusal; thinks, therefore, it had better be kept till he himself arrives in England, when, with his assistance, it may probably be sold to advantage; has many pictures worthy of being proposed to him, but has been so unlucky of late that he is resolved to send no more; never sends a picture by which he [Desenfans] will be out of pocket, and, in sending the Vanni for the low sum of 50*l.*, really meant to do him a service; hopes soon to be in England with a collection of good pictures, including in particular fine works of Polidoro, and, as some of these are of great size, must look out for a large house; Rome, 20 Sept., 1788. f. 7.

4. BIOGRAPHICAL NOTICE of Sir Joshua Reynolds, in the hand of N. J. Desenfans; [1788]. It ends:—'L'impératrice de Russie et M. le Prince Potemkin lui ont commandé deux tableaux,[1] qui viennent d'être envoyés à St. Petersbourg. Si ces ouvrages obtiennent leur approbation, les amis du chevalier Reynolds font les vœux les plus ardens pour que Sa Majesté impériale daigne lui accorder le titre de Baron ou quelque autre marque d'honneur pour preuve de son suffrage.' f. 9.

5. J. BAPTISTE PIERRE LE BRUN to N. J. Desenfans; Paris, 25 Feb., 1789. f. 11.

'Monsieur et cher amy. J'ay pourtant le plaisir de vous aprandre que je souffre moins et que je vien de finir une très belle vente de 728 articles; et en même temps je rasamble les tableaux que je vous destinne, qui partiron cette semainne sie[2] en trois caisse, dont je

[1] The picture painted for the Czarina was the 'Infant Hercules strangling the Serpents,' exhibited at the Academy in 1788. The artist received for it 1,500 guineas and a gold box with Catherine's cypher in diamonds (Leslie and Taylor, *Life and Times of Sir J. Reynolds*, 1865, vol. ii. p. 516).

[2] The writer throughout spells phonetically, with no regard to orthography or grammar.

vous joindré le détaille. Je suis bien facher de ne pas m' estre trouvé à Londres lors de la vente des tableaux de Mr Rigby. Il y avais de belle chauze. Le Sieur Vandergutts [1] m'envoy un Rembrand, qu'il a achetté 150 louis, qui avais eté vendue 500 chez nous, et il n'ent veult pas moin. Parlant de lui, il m'a ecrie une longue épître pour me prouvé que j'avais le plus grand tor de ne pas lui avoir vandue mes Poussin, et qu'il est bin mal à moy de les avoir vandu à son plus grand ennemie, qu'enfin il commencais une établilisement qui avais le plus grand succes, et qu'il voulais reprendre ses correspondance avec moy. Vous devé juger que je vins de lui en répondre sir page, par le quel je lui prouve qu'il veux tout gagner et atrapé les autres. Je lui et [ai] seulement die de prendre garde à faire comme il a déjà fait avec selui de Pall Mall, que quand à moy je ne verais rien; que je me félisittais de ce que sa brouille m'avais procuré le plaisir de vous connoitre et que nous etions fort comptant l'un de l'autre. Je deviens toujour insertain pour savoir sie je pouré aller en Engletaire, quard [car] il me vien de me venir trois vente de conséquence à faire. Dans la premier de Mr le baron d'Holbac [2] il y a une Baitte [bête] unique et superbe de Berchem, un Wowermanse ansamble de la plus grande bauté, une petite fette de villages par Teniers très riche, g[r]avé par Daulé, deux baux Lenain de 4 pids sur 3, une chaste Suzanne du Bourdon, enfin un Poussins qui a une grande réputation, représentant Jupiter et Calistau,[3] gravé daprès ce tableau par Daullé. Il a environ 5 pieds de large sur 4 pieds de hautt. Je n'en suis nullement comptant et ne vous l'enverrais pas. Je serais aize que Vendergutts le fit achetté en cachette. Je l'en et [ai] informé exprais, cela m'amuserais. Parlant de Poussins, votre Davide [4] s'est mon père qui le vendie au vieux Vandergutts pour 8000 livres. Je m'en resouvien bien ; le seul reproche étais que les figures étais les unes sur les autres sans asser de percepective aérienne pour moy. Je l'aime beaucoup et s'est un superbe tableau. . . .

---

[1] Benjamin van der Gucht, a portrait painter and picture dealer residing in London; died in 1794.

[2] Paul Henri Thiry, Baron d'Holbach, the encyclopædist; died 21 Jan., 1789.

[3] Smith's *Catalogue*, no. 183.

[4] Probably 'The Triumph of David,' Smith's *Catalogue*, no. 38; now in the Dulwich Gallery, no. 305.

'N° 1. Primer caisse.

'1. Un superbe le Brun venant de la vente de M^r le Comte de Vaudreuil [1784], de 2800 livres.

'2. La Charitté romainne[1] de l'espagnolette [Spagnoletto] de la vente de Mr de Callonne de 3000 livres. J'envois ses deux tableaux pour que Mr de Callonne se desside s'il le prand ou non ; alors vous seré le maître, s'il vous convienne, ou bien dans le cas contraire vous me les renverré.

'3. Un paysage de Ruisdal et les figures d'Ostade, de la vente Boissette [M. Randon de Boisset. 1777].

'4. Un superbe van Uden et les figures par Teniers de son plus bau faire ; venant de la vente de Horion à Bruxelles.

'5. Un tableaux en travers de Le Nain, no. 193 bis de la vente du 9 Dexembre dernier, dont je vous et [ai] envoié le catalogue.

'6. Une jeune fille en pied, par Vandick.

'7. St Luc paignant la vierge, par Stella. C'étais son morcau de réception à l'académie de St Luc, qui fu vandu lors de la destruction de cette accadémie il y a 7 à 8 anns.

'8. Un brouillard par Vernet, pint en Italie, que je ne [n'ai] pas hu le temps de faire rentoillé.

'Tout ces tablau sont de 3 à 4 pieds de long sur 2 à 3 de haut.'

The list of the contents of the other two cases appears to be lost, as well as the end of the letter.

6. J. B. P. LE BRUN to N. J. Desenfans ; Paris, 14 Dec., 1789. f. 13.

'Monsieur et amy. Ce n'est pas sans peinne que je prie le partie de vous envoler la notte que vous aller trouvé sic joientte. Vous devé facillement consevoir ce que sais [c'est] que de se deffaire d'aubejets que l'on a gardé depuis sie longtemps, où l'on n'a pas et-parger [épargné] l'argent pour ce les procurer, et enfin s'en deffaire au moment où nous alions en jou[i]r : Je dis nous, par ce que ma

[1] Included in the sale catalogue of the collection of M. de Calonne, London, 1795, 4th day, no. 51.

femme[1] partagais bien cette jouissance. Jé [j'ai] differé tant que je pu à vous emparler et à vous l'anvoier, expérant toujour que quelque rentre [rentrée] m'éviterais se sacriffice. Mon expoir n'est pas remplie. Je prend donc cette résolution telle qu'[u]n malade est forcé d'avallé un médicament bien amer pour retrouvé la santer ; au moin aureje la consolation, qu'il seron dans les mains d'une ami qui en jouira comme moy et qui saura les aprécier tout, chacun dans leur genre de beauté. En fesans la liste je ne voulais i mestre aucun prie separé ; sependant je crois nécesaire de vous en donné une apersue, afin que vous puissier dirriger plus facillement votre opinion sur cette masse.

'1°	Poussin	20000	48000 livres.
2°	Le Sueur	2400	
3°	C. du Jardin	4800	
4°	G. Sequalque	1200	
5°	Wina[n]tse	1000	
6°	Teniers	1500	
7°	Alexandre Veronese	3000	
8°	A. Correge	1000	
9°	Rubense Asomption	2400	
10°	Ph. Coning	1000	
11°	Rembrant	1700	
12°	G. Dow	1200	
13°	Guide	2000	
14°	2 Rubens	800	
15°	Sequedon	2000	
16°	Salvator Rosa	2000	

Partie des tableaux que je gardais depuis longtemps pour ma gallery, et que l'honneur me force à vandre.

'1° Le fameux Baccanalle[2] du Poussin venant du pallais delassé de Mr Rendon de Boisset et de Mr de Veaudreuil. Je [j'ai] toujour die que je ne l'avais pas, surtout à Mr de Callonne, à qui je die qu'il apartenais à Mr du Breuil, l'un de nos amateur et de mes bons amis. Et lui en fit offrire mill louis, et Vandergutts m'en a offert viengt

[1] See above, p. 210, n. 3. From what he says further on it may be inferred that the sale was necessitated by losses at play ; and the letter thus confirms Mad. Le Brun's account of the state of their affairs in 1789, and its cause.

[2] Smith's *Catalogue*, no. 221 ; now in the National Gallery, no. 62. Most of the pictures in this list are included in the sale catalogue of M. de Calonne's collection, London, 1795.

mille livres; quatres autres m'on demandé de fixer un prie et qu'il étais vendu. Hauteur 3 pieds ½; largeur 4 pieds 5 pouces. T[oile].

'2° Une St famille par Le Sueur, figures vu à mie corps, de son plus beau et de son plus précieux. Il se trouve gravé par Rousselet. Il m'a coutté près de 3 mil livres à la vente de Mr Collet il y a 4 année. Hauteur 13 pouces 3 lignes; largeur 15 pouces. B[ois].

'3° Une mache [marche?] d'animeaux,[1] qui traverse à guet une rivier basse, une fem, un enfant, &c., par Karel Du Jardin. La premier penser de ce tableau se trouve gravé dans son œuvre, s'est sa plus grand estempes. S'est un de ses ouvrages le plus parfait. Je le acquis à la vente de Mr le Chr de Clenne [Clène, 1786] 4800 livres. Hauteur 14 pouces; largeur 15 pouces.

'4° La Madeleinne à genoux en prier,[2] presque de grandeur naturel, chef d'œuvre de se maître. Il est gravé pasemitts [par Smith] en manier noir; l'estempes se van [vend] 36 [livres], quand el est belle—de Sequalken. J'achetté se tablau à la Hay 1500 florins. Hauteur 4 pied ½; largeur 3 pied, 5 pouces. T[oile].

'5° Par Winants. Un paysage[3] en hauteur avec figures et animeaux de la plus grande beauté. Il vien de la collection de Mr de Boisset, no. 55, vendu 1510 livres. Hauteur 19 pouces; largeur 17 pouces.

'6° David Teniers. Un dentiste,[4] composition de quatre figures de 9 pouces de p[r]oportion; tablau finie comme Gerardow, du plus parfait. Hauteur 15 pouces; largeur 11 pouces. [Bois]. Je l'achetté a Enverse [Anvers] 1800 livres à Beckmans.

'7° Alexandre Veroneze. Hercules et Onphal, riche et belle composition des plus agréable, de 7 figures, digne des plus beau Carracho. Hauteur 4 pieds un pouce ½; largeur 6 pieds 2 pouces; les figures de 4 pied de proportion.

'8° Antoinne Correge. Un vray tableau de se maître représentant St Sebastien atachée à un arbre. Hauteur 2 pieds 9 pouces; largeur 2 pieds 2 pouces; la figure a plus de 24 pouces de proportion. Sie le sujet n'est pas agréable, il fault consulter la rareté du maître.

'9° P. P. Rubens. L'asomption de la vierge, esquisse avanser du

---

[1] Smith's *Catalogue*, no. 41?

[2] 'The Magdalen and Lamp,' by Schalken; Smith's *Catalogue*, no. 44. Engraved by John Smith, 1793 (Nagler, no. 347).

[3] Smith's *Catalogue*, no. 20.

[4] Smith's *Catalogue*, no. 203?

tableau, qui est à la gallery de Dresde. Hauteur 3 pieds 2 pouces; largeur 2 pieds 3 pouces. B[ois].

'C'est une chause bien capital, que j'achetté a Enver plus de cent louis du Sieur Vergelot.

'10° Un paysage de Philipe Coning [P. de Koningk]; l'un des plus finie et des plus beau. Il a tout l'effet de Rembrand avec plus de finie et de verittė. Hauteur 22 pouces; largeur 31 pouces. T[oile]. S'est un vray chef d'œuvre.

'11° Rembrandt. Le charitable St Maritain,[1] très connu par l'estempes à la queu blanche, qui se vand 3 à 4 cent livres. Ce tableau vien du cabinet de Choiseul, n° 9, où il est gravé dans le receuil [de P. F. Basan, 1771, n° 43], et de la collection de Julien [Julienne, 1767] avant. Hauteur 9 pouces ½; largeur 7 pouces ½. B[ois].

'12° Gerardow [Gerard Dow]. Un jeune homme vue de profil,[2] avec toque et os colle [haut col], du plus beau de se maître. Il vien de la vente de Mr de Gagny, no. 106, vendu 1310 livres. Hauteur 5 pouces 3 lignes; largeur 4 pouces; de forme oval. B[ois].

'13° Guide. Leandre et Herauld [Hero], figures de grandeur naturel, tablau très capital de la vigeur de Guerchin, et d'une exécution ferme. Hauteur 4 pieds 7 pouces; largeur 6 pieds 3 pouces. T[oile].

'14° Rubens. Deux belles esquisse[3] du plafond des Jésuitte d'Anvers, qui on été brulé. L'un est la reine de Sabat [Sheba]; et Ester devan Asuerus. Ils son gravé daprès ses esquisse dans la suitte du plafond des Jésuitte. Il vienn du Cabinet de Julienne. Hauteur 18 pouces; largeur 17 pouces. B[ois].

'15° Sequedon [Bart. Schedone]. Une S^t famille[4] à my corps, tableau vray et des plus beau de se maître. Hauteur 2 pieds; largeur 18 pouces. C'est aussi rare que les Correge. B[ois].

'16° Salvator Roza. Un magnifique paysage des plus capital et claire. S'est celui que je vous avais proposer de troquer. Il est san bordure. Hauteur 6 pieds; largeur 9 pieds. T[oile].

'17° L'intérieur d'une chambre[5] par Adrien Ostade, dont je vous

---

[1] 'The Good Samaritan,' Smith's *Catalogue*, no. 119.

[2] The description answers to that of no. 47 in Smith's *Catalogue*, sold at M. Blondel de Gagny's sale, 1777, for 1,320 livres; but the measurement differs.

[3] Smith's *Catalogue*, nos. 642, 643.

[4] Probably no. 63 in the Calonne sale, 4th day.

[5] Smith's *Catalogue*, no. 57. Engraved in Le Brun's *Galerie des Peintres Flamands, Hollandais et Allemands*, Paris, 1792, vol. i. p. 73.

fait passer l'estempes, gravé pour ma collection. S'est l'un des plus beau qui existe. Il vien du cabinet de Fisan d'Amsterdame, où il a coutté 14000 livres, et enfin de la vente de Mr de Boisset, no. 69. Hauteur 15 pouces 9 lignes; largeur 21 pouces. B[ois]. Prix 7200 livres. C'est un chef d'œuvre d'armonie et de couleur. Il est très rare de trouvé des femmes [?] dans ses tableaux. Opservé que tout ce qui vien de Mr de Boisset étais le cabinet le plus choisi qu'est [ait] existé.

'18° Un tableau du plus précieux de Philipe Wowermanse, gravé dans son œuvre par Jean Moyreau, no. 28, intitulé 4iers rafréchissement.[1] Il vien de Mde la comtesse de Verrue; de Mr de Ravanne; et Mr de Callonne voulu bien l'achetté pour moy de Mr Servat amateur pour 6000 livres. Hauteur 18 pouces; largeur 24 pouces. T[oile]. L'on y conte plus de 30 figures principalle, &c. [Prix] 6000 livres.

'Vous jugé bien qu'il n'en n'est aucun que je n'u vendue à bon bénéfisse, sie j'u voulu m'en deffaire. Je [j'ai] refuser pour plusieur de grand prie.

'Il est inutille, que je vous dise, qu'il n'i a rien d'équivoque et que tout est de la plus belle conservation. S'est, je crois, vous en dirre asser que de vous dirre que je les réservais depuis longtemps pour moy et en orné ma gallery. Je vous donneré tout cette partie[2] pour deux mill Louis; je seré loin de gagne. Je veux vendre tout cette partie ensemble :—1°, parceque j'e [j'ai] besoin de cette somme, que je tirrerais en quatre partie de mois en mois; 2°, parceque, déparan tout ma collection et i renonsan, il fault que je place tout. Vous verré que seux qui sont grand ou que seux qui pourrais vous moin convenir, je [j'ai] hu soin de faire de grand sacriffice, affin que vous puissier y faire un bon bénéfisse même en le vendant mal.

'Le Poussin seul peut et dois vous paier toute cette partie, aprais quoy il vous retira six tableaux plus beau les un que les autres dans leur genre.

'Je vous demandré ausie sie vous ne pourier pas me faire placé une collection de pierre gravé antiques en relief et en creux. C'est un choix bien rare, &c.

---

1 'Quartiers de Rafraîchissement,' Smith's *Catalogue*, no. 333.

2 Exclusive apparently of nos. 17 and 18, which were an after-addition, and are priced separately.

'M^de^ Le Brun[1] vien d'estre resue des académie de Parme, Bologne, &c. El est à Rome. Je ne [n'ai] pas le projets d'aller dans se pais sesie tault [ce pays-ci si tôt]. Tout à vous, Le Brun.'

7. J. B. P. LE BRUN to N. J. Desenfans: sees by his letter of the 19th inst. that it is thought that the Palais Royal collection will come to England, but believes that all idea of this is given up; sends him the pictures as below, 'pour m'aquitté avec vous de la lettre de change de 3696 livres'; Paris, 27 Oct., 1790. f. 17.

The pictures are eight in number:—'La transfiguration, tableau capital du Sequedon, d'environ 3 pieds de hauteur sur 2 pie[ds] 4 pouces de largeur'; 'La vierge tenant l'anfan Jésus, par Simon da Contariny, die le Pezarese. Il a gravé lui même se tableau à l'au forte'; 'St Cicille touchan de l'orgue,[2] figures de grandeur naturel, dans le hautt une gloire d'anges, par Augustain Carrache. Ce tableau a été un peu frotté, mais cen cela il vaudrais 10000 livres. Hauteur 5 pieds; largeur 3 pieds 3 pouces'; 'La vierge, l'enfan Jésus et St Jean par Salsauferatte, très beau tableau dans le genre de la Madonna del Sedia de Raphael. Vandergutts a vu ce tableau et voulais me l'achetté. Comme je vous le reservais avec les autres je ne pas voulu lui vendre. Hauteur 3 pieds; largeur 2 pieds'; 'Un repas composé de 3 figures à mie corps qui fon de la musique,[3] par Le Nain. Hauteur 12 pouces; largeur 15 pouces'; 'Un paisage par Akert [Hackert] enrichie de figures, barque, &c., par Vernet. Hauteur 2 pieds 4 pouces; largeur 2 pieds 9 pouces'; 'Le Christe, composition de 4 figures, par Jacques Stella. Hauteur 2 pieds; largeur 16 [pouces]'; 'Un paisage eclairé au soleil couchan, par Pinaquer [Pijnacker] en Italie, du plus beau stile. Hauteur 2 pieds ½; largeur 3 pieds ½.'

8. JOHN POPKIN to his brother, Pan. Popkin, at Chelsea,

[1] Mad. Le Brun left Paris in Oct., 1789. Her name was inscribed on the list of *émigrés*, and she passed the next twelve years in Italy, Germany and Russia. She was permitted to return to France at the end of 1801.

[2] Apparently no. 334 in the Dulwich Gallery; ascribed in the new catalogue to an unknown artist of the Bolognese school, and said to have been formerly ascribed to Annibale Carracci.

[3] Dulwich Gallery, no. 158.

declining to accept from the latter a seal given him by Noel Desenfans; Swansea, 12 Feb., 1794. f. 19.

9. 'PICTURES to be sold': a list, in the hand of N. J. Desenfans, of three hundred and seventy pictures, arranged according to the rooms in which they were hung, with prices attached; no date. f. 21.

The prices are generally low, the largest sum being for no. 170, 'Samson and Delila,' by Rubens [Dulwich Gallery, no. 168. After Rubens], 800 guineas. A few other pictures now at Dulwich may perhaps be included.

10. 'CATALOGUE d'une collection précieuse de [74] tableaux des trois écoles, provenants des plus belles et anciennes collections qu'il y ait eu en France, appartenant au citoyen Viller, qui vendra le tout ensemble ou par école seulement si l'on en préféroit une ou deux. Il ne vendra qu'en Guinées'; [*circ.* 1795]. With critical remarks in the margin in the hand of J. B. P. Le Brun. In pamphlet form, stitched. f. 27.

11. MEMORIAL from Noel [Joseph] Desenfans, 'ci-devant Consul Général de Pologne en Angleterre,' to Paul I., Emperor of Russia, praying him to discharge a debt of 623*l.* sterling, being the unpaid balance, with interest, of a sum of 1,800*l.* advanced by him on behalf of the government of Stanislaus, King of Poland, in 1793, to the Chevalier Bukaty, Polish minister in England; London, 6 May, 1798. *Copy*, in the hand of Desenfans. f. 40.

12. 'MÉMOIRE' addressed by N. J. Desenfans to Alexander I., Emperor of Russia: In 1790 the Prince Primate, brother and first minister of Stanislaus, King of Poland, persuaded the memorialist to give up his business (by which he was making between 2,000*l.* and 3,000*l.* a year), and devote himself to the service of Poland, 'en l'assurant que pour l'en dédommager Sa Majesté Polonnoise lui donneroit une charge publique à Londres et celle de chercher et d'achetter pour elle les beaux tableaux qu'on offriroit en vente à des prix raisonables'; began, therefore, to form the desired collection, and, some time after, received from the King a patent of nobility and the rank of colonel, together with the appointment of Polish Consul-General for Great Britain, but this office, far from being profitable, was only a source of expense and trouble; at the request of the Prince Primate advanced 1,800*l.* to the Chevalier Bukaty, Polish minister, to enable him to quit England, and incurred also a heavy outlay in relieving a crowd of Polish refugees after the revolution at Warsaw, in return for which the King, in spite of his distress, sent him two sums amounting together to a little more than 1,300*l.*, assuring him at the same time that when his own affairs were re-established all his expenses should be paid; although matters went from worse to worse, still hoped for ultimate payment for the collection, which had already cost 9,000*l.*, but on the King's death claimed the protection of the English Government, and prayed them to use their interest in his favour with the Russian Court; Lord Grenville, Secretary of State, having admitted the justice of his claim, requested Lord Whitworth, ambassador at St. Petersburg, to support it, and sent him the proofs, letters, and memoir, but unfortunately the harmony between the two Courts soon after came to an end, and Lord Whitworth returned, leaving all the papers among the archives of the Embassy; when the archives were afterwards burnt, to prevent their falling into the hands of the Russian Government, the proofs of his claim perished with them, but the facts are within the memory of Lord Grenville and Lord Whitworth, and can be otherwise established; prays, therefore, for a sum of about 4,000*l.*, to compensate him for the loss of his business, advances of money, expenses, with interest, on account of the pictures, and his charges and lack of emoluments as Consul-General. When Lord Grenville, towards the end of 1799, sent the memorialist's first memoir to St. Petersburg, an offer of the collection was made to the late Emperor for about 9,000*l.*, its then value at cost price; to make it more complete, has since added to it some fine pictures of the Italian school, bringing the cost up to 12,000 guineas, and offers it for this sum; if the Emperor is unwilling to add these pictures to his gallery, must put them up to auction, but, as sales by auction cost ten per cent. including Government dues, this will cause an expense of more than 1,000*l.*, which he prays the Emperor to allow him, for, having expended so much care and trouble in forming the collection, 'il seroit dur pour lui être aujourd'hui à de tels fraix pour s'en défaire;' his claim, therefore, amounts in all to 5,000*l.*, the recovery of which he solicits with confidence 'de l'auguste Souverain qui possède et règne aujourd'hui sur les états au service desquels cette dette fut contractée,' &c.; London, 22 June, 1801. *Copy.* Preceded by a draft, in the hand of N. J. Desenfans, of the earlier portion of the memorial, somewhat differently worded. ff. 41, 42.

13. LORD WHITWORTH[1] to N. J. Desenfans, in answer to a request for the return of his papers, to the effect that they were left with the rest of the archives of the English Embassy when he quitted St. Petersburg, and possibly shared the fate of the other correspondence when the archives were destroyed, some time after his departure, to prevent their

[1] Charles Whitworth, cr. Lord Whitworth 1800, Viscount Whitworth 1813, and Earl Whitworth 1815; died 1825.

falling into the hands of the Russian Government; will, however, desire his former secretary, Rev. Mr. Pitt, who is returning to Russia, to search for them and let him know the result; Knowles, 14 June, 1801. In duplicate, both *copies*. ff. 46, 48.

Printed, Blanch, *Hist. of Camberwell*, 1875, p. 481.

14. N. J. DESENFANS to Lord Whitworth, acknowledging the above, and requesting him to certify, under the enclosed memorial, the receipt of the papers from the Secretary of State's office, and also to give him two or three lines for Lord Hawkesbury; London, 22 June, 1801. *Copy*. f 46*b*.

15. LORD WHITWORTH to N. J. Desenfans, enclosing a certificate that he received from Lord Grenville, Foreign Secretary, in 1799, the papers referred to in the memorial, and that they were left at St. Petersburg and probably destroyed with the rest of the archives after his departure; London, 24 June, 1801.[1] *Copy*. f. 47.

16. 'TO BE INSURED at the Fire Insurance office the following pictures, the property of Noel [Joseph] Desenfans, esq., at his houses, nos. 38 & 39 Charlotte St., Portland Place, London, July 6th, 1804, & supposed to be painted by the following masters and valued as under.' f. 49.

The list is as follows, the numbers in brackets being those attached to the same pictures in the Dulwich Gallery, according to the new catalogue[2]:—

---

[1] For a history by Desenfans of the Polish collection, with an account of the above correspondence (artt. 11–15), see the introduction to his *Descriptive Catalogue*, 1802, reprinted in the *Catalogue of the Dulwich Gallery*, 1880, App. *A*, p. 199.

[2] Some of the unnumbered pictures may also be at Dulwich, but, owing to the brevity of the descriptions here given, it is impossible to identify them.

		£
1.	St. Cecilia with Angels—S. Rosa	150
2.	Portrait of Mrs. Siddons as the Tragic Muse [340]—Reynolds	200
3.	Our Lady of the Rosary [347]—Murillo	1,200
4.	St. Sebastian [339. After Guido]—Guido	500
5.	Christ going to Mount Calvary [329. Spanish school] Moralez	300
6.	Infant Samuel [285]—Reynolds	100
7.	A Cardinal [333]—Paul Veronese	600
8.	Beggar Boys [283]—Murillo	600
9.	Ditto [216]—Ditto	400
10.	The Shepherds' Offering [1]—Carracci	1,200
11.	Flower Girl [248]—Murillo	800
12.	Madonna and Child [255. After Correggio]—Correggio	500
13.	A Saint [306]—Raphael	150
14.	Ditto [307]—Ditto	100
15.	Cupids reaping [117. After Rubens]—Rubens	100
16.	Child asleep [330. School of Murillo]—Murillo	100
17.	A Nymph and Cupid—Titian	800
18.	The Annunciation—Zucarelli	40
19.	Holy Family [302. School of Schedone]—Schidone	100
20.	A Woman and child in a cradle—Maas	30
21.	St. Ignatius exorcising [2]—Rubens	300
22.	Good Shepherd [262. After Murillo]—Murillo	150
23.	A Landscape [11]—Wynants	50
24.	Ditto [12]—Ditto	50
25.	The Assumption [341? After Murillo]—Murillo	100
26.	Achilles contemplating armour—Rubens	60
27.	Venus and Cupid [226? Italian school]—Dominechino	300
28.	A Spanish Shepherd—Murillo	200
29.	A small Landscape [207? After Rubens]—Rubens	100
30.	A Corps de Garde [50]—Teniers	150
31.	A Landscape and Cattle [192]—Cuyp	100
32.	Philip the 4th [309]—Velasquez	200
33.	A small Landscape [76]—Cuyp	250

[1] Desenfans' *Descriptive Catalogue*, 1802, no. 1.

[2] Desenfans' *Catalogue*, no. 83.

		£
34.	A Peasant [148?]—Teniers	30
35.	Ditto [149?]—Ditto	30
36.	A Madonna—Italian	80
37.	A Landscape [202]—Vernet	80
38.	A Sea Piece [?]—Vanderveldt	400
39.	A Landscape with Pigs [60]—Teniers	100
40.	A large Landscape—N. Poussin	500
41.	A small ditto—Ditto	150
42.	The Landlord—Teniers	50
43.	The Chimney-sweeper—Ditto	50
44.	Dutch Boors [190]—A. Ostade	300
45.	A Holy Family [165. After Albani]—Albano	100
46.	A Ball [210]—Watteau	200
47.	A Conversation—Ditto	150
48.	A small Holy Family [249]—N. Poussin	200
49.	Wise Men's Offering [291]—Ditto	1,200
50.	Jupiter and Antiope [325. School of Poussin]—Ditto	200
51.	Apollo and a Poet [295]—Ditto	500
52.	Triumph of David [305]—Ditto	1,200
53.	Flight into Egypt [310]—Ditto	400
54.	Renaldo and Armida [315]—Ditto	500
55.	Nursing Infant Jupiter [300]—Ditto	1,000
56.	The Education of Bacchus [115. School of Poussin]—Ditto	350
57.	A Landscape with Horses and Figures—Both	600
58.	A Young Lady [182?]—Rubens	150
59.	Lord Ligonier on Horseback [1]—Reynolds	100
60.	A large Landscape with Shepherds [163?]—Cuyp	600
61.	A Young Prince on Horseback [194. After Velasquez] Velasquez	400
62.	A Landscape—Vandermeulen	150
63.	A large Landscape [175? After Rubens]—Rubens	500
64.	A Landscape with Sheep [46]—Teniers	200
65.	Smugglers Defeated [2]—Sir F. Bourgeois	100
66.	A Little Girl—Sir Joshua Reynolds	100

[1] Desenfans' *Catalogue*, no. 187; now in the National Gallery, no. 143.

[2] Desenfans' *Catalogue*, no. 184.

		£
67.	A Little Girl—Sir Joshua Reynolds	100
68.	A Funeral Procession [82]—Sir F. Bourgeois	100
69.	Man's Head—Leonardo da Vinci	150
70.	A Sea Piece [275 ?]—Claude	500
71.	A Landscape [264 ?]—Ditto	600
72.	A Sea-port [270 ?]—Ditto	400
73.	A large Landscape [202]—Vernet	200
74.	Pluto and Proserpine [284. Venetian school]—Mola	80
75.	St. John in the Desert—Ditto	80
76.	St. Francis at the Altar [296. Ag. Carracci]—L. Carracci	150
77.	An Old Woman Eating[1] [85]—Brakelmkemp.	80
78.	A Landscape with Fishermen [163 ?]—Cuyp	100
79.	A Landscape with Sheep [147]—Weeninx	100
80.	Murder of the Innocents [252]—Lebrun	500
81.	A Flower Piece—Young Vanhuysum	150
82.	A Landscape with Horses—Wouvermans	500
83.	A Cart and Figures in a Landscape [228]—Ditto	600
84.	Return from the Chase [136]—Ditto	400
85.	Flower Piece—Old Vanhuysum	500
86.	Mary de Medicis [187. After Rubens]—Rubens	150
87.	An upright Landscape [160 ?]—Berchem	200
88.	A Girl [206]—Rembrandt	500
89.	A Landscape [62 ?]—Karel du Jardin	150
90.	A Farmyard [185]—Teniers	300
91.	St. Cecilia [324. B. Gennari]—Guercino	200
92.	A large Landscape with Cattle—Paul Potter	400
93.	A Magdalen [332. School of Guido]—Guido	200
94.	A Frost Piece [116]—Teniers	150
95.	A Landscape [131 ?]—Hobbima	250
96.	Recovery of a Child [143]—Reynolds	50
97.	Salvator Mundi [328. Bolognese school]—Guercino	30
98.	A Madonna—Guido	30
99.	Sampson and Dalilah [168. School of Rubens]—Rubens	800
100.	The three Graces—Vanderwerff	800
101.	Saints [78. School of Rubens]—Rubens	80

[1] Described in Desenfans' *Catalogue*, no. 129, as by Gerard Dow. It is also under his name in the new catalogue of the Dulwich Gallery; but the editor, Dr. J. P. Richter, expresses his doubts whether it is really by that master. Quirijn van Brekelenkamp was a pupil of Dow.

		£
102.	Horses and Figures [114?]—Cuyp	100
103.	Ditto [156?]—Ditto	80
104.	A small Landscape with Cows [22. After P. Potter] P. Potter	50
105.	Ditto with Cattle [72]—A. Vandevelde	50
106.	Landscape with Monks [159]—S. Rosa	200
107.	Two Saints in a Landscape [265]—Carracci . . .	60
108.	An upright Landscape—Teniers	100
109.	Ditto—Ditto	100
110.	Horatius defending the Bridge [319]—Lebrun	500
111.	Virgin and Infant Saviour [135]—Vandyke .	800
112.	An Emblematical [124? School of Vandijck]—Ditto	400
113.	A Landscape, Cattle, and Figures—Cuyp . .	1,000
114.	A large Landscape—Teniers	300
115.	Ditto with Cattle—Ditto	300
116.	Holy Family [327. After A. del Sarto]—A. del Sarto	400
117.	A small Sea Piece—Vandeveldt	100
118.	A Lady playing on the Harpsicord [106]—G. Dow	500
119.	A small Landscape—Teniers	100
120.	Ditto—Ditto	100
121.	Landscape with Figures—P. Potter	200
122.	A Conversation [107]—A. Ostade	300
123.	Cornucopia [171]—Rubens	100
124.	Venus and Adonis [263. After Titian]—Titian .	500
		£37,370

'I declare that the above-mentioned pictures are either marked at or under their value; London, July 6th, 1804.'

17. ISÂC BOURGEOIS to N. J. Desenfans, introducing 'une jeune élléve qui est sy neuve que sy elle sortoit d'un cloitre,' probably his daughter and the sister of Sir P. F. Bourgeois; no date. f. 52.

18. TH. BOURGEOIS to her cousin, Sir P. F. Bourgeois, requesting his aid to facilitate her return to her sister Kitty in Switzerland; Dublin, 25 July . . . . f. 54.

19. SIR PETER FRANCIS BOURGEOIS to the Duke of Portland, stating his desire to purchase the reversion in fee, at the end of a term of 97 years from 25 Mar., 1777, of two houses in Portland Road and an adjoining house in Charlotte Street, with the view of completing his present intentions, 'which are to bequeath the whole of the late Mr. Desenfans' collection, with the additions which I have made thereto, in such manner that the same, supported by funds which I mean to appropriate for that purpose, may be gratuitously open under certain regulations to artists as well as to the public, and thus form not only a source of professional improvement, but also an object of national exhibition,' &c.; Jan., 1810. *Copy.* f. 57.

Printed, in great part, together with the answer, in the *Catalogue of the Dulwich College Gallery*, 1880, App. C, p. 205.

On f. 56 is a note :—'These three papers [artt. 19–21] were given to me on March 4th, 1811, by Mr. J. H. Greenwell, one of the executors of Sir P. F. Bourgeois, with a request that they might be deposited in the Library of Dulwich College. T[homas] J[enyns] S[mith, Preacher-fellow].'

20. THE DUKE OF PORTLAND[1] to Sir P. F. Bourgeois, replying that he has neither the power nor the inclination to comply with his request; Welbeck, 4 Jan., 1810. Signed, 'Scott Portland.' f. 59.

21. ATTESTED COPY of the will of Sir Peter Francis Bourgeois, knt., R.A., bequeathing a life interest in his estate, real and personal, to Margaret, widow of N. J. Desenfans, with reversion of the whole, including his collection of pictures, in trust to the Master, Warden, and Fellows of Dulwich College; 20 Dec., 1810. f. 61.

Printed, in part, *Cat. of the Dulwich College Gallery*, 1880, App. B, p. 202.

Small folio, ff. 65.

[1] William Henry Cavendish Bentinck, succ. as fourth Duke 1809, died 1854. He married Henrietta, dau. and co-heir of Gen. John Scott, of Balcomie.

MS. No. XVII.

'A BRIEF CATALOGUE of Pictures late the property of Sir [Peter] Francis Bourgeois, R.A., with the sizes and proportions of the pictures,' by J[ohn] Britton [the antiquary, b. 1771, d. 1857]; 24 May, 1813.

'J. Britton submits this as a very concise and imperfect catalogue of the collection of pictures; and has adopted the names of many of the artists and the subjects of their works generally from the late Sir Francis Bourgeois' communications to Jas. Gill, his servant.'

The pictures are three hundred and seventy-one in number, and are catalogued according to their position on the walls of the several rooms, &c., as shown in a plan at the top of each page.

Small quarto, ff. 34.

MUNIMENTS.

(SECTION I.)

DOCUMENTS relating to the Theatre and Bear Garden; 1546–1662:—

1. BARGAIN AND SALE[1] by Rauf Symondes, of Cley, co. Norfolk, gent., to Thomas Langham, of London, fishmonger, for 80*l.*, of 3 tenements, in the tenure of Richard Richardson, John Bucke, and John Edmondes, in Goldingelane, and one tenement, in the tenure of William Gill, in Whitecrosse Strete, in the parish of St. Giles without Cripplegate, London. Dat. 12 July, 38 Hen. VIII. [1546]. *Copy.*

2, 3. BARGAIN AND SALE by Thomas Langham, of London, fishmonger, and Robert Langham, his son and heir, to William Gill, of the parish of St. Giles without Cripplegate, gardener, for 100*l.*, of 3 tenements, &c., in the same parish, two on the east side of Goldingelane and the third on the west side of Whitecross Street, in the tenure of the same Will. Gill or his assigns. Dat. 29 Jan., 8 Eliz. [1566]. Signed; with one seal. Followed by a copy of the same.

4. FEOFFMENT from Thomas Langham and Robert Langham, his son, to William Gill, of the same three tene-

[1] This is the first deed entered by E. Alleyn in the list of 'evidences' for the Fortune Theatre in MS. viii., above, f. 27.

ments, &c. Dat. 29 Jan., 8 Eliz. [1566]. *Lat.* Signed; with seals.

5, 6. FINE by Thomas Langham and Elizabeth, his wife, to William Gill of the same three tenements, &c., for 100*l.* Dat. Mich. term, 10 Eliz. [1568]. *Lat.* In duplicate.

7. LETTERS PATENT of Qu. Elizabeth, granting to Raphe Bowes,[1] esq., the office of master of 'our game pastymes and sportes, that is to saie of all and everie our beares bulles and mastyve dogges,' in 'as large and ample manner and forme as Cuthbert Vaughan or Sir Richard Longe, deceased.' Dat. 2 June, aº 15 [1573]. Exemplified at the request of Morgan Pope, merchant, 18 Nov., aº 28 [1585].

8. LEASE[2] from Ambrose Nicholas and William Boxe, aldermen, and other parishioners of St. Mildred, Bread Street, London, to William Gryffyn, of London, vintner, of a messuage, &c., called the 'litle Rose,' with two gardens adjoining, in the parish late called St. Margaret's, then and now in the parish of St. Saviour, Southwark, for 31 years at a rent of 7*l.*, the same having been granted to the par. of St. Mildred, 3 Dec., 1552, by Thomasyn, widow of Raphe Symonds, of London,

---

[1] See above, MS. ii. art 1. The original patent appears to be in the possession of Mr. Collier (*Mem. of Edw. Alleyn*, p. 70). He speaks of it, however, as granted to John Dorrington, instead of Ralph Bowes; but the date, which is the same as that of the above document, shows that he must be in error. He mentions this exemplification (p. 60), but wrongly dates it 8 Nov., 1586, and makes this the date not of the exemplification, but of the actual grant. Neither the original patent nor the exemplification is included by Edw. Alleyn in the list of 'Wrightings of the beargarden' in MS. viii. f. 43*b*. This list contains thirty-three deeds, together with ten bonds, but not one of the number is to be found among the Muniments. Morgan Pope seems to have derived his interest in the garden from several parties, including Ralph Bowes and Edward Bowes, and to have made it over to one Hayes, from whom it passed to Burnabie, and so to Edw. Alleyn. See above, p. 67, n. 4, and *Alleyn Papers*, p. xvii.

[2] See the note in *Mem. of Edw. Alleyn*, p. 189, concerning this and following deeds relating to the Rose.

fishmonger. Dat. 20 Nov., 17 Eliz. [1574]. Signed; with seals. Endorsed by Edw. Alleyn, 'ye lease of St Myldredes of ye rose.'

9. WILL of William Gill, of the parish of St. Giles without Cripplegate, London, gardener, bequeathing, *inter alia*, his dwelling-house and four tenements in Gouldinglane, lately purchased from Thomas Langham, to Katherine, his wife, for life, and after to Daniel Gill, the elder; and four other tenements to Richard Yaton in tail, with remainder to Daniel Gill, the younger. Dat. 21 Apr., 1575. With probate, 5 Nov., 1576.

10. ASSIGNMENT by William Griffen, of London, vintner, to Robert Withens, of London, vintner, for 105*l.*, of his lease of 'the litle rose,' as above, no. 8. Dat. 11 Dec., 1579. Signed; with seal.

11. POWER OF ATTORNEY from Daniel Gill, the elder, and Daniel Gill, the younger, of the Isle of Man, to Patrick Brewe, one of the overseers of the will of William Gill, to receive from Katheryn, widow of William Gill, and his co-overseers all deeds, &c., relating to tenements bequeathed them in Golden Lane and the balance of a legacy of 25*l.* Dat. 14 Feb., 22 Eliz. [1580]. Signed.

12, 13. LEASE from Daniel Gill, the elder, of the Isle of Man, yeoman, to Patrick Brewe, of London, goldsmith, of six messuages, &c., five on the east side of Gouldinge Lane, and the other on the west side of Whitecrosse Street, in the parish of St. Giles without Cripplegate, co. Midd., late belonging to William Gill, and before to Thomas Langham and Rafe Symondes, for 41 years for 13*l.* 6*s.* 8*d.* in hand and a rent of 12*l.* Dat. 11 July, 26 Eliz. [1584]. Signed; with seal. Followed by the counterpart.

14. FEOFFMENT from Daniel Gill, the elder, to Daniel Gill, clerk, his son, of the same six messuages, &c., late belonging to William Gill and in the tenure of Patrick Brewe. Dat. 10 Oct., 26 Eliz. [1584]. *Lat.* With seal.

15. ASSIGNMENT by Robert Withens, of London, vintner, to Philip Hinchley [Henslowe], of London, dyer, of the lease of the 'Little Rose,' in the parish of St. Saviour, Southwark, as above, no. 8.[1] Dat. 24 Mar., 27 Eliz., 1584[5]. Signed; with seal of arms.

16. DEED of partnership between Philip Hinshley [Henslowe], of London, dyer, and John Cholmley, of London, grocer, for 8¼ years, in a parcel of ground on the Bankside in the parish of St. Saviour, Southwark, and in a playhouse to be erected thereon at the cost of Phil. Henslowe by John Grygges, carpenter; the said John Cholmley to pay 816*l.* in quarterly instalments of 25*l.* 10*s.*, to have half the receipts, and to hold a small tenement at the south end of the ground near Maiden Lane and Rosse Alley, 'to keepe victualinge in, or to putt to any other vse.' Dat. 10 Jan., 29 Eliz., 1586[7]. Signed by John Cholmley.

17. WILL of Daniel Gill, of St. Andrew's, Isle of Man, clerk, containing bequests to Daniel Gill, his father, Katherine, his mother, William and Edward, his brothers, Jony, his sister, and others, and leaving his lands, tenements, &c., in London in trust for Katherine, Elizabeth, Jane and Margaret, his daughters, with a charge of 6*l.* yearly for life to Elizabeth,

[1] The rent of 7*l.* on this lease 'pd. unto St Mildreds' is included by Henslowe in a list of his yearly rents in 1602 (*Diary*, p. 263).

his wife. Dat. 25 May, 1592. Paper. Signed; with seal. Proved at Douglas, 28 Nov., 1592.

18. LETTERS PATENT of Queen Elizabeth, granting to Philip Hensley [Henslowe], esq., upon the surrender of a former patent to Raphe Bowes, the office of master 'of our games pastymes and sports,' &c. [see above, no. 7]. Dat. [*ante* June, 1598]. *Not executed.* With alterations by Henslowe, adapting the wording to the reign of James I., the grant to be in succession to John Dorntone [Dorrington].

Printed, *Mem. of Edw. Alleyn*, p. 213.

19. WARRANT from Jacob Meaden [Meade], keeper of the Queen's 'gayme of Beares, Bulls and dogges,' commissioning John Cullyver to act as his deputy, to take up mastiff dogs, &c., for the Queen's service, and to bait in any place within her dominions. Dat. 24 Nov., 42 Eliz. [1599].

20. ASSIGNMENT by Patrick Brewe, of London, goldsmith, to Edward Allen, of St. Saviour's, Southwark, gent., of the lease from Daniel Gill, sen., as above, nos. 12, 13. Dat. 22 Dec., 42 Eliz., 1599. Signed; with seal. With bond in 250*l.* attached.

21. DRAFT of the preceding assignment. Paper, 4 sheets. *Imperfect.*

22. CONTRACT by Peter Streete, of London, carpenter, with Philip Henslowe and Edward Allen, of St. Saviour's, Southwark, gentlemen, to erect, for the sum of 440*l.*, a 'newe howse and stadge for a Plaiehowse .. nere Goldinge Lane in the parishe of Ste Giles withoute Cripplegate of London,' the same to be 'sett square,' 80 feet each way without and 55 feet each way within, and to be three storeys in height, and, in its arrangements, like 'the late erected Plaiehowse on the Banck in the saide parishe of S[te] Saviours called the Globe.' Dat. 8 Jan., 42 Eliz., 1599 [1600]. Counterpart; signed 'P. S.' On the back are acquittances and notes of payments on account, 8 Jan., 1599 [1600]–11 June, 1600.

Printed, Malone, *Shakespeare*, 1821, vol. iii. p. 338; Halliwell, *Illustrations*, p. 81.

23, 24. LEASE from Daniel, William and Edmond Gill, of the Isle of Man, yeomen, to John Garrett, of London, clothworker, for 21 years, at a rent of 12*l.*, of the premises as above, nos. 12, 13, the term to begin at the expiration of the lease to Patrick Brewe. Dat. 30 June, 43 Eliz., 1601. Signed; with seals. Followed by the counterpart.

25. LETTERS PATENT of James I., granting to John Darrington [Dorrington], gentleman pensioner, the office of master of 'our game and pastimes and sportes' of 'beares bulles and mastiffe dogges,' with a fee of 10*d.* a day and 4*d.* for his deputy, in confirmation of his patent of 11 Aug., 40 Eliz. [1598]. Dat. 14 July, a° 1 [1603]. *Official copy.*

26. BOND from Abraham Savere, of Westminster, gent., to Francis Hensley [Henslowe] and James Browne, of Southwark, gentt., in 40*l.*, to secure the payment to Josua Speed, of Westminster, gent., of 10*l.*, for which they are jointly bound. Dat. 25 Oct., 2 Jas. I., 1604. Signed; with seal.

27, 28, 29. AWARD by William Norres, clerk, vicar of Kirke Lonan, Isle of Man, Nicholas Moore, yeoman, William Crowe, parson of Kirke Bride, John Vescye, Constable of Rushen Castle, and John [Philips, 1605–1633], Bishop of Sodor and Man, in a dispute between Daniel Gill, the elder, and Katherine, Elizabeth, Jane and Margaret, daughters of Daniel Gill, the younger, his son, deceased, whereby land, tenements, &c., in Whitecrosse Street and Goldingelane, in the par. of St. Giles without Cripplegate, London, are divided between William Gill and Edmond Gill, sons of Daniel Gill, the elder, and the said Katherine, Elizabeth, Jane and Margaret, with a proviso that the said Daniel Gill and Isabell, wife of William Norres and widow of Daniel Gill, the younger, shall not be molested in their life-interest in their several moieties of rent, and that 32*l.* shall be paid by Daniel, William and Edmond Gill to the said Katherine, Elizabeth, Jane and Margaret. Dat. 19 Dec., 3 Jas. I., 1605. Signed; with seals. Followed by the counterpart and a copy, the latter having attached to it a copy of the bond as above, MS. i. art. 43.

30. LEASE from Thomas Towne, of St. Saviour's, Southwark, gent., to William Pearls, of Lambeth, waterman, of a tenement, &c., in Lambeth marsh for 21 years, for 3*l.* in hand and a rent of 26*s.* 8*d.* Dat. 5 May, 5 Jas I., 1607. Counterpart, signed; with seal.

31. LEASE from Thomas Garland, of St. Saviour's, Southwark, gent., to Philip Henslowe and Edward Alleyn, esquires, of 3½ acres of pasture called 'Longe Slippe,' in the par. of Lambeth, for 14¼ years, for 7*l.* 10*s.* in hand and a rent of 6*l.*, the same being held by the said Thomas Garland on lease from Mathye Bradburye. Dat. 28 June, 6 Jas. I., 1608. Signed; with seal. Endorsed by Edw. Alleyn, 'beargarden.'

32. GRANT from Edward Alleyn, of Dulwich, esq., to Thomas Towne, of St. Saviour's, Southwark, gent., and Agnes, his wife, of an annuity of 12*l.* for 31 years, charged upon Dulwich manor and other his lands, &c., in Camberwell, in consideration of 90*l.* in hand and the surrender of copyhold lands, &c., in Kennington manor to the use of themselves for life, and after to the use of the said Edw. Alleyn, his heirs and assigns for ever. Dat. 28 Oct., 6 Jas. I., 1608. Counterpart, signed.

33, 34. LEASE from Philip Henslowe and Edward Alleyn, of St. Saviour's, Southwark, esquires, to Thomas Downton, of St. Giles', Cripplegate, gent., of one-eighth of a fourth part of all 'clere gaines in monye' arising from 'any stage play-inge or other exercise commoditye or use . . . . within the playhowse . . . . commonly called the Fortune,' to hold the same for 13 years, for a yearly rent of 10*s.* and 27*l.* 10*s.* in hand, the said Thomas Downton covenanting to pay a pro-portionate part of all 'necessarye and needfull charges,' and to play 'to the best and most benefitt he can within the play howse aforesaid' and in no other 'common playhowse nowe erected or hereafter to be erected within the said cittye of London or twoe myles compasse.' Dat. . . . . 6 Jas. I., 1608. *Not executed,* being without date of month, signatures, or seals. Followed by the counterpart.

Printed, *Mem. of Edw. Alleyn,* p. 86.

35. LEASE from Edward Alleyn, of St. Saviour's, South-wark, esq., to Edmond Williams, of the parish of St. Giles without Cripplegate, 'packthredmaker,' of two messuages in Whitecrosse Street, in the par. of St. Giles, in the tenure of the said Edmond Williams and Roger Barffeilde, for 14 years, at a rent of 3*l.* Dat. 28 Feb., 7 Jas. I., 1609[10]. Counter-part, signed; with seal.

36. ASSIGNMENT by John Garratt, of London, cloth-worker, to Edward Alleyn, of St. Saviour's, Southwark, esq., for 100*l.*, of his lease in reversion of six messuages, &c., in Golding Lane and Whitecrosse Streete, as above, nos. 23, 24. Dat. 1 May, 8 Jas. I., 1610. Signed; with seal of arms.

37. ASSIGNMENT by Edward Alleyn, of St. Saviour's, Southwark, esq., to Philip Henslowe, of the same, esq., of leases of six messuages, &c., in Goulding Lane and Whitecross Street, granted, at a rent of 12*l.*, by Daniel Gill, the elder, 11 July, 1584, to Patrick Brewe for 41 years as above, nos. 12, 13; and by Daniel Gill, William Gill and Edmond Gill, 30 June, 1601, to John Garratt for 21 years as above, nos. 23, 24; with a proviso for voiding the assignment by the payment of 5*s.* Dat. 4 May, 8 Jas. I., 1610. Signed; with fragment of seal of arms.

38. BARGAIN AND SALE by Daniel Gill, the elder, William and Edmond Gill, his sons, William Clarke and Elizabeth, his wife, Philip Moore and Katheryn, his wife, Donald Qualtrough and Margaret, his wife, and Hugh Cannell and Jane, his wife (the said Elizabeth, Katheryn, &c., being daughters and co-heirs of Daniel Gill, the younger), to Edward Alleyn, for 340*l.*, of 12 tenements and all that 'their Playhouse, comonlie called or knowen by the name of the Fortune,' in the par. of St. Giles without Cripplegate, London, six tenements being on the east side of Goldinge Lane and six on the west side of Whitecrosse Streete. Dat. 30 May, 8 Jas. I., 1610. Signed; with seals.

39. BOND from the same parties to Edw. Alleyn in 800*l.*, to observe covenants as above. Dat. 30 May, 8 Jas. I., 1610. Signed; with seals.

40. BOND from Edward Alleyn and Thomas Towne, of London, gent., to Edmond Gill, of the Isle of Man, yeoman, in 540*l.*, for the payment of 273*l.* 6*s.* 8*d.* at the 'Vtter Pentice,' in Chester, on 1 May, 1611. Dat. 2 June, 8 Jas. I., 1610. Signed.

41. BOND from Edward Alleyn to Edmond Gill, of the Isle of Man, yeoman, in 40*l.*, for the payment of 20*l.* at the house of Tho. Sparke, in Ivye Lane, on 29 Sept., 1610. Dat. 2 June, 8 Jas. I., 1610. Signed.

42. RELEASE by Daniel Gill and others as above, no. 38, to Edward Alleyn of all rents and arrears of six messuages, &c., in the parish of St. Giles without Cripplegate, London, leased 11 July, 1584, by Daniel Gill to Patrick Brewe. Dat. 4 June, 8 Jas. I., 1610. Signed; with seals.

43, 44. FINE by the same to Edward Alleyn of 14 messuages and 10 gardens in the parish of St. Giles without Cripplegate for 300*l.* Dat. Mich. term, 8 Jas. I. [1610]. *Lat.* In duplicate.

45. RELEASE by Daniel Gill, the elder, and Katherine, his wife, William Gill and Isabella, his wife, Edmond Gill and Katherine, his wife, and others as above, no. 38, to Edward Alleyn, for 340*l.*, of 14 messuages and 10 gardens in the par. of St. Giles without Cripplegate, co. Midd. Dat. 20 Oct., 8 Jas. I., 1610. *Lat.* Signed; with seals.

46. WARRANT from Philip Henslowe, 'one of the sewers of his highnes [the King's] chamber,' and Edward Alleyn, 'seruant to the high and mightie prince of Wales,' joint masters of the King's game of bears, bulls, &c., by patent dated 24 Nov., 1608, commissioning Thomas Radford to act as their deputy to take up mastiff dogs, bears and bulls for the King's service, and to bait in any place within his dominions. Dat. 11 May, 9 Jas. I., 1611. Signed; with seals.

47. BOND from John Townsend, William Barksted, Joseph Tayler [Taylor], William Egleston [Eccleston], Giles

Gary, Robert Hamlyn [Hamlen], Thomas Hunte, Joseph Moore, John Rice, William Carpenter, Thomas Basse [Besse ?], and Alexander Foster, of London, gentlemen, to Philip Henslowe, of St. Saviour's, Southwark, esq., in 500*l.*, to perform 'certen articles' of the same date. Dat. 29 Aug., 1611. Signed (the spelling within brackets being that of the signatures); with six seals.

Printed, *Mem. of Edw. Alleyn*, p. 98.

48. LEASE from Edward Alleyn, of Dulwich, esq., to Robert Johnson, of London, merchant-tailor, of a tenement, &c., in Gouldinge Lane, in the parish of St. Giles without Cripplegate, London, in the tenure of Paule Lany and another, for 18 years, for a fine in hand of 22*s.* and a rent of 4*l.* and a 'good fatt and sweete capon.' Dat. 6 Jan., 10 Jas. I., 1612[3]. Counterpart; with seal.

49. CONTRACT of Gilbert Katherens, of St. Saviour's, Southwark, carpenter, with Philip Henslowe, esq., and Jacob Maide [Meade], waterman, covenanting, for 360*l.*, to pull down the old Bear Garden 'vppon or neere the Banksyde in the saide parishe of St. Saviour,' and to build before 30 Nov. 'one other game place or plaiehouse fitt and convenient in all thinges bothe for players to plaie in and for the game of Beares and bulls to be bayted in the same, and also a fitt and convenient tyre house and a stage to be carryed or taken awaie and to stand uppon tressels,' &c., the whole to be 'of suche large compasse, fforme, widenes and height as the plaie housse called the Swan in the libertie of Parris garden in the saide parishe of St Saviour now is.' Dat. 29 Aug., 1613. Signed, 'G. K.'

Printed, Malone, vol. iii. p. 343. See also Collier, *Hist. of Dram. Poetry*, vol. iii. p. 99.

50. BOND from Gilbert Katherens to Phil. Henslowe and Jacob Maide in 600*l.*, to observe the covenants in the preceding contract. Dat. 29 Aug., 11 Jas. I., 1613. Signed; with seal.

51. ARTICLES between Gilbert Katherens and John Browne, of St. Saviour's, Southwark, bricklayer, whereby the latter, for 80*l.*, covenants to make the brickwork of 'one Game place or plaie house, a bull howse and a stable neere or vppon the place whereas the Game place of the Beare garden now or latlie stoode,' which the said Gilbert Katherens was under contract of 29 Aug. to build for Philip Henslowe and Jacob Maide [Meade], the same to be 'of as large a compasse and height as the plaie howse called the Swan in the libertie of Parris Garden in the said parishe of St. Saviour now ys.' Dat. 8 Sept., 1613. Signed by J. Browne. Witnesses, Phil. Henslow, Jacob Mede.

52. ARTICLES 'on the parte and behalfe of Phillipp Henslowe, esquier, and Jacob Meade, waterman, to be perfourmed touchinge and concerninge the company of players which they haue lately raised,' the said company being represented by Nathan Feilde. No date [*circ.* 1613]. *Mutilated* and *imperfect.*

Printed, *Mem. of Edw. Alleyn*, p. 118; but Mr. Collier's transcript, besides containing a number of minor inaccuracies, omits after 'company,' on p. 119, l. 8, the words 'to be chosen by the saide Phillipp and Jacob or one of them.' The blank in l. 16 should be filled up with the words 'vnder their handes.'

53. ASSIGNMENT by Agnes, widow and executrix of Philip Henslowe, to Gregory Francklyn, saddler, Drewe Stapley, grocer, and John Hamond, merchant-tailor, of London, of leases (*a*) from Edward Alleyn to Philip Henslowe, 4 Apr., 1601, of a moiety of the Fortune playhouse for 24 years, at a rent of 8*l.*; (*b*) from Richard Woar to James Russell, 3 Aug., 1593, of a messuage, &c., in the parish of St. Saviour, Southwark, for 34¾ years, at a rent of 14*l.*; and (*c*) from Leonard Bilson, of Bishop's Waltham, co. Southampton, to Philip Henslowe, 1 Dec., 1612, of a messuage called the 'James,' or the 'Fooles head,' in the liberty of the Clink, for 20 years, at a rent of 4*l.* Dat. 15 Feb., 13 Jas. I. [1616]. *Not executed.*

54. LEASE from Edward Alleyn, of Dulwich, esq., to Henry Smith, of co. Midd., cook, of a messuage, &c., in Gouldinge Lane, co. Midd., for 21 years, at a rent of 6*l.* and a 'good fate and sweet capon.' Dat. 24 Apr., 16 Jas. I., 1618. Signed; with seal of arms. With note of surrender on the back, 4 Aug., 1621.

55. LEASE from Edward Alleyn, of Dulwich, esq., to Richard Hudson, of Goulding Lane, in the parish of St. Giles, co. Midd., 'vittler,' of a messuage, &c., in Goulding Lane, with license 'to have a dore way or passage towardes the playhows,' for 31 years, at a rent of 6*l.* and a 'good fatt and sweet capon.' Dat. 1 July, 16 Jas. I., 1618. Counterpart, signed; with seal. With bond in 20*l.* to perform covenants attached.

56. LEASE[1] from Edward Alleyne, of Dulwich, esq., to Edward Jubye, William Bird *al.* Bourne, Franck Grace, Richard Gumnell, Charles Massie, William Stratford, William Cartwright, Richard Price, William Parre, and Richard Fowler, gentlemen, of 'all that his great building now vsed for a playhowse and comonly called by the name of the Fortune ....

[1] See Alleyn's *Diary* (MS. ix., above), 31 Oct., 1618, and *Mem. of Edw. Alleyn*, p. 155.

betweene Whitecrosse Street and Golding Lane,' in the par. of St. Giles without Cripplegate, London, with a taphouse, in the occupation of Mark Brigham, and piece of ground adjoining, to hold the same for 31 years at a rent of 200*l.* and 'two rundlettes of wyne, the one sack and the other clarett, of ten shillinges a peece price'; with provisions that, if the said Edw. Alleyn die within the term, the rent be reduced to 120*l.* for the residue, and that the lessees shall not 'convert the said playhowse to any other vse or vses then as the same is now vsed,' and that they shall receive a rent of 24*s.*, to be reduced to 4*s.* at Alleyn's death, due from John Russell on a lease for 99 years of a tenement of two rooms adjoining the playhouse. Dat. 31 Oct., 16 Jas. I., 1618. Counterpart, signed; with five seals. Witnesses, Leonell Tychebourne, Thomas Downton, George Brome.

57. BOND from the lessees as above to Edward Alleyn in 60*l.* to observe covenants. Dat. 31 Oct., 16 Jas. I., 1618. Signed; with remains of seals.

58. LEASE from Edward Alleyn, of Dulwich, esq., to Charles Massy, of London, gent., of one twenty-fourth part of a 'parcell of ground vpon part whereof lately stood a Playhouse or building called the Fortune with a taphouse belonging to the same,' and other tenements, &c., in the occupation of Mark Briggum, John Russell, William Bird *al.* Bourne, and John Parson, 'all scituate lying and being betweene Whitecrosse Streete and Golding Lane in the parish of St. Giles without Creeplegate,' to hold the same for 51 years, paying towards the erection of a new playhouse 41*l.* 13*s.* 4*d.* and a yearly rent of 5*l.* 6*s.* 11*d.* Dat. 20 May, 20 Jas. I., 1622. Counterpart, signed; with fragment of seal.

Printed, *Mem. of Edw. Alleyn*, p. 167.

59. LEASE from Edward Alleyn to Richard Price, of London, gent., of one twenty-fourth part of the ground and tenements as above, on the same terms.. Dat. 20 May, 20 Jas. I., 1622. Counterpart, signed; with seal.

60, 61. LEASE from Edward Alleyn to William Gwalter, of London, innholder, of a sixth part of the ground and tenements as above, for 51 years, paying towards the erection of a new playhouse 166*l.* 13*s.* 4*d.* and a yearly rent of 21*l.* 7*s.* 8*d.* Dat. 20 May, 20 Jas. I., 1622. Endorsed with a note that the present lease was surrendered to Edw. Alleyn on 19 June, 1623, and that, on 20 June, a new lease was granted of a moiety of the same sixth part to William Gwalter and another lease of a moiety to Robert Leigh. Followed by the counterpart.

62. LEASE from Edward Alleyn to Anthony Jarman, of London, carpenter, of a twelfth part of the premises as above, for 51 years, paying towards the erection of a new playhouse 33*l.* 6*s.* 8*d.* and a yearly rent of 10*l.* 13*s.* 10*d.* Dat. 20 May, 20 Jas. I., 1622. Counterpart, signed.

63. LEASE from Edw. Alleyn to Margaret Grey, of London, widow, of a twelfth part of the 'newe Playehouse or building called the Fortune, with a Taphouse belonging to the same, in the occupation of Rob. Hart, and five other tenements in Whitecross Street and Goulding Lane, for 49½ years, at a rent of 10*l.* 13*s.* 10*d.* Dat. 29 Jan., 21 Jas. I., 1623[4]. Witnesses, Thomas Alleyn, Charles Massye, &c. Counterpart, signed; with seal.

64. LEASE from Edward Alleyn to George Bosgrave, of the parish of St. Giles without Cripplegate, gent., of half a twelfth part of the premises as above, no. 63, for 49½ years, at a rent of 5*l.* 6*s.* 11*d.* Dat. 20 Feb., 21 Jas. I., 1623[4]. Counterpart, signed; with seal.

65. EXTRACT from the roll of the Court Baron of the Mayor and citizens of London, lords of the manor of Finsbury, of the enrolment of the evidence of Thomas Allen and Matthias Allen, Master and Warden of the College of God's Gift in Dulwich, to the effect that lands and tenements in Whitecrosse Streete and Golding Lane, 'vna cum domo lusorio [*sic*], anglice a Playehowse, vocato le Fortune,' lately belonging to Edward Allen, had been given by him, under license in mortmain, for the support of the poor in the said college. Dat. 6 Oct., 5 Chas. I., 1629. *Lat.*

66. BILL in Chancery of Thomas [Tobias] Lisle against Dulwich College, praying for relief against actions at law by the College for the recovery of 60*l.*, arrears of rent due on two leases held by the complainant, dated 16, 22 July, 1639,—the one of one-twelfth part of the Fortune playhouse for 21 years, for 18*l.* 4*s.* 2½*d.*, arrears of rent due on a former lease from Edward Alleyn to Mary Bryan, and 10*l.* 3*s.* 10*d.* yearly rent; the other of one-eighth part of the same for 21 years for 50*l.* [*sic*] 6*s.* 10*d.*, arrears on former leases to Margaret Gray, and 16*l.* 0*s.* 9*d.* yearly rent,—the complainant alleging that he was trustee for Mary Mynshowe and Susan Cade, nieces of John Ball, a lunatic in his charge; followed by the answer of the defendants and proofs. Endorsed, 'Rolls, Thursday, 26 Nov., 1646.' Paper, 6 sheets.

67, 68, 69. BILL in Chancery of Dulwich College against Tobias Lisle and Thomas Grymes, claiming arrears of rent for shares in the Fortune playhouse, with answers, proofs, and counsel's notes. Three copies, the first two endorsed 1647 and the third 1649. Paper, each six sheets.

The substance of Tobias Lisle's answer is that, at the entreaty of the College, he took in trust for A. Minshawe and S. Cade the two leases forfeited by Mary Bryan and Margaret Gray, as above, no. 66, paying 18*l.* 14*s.* 2*d.* and 55*l.* 6*s.* 10*d.* for arrears, on condition that the College procured the surrender of the original leases made to Bryan and Gray, and that, if 'the partes of the playhouse should not arrise and make more proffitt then the rentes to be reserved and repaiers and interest of the moneys att 8^{li} per centum for the disbursmentes of the arreres, that the Master, Warden, &c., would repaye the 55^{li} 6^{s} 10^{d} and the 18^{li} 14^{s} 2^{d}, with the rentes the defendant should paye for the partes in the meane time and interest'; these conditions not having been observed by the College, although 'before he had raysed 5^{li} profitt the Parliament putt downe playes, soe, his covenaunt restreyninge him from putting them [the premises] to other vses, and Gray and Bryan not surrenderinge their leases, he was disabled to make any proffitt.'

He also mentions that 'about 9 yeares synce' he became assignee of a half-share in trust for Elizabeth Shanckes, his interest in which, at the request of the same Elizabeth and her husband, he afterwards made over to Winifred Shanckes.[1]

Thomas Grymes denies that he has any lease or assignment, but states 'that he, having a very great stock of Apparrell both for men and women, did furnishe the actors of the playhowse, and therfore they allowed him a part or share out of the playhowse and paid him other somes of money out of the proffittes of the howse and still [are] indetted to him.'

According to the preamble of the bill the Fortune was divided by Edw. Alleyn in 1622 into twelve shares, and on the 20 May, 1622, leases of whole shares for 51 years at a rent of 10*l.* 13*s.* 10*d.* were granted to Richard Gunnell, Edw. Jackson, Thomas Sparkes, and Anthony Jarman, and leases of half-shares for 51 years at a rent of 5*l.* 6*s.* 11*d.* to Frances Juby, George Massey, Richard Price, John

[1] John Shank, Schanke, or Shankes, the actor, had a daughter Winifred, baptised at St. Giles, Cripplegate, 3 Aug., 1623 (Collier, *Memoirs of Actors*, 1846, p. 277). She seems, however, to have died in infancy, as the baptism of another daughter Winifred is registered on 19 May, 1626. This Winifred, again, was buried on 16 June, 1629, so that the Winifred Shankes here mentioned must be a third daughter of the same name, perhaps by a different mother, the Elizabeth Martin whose marriage to a John Shanke is registered on 26 Jan., 1630–1. John Shankes himself was buried 27 Jan., 1635–6; and it may be inferred, from the mention of the husband of Elizabeth Shankes at a later date, that she had married again.

Fisher, Thomas Wigpitt, and Charles Massey. Further leases at the same rents were made to Margaret Graye of a half-share for 50 years, 1 Aug., 1623, and a whole share for 40½ [49½] years, 29 Jan., 162¾; to George Bosgrave and John Blak of half-shares for 49½ years, 20 Feb., 162¾; to Mary Bryan of a whole share for 49¼ years, 24 Mar., 162¾; and to Thomas Gibborne of a whole share for 40¼ [49¼] years, 21 Apr., 1624.

70. ANSWER of Thomas Alleyn, Master of Dulwich College, to the bill of complaint of Arthur Minshawe, Mary Minshawe, and Suzan Cade, denying that Tobias Lisle had been persuaded by himself or Matthias Alleyn to take a lease [of shares in the Fortune playhouse] in trust for Mary Minshawe and Suzan Cade, and to pay arrears of rent on former leases to Mary Bryan and Margaret Gray, on the conditions recited above, nos. 67–69. Dat. Nov., 1649. Paper, 9 sheets.

71. BILL in Chancery of William Beaven against Dulwich College, as above, MS. i. art. 131. Dat. [Nov., 1661]. Paper, 12 sheets.

72. DRAFT of a lease from Dulwich College to William Beaven of nineteen messuages, 'by him lately new built and erected on the ground whereon ye late demolished Fortune playhowse and taphowse heretofore stood and vpon the wast ground therevnto belonging,' for 21 years, at a rent of 34*l.* 10*s.*, with covenant for renewals for 21 years and 3 years. Dat. [Mar.] 1661[2]. Paper, 22 sheets.

(*SECTION II.*)

DOCUMENTS relating to Bishopsgate, Southwark, Kennington manor, &c.; 1537–1626:—

73. LEASE[1] from Thomas Marowe, of Wolstone, co. Warwick, esq., to William Parker, of London, merchant-tailor, of a tenement, &c., late in the tenure of Robert Fyssher, 'gurdeler,' in the parish of 'St Botulphe without Bisshoppesgate of London,' for 50 years, at a rent of 20*s*. Dat. 4 May, 29 Hen. VIII., 1537. Signed; with seal. With bond in 40*l*. to perform covenants attached.

74. GRANT from William Parker, of London, merchant-tailor, to Cornelys Parker, his son, of his interest in the lease as above. Dat. 21 Sept., 33 Hen. VIII. [1541]. With seal.

75. BARGAIN AND SALE by Thomas Marowe, of Stebunhethe [Stepney], co. Midd., gent., son and heir of Thomas Marowe, of Wolstone, to William Parker, of London, merchant-tailor, of the same tenement, for 41*l*. Dat. 26 Sept., 33 Hen. VIII. [1541]. Signed; with seal.

76. LETTERS PATENT of Henry VIII. granting to David Vyncent, groom of the Privy Chamber, a lease of the manor of Kenyngton, co. Surrey,[2] for 40 years, at a rent of 27*l*., the term to begin at Michaelmas, 1559, at the expiration of a lease to William Dauncer, granted 26 June, 1527, to begin at Michaelmas, 1538. Dat. 15 Nov., a° 38 [1546]. *Lat.* With the Great Seal.

---

[1] This is the first deed entered by E. Alleyn in the list of 'deeds of my howses in bushopsgat streat' in MS. viii., above, f. 42.

[2] See above, MS. iii. art. 41, n.; and below, Mun. 156.

77. BOND from Mary Nevell, of the parish of St. Sepulchre, London, to Edward Alleyn [the elder], of London, yeoman, in 30*l.* for the payment of 16*l.* on 28 May. Dat. 30 Apr., 1 and 2 Phil. and Mary [1555].

78. ASSIGNMENT by William Thackewell, of New Windsor, gent., to Edward Allayne [the elder], of London, yeoman, of a lease, dat. 8 Nov., 1555, from John Fulham and Stephen Belle, of Chuckford, co. Essex, yeomen, of a messuage, lands, &c., at Buckershill, in Chigwell, co. Essex, for 5 years, at a rent of 5*l.* Dat. 20 Jan., 3 and 4 Phil. and Mar., 1556[7]. With bond in 20*l.* to perform covenants attached.

79. LEASE from John Bowyar, of Lincoln's Inn [and Camberwell], gent., to Henry Brigges, of Peckham, carpenter, of a messuage, &c., in Peckham in the tenure of Alice Brigges, his mother, for 20 years, at a rent of 46*s.* 8*d.*, two bushels of rye, and two hens. Dat. 26 Aug., 1 Eliz. [1559]. Signed.

80. BARGAIN AND SALE by Cornelys Parker, of London, salter, to Edward Allen, of London, innholder, and Margaret, his wife, for 90*l.*, of a messuage in the parish of 'St. Botholphe without Bisshoppesgate of London,' in the tenure of John Jeele, purchased by William Parker, his father, of Thomas Marrowe, of Stepney, as above, no. 75. Dat. 5 Mar., 8 Eliz., 1565[6]. Signed; with seal.

81. FEOFFMENT from Cornelius Parker to Edward Allen of the same tenement, &c. Dat. 23 Mar., 8 Eliz., 1565[6]. *Lat.* Signed; with seal. With bond in 200 marks to perform covenants attached.

82. WILL of Edward Allen, of the parish of St. Botolph without Bishopsgate, London, innholder, giving all his lands and tenements to his wife, Margaret, for life, and at her death to be divided among his children equally, and all his 'goodes, leases and redy mony,' half to his wife and half among his children equally. Dat. 10 Sept., 1570. *Copy*; with probate, 22 Sept., 1570, having remains of seal attached.

Printed, *Mem. of Edw. Alleyn*, p. 197.

83. BOND from Bartholomew Toker, of Barnstaple, fuller, to John Wilkey, sen., in 10*l.*, for the payment of 4*l.* 10*s.* Dat. 10 Aug., 13 Eliz. [1571].

84. LEASE from John Browne, of London, haberdasher, and Margaret, his wife, widow of Edward Allen, of London, innholder, to Margaret, widow of Jasper Fisher, of London, esq., of a piece of ground on the south side of a messuage in her occupation in the parish of St. Botolph without Bishopsgate, for 99 years, at a rent of 12*d.* Dat. 12 Feb., 22 Eliz. [1580]. Counterpart, signed; with seal.

85. LEASE from Edward Jarvys, of London, leather-seller, to Johan Gravesende, of St. Saviour's, Southwark, widow, of part of the messuage 'sometyme called the Barge,' in the parish of St. Saviour, for 14 years, at a rent of 33*s.* 4*d.* Dat. 8 Apr., 24 Eliz., 1582. Signed by a mark.

86. COVENANT between Philip Hensley [Henslowe], of London, dyer, and Richard Nicolson, of St. Saviour's, Southwark, leather-dresser, relative to the payment of 70*l.* for a joint purchase of 60 dozen goat-skins and the dressing and sale of the same. Dat. 14 June, 26 Eliz., 1584. Counterpart, signed by a mark.

87. COVENANT between the same, relative to the payment of 168*l.* 6*s.* for a joint purchase of 153 dozen goat-skins and the dressing and sale of the same. Dat. 18 June, 26 Eliz. [1584]. Counterpart, signed by a mark; with seal.

88. BARGAIN AND SALE by John Browne, of London, haberdasher, and Margaret, his wife, to John and Edward Allyn, of London, yeomen, sons of Edward Allyn, deceased, and of the said Margaret, of four messuages in 'Busshopesgate Streete without Busshopesgate,' in the suburbs of London, lying next the house of the Earl of Oxford.[1] Dat. 28 Oct., 27 Eliz. [1585]. *Lat.* Signed; with seals. With note of seisin, witnessed by James Tvnstall, &c.

89. RELEASE by the same to the same of the four messuages, as above. Dat. 28 Oct., 27 Eliz. [1585]. *Lat.* Signed; with seals.

90. DEFEASANCE by Hugh Woodcock, of London, salter, of a statute-staple bond from Edward Allen and John Allen, of London, gentt., in 60*l.*, conditional upon the payment by instalments of 30*l.* [in connexion with Alleyn's houses in Bishopsgate Street, MS. viii. f. 42*b*]. Dat. 5 Nov., 27 Eliz. [1585]. Signed; with seal. With acquittances on the back.

91. ASSIGNMENT by Richard Bolton, of Blackfriars, London, shoemaker, to Philip Hinsley [Henslowe], of St. Saviour's, Southwark, dyer, as security for a debt of 5*l.*, of a lease from Richard Alforde, of Blackfriars, dat. 27 Mar., 1585, of a shop, &c., in Blackfriars for 4¼ years, at a rent of 5*l.* 10*s.* Dat. 28 April, 28 Eliz., 1586. Signed by a mark.

---

[1] This was the same house which was also called Fisher's Folly (see below, Mun. 167, note).

92. DEFEASANCE by Hugh Woodcocke, of London, salter, of a statute-staple bond from Edward Allen and John Allen, of London, gentt., in 60*l.*, conditional upon the payment by instalments of 24*l.* Dat. 11 Feb., 29 Eliz. [1587]. Signed; with seal.

93. LETTERS of administration of the goods,[1] &c., of Richard Browne, late of the parish of All Saints, Lombard Street, granted by Richard Cosen, LL.D., Dean of Arches, to John Allen, of St. Botolph's without Bishopsgate, innholder. Dat. 23 Jan., 1587[8]. *Lat.* With seal; and signature of Will. Ferrand, surrogate.

94. BOND from William Bradley, of London, yeoman, to John Allen, of London, innholder, in 40 marks, for the payment, on 25 Aug., of 14*l.* Dat. 8 Mar., 30 Eliz. [1588]. Signed; with seal.

95. ASSIGNMENT by Edward Vaughan, of London, gent., to James Skevington, of Hampstead, gent., of a bond from Richard Beamond and Myls Barker, dat. 15 Feb., 1589, in 500*l.*, for the performance of covenants. Dat. 25 June, 31 Eliz. [1589]. Counterpart, signed; with seal.

96. BOND from John Peirce, of London, cook, to John Alleyn, of London, innholder, in 5*l.*, for the payment of 10*s.* at Michaelmas for the rent of two rooms in the parish of St. Botolph without Bishopsgate. Dat. 24 July, 31 Eliz., 1589. With seal.

97. RELEASE by John Allen, of London, innholder, son of Edward Allen, innholder, deceased, to Edward Allen, of London, yeoman, his brother, of a messuage in the parish of

[1] For the inventory see above, MS. iv. art. 19.

St. Botolph without Bishopsgate, London, late in the occupation of John Jeele, merchant-tailor, and now divided into six tenements in the occupation of Rich. Glynne, Ralph Hudson, and others. Dat. 6 July, 32 Eliz., 1590. Witnesses, James Tvnstall, &c. *Lat.* Signed; with seal.

98. MORTGAGE by John Allen, of London, innholder, and Edward Allen, of London, yeoman, sons of Edward Allen, innholder, deceased, to William Horne, of London, grocer, for 80*l.*, of six tenements, in the tenure of Richard Glyn and others, in the parish of St. Botolph without Bishopsgate, London. Dat. 8 July, 32 Eliz., 1590. Witnesses, Jas. Tvnstall, &c. Signed.

99. ARTICLES whereby Thomas, son of John Lamboll, of Chichester, tailor, is apprenticed to John Alleyn, of London, innholder, for seven years. Dat. 10 June, 33 Eliz., 1591. *Lat.* Signed; with seal.

100. EXTRACT from the court-roll of Leigham manor, co. Surrey, of grant of license to Nicholas Knighte to cut wood on lands in Streatham. Dat. 16 May, 35 Eliz. [1593]. *Lat.*

101. LEASE from Richard Woar, of London, dyer, to James Russell, of St. Saviour's, Southwark, shipwright, of a messuage, &c., in the parish of St. Saviour, for 34 years, at a rent of 14*l.* Dat. 3 Aug., 35 Eliz., 1593. Signed; with seal.

102. RELEASE by Alice Sprigge, of West Langton, co. Leic., widow, and Richard Sprigge, of the same, husbandman, to James Ansley, of West Langton, gent., of a messuage, &c., in West Langton, and a lease of the same granted to Thomas Sprigge, late husband of the said Alice. Dat. 20 Sept., 35 Eliz. [1593].

103. General Release from John Typler, of London, weaver, and Johan, his wife, to John Allen, of London, innholder; 27 May, 36 Eliz., 1594. Signed; with seal.

104. General Release from Robert Kyrkham, of London, haberdasher, to John Allen, of London, innholder, 6 Oct., 36 Eliz., 1594. Signed; with seal.

105. Lease from James Russell, of St. Saviour's, Southwark, shipwright, to John Smythe, of the same, waterman, of a tenement, &c., in the parish of St. Saviour, part of the messuage inhabited by him, the said James Russell, for 32 years, at a rent of 40*s*. Dat. 2 Jan., 37 Eliz., 1594[5]. Counterpart.

106. Bargain and Sale by John Allen, of London, innholder, to Edward Allen, of London, 'musicion,[1]' his brother, of a moiety of a messuage, sometime in the tenure of John Jeele, in the parish of 'St. Buttolphe without Bushoppesgate,' London, held by them jointly by virtue of the will of Edw. Allen, their father. Dat. 26 Apr., 37 Eliz., 1595. Witnesses, William Harris, Arthur Langworth, Philip Henslowe. Signed; with seal. With bond in 200*l.* to perform covenants attached.

107. Release by John Allen, of London, innholder, son of Edward Allen, of London, innholder, deceased, to Edward Allen, of London, yeoman, of the same messuage, &c. Dat. 16 June, 37 Eliz., 1595. Witnesses, Edward Mathewe, Philip Henslow. Signed.

108. Indenture whereby Charles Gilberte, of the parish of St. Botolph without Aldgate, carpenter, contracts with John

[1] This is the only occasion upon which Alleyn is so designated. See above, p. 9, note 1.

Sotherton, Baron of the Exchequer, Sir William Webb, knt., Olyver St. John, Edward Bowier, Bartholomew Scott, and John Chapman, commissioners, to survey 'all the Thamis walls, banckes, ditches, sluces,' &c., from Ravensborne, co. Kent, to Kingston, co. Surr., to take up the 'sluce called Heathes wall sluce' in Batrichsea [Battersea] and 'new make frame and laie a new sluce of good stronge and substanciall new tymber of elme' for 44*l.* Dat. — Sept., 37 Eliz., 1595. *Not executed.*

109. ASSIGNMENT[1] by Arthur Langworth, of Ringmere, co. Sussex, gent., to Edward Allen, of St. Saviour's, Southwark, gent., of a lease from the Dean and Chapter of Chichester, dat. 7 May, 1571, of the parsonage, glebe, tithes, &c., of Firles [Firle], co. Sussex, for 50 years (to begin at the expiration of a lease to John Barnerde for 50 years from 1548), at a yearly rent of 31*l.* 12*s.* 4*d.* Dat. 16 Mar., 38 Eliz., 1595[6]. Counterpart, signed; with seal.

110. LETTERS OF ADMINISTRATION to Margaret Allen of the goods, &c., of John Allen, her husband, late of the parish of St. Andrew, Holborn, deceased intestate. Dat. 5 May, 1596. *Lat.* Signed by Thomas Crake, LL.D., official of the Archdeacon of London.

111. GENERAL RELEASE by Margarett Allen, of the parish of St. Botolph without Bishopsgate, widow of John Allen, late of London, innholder, to Edward Allen, of the parish of St.

1 No. 8 in Alleyn's list of 'the Wrightings of Firles,' in MS. viii., above, f. 45 (*Alleyn Papers*, p. xviii.) According to his statement, 'What y[e] parsnage of Firles coste me,' in MS. viii. f. 6 (p. xiii.), he paid for it in all 1,323*l.* 6*s.* 8*d.*, and received from it 873*l.* 6*s.* 8*d.* The account ends, 'Sowld this parsnage to M[r] Homden and M[r] Bunc about Cristid [Christmas], 1605, for 1,300[l].' See above, MS. iii. art. 16, and Mun. 144.

Saviour, Southwark, gent., brother of the said John. Dat. 2 July, 38 Eliz., 1596. Witnesses, William Harris, scrivener, Philip Henslow, Edward Harris. Signed by a mark; with seal.

On the back is a note of the special release of a rent of 40*s.* 'vppon a lease[1] graunted frome Julian Crapwell, widdowe, mother of Margaret Allen.'

112. LEASE from Robert Lyvesey, of Tooteingebeake, co. Surrey, esq., and Gerrard Gore, of London, merchant, with consent of Isabell, wife of Thomas Keye, *al.* Keyes, 'one of the cookes of her Maiesties kitchen,' to Edward Addyson, of St. Saviour's, Southwark, waterman, 'servant to her Maiestie,'[2] and Joane, his wife, of a tenement, seven cottages, and a wharf, &c., on the Bankside, in the parish of St. Saviour, adjoining the Bear Garden and Unicorn's Alley, for 21¼ years, at a rent of 9*l.* 10*s.* Dat. 20 Aug., 38 Eliz., 1596. Signed.

113. LEASE from the same to William Teyken, of St. Saviour's, Southwark, yeoman, of a messuage, &c., on the Bankside, in the parish of St. Saviour, for 18¾ years, at a rent of 40*s.* Dat. 20 Aug., 38 Eliz., 1596. Counterpart, signed by a mark.

114. LEASE from the same to Gilbert Rockett, of St. Saviour's, Southwark, yeoman (on the surrender of a former lease to Elizabeth Wystoe, widow, now his wife), of a messuage, &c., on the Bankside, in the parish of St. Saviour, for 20¼ years, at a rent of 43*s.* 4*d.* Dat. 20 Aug., 1596.

---

[1] This refers probably to the Boar's Head, on the Bankside, of which 'a lease from Julyan Cropwell to John Alen' is mentioned in MS. viii. f. 43 (*Alleyn Papers*, p. xvii.)

[2] The original warrant for his appointment as one of the Queen's watermen, dat. 6 June, 1569, is in Brit. Mus., Add. MS. 5750, f. 31.

115. DEFEASANCE by Alexander White, of Putney, baker, of a statute-staple bond from Philip Henslowe, gent., in 100 marks, conditional upon the payment by instalments of 460*l.* to Isabell, wife of Thomas Key, *al.* Keys, 'one of the cookes of her Maiesties kitchen.'[1] Dat. 1 Dec., 39 Eliz., 1596. Witnesses, Arthur Langworthe, Edward Alleyn. Signed; with seal.

116. ASSIGNMENT by Edward Allen to John Langworth, of Ringmere, co. Sussex, gent., of the lease as above, no. 109. Dat. 16 Dec., 39 Eliz. [1596]. Counterpart, signed. With a note below of the intention that, in case of the non-performance of the terms of a defeasance of a statute-staple bond from Arthur and John Langworth to Edward Allen, 'then the said lease and premisses might be lyable and extendable to the said statute.'

117. BARGAIN AND SALE by Robert Ballard, of Hollington, co. Sussex, husbandman, to Arthur Langworth, of Ringmere, esq., for 16*l.*, of a messuage called Bukstedes or Buk stade, in West Firles, co. Sussex. Dat. 20 Oct., 41 Eliz. [1598]. Signed; with seal.

118. LEASE from Edward Nowell, of London, haberdasher, to William Frythe, of London, haberdasher, of a messuage, 52 acres of land, &c. (held by the lessor of the Bishop of London), in the manor of Passick, *al.* Patteswicke, co. Essex, for 21 years from Easter, 1602, for 100*l.* in hand and a rent of 24*s.*, voidable by payment of 120*l.* on 21 Apr., 1691. Dat. 3 April, 41 Eliz., 1599. Signed.

[1] Notes of payments for Mrs. 'Keayes,' and of receipts 'of reant of her howsses at Westmester sence I gathered the reante,' 22 Apr., 1599, are entered by Henslowe in his *Diary*, ff. 42*b*, 43. See also MS. iii. artt. 1, 2.

119. BOND from Arthur Langworth, of Ringmere, co. Sussex, gent., to Edward Allen, of London, gent., in 16*l.*, for the payment of 8*l.* on the 28 Nov. Dat. 20 Nov., 42 Eliz., 1599. Signed.

120. LEASE from James Skevington, of Badger, co. Salop, esq., to William Symons, of Lambeth, shipwright, of a wharf, house, &c., in Lambeth, parcel of the manor of Kennington, for 20 years, at a rent of 20*s.* Dat. 1 May, 42 Eliz. [1600]. Signed; with seal of arms.

121. ASSIGNMENT by John West, of London, woodmonger, to Robert Bromfeild, of St. Saviour's, Southwark, woodmonger, for 110*l.*, of a lease, dat. 13 Nov., 1586, from Anthony [Browne], Viscount Montagu, to John West, his bailiff, father of the above John West, of a wharf, &c., in 'the closse of St Mary Overies in Surrey,'[1] for 26 years from Michaelmas, 1590, at a rent of 5*l.* Dat. 27 Apr., 43 Eliz., 1601. Signed; with seal.

122. ASSIGNMENT by Robert Bromfeild to Edward Allen, for 100*l.*, of the lease as above. Dat. 28 April, 43 Eliz., 1601. Signed; with seal.

123. LEASE from James Russell, of St. Saviour's, Southwark, shipwright, to Robert Mount, of London, basket-maker, of two cottages and land on the Bankside, in the parish of St. Saviour, for 25 years, at a rent of 50*s.* Dat. 20 June, 43 Eliz., 1601. Counterpart, signed.

124. RELEASE by Arthur Langworth, of Ringmere, co. Sussex, esq., to Edward Alleyn of his estate in the parsonage of Fyrles, co. Sussex, held on lease from the Dean and Chapter

[1] See MS. viii. f. 41*b* (*Alleyn Papers*, p. xvii.):—'My deeds for ye wharfe in ye close. Lo: Mountagues lease to West:—Young West to Robert Bromfeeld indentur:—Ro. Bromfeeld to me by pole dede. Itt cost me 115^l^.'

of Chichester. Dat. 2 July, 43 Eliz., 1601. Witnesses, John Longworth [*sic*], Philip Henslowe, Richard Langworth. Signed; with seal.

125. BOND from Edward Allen, of London, gent., and John Longworth [Langworth], of Wells, D.D., to Laurence Wetherall, of London, cloth-worker, in 120*l.*, for the payment of 70*l.* on 29 Sept. Dat. 3 July, 43 Eliz., 1601. Signed.

126. BOND from Edward Allen to John Longworth, D.D., in 120*l.*, for the payment to Laurence Wetherall of the same 70*l.* Dat. 3 July, 43 Eliz., 1601. Signed.

127. BOND from Edward Nowell, of London, haberdasher, to Edward Allen, of London, gent., in 300*l.*, in warranty of a tenement called 'the scite of the mannour of Patteswicke,' co. Essex, with land, &c., in Patteswicke, lately surrendered to the use of the said Edw. Allen on mortgage. Dat. 12 May, 44 Eliz., 1602. Witness, Nicholas Kempe. Signed; with seal.

128. MORTGAGE by James Russell, of St. Saviour's, Southwark, shipwright, to Cuthbert Hackett, of London, dyer, for 100*l.*, of a lease from Richard Woar, dat. 3 Aug, 1593, of a messuage, &c., in the parish of St. Saviour, as above, no 101. Dat. 18 Sept., 44 Eliz., 1602.

129. ASSIGNMENT by James Russell to Philip Henslowe, of St. Saviour's, Southwark, esq., for 210*l.*, of the same lease.[1] Dat. 5 Mar., 45 Eliz., 1602[3]. Signed; with seal.

130. LEASE from Philip Henslowe to Edward Addyson, of St. Saviour's, Southwark, waterman, of a tenement, &c., on the Bankside, in the parish of St. Saviour, for 15 years, at a

[1] For a list of 'the tenantes of Jemes Russelles leace' see Henslowe's *Diary*, p. 265.

rent of 40*s.* Dat. 30 Nov., 1 Jas. I., 1603. Counterpart, signed by a mark.

131. BOND from Edward Allen and Philip Henslowe, esquires, to James Skevington, esq., in 400*l.*, for the payment of 200*l.* on 28 Feb., 1605. Dat. 30 Nov., 2 Jas. I., 1604. Signed; with seals of arms.

132. BARGAIN AND SALE by Thomas Keyes, of Richmond, cook, and Thomas Newman, of London, gent., and [Katherine] his wife, to Philip Henslowe, esq., of their estate in messuages, lands, &c., on the Bankside, in the parish of St. Saviour, Southwark, bought by the said Philip of Thomas Challoner, esq. Dat — April, 3 Jas. I., 1605. *Not executed.*

133. COVENANT by Philip Henslowe, of St. Saviour's, Southwark, esq., to deliver to Thomas Newman, of the Inner Temple, and Katherine, his wife, money, goods, chattels, &c., belonging to Isabel Key, deceased, widow of Thomas Key, *al.* Keyes, and mother of the said Katherine. Dat. 13 May, 3 Jas. I. [1605]. Counterpart, signed; with seal of arms.

134. ASSIGNMENT by Philip Henslowe to Thomas Newman and Katherine, his wife, of a lease, dat. 20 June, 1601, from Corpus Christi College, Cambridge, of a mansion-house, three messuages, &c., in Longeditche Street, in Westminster, for 40 years. Dat. 14 May, 3 Jas. I., 1605. Counterpart, signed; with seals.

135. LEASE from Lodovic [Stuart], Duke of Lennox, through Sir Thomas Lascelles and others, his commissioners, to Thomas Dent, of Symondstone, co. York, yeoman, of a messuage, farm, &c., in Symondstone,[1] for 21 years, for a fine of 32*l.* 2*s.* 6*d.* and a rent of 21*s.* 5*d.* Dat. 19 Sept., 3 Jas. I.

[1] Simondstone, or Simonstone, in the parish of Aysgarth, 1½ mile from Hawes.

[1605]. Witn., Sir Tho. Lascelles, Sir Rob. Dolman, &c. Counterpart, signed by a mark.

136. LEASE from Lodovic [Stuart], Duke of Lennox, to Cuthbert Shaw, of Helbecklandes, co. York, yeoman, of a messuage, farm, &c., in Helbecklands [Helbeck Lunds] for 21 years, for a fine of 8*l.* and a rent of 4*s.* 4*d.* Dat. 19 Sept., 3 Jas. I. [1605]. Counterpart, signed by a mark.

137. LEASE from Lodovic [Stuart], Duke of Lennox, to James Metcalfe, of Nappayskar, in Wensladaill [Nappa Scar, in Wensleydale], co. York, yeoman, of a messuage, farm, &c., in Symondstone, in the manor of Dailgraunge, co. York, for 21 years, for a fine of 30*l.* and a rent of 20*s.* Dat. 19 Sept., 3 Jas. I., 1605. Counterpart, signed.

138. LEASE from Lodovic [Stuart], Duke of Lennox, to James Pratt, of Brockelcot [Brockhill Cote], co. York, yeoman, of messuages, farms, &c., at Brockelcot and Helme, in the manor of Dailgraunge, co. York, for 21 years, for a fine of 32*l.* 10*s.* and a rent of 21*s.* 8*d.* Dat. 19 Sept., 3 Jas. I., 1605. Counterpart, signed.

139. LEASE from Lodovic [Stuart], Duke of Lennox, to Christopher Blaides, of Helbecklandes, co. York, yeoman, of a messuage, lands, &c., in Helbecklandes, for 21 years, for a fine of 60*l.* and a rent of 32*s.* 6*d.* Dat. 19 Sept., 3 Jas. I. [1605]. Counterpart.

(Whitaker, *Richmondshire*, 1823, vol. i. p. 414). It formed part of the manor of Dale Grange, the name given after the Dissolution to the site of Jorvaulx Abbey, which was granted in 36 Hen. VIII. to Matthew Stuart, Earl of Lennox, and Margaret, his wife, niece to King Henry (Dugdale, *Monasticon*, ed. 1817–30, vol. v. p. 567). The other places mentioned in the leases following are in the same neighbourhood, and the whole doubtless were comprised in the estate in Yorkshire purchased by Edw. Alleyn in 1626. See above, p. 116, n. 1, and *Alleyn Papers*, p. xxv.

140. LEASE from Lodovic [Stuart], Duke of Lennox, to Christopher Metcalf, of Newhouse, co. York, yeoman, of a farm in Newhouse for 21 years, for a fine of 31*l.* and a rent of 20*s.* 8*d.* Dat. 19 Sept., 3 Jas. I. [1605]. Counterpart, signed by a mark.

141. LEASE from Lodovic [Stuart], Duke of Lennox, to George Skarr, of Seebusk [Sedbusk], yeoman, of a messuage, farm, &c., in George Skarr [*sic*], in the manor of Dale Grange, co. York, for 21 years, for a fine of 20 marks and a rent of 13*s.* 4*d.* Dat. 19 Sept., 3 Jas. I., 1605. Counterpart, signed.

142. LEASE from Lodovic [Stuart], Duke of Lennox, to George, John, and Thomas Atkinson, of Askrige [Askrigg], co. York, labourers, of houses, land, &c., in Askrige, for 21 years, for a fine of 3*l.* 10*s.* and a rent of 2*s.* 4*d.* Dat. 26 Oct., 3 Jas. I., 1605. Counterpart, signed by marks.

143. LEASE from Lodovic [Stuart], Duke of Lennox, to Ellynor Maysson, of Askrigge, co. Yorke, spinster, of a messuage, farm, &c., in Askrigge, for 21 years, for a fine of 27*s.* 6*d.* and a rent of 10*d.* Dat. 30 Oct., 3 Jas. I., 1605. Counterpart, signed by a mark.

144. ASSIGNMENT by Edward Allen, of St. Saviour's, Southwark, gent., to Robert Holmden, of London, leather-seller, for 1,200*l.*, of a lease from the Dean and Chapter of Chichester of the parsonage, glebe, tithes, &c., of Firles, co. Sussex, for 50 years, the same having come to the said Edw. Allen from Arthur Langworth, and having been assigned by him to John Langworth, and by the latter again to him re-assigned as above, nos. 109, 116. Dat. 25 Nov., 3 Jas. I. [1605]. Witnesses, Philip Henslowe, Thomas Towne, and others. Counterpart, signed; with seal.

145. COVENANT by Edward Allen to surrender to the use of Robert Holmden, for 100*l.*, a copyhold messuage and land in the manor of West Firles, co. Sussex, with license to put in suit two bonds, the one for the assurance of the same copyhold from Nicholas Weller, of Balcom, and the other for the assurance of the parsonage of Firles from John Langworth, of Ringmere. Dat. 25 Nov., 3 Jas. I. [1605]. Counterpart, signed.

146. LEASE from Philip Henslowe, esq., to John Darbey, of St. Saviour's, Southwark, glover, of a messuage and yard on the Bankside, in the parish of St. Saviour, in the tenure of Christopher Lylle and John Haynes, for 21 years, at a rent of 3*l.* and 'one very good new paire of kiddes lether gloves sufficiently wrought fitt for the hande of the saide Phillipp, worth in value twoe shillinges' on the F. of the Circumcision, 'comonly called new yeres day only.' Dat. 19 Aug., 4 Jas. I., 1606. Signed.

147. BOND from Edward Alleyn, of Dulwich, esq., and Philip Henslowe, of St. Saviour's, Southwark, esq., to John Elliotson, of St. Olave's, Southwark, cooper, in 100*l.*, for the payment of 52*l.* 10*s.* Dat. 20 Dec., 4 Jas. I., 1606. Signed; with seals of arms. With note of payment, 22 June, 1607.

148. BOND[1] from Philip Henslowe, of St. Saviour's, Southwark, gent., to Thomas Burnett, of London, gent., in 400*l.*, to surrender at request the office of Sewer of the King's Chamber, conditional upon the payment by Thomas Burnett to Edward Allen of 220*l.* before 8 Oct. and his procuring 'my lord chamberleins good will for the said office.' Dat. 3 Oct., 5 Jas. I., 1607. Witnesses, Edw. Alleyn, Alexander Nairne, &c. Signed.

[1] See letters of Burnet, Nairne, and Alleyn, MS. iii., above, artt. 88, 89.

149. LEASE from Philip Henslowe to John Serieant, of St. Saviour's, Southwark, waterman, of 'twoe lowe romes.... in a place called Mouldstrand,' in the parish of St. Saviour, with a piece of land 'under the parlor windowe' of William Warner, waterman, for 20 years, at a rent of 40*s.* Dat. 25 Oct., 6 Jas. I., 1608. Counterpart, signed by a mark; with seal.

150. NOTE by Edw. Alleyn for the repayment to Edward Bromfeeld, within 14 days, of a loan of 100*l.* Dat. 10 Dec., 1608. Signed.

151. BOND from Robert Bromfeilde, of Sevenoaks, gent., and Edward Alleyn, esq., to Elizabeth Feltham, of South wark, widow, in 200*l.*, for the payment of 104*l.* 10*s.* on 16 June, 1609. Dat. 15 Dec., 6 Jas. I., 1608. Signed.

152. BOND from Robert Bromfeilde to Edward Alleyn, in 400*l.*, for the payment to Elizabeth Feltham of the same 104*l.* 10*s.* Dat. 15 Dec., 6 Jas. I., 1608. Signed.

153. BOND from Edward Alleyn to Sir Baptist Hyckes, of London, knt., in 70*l.*, for the payment of 42*l.*[1] Dat. 28 Feb., 1608[9]. Signed; with seal. With note of payment, 15 Apr., 1609.

154. BOND from Edward Alleyn, of St. Saviour's, Southwark, esq., to Henry Leake, of Much Bromley, co. Essex, gent., in 200*l.*, for the payment of 165*l.* on 6 Dec. Dat. 3 June, 7 Jas. I., 1609. Signed; with fragment of seal.

155. BOND from Robert Bromfeild, of Sevenoaks, gent., to Edward Alleyn, of Dulwich, esq., in 500*l.*, for the payment to Elizabeth Feltham, of Southwark, widow, of 104*l.* 10*s.*, for

[1] See above, MS. ii. art. 12.

which they are jointly bound. Dat. 16 June, 7 Jas. I., 1609. Signed.

156. ASSIGNMENT by Edward Alleyn, esq., to Sir Francis Calton, knt., for 2,000*l.*, of two leases from the Crown of the site and demesne lands of Kennington manor, co. Surrey—the one, dat. 14 Feb., 1589, to Richard Beamond and Myles Barker, two of the Queen's 'Gonners,' for 21 years from Michaelmas, 1599; and the other, dat. 27 June, 1600, to Thomas Webber, 'one of the yomen of her highnes mouth,' for 31 years from Michaelmas, 1620—both at the yearly rent of 16*l.* 10*s.* 9*d.* Dat. 6 Sept., 7 Jas. I., 1609. Counterpart, signed; with seal of arms.

157. RE-ASSIGNMENT by Sir Francis Calton to Edward Alleyn of the same leases, by way of assurance to the latter of the peaceable possession of the manor of Dulwich until 8 May, 1612. Dat. 7 Sept., 7 Jas. I. [1609]. Signed.

158. SCHEDULE of deeds relating to Kennington manor to be delivered by Edward Alleyn to Sir Francis Calton according to a covenant in the assignment above. Dat. [7 Sept., 1609]. Signed by Sir Fran. Calton.

159. BOND from Philip Henslowe, of St. Saviour's, Southwark, esq., and Edward Allen, of Dulwich, esq., to Robert Banckworth, of London, scrivener, in 100*l.*, for the payment of 52*l.* 10*s.* on 6 April, 1610. Dat. 4 Oct., 7 Jas. I., 1609. Signed.

160. BOND from Edward Allen, of St. Saviour's, Southwark, esq., to Henry Leake, of Much Bromley, co. Essex, gent., in 200*l.*, for the payment of 165*l.* on 8 June, 1610. Dat. 6 Dec., 1609, 7 Jas. I. Signed.

161. ASSIGNMENT by James Pratt, of London, dyer, to William Graue, of London, joiner, of a lease of 'parcell of the tenement in the wharffe within the Lord Mountagues close in the parishe of St Savior,' Southwark, granted to him by William Penfold and William Champion, of Southwark, woodmongers, 12 July, 1603, for 11 years, at a rent of 12*l.* Dat. 21 May, 1610. Signed.

162. BOND from Edward Alleyn to Henry Leake in 200*l.*, for the payment of 102*l.* 10*s.* on 10 Sept. Dat. 8 June, 8 Jas. I., 1610. Signed.

163. BOND from Simon Malorye, of Woodford, co. Northampton, gent., to Philip Henslow, one of the sewers of the King's Chamber, and Edward Alleyn, esq., servant to the Prince of Wales, in 20*l.*, to perform covenants in indentures of the same date. Dat. 25 Nov., 7 Jas. I., 1609. Signed.

164. BARGAIN AND SALE by Philip Henslowe, esq., one of the six governors of the Free Grammar School of the parish of St. Saviour, Southwark, to John Bingham,[1] George Payne, John Treherne, sen., Randall Carter, and Richard Yearwood, the other five governors, and their successors, for 120*l.*, of a messuage, &c., in the tenure of Joan White, widow, and Michael Spencer, oar-maker, on the Bankside, near the Thames, in the parish of St. Saviour, bounded on the west by Robinhood, late Bullheade, Alley and on the east by another alley and a tenement, the inheritance of Sir Allen Pearcye. Dat. 28 April, 10 Jas. I., 1612. Counterpart; with seal of St. Saviour's Grammar School.

[1] The names of John Bingham, saddler to Qu. Elizabeth and James I. (d. 1625), and of Randal Carter, tallow-chandler (d. 1646), are both recorded as benefactors to the Free School (Stow's *Survey*, ed. Strype, 1720, bk. iv. pp. 13, 14). In the same work (p. 11) is a curious metrical epitaph on J. Treherne, who was gentleman porter to James I.

165. ARTICLES of the apprenticeship of William Wooding, son of Thomas Wooding, of Bridgnorth, weaver, to John Marshall, of London, cook. Dat. 24 Oct., 12 Jas. I., 1614. Signed. With note of assignment to Edward Alleyn, 18 Oct., 1620.

166. BOND from Edward Alleyn, of Dulwich, esq., to Edward Hilliard, of London, 'imbroderer,' in 300*l.*, for the payment of 200*l.* on 8 Nov., 1615. Dat. 7 Nov., 12 Jas. I., 1614. Signed.

167, 168. LEASE from Edward Alleyn to Henry Harris, of St. Botolph's, Bishopsgate, shoemaker, of two messuages in the occupation of John Toppin and Humphrey Chesson, lying next the mansion-house called Fisher's Folly,[1] in Bishopsgate Street, with an alley and garden and eight small tenements adjoining, for 41 years from Christmas, 1616, at a rent of 30*l.* and two fat capons. Dat. 19 June, 13 Jas. I., 1615. Endorsed, 'Pye Alley, in Bishopsgate street, now Mr Phillips.' Followed by the counterpart, signed; with seal.

---

[1] 'The other side of this high street from Bishopsgate and Houndsditch, the first building is a large Inne for receipt of trauellers; then a faire house of late builded by the Lord John Powlet. Next to that, a farre more large and beautifull house with gardens of pleasure, bowling alleyes, and such like, builded by Iasper Fisher, free of the Goldsmithes, late one of the sixe clearkes of the Chauncery, and a Justice of peace. It hath since for a time beene the Earle of Oxfords place. The Queenes Maiestie Elizabeth hath lodged there. It now belongeth to M. Cornewallos. This house, being so largely and sumptuously builded by a man of no greater calling or possessions, was mockingly called Fishers Folly, and a Rithme was made of it and other the like in this manner, Kirkebies Castle and Fishers Folly, Spinilas Pleasure and Megses Glorie,' &c. (Stow, *Survey of London*, 1598, p. 128). In subsequent editions it is said to belong to Sir Roger Manners (ed. 1603) and to the Earl of Devonshire (ed. 1633). According to Fuller (*Worthies*, ed. 1840, vol. ii. p. 385), it was 'near Devonshire House, where now is the sign of the Pie,' that Alleyn was born. The name is still preserved in Devonshire Square.

169. ASSIGNMENT[1] by Edward Alleyn, of Dulwich, esq., to Sir Francis Calton, of Havering, co. Essex, knt., of a lease, for 31 years, of a messuage near the 'Parke corner of East Greenewiche,' originally granted, 4 Oct., 1604, by James I. to Robert Cecil, Earl of Salisbury, and assigned by him, 17 Dec., 1606, to Myles Whitacres, his 'gentleman servant,' at a rent of 40*s.*, and by the latter, 26 May, 1608, to the said Edward Alleyn. Dat. 8 Feb., 13 Jas. I., 1615[6]. Counterpart, signed; with seal of arms.

170. DISCHARGE from the Commissioners for 'new buildinges,' &c., to Henry Harris, of Bethlem, in the parish of St. Botolph without Bishopsgate, for erecting 'five tenementes of brick neare Fishers folly in the parish aforesaid vppon new foundacions,' on a composition of 10*l.* Dat. 1 Mar., 13 Jas. I., 1615[6]. Signed by [Sir] Julius Cæsar, [Sir] Francis Bacon, and others; with seals of arms.

171. LEASE from William Henslowe, of Bucksted, [Buxted], co. Sussex, gent., to Jacob Meade, of St. Saviour's, Southwark, waterman, of a messuage, divided into two tenements, in the tenure of William Parsons, waterman, and Joan Nutt, *al.* Chancey, widow, on the Bankside, in the parish of St. Saviour, for 21 years, at a rent of 30*s.* Dat. 20 June, 15 Jas. I., 1617. Counterpart, signed.

172. LEASE from Edward Alleyn to Richard Wigginton, of London, dyer, of a tenement, &c., in the parish of St. Saviour, Southwark, for 21 years, at a rent of 4*l.* and two fat capons. Dat. 15 Nov., 15 Jas. I., 1617. Counterpart, signed; with seal.

---

[1] For letters relating to this transaction see above, MS. iii. artt. 22, 23, 27, 28.

173. LEASE from Edward Alleyn to Peter Meecup,[1] of Saviour's, Southwark, bricklayer, of a messuage, tenement, &c., on the Bankside, in the parish of St. Saviour, Southwark, for 21 years, at a rent of 3*l.* 10*s.* Dat. 20 May, 16 Jas. I., 1618. Counterpart. With bond to pay rent attached.

174. LETTERS PATENT of James I., appointing Robert Bromfeild, John Hunt, Lionel Tichborne, and William Day to determine the boundaries of the Unicorn and other messuages, &c., in the parish of St. Saviour, Southwark, late in the tenure of John Allen and others, and now in dispute between the Attorney-General on the one part and William Henslowe and Jacob Meade on the other part, the same being parcel of lands, &c., conveyed by Henry Polsted to the Crown in 1552 and leased by Qu. Elizabeth, 11 Oct., 1595 (reserving therefrom 'the Queenes Pike Garden'), to Robert Livesey and Gerard Gore for 50 years, at a rent of 37*l.* 14*s.* 10*d.* Dat. 25 June, a° 16 [1618]. *Lat.*

175. LEASE from Edward Alleyn to Luce [Lucy] Tytone, of the Bankside, in the parish of St. Saviour, Southwark, of a messuage, &c., on the Bankside for 21 years, at a rent of 50*s.* Dat. 31 July, 16 Jas. I., 1618. Counterpart.

176, 177. RELEASE by Sir Thomas Gardiner, of Peckham, knt., to Edward Alleyn, esq., of a recognisance from Sir Francis Calton in 400*l.* on a sale, dat. 18 Nov., 1596, to William Gardiner and William Gardiner, his son, of Calton Woods, in Lewisham, co. Kent. Dat. 5 Dec., 16 Jas. I. [1618]. Followed by the counterpart. *Not executed.*

---

1 According to a return of foreigners in London in 1618, a native of Ostend, resident in England for 15 years, and a member of the Dutch Church (W. D. Cooper, *Foreign Protestants and Aliens resident in England*, 1618–1688, Camden Soc., 1862, p. 97).

178. LEASE from John Millen, of Ouldstreete, in the parish of St. Giles without Cripplegate, son and heir of John Millen, brickmaker, to Edward Alleyn, in furtherance of his design to 'erect certaine almeshowses' thereon,[1] of a piece of land, measuring 140 by 90 feet, in the 'feild called Irish feild, *al.* the Common feild,' in the parish of St. Giles, near the 'Pesthowse,' for 1,000 years, at a rent of 1*d.* Dat. 28 June, 18 Jas. I., 1620. Witnesses, Francis Michell, William Lambe, Anthony Jeffes, &c. Signed; with seal of arms.

179. BOND from Edward Alleyn and Thomas Alleyn, of London, barber-surgeon, to Anthony Bennet, of East Greenwich, esq., in 200*l.*, for the payment of 105*l.* 10*s.* on 24 Feb., 1621–2. Dat. 22 Nov., 19 Jas. I., 1621. Signed.

180. BOND from Sir Francis Calton, of Havering Le Bower, co. Essex, knt., and Edward Allen, of Dulwich, esq., to Magdalen Vaughan, of London, in 100*l.*, for the payment of 52*l.* 10*s.* on 30 Nov. Dat. 28 May, 20 Jas. I., 1622. Signed.

181. ARTICLES whereby Edward Alleyn, son of Godfrey Alleyn, of Norwich, gent., is bound apprentice to Edward Alleyn, of Dulwich, esq., for 7 years. Dat. 26 Dec., 1622. Signed. Witnesses, [Sir] Geo. More, [Sir] Tho. Grymes, and other justices, 17 Jan., 1622–3.

182. BILL of complaint in Chancery of William Persons [Parsons], of Southwark, waterman, and Anne, his wife, against Edward Allen, praying for an injunction to stay his suit against them on a bond for 500*l.*, on the ground that he had obtained the same by an unfulfilled promise to

[1] See above, pp. 185, 189. The first brick was laid 13 July, 1620, and the almshouses were opened 30 April, 1621.

procure for them from Agnes Henslowe a lease for 21 years, or the term of her life, of messuages, &c., called the 'Boares head,' on the Bankside, in Southwark, which had been bequeathed her by Philip Henslowe, her husband, for life, with remainder to the said Anne Persons, his niece. Dat. 18 May, 1625. Paper, 20 sheets.

183. ANSWER by Edward Allen, joint defendant with Sir John Wildgosse, to a bill of complaint of Thomas Farrefoulde, denying all knowledge of a lease alleged to have been made by Thomas Wildgosse to Richard Knell, and assigned to the complainant, of lands in the manor of Lewisham, which were in possession of the said Edw. Allen by virtue of a lease of the manor for 24 years from Richard Sedlye, dat. 14 Dec., 1620. Dat. [1625 or 1626]. Paper, 6 sheets. *Imperfect.*

184. BILL in Chancery of Edward Allen, of Dulwich, esq., against Edmond Travis, of London, haberdasher, and Susanna, his wife, for the non-performance of a covenant to levy to him a fine of messuages, &c., in the parish of St. Anne, Blackfriars, a lease of which they had granted him, 26 Mar., 1617, for 50 years at a rent of 160*l.*, and upon the repair of which he had expended 1,500*l.* Dat. [1625 or 1626]. Paper, 14 sheets.

(*SECTION III.*)

DOCUMENTS relating to Dulwich manor and the foundation of Alleyn's College of God's Gift; 1323–1626:—

185. GRANT from Richard de Langeforde, 'dictus le clerke,' of Suthwerke, and Johanna, his wife, and Simon de Paris and Agatha, his wife, dau. of the said Richard and Johanna, to Robert le Mareschal, of Suthwerke, Cristiana, his wife, and Mariona and Isolda, their daughters, of a messuage and land in Dilewysshe, in the par. of Camerwelle. Witnesses, Steph. de Bekewelle, Will. le Mareschal, Tho. ate Grene, &c. Dat. Sunday before the Feast of St. Gregory the Pope [12 Mar.], 16 Edw. II. [1323]. *Lat.* With four seals, that of Simon de Paris bearing his arms.

186. GRANT from Richard de Langeford, 'dictus le Clerk,' of Suthwerk, to Robert le Mareschal, of Suthwerk, Cristiana, his wife, and Mariona and Isolda, their daughters, of the same messuage and land in Dilewysshe. Witnesses, Steph. de Bekewell, Will. le Mareschal, Tho. atte Grene, &c. Dat. Sund. after the F. of St. Gregory [12 Mar.], 16 Edw. II. [1323]. *Lat.* With fragment of seal.

187. GRANT from Alan, son and heir of Hugh Gerarde, of Dylewyssche, to Roger Berlynge, of Dylewyssche, and Matilda, his wife, of a tenement next the Eststrete and land in a field called Pirifelde, in Dylewyssche, inherited by the grantor from Hugh, his father. Witnesses, Steph. de Bokewelle, Will. Roce, Will. le Mareschall, &c. Dat. 13 Apr., 3 Edw. III. [1329]. *Lat.*

188. DEED OF SALE by Alan Gerard, of Dilewysshe, and Golda, his mother, to Amiel le Meleward and Juliana, his wife, of all their moveable goods in the messuage which the vendees had of the grant of Roger Berlyngge and Matilda, his wife, [in Dilewysshe]. Witnesses, Will. Roce, Will. le Mareschal, Tho. atte Grene, &c. Dat. Tuesd. after the F. of SS. Simon and Jude [28 Oct.], 4 Edw. III. [1330]. *Lat.* With seals.

189. GRANT from John Le Herde, of London, butcher, to Thomas de Hockele of land, &c., called Gerardes Rudene, in Dyluyshe, acquired by grant from Henry Horpol, of London, armourer. Witnesses, Steph. de Bekwelle, Hen. [de] Bekwelle, Will. Roce, &c. Dat. F. of the Exaltation of the H. Cross [14 Sept.], 7 Edw. III. [1333]. *Lat.* With seal.

190. GRANT from Juliana, dau. of Nicholas atte Grene, of Dilewyssche, to William Bussche, of Dylewyssche, of her part of a messuage, garden, &c., in Dylewyssche, in the par. of St. Giles of Camerwelle. Witnesses, Will. le Maschal, Rich. Rotholf, Amyel le Melleward, &c. Dat. Sund. after the F. of St. Augustine [26 May], 11 Edw. III. [1337]. *Lat.*

191. RELEASE from William Mab, marshal of co. Stafford, to John Leuerich, of Waltham Holy Cross, co. Essex, of all his lands and tenements in Est Dilewissh, in the par. of Camerwelle, co. Surrey. Witnesses, Will. de Carleton, Walt. Turk, Will. Clapitus, Rich. de Pynnore, &c. Dat. Est Dilewissh, Sunday after the F. of St. Bartholomew [24 Aug.], 14 Edw. III. [1340]. *Lat.* With seal.

192. GRANT from Nicholas de Strode, of Camerwelle, to Geoffrey de Chykewelle and Johanna, his wife, of a messuage, &c., in Suthdilewysshe, acquired by the grantor from John de Strode, his father. Witnesses, Hen. de Bokewelle, Tho. de Hockele, Peter de Bokewelle, &c. Dat. Thursd. after the F. of St. Ambrose [4 Apr.], 28 Edw. III. [1354]. *Lat.* With seal.

193. GRANT from John Bosshe and Juliana, his wife, of Dilwysche, to Helena, dau. of William de Portusmouthe, of a messuage, garden, &c., in Dilwissche. Witnesses, Rich. Chaundelar, John Wynchestre, John Gaunt, &c. Dat. London, F. of SS. Philip and James [1 May], 37 Edw. III. [1363]. *Lat.* With two seals, one a fine seal of arms.

194. GRANT from Richard de Bailay to Laurence de Merkyngfeld and Ralph, son of Richard de Augtone, of co. Lanc., of all their lands, &c., in Dylwyche, in the par. of Camerwelle, except thirteen acres held 'per virgam' of the manor of Dylwyche. Witnesses, Hen. de Bekwelle, Will. de Depham, Will. Lede, &c. Dat. 20 Apr., 43 Edw. III. [1369]. *Lat.* With seal of arms.

195. RELEASE from Mary, widow of Sir Richard Bailay, knt., to Robert de Boxford, of London, cloth-worker, of her right of dower in lands, &c., at Dilewysshe, in Camerwelle. Witnesses, Hen. Beckewelle, Ralph de Burnham, Will. Depham, &c. Dat. 13 Mar., 44 Edw. III. [1370]. *Lat.* With seal.

196. GRANT from Robert de Boxford, cloth-worker, and Robert de Kent, citizens of London, to John Pere, of London, merchant, and Alice, his wife, of all lands, tenements, &c., at Dilewisshe, in the par. of Camerwelle, which they lately purchased from Laurence de Merkyngfeld and Ralph, son of Richard de Aughton, of co. Lanc. Witnesses, Hen. Bekwelle, Ralph de Burnham, Will. Leed, &c. Dat. Dilewisshe, Tuesd.

after the F. of H. Trinity, 44 Edw. III. [1370]. *Lat.* With two seals.

197. GRANT from Nicholas Strode, of Lombhithe [Lambeth], to Edward Palee, of Camerwelle, and Agnes, his wife, of land in Camerwelle, in a field called Peryfeld, extending on the W. and N. to the road called Aspole. Witnesses, Hen. Bokewelle, John Peere, Rich. Ode, &c. Dat. Sund. after the F. of St. Luke [18 Oct.], 47 Edw. III. [1373]. *Lat.* With seal.

198. GRANT from John Pere, of London, and Alice, his wife, to Gilbert Meldeborne, of London, and Stephen Sexteyn, of Frythendene, of all their lands, &c., at Dilewisshe, lately bought of Robert de Boxford and Robert de Kent. Witnesses, Pet. Sandone, John Carter, John Fippe, &c. Dat. 26 Oct., 48 Edw. III. [1374]. *Lat.* With seals.

199. GRANT from Gilbert Meldeborne and Stephen Sexteyn to Adam Fraunceys, alderman of London, Adam de S. Ivone [St. Ives], William Canele, and others of the same lands, &c. Witnesses, as above. Dat. 20 Nov., 48 Edw. III. [1374]. *Lat.* With two seals, one having the arms of Gilb. Meldeborne.

200. RELEASE from Katerine, widow of Nicholas Strode, of Lombhithe, to Edward Paule, of Camerwelle, of her dower in land in a field called Peryfeld, in Camerwelle, bought by the said Edward and Agnes, his wife, of the said Nicholas Strode. Witnesses, Tho. Balsham, Rich. Ode, Rich. Dene, &c. Dat. 10 Apr., 50 Edw. III. [1376]. *Lat.* With seal.

201–210. EXTRACTS from the court-roll of Dulwich manor, being the title-deeds of 11 acres of land at Howlettes Bridge, passing, by conveyance or inheritance, through the hands of William Brand, Christiana Mortlake and Walter, son of John Mortlake, Walter Godman, Thomas Dybbyll and Alice, his wife, William Ode and Johanna, his wife, Henry Ode and Thomas Ode to Edmond Bowyer. Dat. Wedn. after the F. of All Saints [1 Nov.], 4 Rich. II. [1380]—22 Oct., 28 Eliz. [1586]. *Lat.* Endorsed by Edw. Alleyn, '10 copies of Sr Edm. Bowyars copiehold landes surendred to me E. A.'

211. GRANT from John Gaunt, of Dilewisshe, and Johanna, his wife, widow of Geoffrey de Chikewelle, to John Knyghte, of Camerwelle, of a messuage, garden, &c., in Southdilewisshe, acquired by the said Geoffrey and Johanna from Nicholas de Strode. Witnesses, Rich. Wode, Rich. Courteour, Will. Walsche, &c. Dat. F. of the Innocents [28 Dec.], 13 Rich. II. [1389]. *Lat.* With seal of arms, and another.

212. RELEASE from Peter Borne, of London, tailor, and Dionisia, his wife, to John Knyghte, of Camerwelle, of the same messuage, garden, &c., in Southdilewisshe, in Camerwelle. Dat. F. of St. Thomas the Martyr [29 Dec.], 13 Rich. II. [1389]. *Lat.* With seal of arms, and another.

213. RELEASE from John Freman, clerk, of London, and Idonia, his wife, to John Knyghte, of Camerwelle, of the same messuage, garden, &c. Dat. F. of St. Thomas the Martyr, 13 Rich. II. [1389]. *Lat.* With seals.

214. COVENANT whereby the grant from John Gaunt and Johanna, his wife, to John Knyghte of a messuage, &c., in Southdilewisshe, as above, no. 211, is made conditional upon the enjoyment by the said Johanna of a parcel of the premises for life. Dat. 1 Jan., 13 Rich. II. [1390]. *Lat.* With seal of arms, and another.

215. POWER OF ATTORNEY from Robert Braybroke, Bishop of London, Sir John de Cobham, knt., and John Seymour, of London, to John Drewe, clerk, to deliver seisin to

David de Bikeleghe of the manor of Dulwyche. Dat. Frid. after the F. of All Saints [1 Nov.], 17 Rich. II. [1393]. *Lat.* With fragments of seals of arms.

216. RELEASE from John Hockle, son and heir of Robert Hockle, to Thomas Sakeville, of co. Sussex, John Cokyn, John Drewe, parson of Harple, and others of all the lands, &c., in Camerwelle and Lambehethe, lately belonging to Thomas Hockle, his uncle. Witnesses, John Sandyford, John Warynge, Rich. Courteour, &c. Dat. 26 Jan., 21 Rich. II. [1398]. *Lat.*

217. GRANT from Thomas Eyllesham, of Dylwisshe, and Agnes, his wife, to Henry Bromford, William Bekwelle, John Erehethe, Richard de Ouere, and Henry Hardele of two houses in Dylwisshe, had respectively by grant from William Bythewode and Alice, his wife, and John Role and Johanna, his wife. Witnesses, John Sonnyngford, Rich. Ode, Rich. Courteour, &c. Dat. 5 Mar., 1 Hen. IV. [1400]. *Lat.*

218. RELEASE from William Knyghte, of Lambhithe, to Thomas Aylesham, of Delewiche, and William Bekewelle, of London, vintner, of a messuage, &c., in Delewiche, had by grant from Thomas Short and Alice, his wife. Witnesses, John Sandyngford, John Horle, Rich. Corteour, &c. Dat. 8 Apr., 2 Hen. IV. [1401]. *Lat.* With seal.

219. GRANT from Elena Portusmouthe, widow, dau. of William Portusmouthe, of co. Surrey, to William Wedene, of Dilwysshe, and Johanna, his wife, of a messuage, garden, &c., in Dilwysshe, between the tenement of Sir Robert Denny, knt., and the highway, and between 'Dilewysshe wode' and a field of the same Sir Robert. Witnesses, John Sonnyngforde, John Horlee, Rich. Ode, &c. Dat. 19 Apr., 6 Hen. IV. [1405]. *Lat.* With seal.

220. GRANT from Sir Robert Denny, knt., and Amy, his wife, to Sir John Cornewaylle, knt., John Cokeyn, Sir William Berdewelle, knt., Thomas Geney, esq., John Sayere, of London, and John Hals of all their lands, tenements, &c., in Delewisshe and the parishes of Camerwelle and Lambehethe, co. Surrey. Witnesses, Nich. Carreu, John Grene, John Sonyngford, &c. Dat. 5 Jan., 9 Hen. IV. [1408]. *Lat.* With fine seal of arms, and another.

221. GRANT from William Wedene, of co. Surrey, and Johanna, his wife, to John Sondeford and Alice Shrewesbery of a messuage, garden, &c., in Delewysshe. Witnesses, John Horle, Rich. Ode, John atte Bregge, &c. Dat. 20 Apr., 9 Hen. IV. [1408]. *Lat.* With seal of arms.

222. GRANT from John Sondeford and Alice Shrewesbury, widow, to William Bergh, clerk, William Weston, of London, cloth-worker, John Mathewe, clerk, and Thomas Jue [or Ive], of London, cloth-worker, of a messuage, garden, &c., in Delewisshe, next the tenement of Sir Robert Denny, knt. Witnesses, John Horlee, Rich. Ode, John Brigges, &c. Dat. 21 Jan., 11 Hen. IV. [1410]. *Lat.* With two seals.

223. GENERAL RELEASE from John Sondeford, of Camerwelle, to Simon Dokkyng, of Delewysshe. Dat. 23 Aug., 4 Hen. V. [1416]. *Lat.*

224. EXTRACT from the court-roll of Dulwich manor, of the surrender by Thomas Sampsone, of London, butcher, of three tenements, late belonging to John Reygate and others, to the use of Thomas Haukyne, of London, butcher. Dat. Mond. after the F. of Corpus Christi, 10 Hen. V. [1422]. *Lat.*

225–228. Extracts from the court-roll of Dulwich manor, whereby a tenement called Brounyng, or Brounnyngges, and four acres of land are surrendered by John Lilleborne to the use of Isabella, his wife; by her to the use of Robert Wade; by him to the use of John Elys and Johanna, his wife; and by them to the use of John Brutone. Dat. Mond. after the F. of Corpus Christi, 10 Hen. V. [1422]—Mond. before Mich[s], 3 Hen. VI. [1424]. *Lat.*

229. Extract from the court-roll of Dulwich manor, of the surrender by Elienora Wodesere of 1½ acre of land in 'le aps,' near Langebourne, to the use of Henry Lake. Dat. Thursd. before the F. of St. Faith [6 Oct.], 3 Hen. VI. [1424]. *Lat.*

230. Defeasance of a grant from Simon Dockyng, of Camerwell, tile-maker, to John Drynkwater, the elder, and John Drynkwater, the younger, of a messuage, &c., in the par. of Camerwelle, conditional upon the payment, by yearly instalments, of 23*l.* 6*s.* 8*d.* Dat. 26 Sept., 6 Hen. VI., 1427. *Lat.* With seal.

231. Grant from Simon Dockyng to John Drynkewater, of Pecham, the elder, and John Drynkewater, the younger, of a tenement, &c., in Delewyche. Witnesses, Will. Westone, Tho. Gryme, John Colkoc, &c. Dat. Mich[s], 6 Hen. VI. [1427]. *Lat.* With seal.

232–242. Extracts from the court-roll of Dulwich manor, showing the descent of a messuage and lands from father to son from William Lane to Thomas, John, Richard, John and Richard Lane, and from the last-named to John Crofte and Thomas Crofte, his son. Dat. Thursd. after the F. of St. Martin, 8 Hen. VI. [1429]—22 Oct., 28 Eliz. [1586]. *Lat.*

243. GRANT from William More, of Bekynham, co. Kent, to Roger Hundirwode, of Dyllewyche, of a house and 4½ acres of land in a field called Canelcroft, in the par. of Camerwelle, had by grant from Richard Knyghte, of Lambehythe, and Edward FitzSymondes, of Camerwelle. Witnesses, Rich. Ode, Rich. Depeham, Tho. Gryme, &c. Dat. 1 Apr., 9 Hen. VI. [1431]. *Lat.*

244. EXTRACT from the court-roll of Dulwich manor, of the surrender by Edith, widow of Henry Lake, and William, son of the same, of a croft near Langbourne, formerly belonging to Richard Wodesere, to the use of Roger Tornour. Dat. Mond. after the F. of St. Andrew [30 Nov.], 11 Hen. VI. [1432]. *Lat.*

245. EXTRACTS from the court-roll of Dulwich manor, of surrenders to the use of Roger Tornour—(1) as above, no. 244; (2) by Richard Depeham of an acre called Canell acre; and (3) by Simon Dokkyng of 1½ acre in Purifield. Dat. 11 Hen. VI. [1432]. *Lat.*

246. GRANT from Simon Dokkyng, of Dilwyssh, tilemaker, to William Dokkyng and Johanna, his wife, of a messuage known as Coppedhalle, &c., in Dilwysshe, had by the said Simon and Johanna, his wife, by grant from Andrew Heriard, of London, tiler. Witnesses, Tho. Yngolf, John Colkok, John Carter, &c. Dat. 10 Feb., 13 Hen. VI. [1435]. *Lat.* With seal.

247. DEMISE by John Drynkwater, the elder, and John Drynkwater, the younger, to Thomas Wakefeld, of London, gent., and Johanna, his wife, of a messuage, &c., in Dilwyche, conditional upon the payment of 10*l.* in the parish church of Camerwelle on Easter Day, 1437. Witnesses, Rich. Baker,

John Fairwyner, Tho. Ingham, &c. Dat. 27 Feb., 13 Hen. VI. [1435]. *Lat.* With seals.

248. GRANT from Thomas Wakefeld, of London, gent., and Johanna, his wife, to William FitzWalter, gent., William Albertone, gent., Henry Appultone, gent., and William Appultone, his brother, of a messuage, &c., in Dilwych. Witnesses, Rich. Bakere, John Fayrewyne, Tho. Ingham. Dat. 1 Mar., 13 Hen. VI. [1435]. *Lat.* With seals.

249. EXTRACT from the court-roll of Dulwich manor, of grant of seisin to John Knyght, younger son of Cristiana Knyght, of 2 acres of land in le Napce and Crokstrete, inherited from his mother. Dat. Thursd. after the F. of St. Andrew [30 Nov.], 14 Hen. VI. [1435]. *Lat.*

250. EXTRACT from the court-roll of Dulwich manor, of the surrender by William Haukyn of a messuage and 30 acres of land, late belonging to Thomas Haukyn, his brother, to the use of Robert Claptone, of London, cloth-worker. Dat. 14 Hen. VI. [1435]. *Lat.*

251. FEOFFMENT from Cecilia, widow of John Horle, of Camerwelle, and Richard Baker, of Pekham, to John Brutone, of Camerwelle, of land in a field called Peryfeld, in Camerwelle, adjoining the road called Aspole. Witnesses, Rich. Ode, Will. Ode, Rich. Depeham, &c. Dat. 31 Oct., 15 Hen. VI. [1436]. *Lat.* With seals.

252. EXTRACT from the court-roll of Dulwich manor, of the surrender by Robert Clopton, of London, cloth-worker, of a messuage and 30 acres of land to the use of William Fayrher and Juliana, his wife. Dat. Mond. after the F. of St. Katherine [25 Nov.], 15 Hen. VI. [1436]. *Lat.*

253. EXTRACT from the court-roll of Dulwich manor, of the surrender by Simon Dockyng of 1½ acre of land in Puryfield to the use of Roger Tornour. Dat. 15 Hen. VI. [1436]. *Lat.*

254, 255. EXTRACTS from the court-roll of Dulwich manor, of the surrender of 2 acres of land in Lytel Crofte by Lucy Bakere to the use of Richard Wythyr and Lucy, his wife, and by Richard Wythyr to the use of John Brutone. Dat. 15 Hen. VI. [1436], 28 Hen. VI. [1449]. *Lat.*

256. EXTRACT from the court-roll of Dulwich manor, of the surrender by John Aleyne of 7 acres of land in Frenchefelde, late Richard Aleyne's, to the use of Walter Marys and Richard Wyther. Dat. F. of SS. Fabian and Sebastian [20 Jan.], 16 Hen. VI. [1438]. *Lat.*

257. DEFEASANCE of a grant from William Dokkyng, of Dilwysshe, and Johanna, his wife, to John Drynkwater, the younger, Richard Baker, of Pekham, and John Knyght, of the messuage called Coppedhalle, &c., in Dillwysshe, conditional upon the payment, by instalments, of 13*l.* 6*s.* 8*d.* Dat. 30 Oct., 19 Hen. VI. [1440]. *Lat.*

258. RELEASE by John Knyght, of Delewysshe, to John Drynkwater, the younger, and Richard Baker, of Pekham, of lands, &c., in Delewysshe, held by the three jointly by grant from William Dokkyng and Johanna, his wife. Witnesses, John Brutone, Rich. Ode, Will. Ode, &c. Dat. 26 Oct., 20 Hen. VI. [1441]. *Lat.*

259, 260. EXTRACTS from the court-roll of Dulwich manor, of the surrender by John Baker, and re-grant to the same and William Knyght, of London, butcher, of a messuage and 30 acres of land, lately belonging to William Hawkyne and William Clopton. Dat. Wedn. after the F. of St. Barnabas [11 June], 21 Hen. VI. [1443]. *Lat.*

261, 262. GRANT from Thomas Wakefeld, of Southwark, and Johanna, his wife, to William FitzWater, Johanna, his wife, dau. of the said Johanna, Elias Davy, and others of all their lands, &c., in Dylwyche and Camerwelle, reserving an annual rent of 4*l.* 6*s.* 8*d.* to the grantors or the survivor of them for life. Witnesses, Rich. Baker, John Drynkwater, John Brutone, &c. Dat. 2 Nov., 24 Hen. VI. [1445]. *Lat.* Followed by the counterpart, having five seals.

263. FEOFFMENT from Roger Wynter and John Colford to John Brutone and John Bakere of 5 acres of land in Puryfeld, in Delewysshe. Witnesses, Will. FitzWater, Rich. Baker, Will. Ottele, &c. Dat. 31 Dec., 25 Hen. VI. [1446]. *Lat.* With fragments of seals.

264. FEOFFMENT from John Drynkwater, the younger, Richard Baker, of Pekham, and John Knyght to William FitzWater, Elias Davy, Thomas Warham, and others of the messuage called Coppedhalle, &c., in Dilwish, had by grant from William Dokkyng and Johanna, his wife. Witnesses, John Maynell, esq., John Brutone, Rich. Wode. Dat. 1 July, 25 Hen. VI. [1447]. *Lat.* With seals.

265. POWER OF ATTORNEY from John Drynkwater, the younger, Richard Baker, and John Knyght to John Brathewelle to deliver seisin to William FitzWater, Elias Davy, Thomas Warham, and others of the messuage, &c., as above. Dat. 1 July, 25 Hen. VI. [1447]. *Lat.* With three seals.

266. RELEASE from John Drynkwater, the younger, Richard Baker, and John Knyght to William FitzWater, Elias Davy, Thomas Warham, and others of the same messuage, &c. Dat. 10 July, 25 Hen. VI. [1447]. *Lat.* With seals.

267. EXTRACT from the court-roll of Dulwich manor, of the grant of seisin to Felix, widow of Walter Knyght, of 2 acres of land in le Naps for life, with remainder to John, her elder son. Dat. 17 Apr., 26 Hen. VI. [1448]. *Lat.*

268. EXTRACT from the court-roll of Dulwich manor, of the surrender by Richard Dereham of 2 acres of land to the use of John Brutone and William Ode. Dat. 17 Apr., 26 Hen. VI. [1448]. *Lat.*

269. GRANT from Roger Hundirwode, of Dyllewych, to William Knyght, the elder, of London, butcher, and John Carter of a house and land in Dyllewych in a field called Canelcroft, had by grant from William More, of Bekenham. Witnesses, John Brutone, John Warene, Tho. Lane, &c. Dat. 14 Feb., 31 Hen. VI. [1453]. *Lat.* With seal.

270. EXTRACT from the court-roll of Dulwich manor, of the surrender by Henry Perrour to the use of John Brutone and Elias Ingolf of lands, &c., late belonging to John Wynter. Dat. 4 June, 31 Hen. VI. [1453]. *Lat.*

271. RELEASE from William Dokkyng, of Dylwyssh, and Johanna, his wife, to William FitzWater, Elias Davy, Thomas Warham, and others of a messuage called Coppedhalle, with lands, &c., in Dylwysshe, held by the latter parties by feoffment, as above, no. 264. Dat. 27 Feb., 32 Hen. VI. [1454]. *Lat.* With two seals.

272. GRANT from Roger Vndrewode, of Dilwich, to William Knight, the elder, of London, butcher, of half an acre of land in Canelfeld, in Dilwich, had by grant from Johanna Balle, widow. Witnesses, John Brutone, Tho. Lane, John Carter, &c. Dat. 26 Mar., 32 Hen. VI. [1454]. *Lat.* With seal.

273. RELEASE from Johanna Balle, of Dilwiche, widow, to William Knighte, the elder, of the land as above. Dat. 30 Mar., 32 Hen. VI. [1454]. *Lat.* With fragment of seal.

274. FEOFFMENT from William FitzWater, Johanna, his wife, dau. of Thomas Wakefeld, Elias Davy, Thomas Warham, and others to John Braythewelle, Agnes, his wife, Nicholas Marchall, and John Andrewe of the messuage, &c., in Dulwyche, called Coppedhalle, had by feoffment from John Drynkwater and others, conditional upon the payment, by instalments, of 23*l.* 6*s.* 8*d.* Dat. 28 Aug., 32 Hen. VI. [1454]. *Lat.* With seal and fragments. Much rotted and injured by damp.

275. POWER OF ATTORNEY from William FitzWater and others, as above, to Thomas Dantree and Richard Fereby to deliver seisin to John Braythewelle and Agnes, his wife, Nicholas Marchall, and John Andrewe of all their lands, &c., in Dylwyche, had by grant from Thomas Wakefeld and Johanna, his wife, and also of the messuage, &c., called Coppedhalle, had by feoffment, as above. Dat. 28 Aug., 32 Hen. VI. [1454]. *Lat.* With six seals.

276–281. EXTRACTS from the court-roll of Dulwich manor, relating to two acres called Walkynscrofte, Walkerscroft, Walcardyscrofte, Walkenscrofte or Walcardisecrofte, viz.:—

276. Surrender by Thomas Wakefield to the use of John Braythewelle. Dat. Tuesd. after the F. of All Saints, 33 Hen. VI. [1454]. *Lat.*

277. Surrender by John Hunte to the use of Johanna, his wife, for life, with remainder to John, his son. Dat. 3 May, 21 Edw. IV. [1481]. *Lat.*

278. Surrender by Robert Holonde and Johanna, his wife, widow of John Hunt, to the use of Guy Hunt, with release by John Hunt, jun. Dat. 10 July, 12 Hen. VII. [1497]. *Lat.*

279. Grant of seisin to Henry Hunte, son of Guy Hunte. Dat. 15 Dec., 11 Hen. VIII. [1519]. *Lat.*

280. Surrender by John Hunte to the use of Walter Boyer. Dat. 12 Feb., 8 Eliz. [1566]. *Lat.*

281. Surrender by Walter Bowyer to the use of John Dove. Dat. 14 Oct., 10 Eliz. [1568]. *Lat.*

282. EXTRACT from the court-roll of Dulwich manor, of the surrender by William Knyght and John Baker of a messuage and 30 acres of land to the use of Elias Ingolf, John Carter, jun., Elizabeth, wife of the said William Knyght, and the heirs of the same Elizabeth. Dat. Thurs. after the F. of St. Andrew [30 Nov.], 36 Hen. VI. [1457]. *Lat.*

283. FEOFFMENT from John Carter, of Dyllewyche, to Elizabeth, widow of William Knyght, sen., of London, butcher, Nicholas Boille, of London, 'Wexchaundeler,' and Thomas Fermory, of London, scrivener, of a house and 4½ acres of land in Canelcroft, in the par. of Camerwelle, hald by grant from Roger Hundirwode, of Dyllewyche. Witnesses, John Brutone, John Warene, Tho. Lane, &c. Dat. 5 Aug., 36 Hen. VI. [1458]. *Lat.*

284. RELEASE by Roger Vndrewode, of Dylwyche, to Elizabeth, widow of William Knyght, and others, as above, of a house and land, &c., in Dyllewych, in a field called Canelcroft, had by them by feoffment from John Carter, with half an acre in Canelfeld and other lands, had by grant from the same Roger. Dat. 8 Aug., 36 Hen. VI. [1458]. *Lat.*

285. EXTRACT from the court-roll of Dulwich manor, of the surrender by William Spencer and Agnes, his wife, to the use of John Brutone, of land at Tweycroftes, late belonging to Tho. Gryme. Dat. F. of St. Clement, Pope [17 Nov.], 37 Hen. VI. [1458]. *Lat.*

286, 287. EXTRACTS from the court-roll of Dulwich manor, of the surrender by Roger Vnderwode, *al.* Tornour, of 1½ acre of land in le Aspe, near Langebourne, late Richard and Alianor Wodesere's, 1 acre called Canell acre, late Rich. Depeham's, and 1½ acre near the Waterynges in Puryfeld, late Simon Dokkyng's—the whole to the use of Elizabeth, widow of William Knyght. Dat. F. of St. Clement, Pope [17 Nov.], 37 Hen. VI. [1458]. *Lat.*

288. EXTRACT from the court-roll of Dulwich manor, of the surrender by Elizabeth, widow of William Knyght, of a messuage and 30 acres of land, and of the re-grant of the same to the said Elizabeth, John Veyre, *al.* Feer, of London, goldsmith, her son by Thomas Veyre, late of London, vintner, Edmond Hille, porter of the Weyhous, London, and others. Dat. 28 Nov., 5 Edw. IV. [1465]. *Lat.*

289. EXTRACTS from the court-roll of Dulwich manor, of a similar surrender and re-grant of the land as above, nos. 286, 287. Dat. 28 Nov., 5 Edw. IV. [1465]. *Lat.*

290. RELEASE from William FitzWater and Thomas Warham to John Braythewelle and Agnes, his wife, Nicholas Marchall and John Andrewe of lands, tenements, &c., in Dylwyche, lately belonging to Thomas Wakefeld and Johanna, his wife, and of the messuage called Coppedhalle, &c., in the same. Dat. 11 Oct., 6 Edw. IV. [1466]. *Lat.* With seals.

291. EXTRACT from the court-roll of Dulwich manor, of the surrender by John Bruton of land called 'v daywark,' in Longburne, to the use of John Veyer. Dat. 6 May, 8 Edw. IV. [1468]. *Lat.*

292. EXTRACT from the court-roll of Dulwich manor, of the grant of seisin to Richard Ode of 11 acres of land near Cortemede, as heir of William Ode, deceased. Dat. 15 July, 11 Edw. IV. [1471]. *Lat.*

293. EXTRACT from the court-roll of Dulwich manor, of the grant of seisin to Johanna, wife of John Brutone, and John Dowve, *al.* Brutone, of half a rod of land. Dat. 24 Oct., 11 Edw. IV. [1471]. *Lat.*

294, 295. EXTRACTS from the court-roll of Dulwich manor, of the surrender of a tenement and 10 acres of land by John Barnard to the use of Hugh Alstone and Matilda, his wife, and by the latter to the use of Guy Hunt and Margery, his wife. Dat. 24 Oct., 11 Edw. IV. [1471], 19 Oct., 12 Edw. IV. [1472]. *Lat.*

296. EXTRACT from the court-roll of Dulwich manor, of the surrender by John Veyre, *al.* Feer, and others of the messuage and lands as above, nos. 286–288, and of the re-grant of the same to the said John Veyre alone. Dat. 22 Apr., 12 Edw. IV. [1472]. *Lat.*

297. EXTRACT from the court-roll of Dulwich manor, of the surrender by Thomas Newman and Elizabeth, his wife, of an acre in Twaycrochyn to the use of John Brutone, Johanna, his wife, and John Dove. Dat. 19 Oct., 12 Edw. IV. [1472]. *Lat.*

298. RELEASE from Elizabeth, widow of Thomas Newman, to John Brutone, of Camerwelle, yeoman, of all lands,

&c., in Camerwelle, late belonging to Margaret Pynnour, her mother. Dat. 18 Nov., 13 Edw. IV. [1473]. *Lat.* With seal.

299. EXTRACT from the court-roll of Dulwich manor, of the surrender by John Veyre of the messuage and lands as above, nos. 286–288, to the use of Henry Knyght and Elena, his wife. Dat. Tuesd. after the F. of H. Trinity, 19 Edw. IV. [1479]. *Lat.*

300. EXTRACT from the court-roll of Dulwich manor, of the surrender by Felicia, widow of John Morgan and wife of John Mose, of a field called Frensshfeld and two acres of wood in le Napse, formerly belonging to Walter Knyght, her husband, to the use of John Knyght and Alienor, his wife. Dat. Tuesd. after the F. of H. Trinity, 19 Edw. IV. [1479]. *Lat.*

301. BARGAIN AND SALE by William Braythewelle and John Braythewelle, sons of John and Agnes Braythewelle, to Robert Crosby, of Westminster, gent., of all their lands, &c., in Dylwiche, including the messuage called Coppedhalle. Dat. 8 June, 8 Hen. VII. [1493]. With fragment of seal. With bond in 40*l.* to perform covenants attached.

302. GRANT from William Braythewell, son and heir of John and Agnes Braythewell, to Robert Crosby, of West minster, gent., of all the lands, tenements, &c., late belonging to Thomas Wakefeld and Johanna, his wife, in Dylwyche and Camerwell, together with the messuage called Coppedhalle, &c. Witnesses, John Lye, esq., John Scot, gent., Hen. Knyght, yeoman, &c. Dat. 9 June, 8 Hen. VII. [1493]. *Lat.* With seal.

303. RELEASE from William and John Braythewelle to Robert Crosby of the same lands, tenements, &c., in Dylwyche and Camerwelle. Dat. 11 June, 8 Hen. VII. [1493]. *Lat.* With seal.

304. EXTRACT from the court-roll of Dulwich manor, of the surrender by Edward Bassham and Edith, his wife, of land in a place called Berdye to the use of Thomas Webster. Dat. Thursd. after the F. of St. Mark [25 Apr.], 10 Hen. VII. [1495]. *Lat.*

305. WILL of Guy Huntte, of Dulwyche, making bequests of money to the 'hye awlter' of St. Giles, Camerwell, to the 'brotherhede off Seynt Gylys,' to 'the lyghte off Seynt Jamys,' and to Elizabeth, Annes, Alys, and Jone, his daughters, with the residue to Alys, his wife, and giving his land at Penge to John, his son; his dwelling-house and land adjacent to Alys, his wife, till Edward, his son, reach full age, and then to the latter in tail; his new house, with Walkynscrofte, to Henry, his son, in tail; and his land called 'Gory londe' to William, his son, in tail; the whole with remainders over. Witnesses, 'Syr Wylliam, parysche pryst off Camerwelle,' Hen. Knyghte, Tho. Webster, &c. Dat. 1 Oct., 1503. With probate attached, 18 Oct., 1503.

306. GRANT from Margery Crosby, dau. of George Crosby, kinsman and heir of Robert Crosby, deceased, to Margery, widow of John Lee, of London, goldsmith, Richard Ellys, John Poole, of London, Robert Le, and Nicholas Alwyn, of lands, tenements, &c., in Dylwyche and Camerwelle, late belonging to Thomas Wakefeld, of Suthwerk, and Johanna, his wife, together with a messuage called Coppedhalle, with lands, &c., in Dilwiche. Dat. 13 May, 11 Hen. VIII. [1519]. *Lat.* With seal.

307. EXTRACT from the court-roll of Dulwich manor, of the grant of seisin to Edward Hunte, son and heir of Guy

Hunte, of a tenement and ten acres of land, late belonging to Bernard Johns and afterwards to Guy Hunte, to hold in tail, with remainder to Henry and William, second and third sons of the said Guy. Dat. 15 Dec., 11 Hen. VIII. [1519]. *Lat.*

308. EXTRACTS from the court-roll of Dulwich manor, showing the descent of two messuages and 57 acres of land to Nicholas Knight, son and heir of Henry Knight. Dat. 15 Dec., 11 Hen. VIII. [1519], 3 June, 7 Edw. VI. [1553], 13 Apr., 32 Eliz. [1590]. *Lat.*

309–311. EXTRACTS from the court-roll of Dulwich manor, relating to two acres of land in Mydellfeld, Medyllffeld, or Middlefilde, viz.:—

309. Grant of seisin to Agnes Hunte, dau. of Sibelle Hunte, dau. of Elizabeth Hale, with two other acres to Richard Lane and Margery, his wife, also dau. of Eliz. Hale. Dat. 17 Jan., 12 Hen. VIII. [1521]. *Lat.*

310. Surrender by Agnes Hunte to the use of Henry Ode. Dat. 17 Jan., 12 Hen. VIII. [1521]. *Lat.*

311. Surrender by Thomas, son of Hen. Ode, and Elizabeth, his wife, to the use of John Dove. Dat. 4 May, 6 Eliz. [1564]. *Lat.*

312. BARGAIN AND SALE by Margery, widow of John Lee, of London, goldsmith, and Richard Ellys, her son, to Henry Oode, of Camberwell, yeoman, for 23*l.* 10*s.*, of Coppedhalle and other messuages, lands, &c., in Dylwyche and Camerwelle, co. Surr., which came to the said Margery by grant from Margery, dau. of George Crosby, cousin and heir of Robert Crosby. Dat. 2 July, 13 Hen. VIII. [1521]. With bond to perform covenants attached. With seals.

313. EXTRACT from the court-roll of Dulwich manor, of the surrender by John Dove of lands, &c., called, or lying in,

Hopper crofte, Great and Lytyll Nappys, Longe borne and Greate borne, Aspole, Cambrewell hell and Newlondes, to the use of John Dove, his third son, in tail, with remainder to his other sons, John [*sic*], Henry, and Humfrey Dove, successively in tail, and in default to John Scott. Dat. 29 Nov., 15 Hen. VIII. [1523]. *Lat.*

314. EXTRACT from the court-roll of Dulwich manor, of the grant of seisin to John Webstar, as son and heir of Thomas Webstar, of land called Berdes. Dat. 29 Nov., 15 Hen. VIII. [1523]. *Lat.*

315. LEASE from the Abbot and Convent of Bermondsey to John Scott, Baron of the Exchequer, of the manor of Dulwich, excepting the 'great wood called Dulwich woode and Dulwich common hedgerowes and vnderwoodes,' &c., for 50 years from Michaelmas, 1531, at a yearly rent of 20 marks. Dat. 6 May, 22 Hen. VIII. [1530]. With the signature of Robert,[1] Abbot; and the following names, all of which are written by the same hand: Richard, prior, John Cambryge, sub-prior, Ralph Lincoln, Thomas Gainsborough, John Kinder, John Blanke, Peter Luke, Richard Gylle, John Cuthbert, William Spicer, Reginald Cobbam, Thomas Rocley, Thomas Lewes, William Painter, and William Gardiner, monks.

316, 317. EXTRACTS from the court-roll of Dulwich manor, of the grant of seisin to Thomas Henley, the younger,

[1] Robert Warton, Wharton, or Parfew, abbot in 1525 (Dugdale, *Monasticon*, ed. 1817–30, vol. v. p. 92); made Bishop of St. Asaph in 1536, and translated to Hereford in 1554; died 1557. He surrendered the abbey to the King, 1 Jan., 1637–8, and was granted a pension of 333*l.* 6*s.* 8*d.* In a list of pensions printed in Dugdale, vol. v. p. 103, the names of several of the monks who sign this lease are included—viz. Richard Gile, late prior, 10*l.*; Tho. Gaynesborow, prior of Derby, 7*l.*; John Kinder, sub-prior, 6*l.*; Peter Luke, late chaunter, 6*l.*; John Cutbert, 6*l.*; Tho. Rokeley, 5*l.* 6*s.* 8*d.*; Will. Paynter, 5*l.* 6*s.* 8*d.*

of an acre of land called Wattes crofte. Dat. 14 Jan., 24 Hen. VIII. [1533]. *Lat.* Two copies.

318. EXTRACT from the court-roll of Dulwich manor, of the surrender by John Dove, the younger, deceased, of all his lands, &c., to the use of Katerine, his wife, for life, with remainder to John Dove, his younger son. Dat. 2 Oct., 25 Hen. VIII. [1533]. *Lat.*

319. BARGAIN AND SALE by Edw. Dove, of London, cloth-worker, son and heir of John Dove, the elder, of Dulwich, to Henry Hunte, of Dulwich, husbandman, of all his freehold lands, &c., in Dulwyche, for 36*l.* Dat. 11 Oct., 29 Hen. VIII. [1537]. With seal.

320. BOND from Edward Dove to Henry Hunte, in 40*l.*, to perform covenants as above. Dat. 11 Oct., 29 Hen. VIII. [1537]. Signed; with seal.

321. GRANT from Edward Dove to Henry Hunte of 12 acres of land in Peryfeld, and all his lands, &c., of free tenure in Dulwyche. Dat. 12 Oct., 29 Henry VIII. [1537]. *Lat.* Signed.

322. RELEASE from Edward Dove to Henry Hunte, of the land, &c., as above. Dat. 27 Nov., 29 Hen VIII. [1537]. *Lat.* With seal.

323. RECOVERY by Henry Hunt against Edward Dove of a barn and 14 acres of land, &c., in Dulwich. Dat. 30 Jan., 29 Hen. VIII. [1538]. *Lat.* With seal of court.

324. LETTERS PATENT of Henry VIII., granting to Sir Humfrey Browne, knt., for 848*l.*, the manor of Lockyngton, co. Leic., with lands, tithes, &c., in Lockyngton and Mykkleholme, late belonging to the Monastery of St. Mary de Pré, co. Leicester, at a yearly rent of 5*l.* 4*s.*; and land, &c., called 'Rigates grene,' in 'Dulwiche Commen woode,' co. Surrey, late belonging to the Monastery of St. Saviour, Bermondsey, at a yearly rent of 4*d.* Dat. 27 Apr., a° 34 [1542]. *Lat. Copy.*

325. SALE by Sir Humfrey Browne, knt., to Sir Thomas Pope, knt., and Elizabeth, his wife, for 30*l.*, of land, &c., called 'Rigates grene,' in 'Dulwiche Commen woode,' paying 4*d.* yearly rent to the Crown. Dat. 28 Apr., 34 Hen. VIII. [1542]. *Lat.* Signed; with seal.

326. POWER OF ATTORNEY from Sir Thomas Pope and Elizabeth, his wife, to Thomas Rydley and Thomas Hendleye to receive seisin of the same land. Dat. 28 Apr., 34 Hen. VIII. [1542]. *Lat.* Signed; with gem seals.

327. BARGAIN AND SALE by John Legh, of Stockwell, esq., to Robert Draper, of Camberwell, gent., and Elizabeth, his wife, for 53*l.*, of a tenement, lands, rent, &c., in Dulwich. Dat. 30 April, 34 Hen. VIII. [1542]. Signed. With fine attached of messuages, lands, &c., in Dulwich, Newington, and Walworth, Trin. term, 1542.

328, 329. FEOFFMENT from John Legh to Robert Draper and Elizabeth, his wife, of the tenement, lands, &c., as above. Dat. 6 July, 34 Hen. VIII. [1542]. *Lat.* Signed; with seal. In duplicate.

330. FEOFFMENT from Sir Thomas Pope, knt., to Thomas Calton, of London, goldsmith, and Margaret, his wife, of land, &c., called 'Rigates grene,' in 'Dulwiche commen woode.' Dat. 18 Sept., 36 Hen. VIII. [1544]. *Lat.* Signed; with seal of arms. On the back is a note of seisin, 16 Mar., 1545, one of the witnesses bearing the name Rob. Sharparrowe.

331. LETTERS PATENT of Henry VIII., granting to Thomas Calton, of London, goldsmith, and Margaret, his wife, for 609*l.* 18*s.* 2*d.*, the manor of Dulwyche, with the messuage of Hall Place, the advowson of Camberwell, Dulwyche common wood, &c., in co. Surrey, late belonging to Bermondsey Abbey, at a yearly rent of 33*s.* 9*d.*; and the rectory of Wylley, &c., co. Herts., late belonging to the Friars Preachers of Langley, at a yearly rent of 24*s.* Dat. 11 Oct., a° 36 [1544]. *Lat.* With portions of the Great Seal.

332, 333. FINE from Sir Thomas Pope, knt., and Elizabeth, his wife, to Thomas Calton and Margaret, his wife, of 60 acres of wood called Rygates Grene, in Camerwell, for 40*l.* Dat. Morrow of the F. of All Souls, 36 Hen. VIII. [1544]. *Lat.* In duplicate.

334. 'BYLL' of Rauff Muschampe, esq., admitting that he had illegally felled 'certeyn ookes vpon a grounde called Erber hyll agaynst Lodlynge grene .... vpon the ffreholde of Thomas Calton of London, Goldesmythe, lorde of the manour of Dulwyche,' and renouncing all such claim for the future. Dat. 17 May, 1 Edw. VI. [1547]. Signed; with seal of arms.

335. EXTRACT from the court-roll of Dulwich manor, of the surrender by Henry Hunte of 2 acres of land, late Robert Holland's, and 3 acres called Goryland, and of the re-grant of the same to the said Henry for life, with remainder to John, his son. Dat. 17 May, 6 Edw. VI. [1552]. *Lat.*

336. EXTRACT from the court-roll of Dulwich manor, of the surrender by John Dove, son of John Dove, of lands called Carterscroft and Cartersgarden to the use of Katerine Turnour, wife of John Turnour, for life, with remainder to John Dove, her son. Dat. 3 June, 7 Edw. VI. [1553]. *Lat.*

337. EXTRACT from the court-roll of Dulwich manor, of the admission of John Dove to the reversion of lands, &c., in Northcroftes, Browenynges, le Apse, Denesmede, Midlefeld, &c., after the death of his mother, Katerine, widow of John Dove. Dat. 3 June, 7 Edw. VI. [1553]. *Lat.*

338. PETITION in Chancery of Margaret, widow of Thomas Calton, for a writ of subpœna against John Crofte, Henry Knighte, and John Dove, pretending a title to messuages and land in the manor of Dulwich. Dat. [1558]. Paper, 3 sheets.

339. DEPOSITIONS in behalf of Margaret Calton in the same suit, with interrogatories. Dat. [June, 1558]. Paper, 19 sheets. *Imperfect.*

340. EXTRACT from the court-roll of Dulwich manor, of license to John Dove, the younger, to lease to Walter Symons, for 21 years, a tenement called Morkyns and land called Norcroftes, little Nappes, and Stonye Nappes. Dat. 23 Apr., 4 Eliz. [1562]. *Lat.*

341. EXTRACT from the court-roll of Dulwich manor, of the grant of seisin to John Hunte, as son and heir of Henry Hunte, of a tenement and 16 acres of land formerly belonging to Bernard Johns, a tenement and 2 acres called Walkers crofte, and a parcel called Gorye lande. Dat. 23 Apr., 4 Eliz. [1562]. *Lat.*

342. EXTRACT from the court-roll of Dulwich manor, of the surrender by Henry Henleye to the use of John Dove of a tenement and an acre of land called Wattes crofte. Dat. 14 Oct., 10 Eliz. [1568]. *Lat.*

343. BOND from Matthew Draper, of Camerwell, gent., to Margaret Calton, of London, widow, in 100 marks, not to vex, sue, or implead her on account of the tithe of wood felled in the manor of Dulwich during a lease held by him of the rectory of Camerwell. Dat. 5 Nov., 11 Eliz. [1569]. Signed.

344. COVENANT by Margaret, widow of Thomas Caulton [Calton], of London, and William Caulton, of London, goldsmith, son of the same, to levy a fine to Lord Giles Pawlett and William Chyvall, draper, of the manor, rectory, &c., of Goringe, co. Oxon, the manor of Dulwich, with lands, &c., in Dulwich and Camberwell, co. Surrey, lands, &c., in Chaddesdon and Derby, co. Derby, wood in Lewisham, co. Kent, and the rectory, vicarage, &c., of Willey, co. Herts, the whole to the use of the said Margaret for life, and at her decease to the sons of the said Thomas Caulton—viz. the Willey estate to George and Henry, the Goringe estate to Robert, the Dulwich and Lewisham estates to Nicholas, and the Chaddesdon and Derby estate to George; with remainders over, among others, to the above William Caulton, to Thomas, his son, and his other children by his late wife, Margaret, dau. of Will. Hobson, and to Alys, dau. of Thomas Caulton the elder. Dat. 24 Jan., 12 Eliz. [1570]. Exemplification, 23 Jan., 9 Jas. I. [1612]. *Lat.*

345. FINE from Margaret Caulton and William Caulton to Lord Giles Poulett and William Chyvall, in accordance with the preceding covenant. Dat. Hilary term, 12 Eliz. [1570]. Exemplification, 28 Nov., 9 Jas. I. [1611]. *Lat.* With fragments of seal.

346. STATUTE-STAPLE BOND from Nicholas Calton, of Graveley, co. Camb., gent., to Margaret Calton, of London, widow, Thomas Smalman, of the Inner Temple, gent., Robert Taylour, mercer, and Walter Bowyer, goldsmith, in 5,000*l* Dat. 13 Nov., 12 Eliz. [1570]. Signed by Nich. Calton and

[Sir] Rob. Catelyn [Chief Justice of the King's Bench]; with seals.

347, 348. DEFEASANCE of the preceding statute, conditional upon the observance by the said Nicholas Calton of the terms and intent of a conveyance by the said Margaret Calton and William Calton, her son, of the manor of Dulwich, &c., as above, no. 344. Dat. 13 Nov., 12 Eliz. [1570]. Followed by the counterpart. Signed; with seals.

349. ASSIGNMENT by John Dove, of Westminster, and Henry Dove, of Camberwell, yeomen, to John Levar, of London, fishmonger, of a lease from John Scott of the manor-house of Dulwich, &c., for 20 years from Michaelmas, 1561, at a rent of 11*l.* Dat. 20 Jan., 15 Eliz. [1573]. Signed; with seals.

350. ASSIGNMENT by John Levar to George Robertes, of London, cordwainer, of his estate in the manor-house, demesne lands, &c., of Dulwiche as above, and by assignment from Edward, Acton, and Edgar Scott. Dat. 25 June, 15 Eliz., 1573. Signed; with fragment of seal of arms.

351. BOND from John Dove, of Westminster, gent., to Nicholas Calton, of Keston, co. Hunts, esq., in 40*l.*, to observe an award as to the title to a messuage and six acres of land, copyhold of Dulwich manor. Dat. 24 Nov., 16 Eliz. [1573]. Signed; with seal.

352. ORDER to Nicholas Calton, in pursuance of a decree in Chancery, dat. 22 May, allowing the claim of Matthew Draper and other tenants of Dulwich manor to woods and underwoods upon Dulwich Common 'for theire necessarie fewell and hedgebote.' Dat. 16 June, 16 Eliz. [1574].

353, 354. LETTERS PATENT of Queen Elizabeth, granting license to Nicholas Calton to alienate to William Farren and John Bedell the manor of Dulwich, with lands, &c., in Dulwich and Camberwell, the advowson of Camberwell, and wood in Lewisham, to the use of the said Nicholas for life, with remainders over. Dat. 1 Jan., a° 17 [1575]. *Lat.* With fragment of seal. Followed by a copy of the same, on paper, two sheets.

355, 356. COVENANT by Nicholas Calton, of Dulwich, gent., to levy to William Farren, of Molesworth, co. Hunts, gent., and John Bedell, of Hamerton, co. Hunts, gent., a fine of the manor, lands, &c., as above, to the use of the said Nicholas for life, and, after his decease, one-third to the use of the heirs of his body, one-third to the use of Thomas, his second son, and the heirs of the body of the same Thomas, and one-third to the use of his executors for 12 years to perform his will, and then to the use of his heirs as before. Dat. 12 Jan., 17 Eliz. [1575]. Counterpart, signed; with seals. Followed by a copy, on paper, three sheets.

357, 358. FINE from Nicholas Calton, gent., to William Farren and John Bedell, gentt., of Dulwich manor, &c., as above, no. 353, for 380*l.* Dat. Morrow of the Purif. B. V. M., 17 Eliz. [1575]. *Lat.* In duplicate.

359. LEASE from William, Bartholomew, Acton, and Edgar Scott, of Camberwell, gentlemen, to Henry Brigges, of Peckham, carpenter, of 12 acres of land in Camberwell, called 'Greate Rudlandes,' for 21 years, at a rent of 16*s.* Dat. 1 May, 17 Eliz. [1575]. Signed; with two seals.

360–362. BARGAIN AND SALE by Thomas Oode, of Dulwich, yeoman, to Matthew Draper, esq., of five messuages, three acres of land, &c., in Dulwich. Dat. 3 Nov., 17 Eliz. [1575]. Signed; with seal. Much rotted and injured by damp. Attached is a fine, in duplicate, from Thomas Ode and Elizabeth, his wife, of the same messuages, &c. Dat. Oct. of St. Martin, 18 Eliz. [1575]. *Lat.*

363. ANSWER of Tho. Becke, steward of Dulwich manor, to a bill of complaint of Robert Wyth, with regard to the refusal to accept a surrender by John Hunte of a messuage, &c., to the use of the complainant. Dat. [*circ.* 1572–1574]. Paper, 20 sheets.

364. ANSWER of Joan Calton, widow of Nicholas Calton lord of the manor of Dulwich, to the same bill, stating that the reason for not accepting the surrender was the complainant's refusal to compound for the fine according to the custom of the manor, whereby fines upon surrenders and admissions 'were and had byn vncerten and were and had byn assessed and rated according as the lorde of the sayd manor or his steward shold resonably asses.' Dat. [*circ.* 1575]. Paper, 13 sheets.

365–368. EXTRACTS from the court-roll of Dulwich manor, of the admission (1) of Katherine Wright to $\frac{1}{5}$ of a messuage and 15 acres of land inherited from Richard Wright, her father; (2) of Thomas Warde and Katherine, his wife, to $\frac{1}{4}$ of $\frac{1}{5}$ of the same, inherited by the said Katherine from Elizabeth, her sister; and (3, 4) of Elena and Mary Wright to $\frac{1}{4}$ of the same respectively, inherited from Richard Wright, their father. Dat. 11 Oct., 18 Eliz. [1576], 22 Oct., 28 Eliz. [1586], 17 Apr., 31 Eliz. [1589]. *Lat.*

369. BARGAIN AND SALE by Thomas Ode, of Camerwell, yeoman, to Edmond Bowyer, of the same, esq., of five tenements and three acres of land in Dulwich. Dat. 18 Dec., 20 Eliz. [1577]. Signed; with seal.

370. BARGAIN AND SALE by Henry Knight, of Brookehooles, in Lambeth, gent., to Peter Marshe, of Mestham, gent., for 40*l.*, of 4½ acres of land in Dyllewiche, in a field called Canelcroft. Dat. 19 Jan., 21 Eliz., 1578[9]. Signed; with seal.

371–373. PROCEEDINGS in an action by Joan Calton, widow, against Robert Brokesbye for trespass and cutting of wood in 'Kynges Copyes,' in Dulwich, Mich. term, 21 Eliz. [1579]. *Lat.* In triplicate. Paper, 8 sheets.

374. EXTRACT from the court-roll of Dulwich manor, of the surrender by John Hunte to the use of Robert Withe, esq., of a messüage and 10 acres of land, formerly belonging to Barnard Jones. Dat. 3 Dec., 22 Eliz. [1579]. *Lat.*

375. EXTRACT from the court-roll of Dulwich manor, of the grant of the custody of the person and lands of Nicholas Knight, son and heir of Henry Knight, to Peter Marshe and Johanna, his wife, mother of the said Nicholas, during minority. Dat. 10 June, 23 Eliz. [1581]. *Lat.*

376. COVENANT by Robert Wythe, of the Inner Temple, esq., to carry into effect a surrender of a messuage and land in Dulwich manor to the use of Ellys Parry, of London, weaver. Dat. 29 June, 26 Eliz. [1584]. Signed; with seal.

377. EXTRACT from the court-roll of Dulwich manor, of the grant of seisin to Elizeus Parrye of a messuage and 10 acres of land, late in the tenure of Christopher Heath, and surrendered to his use by Robert Wythe. Dat. 26 Oct., 26 Eliz. [1584]. *Lat.*

378. COVENANT between Johane Calton, of Little Catworth, co. Hunts, widow of Nicholas Calton, gent., and Francis Calton, of Cosenton, in Alseford, co. Kent, her son, for the enjoyment by the latter of Dulwich manor and lands, &c., in Dulwich and Camberwell, co. Surr., and Lewisham, co. Kent, left him by his father, upon assurance to the said Johane of her third part as dower. Dat. 15 May, 28 Eliz. [1586].

379. EXTRACT from the court-roll of Dulwich manor, of the grant of seisin to Francis Fromans of land in le Apps, &c., inherited from Benedicta Fromans, his mother. Dat. 22 Oct., 28 Eliz. [1586]. *Lat.*

380. COVENANT between Francis Calton, lord of the manor of Dulwich, and Edmond Bowyar, Peter Marsh, and others, tenants of the same manor, for the observance of an award by John Baker and others on claims of the said tenants to 'common of pasture, spraye, hedgebote, estovers,' &c. Dat. 14 Nov., 28 Eliz. [1586]. Counterpart, signed; with seals.

381. AWARD by John Baker, of St. Stephen's, Coleman Street, esq., Richard Burton, of Carshalton, esq., Humphrey Donnatt, of Lincoln's Inn, gent., and George Holmeden, of Longfield, co. Surr., gent., in favour of the tenants in the dispute as above. Dat. 29 Nov., 29 Eliz. [1586]. Signed; with seals of arms.

382. ABSTRACT of the bill, answer, and replication in a suit of John Mason, Richard Watford, and other inhabitants of Dulwich, against Francis Calton, Thomas Hopkins, and Thomas Rowse, claiming 'comon of estovers' and sprays of oak, &c., in 'the comon or wast grounde of Dulwiche.' Dat. [*circ.* 1586].

383. LETTERS PATENT of Qu. Elizabeth, granting to Francis Calton, gent., a special livery of manors, lands, &c., inherited by him from Nicholas Calton, his father. Dat. 1 Feb., a° 29 [1587]. *Lat.* With seal.

384. RATIFICATION by Francis Calton, of Cosenton, of an assignment to Johane, widow of Nicholas Calton, his mother, of messuages, lands, &c., in Dulwich and Camberwell, for life, as her dower; with covenant to pay a yearly rent of 52*l.* for a lease of the same, certain excepted, for 40 years, if she so long survive. Dat. 26 Feb., 29 Eliz. [1587]. Injured by damp.

385, 386. COVENANT between Francis Calton and Thomas Calton, his brother, apprentice to Henry Calton, of Westcheap, London, cloth-worker, for the allowing to the tenants of the manor of Dulwich of common of pasture and underwoods on the commons and waste grounds. Dat. 22 June, 29 Eliz. [1587]. Followed by the counterpart, signed; with seals.

387. EXTRACT from the court-roll of Dulwich manor, of the recovery by Ellys Parrye and John Lewys against John Hunte of a cottage, garden, &c., in Dulwyche. Dat. 5 Dec., 33 Eliz. [1590]. *Lat.*

388. COVENANT by Thomas Warde, of Camberwell, carpenter, William Wellfoord, of Earl's Barton, yeoman, and Marie Wrighte, of Lee, co. Essex, for the surrender to the use of Thomas Parie, of Graies Inn, gent., of land, &c., in Dulwich, lately held by copy of court-roll by Richard Wrighte, and inherited by his daughters, Katherin, wife of Thomas Warde, Ellen, wife of William Wellfoord, the said Marie Wrighte, and Annis, wife of Robert Miller. Dat. 4 Feb., 34 Eliz. [1592]. Signed; with seals.

389–391. BONDS from the above Thomas Warde, William Wellford, and Mary Wright to Tho. Parrie, in 50*l.* respectively, for the performance of covenants. Dat. 4 Feb., 34 Eliz. [1592]. Signed; with seals.

392–395. EXTRACTS from the court-roll of Dulwich manor, of the surrender by Mary Wrighte, Thomas Warde and Katerine, his wife, and William Welforthe and Elena, his wife, respectively, of their several fourth parts of a messuage and 15 acres of land, inherited by the said Mary, Katerine, and Elena from Richard Wrighte, their father, to the use of Thomas Parrye, and of the subsequent surrender of the same by the said Thomas Parrye to the use of John Berrye. Dat. 22 Apr., 34 Eliz. [1592], 24 Oct., 37 Eliz. [1595], 7 Mar., 3 Jas. I. [1606]. *Lat.*

396. FEOFFMENT from Francis Calton, of London, esq., to Ellys Parry, of London, weaver, of four acres of land in Dulwiche, adjacent to Crocksted Lane. Dat. 7 Mar., 37 Eliz., 1594[5]. *Lat.* Signed; with seal.

397. BARGAIN AND SALE by Francis Calton to Ellys Parry, for 30*l.*, of the land, as above, in the tenure of Henry Jackson. Dat. 7 Mar., 37 Eliz. [1595]. Signed.

398. BOND from Francis Calton to Ellys Parry, in 100 marks, to perform covenants. Dat. 7 Mar., 37 Eliz., 1594[5]. Signed; with seal.

399. EXTRACT from the court-roll of Dulwich manor, of the grant of license to Nicholas Knight, gent., to lease to William Addams, of the par. of St. Bride, London, a messuage, lands, &c., in Dulwich, late in the occupation of Roger Hamonde, for 21 years. Dat. 12 May, 37 Eliz. [1595]. *Lat.*

400. BARGAIN AND SALE by William Jones, or Johns, of London, merchant-tailor, and Agnes, his wife, dau. and heir of Thomas Hunt, of Dulwich, to Thomas Turner, of London, yeoman, of a messuage and lands called Perifield, &c., in Dulwich, for 200*l.* Dat. 12 Jan., 38 Eliz. [1596]. Signed; with seals.

401. BOND from William Jones to Thomas Turner, in 300*l.*, for the performance of covenants as above. Dat. 12 Jan., 38 Eliz. [1596]. Signed; with seal.

402. FEOFFMENT from William Jones to Thomas Turner of the messuage, lands, &c., as above. Dat. 9 Feb., 38 Eliz. [1596]. *Lat.* Signed; with seal.

403, 404. FINE from William Jones and Agnes, his wife, to Thomas Turner of the messuage, lands, &c., as above, for 80*l.* Dat. Oct. of Purif. B. V. M., 38 Eliz. [1596]. *Lat.* In duplicate.

405. RELEASE by William Jones to Thomas Turner of the messuage, lands, &c., as above. Dat. 27 Feb., 38 Eliz. [1596]. Signed; with seal.

406. FEOFFMENT from Peter Marshe, of the par. of St. Giles without Cripplegate, London, gent., to Nicholas Knight, of Thavies Inn, Holborn, gent., of land called Kennalls, in Dulwich. Dat. 19 Apr., 38 Eliz., 1596. *Lat.* Signed; with seal.

407. RECOVERY by Margery Turner, widow, against Thomas Turner of a messuage, lands, &c., in Dulwich and Camerwell. Dat. 24 May, 38 Eliz. [1596]. *Lat.* With fragments of seal.

408, 409. EXTRACTS from the court-roll of Dulwich manor, of the grant of seisin to John Fromans of a tenement and 14 acres of land, late in the tenure of Francis Fromans, his brother, and of the surrender of the same by John Fromans to the use of John Bowyar and Emma, his wife. Dat. 8 Dec., 39 Eliz. [1596]. *Lat. Mutilated.*

410. FEOFFMENT from Nicholas Knight, of Thavis Inne, in Holborne, gent., to Paul Bushe, clerk, for 92*l.*, of a house and lands called Kennalls, in Dulwich, had by the grantor from Peter Marshe, or by the will of Henry Knight, his father. Dat. 1 Apr., 39 Eliz., 1597. *Lat.* Signed; with seal.

411. WILL of Isabel Savage, of Peckham, widow, giving legacies to Thomas Newman, smith, of Newington, to Mary Savage, and to the poor of Peckham and Camberwell. Dat. 17 April, 1597. With probate, 21 July, 1597, signed by Tho. Ridley, LL.D., Vicar-General of the Bp. of Winchester.

412, 413. EXTRACT from the court-roll of Dulwich manor, of the surrender of a messuage and 11 acres of land by Nicholas Knyght, of Thavies Inn, Holborn, to the use of Ellis Parrye, of London, weaver, and Mariane, his wife. Dat. 20 Apr., 39 Eliz. [1597]. *Lat.* With license attached from Francis Calton, lord of the manor, to Ellis Parrye to lease the same for 10 years. Dat. 3 Feb., 2 Jas. I. [1605].

414. BOND from Nicholas Knight, of Thavys Inn, in Holborn, gent., to Ellis Parye, of London, weaver, in 60*l.*, in warranty of a messuage, land called French field, &c., in Dulwiche, in the tenure of John Shott. Dat. 25 Apr., 39 Eliz., 1597. Signed; with seal.

415. LEASE from Francis Calton, of Stebenheath [Stepney], co. Midd., esq., to John Bone, of Camberwell, yeoman, of a messuage called Hall Place, with land, &c., in

Dulwich, for 21 years, at a rent of 20*l.* Dat. 12 May, 39 Eliz., 1597. Counterpart.

416. LEASE from Thomas Calton, of Dulwich, gent., to John Mathewe, of Camberwell, husbandman, of a messuage and lands in Dulwich, for 21 years, at a rent of 6*l.* and two good hens. Dat. 28 Nov., 40 Eliz. [1597]. Counterpart; with seal.

417. LEASE from Thomas Calton to Henry Mathewe, of Camberwell, husbandman, of a messuage, land, &c., in Dulwich, for 21 years, for 3*l.* 5*s.* in hand and a rent of 40*s.* and two hens. Dat. 20 Mar., 40 Eliz. [1598]. Counterpart; with seal.

418. LEASE from Francis Calton, of Camberwell, esq., to Richard Stoughton, of Streatham, gent., of a messuage, lands, &c., in Dulwich, for 99 years, or the term of the life of the survivor of the said Rich. Stoughton, Elizabeth, his wife, and Edward, his son, at a rent of 9*l.* Dat. 23 May, 40 Eliz., 1598. Counterpart.

419. STATUTE-STAPLE BOND from Francis Calton, of Camberwell, esq., to Giles Sympson, of London, goldsmith, in 200*l.* Dat., 6 Apr., 41 Eliz. [1599]. *Lat.* Signed by Fran. Calton and [Sir] Edmund Anderson [Chief Justice of the Common Pleas].

420. LEASE from Thomas Calton, of London, cloth worker, to Thomas Treene, of London, ale-brewer, of a messuage, land, &c., in Dulwich, for 17 years, at a rent of 8*l.* 5*s.* Dat. 20 May, 41 Eliz., 1599. Signed; with fragment of seal of arms.

421. LEASE from Thomas Townsend, of Farnham Royal, co. Bucks, yeoman, and Rebecca, his wife, Thomas Butterfeild, of Iver, co. Bucks, weaver, and Agnes, his wife, and Mary Shillingford, of Alesford, co. Kent, widow (the said Rebecca, Agnes, and Mary being daughters of Nich. and Eliz. Freind, of Farnham Royal), to Edw. Strange, of Dulwich, gent., of a messuage, &c., in Dulwich, for 21 years, at a rent of 40*s.* Dat. 8 June, 41 Eliz. [1599]. Signed; with seals.

422. LEASE from Thomas Calton, of Dulwich, gent., to George Hethersale, of Mitcham, husbandman, of a messuage, lands, &c., in Dulwich, for 20 years, for 125*l.* in hand and a rent of 40*s.* Dat. 10 Aug., 41 Eliz., 1599. Signed.

423–425. BONDS from Francis Calton, esq., and Edward Wilson, clerk, of Camerwell, to Nicholas Knighte, of Brockholes, gent., in 200*l.*, for three separate payments of 100*l.* Dat. 22 Sept., 41 Eliz. [1599]. Signed.

426. MORTGAGE by Francis Calton, esq., to Thomas Fletcher, of London, merchant-tailor, of lands called Blanch downes, &c., in Dulwich, for 200*l.* Dat. 7 Aug., 42 Eliz. [1600]. *Copy*; paper, 5 sheets.

427. ASSIGNMENT by Thomas Treene, of London, ale-brewer, to Edmond Reynoldes, of Dulwich, of a lease from Thomas Calton, dat. 20 May, 1599, of a messuage, land, &c., in Dulwich, for 17 years, at a rent of 8*l.* Dat. 28 Aug., 42 Eliz., 1600. Signed.

428. BARGAIN AND SALE by Pawle Bushye, of the par. of St. Botolph without Aldgate, London, clerk, to Humphrey Emerson, of Southwark, gent., for 170*l.*, of a messuage and lands called Kennalls, in Dullwiche, with covenant for assurance from himself and Joan, his wife. Dat. 27 Sept., 42 Eliz. [1600]. Signed; with seal.

429. FEOFFMENT from Pawle Bushye to Humfrey Emerson of the messuage, &c., as above. Dat. 27 Sept., 42 Eliz. [1600]. *Lat.* Signed.

430, 431. FINE from Paul Bushye, clerk, and Johanna, his wife, to Humfrey Emerson, gent., of the same messuage, &c., in Dulwyche and Camberwell, for 41*l.* Dat. Morrow of All Souls, 42 Eliz. [1600]. *Lat.* In duplicate.

432. BARGAIN AND SALE by Thomas Calton, of Dulwich, gent., to Humfrie Plessington, of St. Martin's in the Fields, gent., for 104*l.* 3*s.* 4*d.*, of a messuage and 16 acres of land in Dulwich, in the tenure of Thomas Treene. Dat. 8 Sept., 43 Eliz. [1601]. *Copy*; paper, 6 sheets.

433. RELEASE from Thomas Fletcher, of London, merchant-tailor, to Francis Calton, of London, esq., of lands called Blaunchdownes, &c., in Dulwich, mortgaged as above, no. 426. Dat. 3 May, 44 Eliz., 1602. Signed; with seal.

434. MORTGAGE by Francis Calton, of London, esq., to Robert Lee, Lord Mayor of London, of Dulwich Corte, Hall Place, and three other messuages, &c., in Dulwich, for 660*l.*, to be repaid on 20 Dec., 1603; with covenant by Giles Simpson, of London, goldsmith, in default of such payment, to pay 665*l.* on 20 Jan., 1603[4]. Dat. 17 Dec., 45 Eliz., 1602. Signed by Fran. Calton and Giles Simpson; with seals.

435. STATUTE-STAPLE BOND from Francis Calton to Robert Lee for the payment of 1,000*l.* on Christmas Day. Dat. 18 Dec., 45 Eliz. [1602]. *Lat.* Signed by Fran. Calton and [Sir] Edm. Anderson [Chief Justice of the Common Pleas]; with seals.

436. WILL of Henry Olliff, of Peckham, yeoman, making bequests to the children of Richard North and Peter Byrde, Katheryne and Elizabeth, his daughters, Agnes Brande, Oliff Birde, Henry Northe, William Ramsey, William Starky, Edmond Bowyer, Mrs. Foster, John Bowier, and Benjamin Bowier, and appointing Jone, his wife, residuary legatee and executrix, and Edward Wilson, Vicar of Camberwell, and Henry Brigges overseers. Dat. 10 Jan., 1602[3]. With probate attached, 19 Mar., 1602[3].

437, 438. FINE from Francis Calton, esq., to Robert Lee, Mayor of London, of six messuages, lands, &c., in Dulwich, for 300*l.* Dat. Morr. of the F. of the Purif. B. V. M., 45 Eliz. [1603]. *Lat.* In duplicate.

439. BOND from John Ambler, of Dulwich, yeoman, to Francis Calton, esq., in 40*l.*, to perform covenants in indentures of lease. Dat. 20 Feb., 45 Eliz., 1602[3].

440. ASSIGNMENT by Edward Strange, of London, gent., to Robert Crosse, of London, skinner, of a lease, dat. 8 June, 1599, from Thomas Towneshend, Rebecca, his wife, and others, of a messuage, &c., in Dulwich, for 21 years, at a rent of 40*s.* Dat. 18 June, 1 Jas. I., 1603. Signed; with seal.

441, 442. RELEASE from Francis Calton, of London, esq., to Sir Robert Lee, knt., alderman of London, of the messuages of Dulwich Corte and Hall Place, and three other messuages, &c., in Dulwich, mortgaged as above, no. 434. Dat. 21 Dec., 1 Jas. I., 1603. Followed by the counterpart. Signed; with seals.

443–445. BARGAIN AND SALE by Sir Robert Lee to Francis Calton of Dulwich Court and other the premises as above, for 660*l.*, to be paid on 23 Dec., 1604; and in default to Gyles Simpson, of London, goldsmith, for 660*l.*, to be paid on 24 Jan., 160$\frac{4}{5}$. Dat. 22 Dec., 1603. Indenture tripartite, with counterparts. Signed; with two seals.

446. DEFEASANCE of a statute-staple bond from Francis Calton to Sir Robert Lee, in 1,000*l.*, conditional upon the performance of covenants in an indenture of 18 Dec., 1602. Dat. 22 Dec., 1 Jas. I., 1603. Signed.

447. ASSIGNMENT by Simon Crosse, administrator of the goods of Robert Crosse, his brother, to John Ewen, of Dulwich, yeoman, of a lease of a messuage, &c., in Dulwich, assigned as above, no. 440. Dat. 3 Mar., 1 Jas. I., 1603[4]. Signed.

448. LEASE from Emme, widow of Humphrey Emerson, of Southwark, to Henry Roper, of Lincoln's Inn, gent., of a messuage, land, &c., in Dulwich, for 21 years, at a rent of 13*l.* 6*s.* 8*d.* Dat. 24 May, 2 Jas. I., 1604.

449. LEASE from Francis Calton, of East Greenwich, esq., to Thomas Hopkins, of Newington, yeoman, of Blanch dounes and other lands in Dulwich, for 21 years, at a rent of 20*l.* Dat. 6 June, 2 Jas. I., 1604. Signed; with seal.

450. BARGAIN AND SALE by Emme Emerson, of St. Saviour's, Southwark, widow, and Rich. Mellersh, gent., to Hugh Browker, esq., prothonotary of the Common Pleas, and Peter Turner, M.D., for 500*l.*, of the interest of the said Emme in all the lands, messuages, &c. (one dwelling-house excepted), bequeathed to her for life by the will of Humphrey Emerson, her husband, dat. 14 Nov., 1603. Dat. 27 Aug., 2 Jas. I. [1604]. *Copy*; paper, 15 sheets.

451. LEASE from George Addams, of Dulwich, yeoman, and Anne, his wife, widow of Edmond Reynoldes, to John Berrye, of Southwark, gent., of a messuage, lands, &c., in Dulwich, for 12 years, at a rent of 14*l.* Dat. 26 Oct., 2 Jas. I., 1604. Counterpart, signed; with seal.

452. LEASE from Francis Calton, of East Greenwich, esq., to John Hanford, of Lewisham, yeoman, of a tenement and lands in Dulwich and Camberwell in the occupation of John Longe, for 21 years, for 40*s.* in hand and a rent of 6*l.* 13*s.* 4*d.* Dat. 27 May, 3 Jas. I., 1605. Signed.

453. LETTERS PATENT of James I., granting to Sir Francis Calton, knt., Sir Robert Lee, knt., and Mary, his wife, and Giles Sympson license to alienate to Edward Alleyn, esq., six messuages, 300 acres of pasture, 20 acres of wood, &c., in Dulwich, held of the Crown *in capite.* Dat. 2 Sept., a° 3 [1605]. *Lat.*

454. LETTERS PATENT of James I., granting license to Thomas Calton to alienate to John Ewen and Mary, his wife, a messuage, lands, &c., in Dulwich, held *in capite.* Dat. 2 Sept., a° 3 [1605]. *Lat.*

455. COVENANTS between Thomas Calton, gent., John Ewen, yeoman, and Mary, his wife, and John Jackson, scrivener, for the prosecution of a recovery for the assurance to the said John and Mary Ewen of a messuage and lands called Naspe, Little Browninges, &c., in Dulwich, sold to them by Thomas Calton. Dat. 20 Sept., 3 Jas. I., 1605. Signed; with seals.

456. BARGAIN AND SALE by Sir Francis Calton, knt., Sir Robert Lee, knt., and Gyles Simpson, goldsmith, to

Edward Alleyn, of St. Saviour's, Southwark, esq., of messuages called Dulwich Courte and Hall Place and three other messuages, with lands, &c., in Dulwich, for 130*l.* paid to Sir Fran. Calton and 660*l.* to Sir Rob. Lee, the premises being mortgaged to the latter for so much by deed dated 17 Dec., 1602. Dat. 1 Oct., 1605. Signed; with seals of arms.

457. ASSIGNMENT by Sir Robert Lee, of London, knt., to Philip Henslowe, of St. Saviour's, Southwark, esq. (in trust for Edw. Alleyn), of a statute-staple bond from Sir Fran. Calton, in 1,000*l.*, for performance of covenants in a mortgage, dat. 17 Dec., 1602, of Dulwich Court, Hall Place, &c., in Dulwich, since sold to Edw. Alleyn. Dat. 1 Oct., 3 Jas. I., 1605. Signed; with seal of arms.

458, 459. FINE from Thomas Calton, gent., to John Ewen and Mary, his wife, of a messuage, lands, &c., in Dulwiche and Camberwell, for 41*l.* Dat. Morrow of All Souls, 3 Jas. I. [1605]. *Lat.* In duplicate.

460. EXEMPLIFICATION of a fine, morr. of All Souls, 3 Jas. I. [1605], from Sir Robert Lee, knt., and Mary, his wife, to Edward Alleyn, esq., of six messuages, with land, &c., in Dulwich, for 200*l.* Dat. 6 Nov., 3 Jas. I. [1605]. *Lat.*

461. EXEMPLIFICATION of a fine, Mich. term, 3 Jas. I. [1605], from Sir Francis Calton, knt., to Edward Alleyn, esq., of six messuages, with lands, &c., in Dulwich and Camerwell, for 200*l.* Dat. 28 Nov., 3 Jas. I. [1605].

462. BARGAIN AND SALE by Thomas Calton, of Dulwich, gent., to John Ewen, of Dulwich, yeoman, and Marie, his wife, of a messuage and land in Dulwich, in the tenure of Robert Bodger, for 50*l.* Dat. 1 Dec., 3 Jas. I., 1605. Signed; with seal.

463. RECOVERY by John Jackson against John Ewen and Mary, his wife, of the messuage, &c., as above, by way of assurance on the sale of the same by Thomas Calton. Dat. 12 Feb., 3 Jas. I. [1606]. *Lat.* With fragment of seal.

464. LETTERS PATENT of James I., granting license to Thomas Calton and Anne, his wife, to alienate to Sir Francis Calton, knt., messuages, lands, &c., in Dulwich and Camberwell, held *in capite.* Dat. 1 Mar., a° 3 [1606]. *Lat.*

465. BOND from Sir Francis Calton, of London, knt., to Edward Alleyn, of St. Saviour's, Southwark, esq., in 60*l.*, for the payment of 30*l.* on 31 Mar. Dat. 15 Mar., 3 Jas. I., 1605[6]. Signed; with seal of arms.

466, 467. FINE from Thomas Calton, gent., and Anne, his wife, to Sir Francis Calton, knt., of six messuages, with lands, &c., in Camerwell and Dulwiche, for 60*l.* Dat. Easter term, 4 Jas. I. [1606]. *Lat.* In duplicate.

468. BARGAIN AND SALE by Thomas Calton, of Camberwell, gent., to Sir Francis Calton, of London, knt., for 240*l.*, of messuages, lands, &c., in Dulwich and Camberwell, in the tenure of John Mathew and others. Dat. 1 April, 4 Jas. I., 1606. Signed.

469. ASSIGNMENT by Thomas Hopkins, of Newington, co. Surr., yeoman, to Gabriell Jennynges, of Harrington, co. Northton, gent., of a lease, dat. 6 June, 1604, from Francis Calton of lands called Blanchdowns, &c., in Dulwich, for 21 years, at a rent of 20*l.* Dat. 16 Apr., 4 Jas. I., 1606. Signed; with seal.

470. LETTERS PATENT of James I., granting to Sir Francis Calton, knt., and Dorothy, his wife, license to alienate to Edward Alleyn, esq., the manor of Dulwich, &c., in Dulwiche and Camerwell, and the advowson of the vicarage of Camerwell, held of the Crown *in capite*. Dat. 7 May, a° 4 [1606]. *Lat.* With the Great Seal.

471. BARGAIN AND SALE by Sir Francis Calton, of London, knt., and Dorathie, his wife, to Edward Alleyn, of St. Saviour's, Southwark, esq., for 5,000*l.*, of the manor of Dulwich, with the advowson of the vicarage of Camerwell; messuages called Hall place and Dulwich Court; woods called Dulwich common, Woodsyer, Blanchdowne and Hall place groves; lands called Napps, Stony Napps, Little Bornes, and in Newlands; with all other their lands, tenements, rents, &c., in Dulwich and in the parish of Camerwell, cos. Surrey and Kent. Dat. 8 May, 4 Jas. I., 1606. Signed; with seals.

472. GRANT from Thomas Calton, of Dulwich, gent., to Edward Leachland, of London, merchant, and Edward Hilliard, of London, imbroderer, of a messuage and lands in Dulwich, in trust for a jointure to Ann, his wife. Dat. 10 May, 4 Jas. I. [1606]. Signed; with seal.

473. ASSIGNMENT by George Hethersall, of Mitcham, co. Surr., to Edward Alleyn, for 85*l.*, of a lease, dat. 10 Aug., 1599, from Thomas Calton, of Dulwich, of a messuage, lands, &c., in Dulwich, for 20 years, at a rent of 40*s.* Dat. 13 May, 4 Jas. I., 1606. Signed by a mark.

474. BOND from Edward Alleyn, of St. Saviour's, Southwark, to George Hethersall, of Mitcham, husbandman, in 100*l.*, for the payment of 80*l.* on 29 Sept. Dat. 14 May, 4 Jas. I., 1606. Signed.

475. STATUTE-STAPLE BOND from Sir Francis Calton to Edward Alleyn in 8,000*l.* [see below, no. 519]. Dat. 24

May, 4 Jas. I. [1606]. *Lat.* Signed by Sir Francis Calton and [Sir] John Popham [Chief Justice of the King's Bench]; with seals.

476. BARGAIN AND SALE by Thomas Emerson, of the Inner Temple, esq., to Edward Alleyn, of St. Saviour's, Southwark, esq., of a messuage, lands, &c., in Dulwich, sometime known as Kennalls, for 230*l.* Dat. 1 June, 4 Jas. I. [1606]. Signed; with seal of arms.

477. DEFEASANCE of a recognisance from Edward Alleyn to Sir Francis Calton in 5,000*l.*, conditional upon the observance of articles of agreement of the same date. Dat. 1 June, 4 Jas. I., 1606. *Not executed.*

478. EXEMPLIFICATION of a fine, morr. of F. of the Ascension, 4 Jas. I. [1606], from Sir Francis Calton, knt., and Dorothy, his wife, to Edward Alleyn, esq., of the manor of Dulwiche, &c., in Dulwiche and Camerwell, and the advowson of the vicarage of Camerwell, for 500*l.* Dat. 2 June, 4 Jas. I. [1606]. *Lat.*

479, 480. ARTICLES of agreement between Edward Alleyn and Sir Francis Calton relative to the payment by the former of the purchase money for the manor of Dulwich, &c. Dat. 2 June, 4 Jas. I., 1606. *Not executed* and *imperfect*, containing little more than the preamble. Followed by a second copy, also *imperfect.*

481, 482. FINE from Thomas Calton, gent., and Anne, his wife, to Edward Alleyn, esq., of a messuage, cottage, land, &c., in Dulwiche and Camerwell, for 41*l.* Dat. Trinity term, 4 Jas. I. [1606]. *Lat.* In duplicate.

483. BARGAIN AND SALE by Thomas Calton and Anne, his wife, to Edward Alleyn, for 300*l.*, of a messuage and lands called Norcroftes, Greate Bournes, &c., in Dulwich. Dat. 3 July, 4 Jas. I., 1606. Signed; with seals.

484. BOND from Thomas Calton to Edward Alleyn, in 500*l.*, to perform covenants as above. Dat. 3 July, 4 Jas. I., 1606.

485. RECOVERY by Thomas Jackman and Edward Hughes against Edward Alleyn of the manor of Dulwich, &c., by way of assurance for the sale of the same to Edward Alleyn by Sir Fran. Calton as above, no. 471. Dat. 9 July, 4 Jas. I. [1606]. *Lat.*

486. ASSIGNMENT by Hugh Browker, prothonotary of the Common Pleas, and Peter Turner, of London, M.D., to Philip Henslowe, of St. Saviour's, Southwark, esq., of a life interest in a messuage and land in Dulwich sold to them by Emm, widow of Humphrey Emerson, gent.; with covenant by Thomas Emerson for the payment to the said Philip of the rent due on a lease of the same premises to Henry Roper for 21 years. Dat. 16 July, 4 Jas. I. [1606]. Signed; with seal of arms.

487. LETTERS PATENT of James I., granting license to John Ewen and Mary, his wife, to alienate to Edward Alleyn a messuage, lands, &c., in Dulwich, held *in capite.* Dat. 1 Aug., a° 4 [1606]. *Lat.*

488, 489. FINE from Thomas Emerson and Jane, his wife, to Edward Alleyn of the messuage, land, &c., as above, no. 486. Dat. Mich. term, 4 Jas. I. [1606]. *Lat.* In duplicate.

490. BARGAIN AND SALE by John Ewen, of Dulwich, yeoman, and Mary, his wife, to Edward Alleyn, esq., for 80*l.*, of a messuage and lands in Dulwich called Naspe, Pynners meade, Little Browninges, and Carters garden. Dat. 1 Oct., 4 Jas. I., 1606. Signed; with seals.

491. BOND from John Berry, of Dulwich, yeoman, to Edward Alleyn, of Dulwich, esq., in 400*l.*, in warranty of three-fourths of a messuage and lands in Dulwich, surrendered to the use of the said Edw. Alleyn on 16 Oct. Dat. 18 Oct., 4 Jas. I., 1606. Signed; with seal.

492. BOND from Edward Alleyn to John Berry, in 400*l.*, for the payment of 200*l.* on 31 Oct., 1607. Dat. 18 Oct., 4 Jas. I., 1606. Signed.

493, 494. FINE from John Ewen and Mary, his wife, to Edward Alleyn, of a messuage, lands, &c., in Dulwich and Camerwell, for 41*l.* Dat. Morr. of All Souls, 4 Jas. I. [1606]. *Lat.* In duplicate.

495. STATUTE-STAPLE BOND from John Ewen to Edward Alleyn for the payment of 160*l.* Dat. 14 Nov., 4 Jas. I. [1606]. Signed by J. Ewen and [Sir] Edw. Coke [Chief Justice of the Common Pleas]; with seals of arms.

496. DEFEASANCE of the preceding bond from John Ewen to Edw. Alleyn, conditional upon the safe assurance to the latter of the messuage and land sold as above, no. 490. Dat. 14 Nov., 4 Jas. I., 1606. Counterpart, signed; with seal. With the mark of Johan Alleyn, wife of Edw. Alleyn, as a witness.

497. ASSIGNMENT by John Berrye to Edward Alleyn of a lease, dat. 21 July, 1598, from Thomas Calton to Thomas

Parry, *al.* Whettle, of land called Greate Browninges, in Dulwich, for 21 years, at a rent of 20*s.* Dat. 25 Nov., 4 Jas. I., 1606. Signed.

498. Bond from Edward Alleyn, of Dulwich, esq., and Philip Henslowe, of St. Saviour's, Southwark, esq., to John Berry, of Dulwich, yeoman, in 400*l.*, for the payment of 200*l.* on 31. Oct., 1607. Dat. 27 Nov., 4 Jas. I., 1606. Signed.

499. Bargain and Sale by Edward Alleyn, esq., to Edward Wilson, of Camerwell, clerk, for 220*l.*, of the advowson, patronage, &c., of the vicarage of Camberwell, *al.* Camerwell. Dat. 20 Dec., 4 Jas. I., 1606. Counterpart, signed; with seal of arms. Witnesses, Tho. Bolton, Edw. Juby.

500. Bargain and Sale by Thomas Turner, of London, gent., to Edward Alleyn, of Dulwich, esq., for 226*l.* 13*s.* 4*d.*, of a messuage, 12 acres of land, &c., in Dulwich, purchased by the vendor from William Jones and Agnes, his wife, dau. and heir of Thomas Hunte. Dat. 29 Dec., 4 Jas. I., 1606. Signed; with seal.

501, 502. Fine from Thomas Turner and Anne, his wife, to Edward Alleyn of the messuage, land, &c., as above, for 60*l.* Dat. Oct. of St. Hilary, 4 Jas. I. [1607]. *Lat.* In duplicate.

503. Assignment by Richard Scudamore, of London, gent., to Thomas Calton, of Dulwich, gent., of the lease from Francis Calton as above, nos. 449, 469, for the sum of 40*l.*, to be paid by instalments 'att the now shop of John Mylton,[1]

[1] Father of John Milton, the poet, who was born in this house in Bread Street, known by the sign of the Spread Eagle. Bonds for the payment of moneys in the same place are in Lansdowne MS. 241, f. 58, dat. 4 Mar., 1602–3, and Harley Charter 112 D, 19, dat. 2 Dec., 1615. The former is quoted by Prof. Masson (*Life of Milton*, vol. i., 1859, p. 1), but with the erroneous reading of 'new' for 'now.'

scrivener, in Bread street in London.' Dat. 21 Jan., 4 Jas. I., 1606[7]. Signed; with seal of arms. Witnesses, John Milton, scrivener, Rich. Scudamor, John Roch.

504. ASSIGNMENT by George Adams, of Luton, yeoman, and Anne, his wife, widow and executrix of Edmond Reynoldes, of Dulwich, gent., to Philip Henslowe, for 29*l.*, of the leases of a messuage, lands, &c., in Dulwich as above, nos. 420, 451. Dat. 24 Jan., 4 Jas. I., 1606[7]. Signed; with seals.

505. LEASE from Edward Alleyn, of Dulwich, esq., to Mathew Withers, of Camberwell, gardener, of a messuage, lands, &c., in Dulwich, for 31 years, at a rent of 24*l.* Dat. 29 Jan., 4 Jas. I., 1606[7]. Counterpart, signed; with seal.

506. BOND from Edward Alleyn, of Dulwich, esq., and Philip Henslowe, of St. Saviour's, Southwark, esq., to Thomas Turner, of London, gent., in 200*l.*, for the payment of 126*l.* 13*s.* 4*d.* on 20 April. Dat. 5 Feb., 4 Jas. I., 1606[7]. Signed; with seals of arms.

507. ENROLMENT of the recovery as above, no 485. Dat. 12 Feb., 4 Jas. I. [1607]. *Lat.* With seal.

508. EXEMPLIFICATION of the enrolment, Hilary term, 4 Jas. I. [1607], of the proceedings on a fine from Sir Francis Calton, knt., and Dorothy, his wife, to Edward Alleyn, esq., of the manor of Dulwich, with lands, &c., in Dulwich and Camerwell, and the advowson of the vicarage of Camerwell. Dat. 12 Feb., 4 Jas. I. [1607]. *Lat.* With fragment of seal of the Common Pleas.

509. BOND from Edward Alleyn, of Dulwich, esq., to Edward Husbandes, of Dulwich, gent., for the payment of 8*l.* on 24 June. Dat. 22 Apr., 5 Jas. I., 1607. Signed. With note of payment, 29 June, 1607.

510. DEED of conveyance by Thomas Calton, of Dulwich, gent., and Anne, his wife, and Henry Farr, of Great Bursted, co. Essex, esq , and Prudence, his wife, cousin and heir of Humfrey Plesington (being dau. of Margaret Flinte, his sister), to Edward Alleyn, esq., of a messuage, 16 acres of land, &c., in Dulwich, for 152*l.* paid to Thomas and Anne Calton, and 123*l.* 6*s.* 8*d.* paid to Henry and Prudence Farr; with covenants for assurance, &c. Dat. 1 June, 5 Jas. I., 1607. Signed ; with seals of arms.

511. BARGAIN AND SALE by the same to the same of the messuage, lands, &c., as above. Dat. 1 June, 5 Jas. I., 1607. Signed ; with seals.

512. BOND from Edward Alleyn to Henry Farr, in 100*l.*, for the payment of 55*l.* on 20 Oct. Dat. 18 June, 5 Jas. I., 1607. Signed ; with seal.

513, 514. FINE from Thomas Calton and Anne, his wife, and Henry Farre, esq., and Prudence, his wife, to Edward Alleyn, of the messuage, lands, &c., as above, no. 510, for 41*l.* Dat. Trin. term, 5 Jas. I. [1607]. *Lat.* In duplicate.

515. COVENANTS by Henry Farre and Prudence, his wife, cousin and heir of Humfrey Plesington, deceased, with Robert [Cecil], Earl of Salisbury, Master of the Court of Wards and Liveries, and Sir Cuthbert Pepper, surveyor of the same, on sueing out a general livery of the lands, &c., inherited from the said Humfrey in Surrey, Middlesex, and London. Dat. 24 June, 5 Jas. I. [1607]. With schedule attached.

516. BARGAIN AND SALE by Ellis Parrye, of London, weaver, to Edward Alleyn, esq., of 4 acres of land in Dulwich. Dat. 22 Oct., 5 Jas. I., 1607. Signed by a mark.

517. BOND from Ellis Parrey to Edward Alleyn in 500*l.*, in warranty of three tenements, &c., copyhold of Dulwich manor, surrendered to his use by the said Ellis and Marrian, his wife. Dat. 22 Oct., 5 Jas. I., 1607. Signed; with seal of arms.

518. WARRANT for a livery to Henry Farre, gent., and Prudence Flint, his wife, of messuages, lands, &c., in Dulwich, co. Surr., the par. of St. Martin in the Fields, co. Midd., and the parishes of St. Mary Abchurch and St. Mary Outwich, and in Eastcheap, London, inherited by the said Prudence from Humfrey Plesington, gent., *ob.* 1 Oct., 1603. Dat. 28 April, 6 Jas. I. [1608]. *Lat.*

519. DEFEASANCE of a statute-staple bond, dat. 24 May, 1606, from Sir Francis Calton, knt., to Edward Alleyn, esq., in 8,000*l.*, conditional upon the peaceable enjoyment by the latter of the manor of Dulwich from 8 May, 1606. Dat. 26 May, 6 Jas. I., 1608. Signed by Sir F. Calton; with seal of arms.

520. LIST of five bonds from Francis Calton and Thomas Calton to Thomas Flettcher, Giles Sympson, and Humphrey Walcott; with the note, 'Serched from this day [31 May, 1608] to the xxxij[th] of Eliz., and thes are all vndischarged of Record.'

521. LEASE from Edward Alleyn, of Dulwich, esq., to Thomas Fowler, of Dulwich, husbandman, of a messuage, &c., in Dulwich called the 'blew house,' for 10 years, at a rent of 53*s.* 4*d.* Dat. 4 June, 6 Jas. I., 1608. Counterpart, with seal.

522. RELEASE from Thomas Calton, of Dulwich, gent., to Edward Alleyn, esq., for 50*l.*, of lands in Dulwich called

Carters gardeine and Little Browneinges. Dat. 13 June, 6 Jas. I., 1608. Signed; with seal.

523. ASSIGNMENT by William Cockett, late of Dulwich, gent., to Humfrey Abdy, of London, gent., of a lease from Emm Emerson, of Southwark, widow, to Henry Rooper, of Lincoln's Inn, dat. 24 May, 1604, of a messuage, land, &c., at Dulwich, as above, no. 448. Dat. 19 Nov., 6 Jas. I. [1608]. Signed.

524. LETTERS PATENT of James I., pardoning the alienation by Thomas Calton to Humphrey Plessington, 8 Sept., 1601, of a messuage, lands, &c., in Dulwich held *in capite*. Dat. 20 Nov., aº 6 [1608]. *Lat.*

525, 526. BONDS from Edward Alleyn and Philip Henslowe, esqq., to John Bowyer, of Wandsworth, esq., in 200*l.*, for payments of 100*l.* on 14 June and 14 Dec., 1609. Dat. 14 Dec., 6 Jas. I., 1608. Signed.

527. BARGAIN AND SALE by Sir Edmond Bowyer, of Camberwell, knt., to Edward Alleyn, esq., of messuages, lands, &c., in Dulwich, for 1,240*l.* Dat. 1 Jan., 6 Jas. I. [1609]. Signed.

528, 529. FINE from Sir Edmond Bowyer, knt., and Katerine, his wife, to Edward Alleyn of the same messuages, lands, &c., in Dulwich, with warranty against the heirs of Matthew Draper and Robert, his son. Dat. 3 Feb., 6 Jas. I. [1609]. *Lat.* In duplicate.

530. BOND from Edward Alleyn and Philip Henslowe to John Bowyer, of Wandsworth, esq., in 200*l.*, for the payment of 100*l.* on 14 Dec., 1610. Dat. 10 Feb., 6 Jas. I. [1609]. Signed.

531. BOND from Edward Allen and Philip Henslowe to Sir Edmond Bowyer, of Camerwell, knt., in 200*l.*, for the payment of 100*l.* on 28 Apr., 1610. Dat. 26 Nov., 7 Jas. I., 1609. Signed; with seals of arms.

532. BARGAIN AND SALE by Thomas Calton, of Dulwich, gent., to Edward Alleyn, of St. Saviour's, Southwark, esq., of 'comoning and common of estovers and pastures' pertaining to his (the vendor's) dwelling-house and lands in Dulwich. Dat. 21 Dec., 7 Jas. I., 1609. Signed; with seal of arms.

533. LEASE from Thomas Calton to Philip Henslowe, of St. Saviour's, Southwark, esq., of 12 acres of land, called Addington's meadows, in Dulwich, for 150 years, at a peppercorn rent, voidable by the repayment of 60*l.* within three years. Dat. 21 Dec., 7 Jas. I., 1609. Signed; with seal of arms.

534. STATUTE-STAPLE BOND from the same to the same in 120*l.* Dat. 21 Dec., 7 Jas I. [1609]. *Lat.* Signed by Tho. Calton and [Sir] Edw. Coke [Chief Justice of the Common Pleas]; with seals of arms.

535. DEFEASANCE of the preceding statute-staple bond, conditional upon the performance of covenants in the indenture of lease as above, no. 533. Dat. 21 Dec., 7 Jas. I., 1609. Counterpart, signed; with seal of arms.

536. DECLARATION by Philip Henslowe that the lease and bond as above, nos. 533, 534, were held by him in trust for Edward Alleyn. Dat. 21 Dec., 1609. Signed; with seal.

537. COVENANT by Sir Edward Duke, knt., of Cossington, co. Kent, with William Rayner, of Lincoln's Inn, esq., and Thomas Bynwyn, of Stanmore, co. Midd., gent., for a fine and recovery of the manor of Milkwell, with lands, &c., in Camberwell and Lambeth, to the use of the same Sir Edw. Duke, his heirs and assigns. Dat. 2 Jan., 7 Jas. I. [1610]. Certified *copy*. Paper, 9 sheets.

538. Bargain and Sale by Sir Edward Duke, knt., to William Rayner, esq., of the manor of Milkwell, with lands in Milkwell, Camberwell, and Lambeth, co. Surr., lately belonging to the dissolved monasteries of St. Mary Overy and Bermondsey. Dat. 6 Jan., 7 Jas. I., 1609[10]. Certified *copy*. Paper, 4 sheets. Endorsed by Edw. Alleyn, '. . . . for cutting off ye entayle.'

539. Lease from Thomas Calton, of Dulwich, gent., and Anne, his wife, to Walter Ethersoll, of Dulwich, husbandman, of a field called Carter's Hall, &c., in Dulwich, for 31 years, at a rent of 4*l.* Dat. 5 Mar., 7 Jas. I., 1609[10]. Counterpart, signed by a mark.

540. Lease from Thomas Calton to Edmond Pigeon, of Estgrenewich, gent., of a close called 'the three acres' in Dulwich, for 13 years and 12 months of 28 days, at a rent of 3*l.*, and at the end of the term 30*s.* Dat. 30 Apr., 8 Jas. I., 1610. Signed.

541. Lease from Edward Alleyn to Anthony Kitchen, gent., and John Ewen, yeoman, of Dulwich, of Hamondes and Linges Coppices, &c., in Dulwich, for 21 years, at a rent of 6*l.* 8*s.* Dat. 20 Sept., 8 Jas. I., 1610. With note of surrender, 6 Feb., 1614[5].

542. 'The Aunsweare of Sir Frauncys Calton, knight, defendant, to the Bill of Complaint of Edward Allen, esquire complainant.' Dat. [3 June, 1611]. See above, MS. iv., art. 76. *Copy*; paper, 11 sheets.

543. LEASE from Thomas Calton, of Dulwich, gent., and Anne, his wife, to Edward Alleyn, esq., of a field in Dulwich called Carter's Hall, for 500 years, at a peppercorn rent; together with a grant of a yearly rent of 4*l.* due on the lease of the same as above, no. 539. Dat. 18 Oct., 9 Jas. I., 1611. Signed; with seal.

544. LEASE from Edward Alleyn to Richard Pare, of Dulwich, husbandman, of land in Dulwich for 99 years, at a rent of a pullet during the life of Rich. Pare and after of 20*s.* Dat. 20 Oct., 9 Jas. I., 1611. Counterpart, with seal. With note of re-entry, 30 Nov., 1613.

545. LETTERS PATENT of James I., granting license to Thomas Calton to alienate to Edward Alleyn two messuages, with lands, &c., in Dulwich and Camberwell, held *in capite.* Dat. 2 Nov., a° 9 [1611]. *Lat.*

546. MEMORANDUM of the terms of purchase by Edward Alleyn from Thomas Calton, for 500*l.*, of a dwelling-house and lands in Dulwich—viz. the three acres next the house, Addington's meadows, Carter's Hall, and Great Browninges. Dat. 9 Nov., 1611. Signed. With acquittances below from Tho. Calton for 139*l.* in all; 15, 29 Nov., 1611.

547. ASSIGNMENT by Edward Alleyn to Philip Henslowe of the lease from Thomas Calton of a field in Dulwich as above, no. 543; the assignment to be void on payment of 5*s.* Dat. 20 Nov., 9 Jas. I., 1611. Signed; with seal of arms.

548. BARGAIN AND SALE by Thomas Calton, of Dulwich, gent., and Anne, his wife, to Edward Alleyn, of Dulwich, esq., of two messuages, with lands called Carter's Hall, Great Brownings, Addington's meadows, &c., in Dulwich, for 510*l.* Dat. 28 Nov., 9 Jas. I., 1611. Signed; with seal of arms.

549. DEFEASANCE of a bond from Thomas Calton to Edward Alleyn, in 1,000*l.*, conditional upon the performance of covenants in the preceding indenture. Dat. 29 Nov., 9 Jas. I., 1611. Counterpart, signed.

550, 551. FINE from Thomas Calton to Edward Alleyn of two messuages, with lands, &c., in Dulwich and Camerwell, for 41*l.* Dat. Hilary term, 9 Jas. I. [1612]. *Lat.* In duplicate.

552. RECOVERY by Ralph Bovey and John Badger against Edw. Alleyn of 5 messuages, 56 acres of land, &c., in Dulwich and Camerwell, by way of assurance on a sale of the same to Edw. Alleyn by Tho. Calton. Dat. 12 Feb., 9 Jas. I. [1612]. *Lat.* With fragment of seal.

553. LEASE from Edward Alleyn to John Townley, of Gray's Inn, co. Midd., esq., of a messuage, lands, &c., in Dulwich for 31 years, at a rent of 22*l.* Dat. 18 May, 10 Jas. I., 1612. Counterpart, signed. The name of John Townley has been altered throughout to Philip Padmore and Mary, his wife.

554. LEASE from Edward Alleyn to Edmond Mountjoye, of Wetherfield, co. Essex, gent., of a messuage and lands in Dulwich, in the occupation of Anthony Kitchen, for 21 years, at a rent of 12*l.* Dat. 13 July, 10 Jas. I., 1612. Signed. With note of surrender, 5 July, 1620.

555. RECOVERY by Ralph Bovey and John Badger against Edward Alleyn of 10 messuages, 20 acres of land, 20 acres of pasture, and 14 acres of wood, &c., in Dulwich, by way of assurance on a sale of the same to Edward Alleyn by Sir Edmond Bowyer, knt. Dat. 15 Nov., 10 Jas. I. [1612]. *Lat.* With fragm. of seal.

556. RELEASE from Sir Francis Calton, knt., to Edward Alleyn, esq., for 5,000*l.*, of the manor of Dulwich, with messuages, lands, &c., in Dulwich and Camerwell, and the advowson of the vicarage of Camerwell, as sold to the said Edw. Alleyn by deed dat. 8 May, 1606. Dat. 27 Feb., 10 Jas. I., 1612[3]. Signed; with seal of arms.

557. DEFEASANCE of a statute-staple bond from Edward Alleyn to Sir Francis Calton, in 1,000 marks, conditional upon the payment of two sums of 266*l.* 13*s.* 4*d.* when Duke Calton and Henry Calton, sons of the said Sir Francis, respectively attain the age of 16 years, or, in the event of the death of either or both of them, upon the payment of 10*l.* towards the expenses of burial. Dat. 27 Feb., 10 Jas. I. [1613]. Counterpart, signed.

558. INDENTURE of contract between Edw. Alleyn, of Dulwich, esq., and John Benson, of Westminster, bricklayer, for the erection by the latter upon Dulwich Green of 'a certaine buildinge of brick' for 'a chappell, a scholehowse and twelve almshowses,' the payment for the same to be in all at the rate of 40*s.* a rod. Dat. 17 May, 11 Jas. I., 1613. Signed by John Benson. With acquittances on the back for 127*l.* in all; 19 June, 1612--22 Apr., 1614.

Printed, *Mem. of Edw. Alleyn*, p. 215; Blanch, *Hist. of Camberwell*, 1875, Appendix, p. xxxvi.

559. ENROLMENT of the recovery as above, no. 555. Dat. 9 Oct., 11 Jas. I. [1613]. *Lat.* With fragments of seal.

560. BOND from Sir Francis Calton, of Pasloes, in Dagnam, co. Essex, knt., to Edward Alleyn, of Dulwich, esq., in 500*l.*, to procure a surrender by Sir Edward Duke, of Cossington, knt., of lands, &c., in Dulwich manor, held by him, on surrender from Nicholas Knight, in trust for the said Sir Francis, and sold by the latter to Edw. Alleyn. Dat. 25 Oct., 11 Jas. I., 1613. Signed; with seal of arms.

561. BARGAIN AND SALE by Sir Edward Duke, knt., to Peter Scott, of Camberwell, and Edward Allen, of Dulwich, esqq., respectively, of all deeds, &c., relating to 9 acres of land in Camberwell and 18 acres in Lambeth and Camberwell, conveyed by two deeds of feoffment of the same date; with covenant to levy a fine. Dat. 2 Nov., 11 Jas. I. [1613]. Scott's counterpart, signed; with seal of arms.

562. FEOFFMENT from Sir Edward Duke, of Aylesford, co. Kent, knt., to Edward Alleyn, for 160*l.*, of 18 acres of land in Lambeth and Camberwell. Dat. 2 Nov., 11 Jas. I., 1613. *Lat.* Signed.

563. LEASE from Edward Alleyn, of Dulwich, esq., to John Casinghurst and Amy, his wife, of lands called Gilcottes landes and Court Mead, in Dulwich, for .... years, at a rent of 12*l.* Dat. .... 1613. Fragment.

564, 565. FINE from Sir Edward Duke, knt., and Margaret, his wife, to Edward Alleyn and Peter Scott, esqq of 20 acres of land and 20 acres of pasture in Lambeth and Camberwell, for 41*l.* Dat. Easter term, 12 Jas. I. [1614]. *Lat.* In duplicate.

566. LEASE from Edward Alleyn to Marie, wife of John Townley, of Dulwich, esq., of a messuage and 36½ acres of and in Dulwich, for 41 years, for 200*l.* in hand and a yearly rent of 22*l.*, and 'upon the last daye of August one good fatt and sweete Buck of the season.' Dat. 10 Sept., 12 Jas. I., 1614.

567, 568. FINE from Thomas Calton, gent., and Anne, his wife, to Edward Alleyn, esq., of two messuages, with lands, &c., in Dulwich and Camerwell, for 41*l.* Dat. Mich. term, 12 Jas. I. [1614]. *Lat.* In duplicate.

569. ACQUITTANCES from Thomas Calton to Edward Alleyn for 60*l.* in all in full payment of all claims. Dat. 9, 18, 26 Nov., 1614. In the hand of Edw. Alleyn. Signed by Tho. Calton.

570. LEASE from Edward Alleyn to Robert Best, of Dulwich, husbandman, of a messuage and lands in Dulwich, for 21 years, at a rent of 17*l.* 6*s.* 8*d.* Dat. 11 Sept., 13 Jas. I., 1615. Counterpart.

571. LEASE from Edward Alleyn to Robert Cooper, of London, skinner, of a messuage, land, &c., in Dulwich, for 31 years, at a rent of 29*l.* Dat. 11 Sept., 13 Jas. I., 1615.

572. LETTERS TESTIMONIAL of George Abbot, Archbishop of Canterbury, endorsed by Edw. Alleyn, 'The Instrument off Consecracon [1 Sept.] for ye Chapple dedicated to the Honore off Christ in Dullwich with ye Churchyard thervnto belonging.' Dat. 13 Sept., 1616. *Lat.* With seal of the Archbishop.

The form of dedication and the prayers used on the occasion are contained in Archb. Abbot's register at Lambeth, and are printed by Wilkins, *Concilia*, 1737, vol. iv. p. 455.

573. LEASE from Edward Alleyn to Edmond Rogers, of Dulwich, tailor, of a messuage, part of the house called the

Pettes, with land, &c., in Dulwich, for 21 years, at a rent of 3*l.* Dat. 29 Sept., 14 Jas. I., 1616. With note of surrender, 2 July, 1617.

574. LEASE from Edward Alleyn to Thomas Beimane, of Dulwich, gent., of a messuage, land, &c., in Dulwich, for 21 years, at a rent of 12*l.* Dat. 1 May, 16 Jas. I., 1618.

575. LEASE from Edward Alleyn to Thomas Tillesley, of Camberwell, gent., of a close of land in Dulwich, for 25 years from Michaelmas, 1624, at a rent of 3*l.* Dat. 26 Sept., 16 Jas. I., 1618. Signed.

576. LEASE from the same to the same of a messuage, lands, &c., in Dulwich, for 31 years, at a rent of 29*l.* Dat. 26 Sept., 16 Jas. I., 1618. Counterpart, signed; with seal.

577. BOND from Thomas Tillesley to Edward Alleyn, in 100*l.*, for the payment of rent on the lease above. Dat. 26 Sept., 16 Jas. I., 1618. Signed.

578. LEASE from Edward Alleyn to Raphe Canterburie, of Dulwich, wheelwright, of a messuage, land, &c., in Dulwich, for 31 years, at a rent of 3*l.* 13*s.* 4*d.* Dat. 17 Oct., 16 Jas. I., 1618. Counterpart; with seal.

579. LEASE from Edward Alleyn to John Stock, of London, haberdasher, of a messuage and lands called Napps and Stony Napps, in Dulwich, for 21 years, at a rent of 11*l.* Dat. 30 Nov., 16 Jas. I., 1618. Counterpart, signed.

580. ASSIGNMENT by Philip Padmore, of Dulwich, gent., and Marie, his wife, to Samuel Bridges, of London, gold smith, of a lease, dat. 3 Dec., 1618, from Edw. Alleyn, of a messuage, lands, &c., in Dulwich, for 40 years, at a yearly rent of 22*l.* Dat. 26 Dec., 16 Jas. I., 1618. Signed; with seals.

581. LETTERS PATENT of James I. to Edward Alleyn, of Dulwich, esq., chief master of 'our games of Beares Bulles and mastive dogges and mastive bitches,' for the foundation of a college to be called 'The Colledg of Gods Guift in Dulwich,' and to consist of a master, warden, four fellows, six poor brothers, six poor sisters, and twelve poor scholars; with license for its endowment in mortmain with the manor of Dulwich, the manor-house, land, &c., of Hall Place or Knowlis, lands, wood, &c., called Ricotes or Rigates, and all other manors, lands, &c., in Dulwich bought by Edw. Alleyn from Sir Fran. Calton; messuages, lands, &c., in Dulwich bought from Sir Edm. Bowyer, John Bowyer, Thos. Calton, Henry Farr, and others; eighteen acres of pasture in Lambeth bought from Sir Edw. Duke; messuages, lands, &c., in the par. of St. Botolph without Bishopsgate, inherited from Edw. Alleyn, gent., his father; messuages, lands, &c., in Whitecross Street and Golden Lane, in the par. of St. Giles without Cripplegate, called the Fortune, bought from Daniel Gill and others; and all and singular his manors, messuages, lands, &c., in the above places and elsewhere soever as he shall think meet; and with provision that the Archbishop of Canterbury for the time being be the Visitor of the College. Dat. Westminster, 21 June, a° 17 [1619]. With the Great Seal attached.

Printed, Blanch, *Hist. of Camberwell*, 1875, Appendix, p. i.

582, 583. LEASE from Edward Alleyn to William Lawton, of London, haberdasher, of a messuage called Hall Place, with land, &c., in Dulwich, for 51 years, for 40*l.* in hand and a rent of 8*l.* Dat. 22 June, 17 Jas. I., 1619. Followed by the counterpart. Signed; with seals.

584. DEED OF FOUNDATION by Edward Alleyn, of Dulwich, esq., by virtue of the Letters Patent as above, no. 581, of a college to be called and named 'THE COLLEGE OF GODS GUIFT IN DULWICH IN THE COUNTY OF SURREY,' and to 'consist of one maister, one warden, fower fellowes, six poore brethren, six poore sisters and twelue poore schollers.' Dat. 13 Sept., 17 Jas. I. [1619]. Signed, 'E. Alleyn'; with seal of arms. Signed also by the following witnesses:—Fr[ancis Bacon, Lord] Verulam, Chancellor, T[homas Howard, Earl of] Arundell, [Sir] Edw. Cecyll [afterwards Viscount Wimbledon, Lord-Lieutenant of Surrey], [Sir] John Howland [Sheriff of Surrey], [Sir] Edm. Bowyer, [Sir] Tho. Grymes, [Sir] John Bodley, [Sir] J. Tonstall, Inigo Jones, Jo: Finch, Richarde Tailboys, Rich: Jones, Jo: Anthony, Edmond Howes, chronyckler, Leonell Tychebourn, notary public.

Printed, Blanch, *Hist. of Camberwell*, 1875, Appendix, p. vi. See also Alleyn's *Diary* [MS. ix., above], 13 Sept., 1619.

585. LEASE from Edward Alleyn to Richard Needum, of Camberwell, tailor, of land in Lambeth and Camberwell, for 8 years, at a rent of 8*l.* Dat. 21 Oct, 17 Jas. I., 1619. Counterpart, signed; with seal.

586, 587. COVENANT by Edward Alleyn, of Dulwich, esq., to levy a fine to William Allen and William Austen of the manor of Dulwich, with lands, messuages, &c., in Dulwich and Camerwell and in the parishes of Lambeth, co. Surr., and St. Botolph without Bishopsgate and St. Giles without Cripplegate, co. Middlesex, to the use of himself, the said Edw. Alleyn, for life, and after to the use of the 'Colledg of Godes guifte in Dullwich' for ever. Dat. 24 Apr., 18 Jas. I. [1620]. Followed by the counterpart. Signed; with seals of arms.

Printed, Blanch, *Hist. of Camberwell*, 1875, Appendix, p. ix.

588. DRAFT of the preceding covenant, with a few additions and notes in the hand of Edward Alleyn. Paper, 21 sheets. *Imperfect*, and injured by damp.

589. EXEMPLIFICATION of a fine by Edward Alleyn, esq., and Johanna, his wife, to William Alleyn and William Austen of the manor of Dullwich, &c., as above, nos. 586, 587, for 2,100*l.* Dat. Easter term, 18 Jas. I. [1620]. *Lat.* Fragm. of seal.

590. SURRENDER by Samuel Bridges, of London, goldsmith, to Edward Alleyn, esq., of two acres of land in Dulwich included in leases from the latter to Humphrey Abdy, dat. 20, 21 Aug., 1609. Dat. 15 Nov., 18 Jas. I., 1620. Signed.

591. LEASE from Edward Alleyn to William Lewis, of London, goldsmith, for 2*l.* 15*s.* in hand and a rent of 8*s.*, of 'shreddes loppes and topps' on lands, &c., in Dulwich, leased to him, 20 Jan., 1620[1], for 41 years, at a rent of 40*l.* Dat. 16 Mar., 18 Jas. I., 1620[1]. Counterpart, signed.

592, 593. COVENANT by Sir Edmond Bowyer, knt., and Edward Alleyn, esq., to submit to an award as to the payment of tithes for land in Dulwich called 'the cokers,' heretofore 'copice woods and lately converted into earable and tillage.' Dat. 29 Aug., 1626. Signed. Followed by a copy of the same.

594. THE ORIGINAL BOOK of the Statutes and Ordinances of the College of God's Gift in Dulwich, signed by Edward Alleyn, the Founder. Dat. 29 Sept., 1626. With an additional clause, 20 Nov., 1626. Witnesses, Joseph Reding, Matthew Sweetser, Henry Dell, John Casenghurst, George Brome.

Printed, Blanch, *Hist. of Camberwell*, 1875, Appendix, p. xiii.

(*SECTION IV.*)

COURT-ROLLS of Dulwich manor; 1333–1626.

A. From Tuesday before the Feast of the Nativity of St. John Bapt., 7 Edw. III. [1333], to Wednesday after the Feast of St. Augustine, 9 Edw. III. [1335]. Five sheets.

B. From Thursday after the Feast of the Conception of the Virgin, 1 Hen. IV. [1399], to Tuesday before Michaelmas, 13 Hen. IV. [1411]. Thirteen sheets.

C. From Tuesday before the Feast of St. George, 6 Hen. VI. [1428], to the Feast of St. Katherine the Virgin, 24 Hen. VI. [1445]; and from 6 May, 8 Edw. IV. [1468], to 23 Apr., 12 Edw. IV. [1472]. Fourteen sheets.

D. From 19 Jan., 1 Hen. VII. [1486], to 10 July, 12 Hen. VII. [1497]. Eight sheets.

E. From 15 Dec., 11 Hen. VIII. [1519], to 2 May, 30 Hen. VIII. [1538]. Nine sheets.

F. 11 May, 38 Hen. VIII. [1546]. One sheet.

G. From 17 May, 6 Edw. VI. [1552], to Wednesday before the Feast of St. James the Apostle, 1 Eliz. [1559]. Three sheets.

H. From 21 Oct., 3 Eliz. [1561], to 14 Oct., 10 Eliz. [1568]. Seven sheets.

I. From 22 Oct., 14 Eliz. [1572], to 10 May, 16 Eliz., 1574. Two sheets.

K. From 8 Mar., 18 Eliz. [1576], to 26 Oct., 26 Eliz. [1584]. Seven sheets.

L. From 22 Oct., 28 Eliz. [1586], to 27 Mar., 3 Jas. I. [1605]. Nine sheets.

M. From 7 Oct., 4 Jas. I. [1606], to 24 Oct., 2 Chas. I. [1626]. Twelve sheets.

APPENDIX.

MS. No. XVIII.

ALLEYN PAPERS. Vol. VII. Miscellaneous Papers connected with Edward Alleyn and Dulwich College; 1330 1662. Included are:—

1. ATTESTED COPIES from records in the Tower, made in 1638, relating to the Priory and Abbey of St. Saviour, Bermondsey, viz.:—

a. Inspeximus by Edward III. of grants by Henry I. of St. George's Church, Southwark, of Rodereia, Dilewic, &c., and of free-warren, in co. Surrey; of confirmations by Henry I. of grants by Hubert, son of Dudeman, of three 'mansiones' of land and by William II. of Bermondsey and St. Saviour's Church; and of confirmations by Henry II. of the possessions, &c., of the priory generally, and of Camberwell Church, granted by William de Mellent, Earl of Gloucester; Woodstock, 15 July, 4 Edw. III. [1330.] *Lat.* f. 1.

b. Inspeximus by Edward III. of a lease, dat. 4 Feb., from the priory to Thomas Dolsaly, pepperer, of Dilwysshe manor, for life; 21 Feb., 31 Edw. III. [1357]. *Lat.* f. 16.

c. Certificate from the return of benefices in the hands of aliens that Camberwell Church is appropriated to the alien priory of Bermondsey, and is held by Tho. Cortherope, rector of Goleston, at a rent of 20*l.* a year; 48 Edw. III. [1374]. *Lat.* f. 22.

d. Grant by Richard II. to Richard Duntone, Prior of Bermondsey, and his successors of naturalisation in England, the priory no longer to be treated as alien so long as the prior and the majority of the monks shall be English born; 29 May, 4 Rich. II. [1381]. *Lat.* f. 24.

2. 'THAUNSWERE of John Croft to the bill of complaint [Mun. 338] of Margaret Calton, wydowe'; [1558]. f. 31.

3. 'RECEYPTES for mony some tyme called Oggnell mony,' arranged under the heads of 'Camberwell,' 'Peckham,' and 'Dowlytche,' the amounts being respectively 31*s.*, 15*s.* 4*d.*, and 11*s.* 8*d.*; 1562–3. f. 39.

Oggnell or Hognell money is apparently the same as Hock-money, collected on Hock-day or Hoke-day, which was the second Tuesday after Easter, by the women-parishioners, or on the Monday preceding by the men. One of the uses to which it is said to have been put was the repair of the parish churches. See Brand, *Popular Antiquities*, ed. Ellis, 1813, vol. i. p. 156, and *Notes and Queries*, 2nd series, vol. iv. p. 387, 3rd series, vol. iii. p. 423.

4. PROCEEDINGS in an action by Joan Calton against Robert Brokesbye for trespass, &c., in Dulwich [Munn. 371–373]; Trin. term, 21 Eliz. [1579]. f. 41.

5. COMMISSION from James I. to George Buck, esq., Master of the Revels, to take up all property-makers, workmen, and stuff necessary for the service of the Revels, and 'to warne, commaund and appointe . . . . all and every player or players with their play-makers, either belonging to any nobleman or otherwise bearing the name or names of [or] vseing the facultye of playmakers or players of comedyes, tragedyes, enterludes or what other shewes soever, from tyme to tyme and at all tymes to appeare before him with all such playes, tragedyes, comedyes or shewes as they shall have in readines or meane to sett forth and them to present and recite before our said servant or his sufficient deputye,' &c., with power to commit recalcitrants to ward without bail for so long time as he shall think sufficient; [21 June, 1603]. *Copy. Imperfect.* f. 51.

6. RENT-BOOK of Philip Henslowe, containing the names of his tenants of the Boar's Head, James Russell's tenements, the Pike Garden, the Bankside, &c., in Southwark; 1604–1611. f. 62.

7. STATEMENT in the hand of Edw. Alleyn of his expenditure on the Bear Garden and the Fortune; 1602–1608. f. 76.

	‘BEAR-GARDEN.			PLAY HOWSE.		
1602	121^l	11^s	6^d	089^l	05^s	0^d
1603	118	07	0	004	02	0
1604	153	14	0	232	01	8
1605	092	12	4	108	14	3
	486	04	10	434	02	11
1606 pd for ye building				127	00	00
1607 of ye howse wch may				163	00	00
1608 be counted to 360^l				121	06	00
some totall . .	846	04	10	411	06	00
totall .				845	08	11’

8. PAPERS relating to the sale by John Ewen to Edw. Alleyn of lands in Dulwich; 5 Mar., 1609[10], 16, 23 Oct., 1615. With acquittances, &c., 29 Sept., 1618–13 Oct., 1623. Three of the documents (ff. 114, 115, 116) are witnessed by the dramatists Robert Daborne and Philip Massinger. ff. 77, 101–116.

9. BOND from John Townsend, Joseph Tayler, William Egglestone, Giles Gary, Robert Hamlyn, Thomas Hunte, Joseph Moore, John Rice, William Carpenter, Alexander Foster, Francis Waymus, and Thomas Basse, of London, gentlemen, to Philip Henslowe, of Southwark, esq., in 500*l.*, to perform certain theatrical articles of the same date; 29 Aug., 1611. Signed by all the company except G. Gary. For the list of names cf. Mun. 47. One of the witnesses is John Taylor, perhaps the 'water-poet.' f. 78.

10. ANSWER of Thomas Wightman to a bill of complaint of Edw. Alleyn, enumerating the deeds and other documents in his possession relating to Dulwich manor, he having married Joan, widow of Nicholas Calton and mother of Sir Francis; 5 Oct., 1611. f. 79.

11. THOMAS BROOKE, J.P. for co. Chester, to Phil. Henslowe, as Master of the Royal Game, informing him that his servants have been charged with felony by [John] Venables for taking his dog [MS. ii. art. 28], and that, unless he sends down both letters and a pursuivant, they will be hardly used; Thelwall, 9 Aug., 1613. f. 99.

12. PETITION from Edw. Alleyn to James I. for a writ of privy-seal to John Hobdaye to account for 13*l.* 5*s* 5*d.* which had been paid on behalf of the King of France, for a supply of bears and dogs, in 1611 to James Starkey and John Alleyn, and had been advanced by them to the said John Hobdaye for repayment to Phil. Henslowe or Edw. Alleyn in England; *circ.* 1618. *Draft.* f. 136.

13. 'REPLICACION' of Dulwich College to the several answers of Tobias Lisle and Tho. Grimes concerning leases of the Fortune, denying the allegations therein contained

[Munn. 67–69]; 1645. With a 'breviate' in the same suit; 1647. ff. 140, 145.

14. ANSWERS of John Roades [or Rhodes] and Susan Baskerville to a bill of Dulwich College, that they have paid all arrears of rent on their leases of the Fortune up to 1640, but that since then 'stage playes and playhowses have bene suppressed,' and they are therefore not answerable for rent, being forbidden by the terms of their leases to put the premises to any other use; 1648. With a demurrer on the part of the College; 1649. ff. 150, 158.

15. MEMORANDA of leases from Dulwich College to William Beaven of the site of the Fortune, &c., with the bill and decree in Chancery as above, MS. i. artt. 129, 131, 132; 24 July, 21 Nov., 1661, 4 Sept., 1662. ff. 164–218.

Paper, ff. 218. Quarto.

MS. No. XIX.

'THE PLATT of the Secound parte of the Seuen Deadlie Sinns': an outline of the action in the play of *The Seven Deadly Sins*, part ii., by Richard Tarleton, with the names of the performers, including R. Burbage, T. Pope, R. Cowley, A. Phillips, W. Sly, R. Pallant, and 'Ned' [Edward Alleyn?]. Entitled on the outside 'The Booke and Platt,' &c.

Written in a large clear hand on a sheet of paper measuring 16 × 12 inches, with a hole in the centre near the top for the nail or peg by which it was suspended in the theatre. When found at Dulwich, it formed the cover for the play of *The Tell-Tale*, MS. xx.

First printed by Edm. Malone in 1780 in his *Supplement to the Edition of Shakspeare published in* 1778, vol. i. p. 58, accompanied by some remarks by George Steevens, and included also in Malone's *Shakspeare*, ed. Boswell, 1821, vol. iii. p. 348. Printed again by Mr. Collier, *History of Dramatic Poetry*, &c., 1831, vol. iii. p. 394 [ed. 1879, iii. 197].

Mr. Collier considers that the play consisted of pantomime and extemporaneous dialogue on a pre-arranged plot, and he thus describes it:—'It relates to three distinct stories, illustrating the consequences of Envy, Sloth, and Lechery: first, that of Gorboduc and his sons Ferrex and Porrex; secondly, that of Sardanapalus; and thirdly, that of Tereus; and the question arises, in what way Henry VI. and Lidgate were concerned in it. Henry VI. is in his tent, and probably Lidgate is supposed to regulate the performance in his presence, and for his amusement. In the course of the piece, Henry and Lidgate twice talk together, and Lidgate seems to act as chorus, to explain the dumb shows, and to deliver the prologue and epilogue.'

The 'plat' of the first part of the play, which probably dealt with Pride, Gluttony, Wrath, and Covetousness, has not been preserved. As Tarleton was buried 3 Sept., 1588, the piece must have been composed before that date.

MS. No. XX.

'THE TELLTALE,' a comedy in five acts. A part of the fourth act is missing, the leaves being left blank.

The scene is laid in Florence, the chief characters being the Duke, Aspero, his general, Hortensio, a Venetian prince, prisoner of war, Picentio, Bentivoglio, Victoria the Duchess, Isabella, her niece or cousin, and Elinor. The plot turns on the Duke's unfounded jealousy of his wife and the intrigues of Aspero, who on the Duke's reported death obtains the crown, after having, as he supposed, procured the murder of the Duchess and Picentio, her reputed lover, in prison. The title-character is Bentivoglio, as thus explained :—

'*Hort.*—A fellow not worth anger. What's the other—that ould fellow?

'*Asp.*—Lesse vainglorious but much more valiant; and yet as euery man has one ydle humor or another, hee wants not his, and the traine this peacocke ys so proud of ys his tale.

'*Hort.*—Does hee take such pleasure in an ould tale

'*Asp.*—Ould or yong so yt bee in the likenes of a tale yt neuer comes amisse to him. The Duke knowes his humor so well hee giues way, and indeed lenes a kind of priuilege too't and calls him his telltale.'

The name of the author is unknown and the play has not been printed, though it was advertised as being in the press in 1658 and 1661 (Halliwell, *Dict. of Old English Plays*, p. 242). The present unique copy, which is in a hand of the early part of the seventeenth century, appears to have belonged to the actor who played the leading part of the Duke, the word 'mine' being written opposite his first speech.

This MS. and MS. xix., which formed its cover, were included in the sale-catalogue of the library of James Boswell in 1825, but were claimed by the College authorities and given up to them a few days before the sale.

Paper, ff. 25. Small quarto.

MS. No. XXI.

'A BOOKE of a Compte [accompt] from the time of the death of our ffounder, whooe dyed the 25th daie of November beeinge Saterdaie about 8 of the clocke at night, 1626.'

Accounts of expenditure by Matthias Alleyn, the Warden, on behalf of Dulwich College, 26 Nov., 1626–10 Nov., 1627, signed weekly by Thomas Alleyn, the Master, and the four Fellows.

Paper, ff. 30. Narrow folio.

MS. No. XXII.

THEOLOGICAL TRACTS and other pieces in prose and verse, in different hands of the thirteenth and fourteenth centuries:—

1. SERMONS for festivals, from Advent to Quadragesima, in *Latin.* The first sermon, on Isaiah xxxv. 4, begins, 'Ante adventum domini, fratres karissimi, tanta caligine genus hominum uoluebatur.' This and the sermon 'in die S. Stephani' are included in a volume of sermons of St. Bernard in Brit. Mus. Burney MS. 301, but they are not printed among his works. f. 1.

2. EXTRACTS from St. Augustine, sermons on the Nativity, St. Peter, St. Benedict, &c., in *Latin.* ff. 22–23*b*, 24*b*–28.

3. 'MISSA de sancto Antonio.' Inserted in a later hand of the fifteenth century. f. 24.

4. EXPLANATION of the two degrees of excommunication, 'the lesse curse' and the 'more curse,' beginning, 'It is ordeyned by þe covnsel of alle holy chirche first of our holy fader þe pope of Rome and his cardenallys and his counselle and sythyn be erchebyschoppis and byschoppis and alle þe clergie þat euery man of holy chirche þat hath cure of sowlys schuld schewe among þer paryschonyrs fouure tymys in þe ȝere partycles þat be wrytyn in þe generalle sentense,' &c. *Imperfect.* Inserted by the same hand as art 3. f. 28.

5. 'INCIPIT liber qui appellatur Lucidarius': the Elucidarium or Dialogue between a master and pupil on the

Christian faith, attributed to Honorius, Bishop of Autun, St. Anselm, and others. f. 29.

6. 'HIC incipit tractatus Caducani Bargornensis [*sic*, Bangorensis] episcopi de modo confitendi': a treatise on confession, by Cadogan, Bishop of Bangor [1215–1237, *ob.* 1241], beg. 'Notandum quod vere penitentes possunt agnosci.' f. 46.

7. SUMMA de officio sacerdotum, beg. 'Qui bene presunt presbiteri, duplici honore dingni [digni] habeantur.' Attributed in New Coll. MS. 94 to Richard [William] de Montibus, Chancellor of Lincoln [*ob.* 1213], and in Bodley MS. 64 to Richard de Wetherset, Chancellor of Cambridge. W. de Montibus is twice mentioned by name in the body of the work. f. 49.

8. THEOLOGICAL COMMONPLACES and miscellaneous notes, including a series of proverbs in verse, as, *e.g.*, 'Cum sis mendicus, tibi vix erit unus amicus.' A few English sentences also occur, as (f. *76b*), 'If yt so were þat þe ape penyes bere, yet ssolden men seyn in þe gate, wolcome syre ape.' ff. 74–79.

9. POEM on the Life of Christ, in *English*: a fragment, containing the first 519 lines. Written, about 1300, on part of a quire (the two outside leaves of which are lost) originally forming part of another MS. The first three pages remaining (ff. 80–81) contain the end of some theological treatise, notes on the plagues of Egypt, &c., in *Latin*. f. 81*b*.

The poem begins:—

'Sum wyle i was wþt sinne ibunde
Ant sinne me hauid cast to grunde
Bot swete ihesu þine fif wundis?
Lesid me hauis of harde stundis.
Se hu i to þe wende mi þouht.
Pymis to þole greuis me nouht.
Þi ded me hauis of serue al brouht.
Ant loue to þe in me hauis wrouht.'

10. POEM on the Miracles of the Virgin, in *French*: a fragment of about 800 lines, containing part of the stories of Theophilus and his compact with the Devil, and of a monk in Germany, 'ki pur mal guerpir prist puisun.' The hand, though of about the same date, differs from that of art. 9, and the edges of the leaves have been cut, mutilating the text. f. 85.

The same versions are in Brit. Mus., Egerton MS. 612, ff. 27*b*, 41, translated by Adgar *al.* William from a book written by 'Mestre Albri' in the library of St. Paul's, London. The connecting lines here (f. 88*b*) are addressed to a 'dame Mahaut':—

> 'E gente e bone gent senee
> Ki en dev estes asemblee
> E uus dame mahaut premeeres
> A uus dirrai plus uolantiers
> Des miracles des granz succurs
> E [*sic*, ke] fait nostre dame a plusurs
> A tuz e a tutes ki la aiment
> E ki de bon quor la reclaiment.'

Vellum, ff. 89. Small quarto.

MS. No. XXIII.

GULIELMI BRITONIS Vocabularium Biblicum: explanations of words in the Vulgate version of the Bible, with a prologue and epilogue in verse, the former beginning:—

> 'Difficiles studio [studeo] partes quas Biblia gestat
> Pandere, sed nequeo latebras nisi qui manifestat.'

Written in the fourteenth century. With the inscriptions, 'Iste liber datus est comuni armariolo per dominum Reginaldum de Barneby. Quicunque illum alienauerit anathema sit,'

f. 26*b*; and, 'De communi librario monachorum Dunelmensium,' f. 27.

Vellum, ff. 263. Octavo.

MS. No. XXIV.

'MANUEL de Pecche': Robert [Mannyng] of Brunne's *Handlyng Synne,* a poem founded on the *Manuel des Péchés* of William of Wadington.

A fragment, ending at the ninth commandment with the story of Jephtha, being lines 1–2897 of the edition printed for the Roxburghe Club, ed. F. J. Furnivall, 1862. A few lines at the bottom of the first leaf are also torn away. The variations from the printed text are numerous. Written in a rough, ill-formed hand in the early part of the fifteenth century, by a scribe surnamed Rose (f. 16). The lines containing the author's name run as follows:'—

'[To alle crystyn men vndir sunne,
And to gode men of Brunne,] [1]
And specyally alle be name.
Þe felaschepe of Symprynghame.
Robert of Brunne gretiþ ȝow.
In al goodness þ^t may be prow.
Of Brunne Wake [2] in Kesteuene.
Sixe myle fro Sympryngham euene.
I duellyd in þ^t priory.
Xv ȝeer in good cumpany.
In þ^e tyme of goode Dan John.
Of Cameltone [3] þat now is gon.

[1] Ed. Furnivall; MS. torn away.

[2] Ed. Furnivall, Brymwake.

[3] John de Cameltone appears as prior of Sempringham in 1298 (Brit. Mus., Add. Chart. 20652). He cannot therefore, as Sir F. Madden assumed (ed. Furnivall, p. v.), be identical with John de Hamertone, who held office from 1276 until the end of March, 1282. According to Willis (*Mitred Abbeys*, 1719, vol. ii. p. 121) Hamertone was succeeded by Roger de Bolingbrok, who died in

In his tyme was I ther x ȝerys.
And knew and herde of his goode manerys.
Siþþin w^{t} dan John John Clattone.
V ȝeer w^{t} hym gan I wone.
Dan Philipp was mayster þ^{t} tyme.
Þ^{t} I began þis ynglysche ryme.
Þ^{e} ȝeer of grace fil þan to be.
A m^{l}. ccc. and þre.
In þ^{t} tyme turned I þis.
Into ynglysche tunge out of frensche.
Out of a book as I fond þerinne.
Men callyd þe book handlyng of synne.
Of ffrensche þer a clerk it sees.
He callyd it manuel de pecchees.
Manuel is handlyng w^{t} hond.
Pecches arn synnys to vnderstond.
Þese to wurdys þat arn a twynne.
Put hem togedere is handlyng synne.'

Paper, ff. 21. Quarto.

MS. No. XXV.

HOURS of the Virgin, &c., containing a calendar, f. 1; 'quindecim oraciones,' f. 14; commemorations of saints, &c., f. 25; 'hore beate Marie virginis secundum vsum sarrum' [Sarum], f. 45; lauds of the Virgin: 'has videas laudes qui sacra virgine gaudes,' f. 110: 'septem gaudia in honore beate Marie virginis,' f. 126; the five wounds, f. 128*b*; 'oracio venerabilis Bede presbiteri de septem verbis Christi in

1298, and was succeeded by Philip de Barton or Burton. These dates, however, are at variance with the language of Robert of Brunne. If he is to be depended upon, Bolingbrok probably died in 1288, not 1298, and Barton did not become prior until 1303, the same year in which the poem was begun. This would exactly allow the requisite ten years for John de Cameltone, 1288-1298, and five for John Clattone, 1298-1303. For the last name both Mr. Furnivall's MSS. read Clyntone. It has been suggested that John de Glyndone, who was prior from 1332 to 1341, is intended; but his date is obviously too late.

cruce pendentis,' f. 134*b*; 'septem psalmi penitentiales,' f. 146; 'vigilie mortuorum,' f. 174.

Written in the fifteenth century. With illuminated initials, borders, and miniatures.

Vellum, ff. 178. Duodecimo.

MS. No. XXVI.

'A BOOKE of ffees and offices, primo die Augusti, anno primo Regine Marie'; [1553].

A volume of the same nature as MS. xi. (p 198), with the exception that the names of the actual holders of the several offices are here given.

Paper, ff. 86. Large folio.

MS. No. XXVII.

'ESCHINES answer to Demosthenes': a translation of the speech of Æschines περὶ τῆς παραπρεσβείας; 1583.

Preceded by a dedicatory letter in the hand of, and signed by, John Osborne, addressed to Sir Christopher Hatton, Vice-Chamberlain to the Queen and Captain of the Guard, and dated London, 26 Jan., 1582[3]. The writer speaks of an earlier work favourably received by Sir C. Hatton, and adds, 'I meane farther also to translate you two other most excellent workes. Eschines and Demosthenes orations about the coronation of Demosthenes is the one; and the whole volume of Demosthenes orations of state and counsayle is the other.' A translation by him of the speech of Demosthenes against Leptines is in Brit. Mus., Add. MS. 10059. This also was the original presentation copy, and is dated London, 10 Jan., 1581[2].

The translator was probably John Osborne, afterwards Sir

John Osborne, of Chicksand, knt., son of Peter Osborne, Treasurer's Remembrancer of the Exchequer, who married a niece of Sir John Cheke, the first Regius Professor of Greek at Cambridge. John Osborne succeeded his father as Treasurer's Remembrancer in 1592, and died in 1628, aged 76.

Paper, ff. 51. Small quarto.

MS. No. XXVIII.

'WHETHER a Prince or Soueraine Magistrat may, in cases of High Treason, take the lief of his subiect without triall by the ordinary course of his lawes, as in the case of the late D. of Guise hapned in France. With a brief declaration of the tresons complotted by the house of Guise against the K. and state of France'; 1589 or 1590.

Preceded by a dedicatory letter addressed to Sir Christopher Hatton, K.G., Lord Chancellor [1587–1591], signed by the author, Thomas Wilkes, Clerk of the Privy Council. The question is answered in the affirmative, and the dedication concludes, 'Lastlie, I doo applie and compare the actions of the D. of Guise [Henri de Lorraine, Duc de Guise, assassinated at the Royal Château of Blois, 23 Dec., 1588] and his complices to the examples produced, whereby it may appere that the maner of his death in that kinde was not onelie not vnlawfull but necessarie for the saftie of the King and preservacion of his estate.'

The presentation copy, having the signature 'Chr. Hatton, Canc.,' on ff. 1, 50*b*.

Paper, ff. 50. Small quarto.

MS. No. XXIX.

'MILITARY DISCOURSE prouing whether it bee better for England to give an invador present battaile, or to temporize and deferre the same; with a certaine ready and orderly course for the speedy arming and bringing of men together in the shire of Kent at an alarum giuen to the country, which by like proporcion may bee observed in any other shire whatsoeuer throughout England and Wales'; *circ.* 1595.

The writer, who advocates a temporising policy, speaks of another treatise shown by him privately to some of the Lords of the Council in 1585 [ff. 2*b*, 32]. The scope of the earlier work was 'but to perswade you to restrayne the violently and disorderly running downe of the countrie to the sea-side to fight and give battaile to the enemy at landing after the old custome' [f. 28*b*]; and the arguments there advanced having been 'lately impugned by a gentleman of good worth and his discourse committed to print,' he was compelled to uphold and fortify them. He appears to have been a soldier by profession, and had served in France at the siege of Paris and elsewhere, no doubt in the English force under Lord Willoughby sent to the aid of Henry of Navarre in Sept., 1589. Neither of these leaders, however, is mentioned, but the Duke of Parma is continually eulogised, especially for 'the late carriage of his warres in France.'

The writer also refers to the defeat of the Spanish Armada [f. 22], and gives a graphic account as an eye-witness [f. 17] of the tumultuous way in which, upon the firing of the beacons, the country-people rushed down to the shore, 'some with clubbs, some with piked staves and pitchforkes, all vnarmed, and they that were best appointed were but with a bill, a bow and a sheafe of arrowes, noe captaine or commander appointed to direct, lead or order them,' &c.

Several copies of the discourse are in the British Museum, one of which, Harley MS. 4685, is in the same hand as the present MS.

Paper, ff. 36. Folio.

MS. No. XXX.

'BREEF TABLES of vsuall English waightes and measurs, wherin doeth appeare what proporcion they beare one to annother in their kyndes, with certain termes and sizes of waight, measur and number belonging properly to som thinges, and a short table of partes of tyme, not vnfit for eny man that dealith with accomptes of all sortes'; *circ.* 1600.

Among the special tables are the measure of salmon and eels, the number and measure of herrings, the 'number only' of other fish, furs, skins, tanned leather, &c., and the sizes of broad-cloth, narrow-cloth, 'carsies,' cottons, 'frizes and rugges' and flannel, according to the custom of the several places of manufacture.

Paper, ff. 23. Quarto.

MS. No. XXXI.

'TOM TELL TROTH: or a free discourse touching the murmurs of the tyme. Directed to his Majestie by way of humble aduertisement.'

An anonymous political pamphlet, written about the end of the year 1621. See *Calendar of State Papers*, 1619–1623, p. 332.

The writer concludes, 'I shalbe content to remayne vnknowne, soe as I may make your Majestie knowe what false and wicked men keepe from yow, the misfortunes of gouernment and the iust complaintes of your subiectes,' &c.

A copy dated 1621 is in Harley MS. 1220, f. 63. Published in black-letter, without date, quarto, fifteen leaves. Another edition appeared in 1642.

Paper, ff. 84. Small quarto.

MS. No. XXXII.

'THE Lyfe and Raigne of King Edward the Sixth,' by Sir John Hayward; 'Finis, London, 30th November, 1627.'

First printed, London, 1630, 4to. Included in Kennet's *Complete History of England*, 1706, vol. ii. p. 273.

A contemporary copy, written in two hands, neither of which is the author's autograph.

Paper, ff. 84. Folio.

MS. No. XXXIII.

'LES TENURES de Monsineur Littleton': the printed edition, London, 1612, 12mo, interleaved and annotated later in the seventeenth century.

Paper, ff. 195. Quarto.

MS. No. XXXIV.

NOTES of sermons on the two covenants, the mediation of Christ, &c.; having the date July, 1649, on f. 2, and the name 'Mr. [John ?] Strickland' and 'Mr. [Richard ?] Byfeild, June 9, 1650,' on ff. 38, 121*b*.

Paper, ff. 134. Duodecimo.

MS. No. XXXV.

CONTEMPORARY COPIES of three letters 'concerning the lawfullness of taking the oaths to K. William and Q. Mary,' addressed to Captain Hatton, the first [ff. 1–4] and third [ff. 9–52] by J. A., and the second [ff. 5–8] by the Rev. Henry Dodwell, Camden Professor of History at Oxford; 1589.

The last letter of J. A., who advocates submission against Dodwell, concludes, 'I could add many other arguments (of great weight with me) to prove our discharge from the former oath and our liberty to take the new one, but I may well think that they would be tedious and offensive to you who have seen and considered most things that can be offer'd on this side and have probably determined against them in your own judgement; what I have said, I take to be a full answer to M[r] D's. charge of apostasie and perjury,' &c. The initials J. A. possibly mean John Allen, Archdeacon of Chester, 1686–1695 (see above, p. 155). Capt. Hatton is no doubt Capt. Charles Hatton, younger son of the first Lord Hatton. From an entry in Luttrell's Diary, 22 June, 1690, it appears that he was sent to the Tower 'for handing to the presse a treasonable paper against the government.' See also the *Hatton Correspondence*, Camden Soc., 1878, vol. ii. pp. 151 *seqq*.

At the end, f. 53, is an original letter on the same subject, without signature or address, dated Highgate, 22 Aug., 1689.

Paper, ff. 53. Small quarto.

MS. No. XXXVI.

'THE six Satires of A. Persius Flaccus grammatically translated by J. R.' [John Rhodes, usher and school-master Fellow of Dulwich College, 1692–1701 ?].

At the end, reversing the volume, is a 'compendium' of Greek grammar, in a later hand of the eighteenth century, ff. 43–58.

Paper, ff. 58. Small octavo.

INDEX.

LONDON: PRINTED BY
SPOTTISWOODE AND CO., NEW-STREET SQUARE
AND PARLIAMENT STREET

GENERAL LISTS OF WORKS

PUBLISHED BY

MESSRS. LONGMANS, GREEN & CO.

HISTORY, POLITICS, HISTORICAL MEMOIRS, &c.

History of England from the Conclusion of the Great War in 1815. By SPENCER WALPOLE. 8vo. VOLS. I. & II. 1815–1832 (Second Edition, revised) price 36*s*. VOL. III. 1832–1841, price 18*s*.

History of England in the 18th Century. By W. E. H. LECKY, M.A. VOLS. I. & II. 1700–1760. Second Edition. 2 vols. 8vo. 36*s*.

The History of England from the Accession of James II. By the Right Hon. Lord MACAULAY.

STUDENT'S EDITION, 2 vols. cr. 8vo. 12*s*.
PEOPLE'S EDITION, 4 vols. cr. 8vo. 16*s*.
CABINET EDITION, 8 vols. post 8vo. 48*s*.
LIBRARY EDITION, 5 vols. 8vo. £4.

Lord Macaulay's Works. Complete and uniform Library Edition. Edited by his Sister, Lady TREVELYAN. 8 vols. 8vo. with Portrait, £5. 5*s*

Critical and Historical Essays contributed to the Edinburgh Review. By the Right Hon. Lord MACAULAY.

CHEAP EDITION, crown 8vo. 3*s*. 6*d*.
STUDENT'S EDITION, crown 8vo. 6*s*.
PEOPLE'S EDITION, 2 vols. crown 8vo. 8*s*.
CABINET EDITION, 4 vols. 24*s*.
LIBRARY EDITION, 3 vols. 8vo. 36*s*.

The History of England from the Fall of Wolsey to the Defeat of the Spanish Armada. By J. A. FROUDE, M.A.

POPULAR EDITION, 12 vols. crown, £2. 2*s*.
CABINET EDITION, 12 vols. crown, £3. 12*s*.

The English in Ireland in the Eighteenth Century. By J. A. FROUDE, M.A. 3 vols. crown 8vo. 18*s*.

Journal of the Reigns of King George IV. and King William IV. By the late C. C. F. GREVILLE, Esq. Edited by H. REEVE, Esq. Fifth Edition. 3 vols. 8vo. price 36*s*.

The Life of Napoleon III. derived from State Records, Unpublished Family Correspondence, and Personal Testimony. By BLANCHARD JERROLD. In Four Volumes, 8vo. with numerous Portraits and Facsimiles. VOLS. I. to III. price 18*s*. each.

Russia Before and After the War. By the Author of 'Society in St. Petersburg' &c. Translated from the German (with later Additions by the Author) by EDWARD FAIRFAX TAYLOR. Second Edition. 8vo. 14*s*.

Russia and England from 1876 to 1880; a Protest and an Appeal. By O. K. Author of 'Is Russia Wrong?' With a Preface by J. A. FROUDE, M.A. Portrait and Maps. 8vo. 14*s*.

The Early History of Charles James Fox. By GEORGE OTTO TREVELYAN, M.P. Third Edition. 8vo. 18*s.*

The Constitutional History of England since the Accession of George III. 1760–1870. By Sir THOMAS ERSKINE MAY, K.C.B. D.C.L. Sixth Edition. 3 vols. crown 8vo. 18*s.*

Democracy in Europe; a History. By Sir THOMAS ERSKINE MAY, K.C.B. D.C.L. 2 vols. 8vo. 32*s.*

Introductory Lectures on Modern History delivered in 1841 and 1842. By the late THOMAS ARNOLD, D.D. 8vo. 7*s.* 6*d.*

On Parliamentary Government in England. By ALPHEUS TODD. 2 vols. 8vo. 37*s.*

Parliamentary Government in the British Colonies. By ALPHEUS TODD. 8vo. 21*s.*

History of Civilisation in England and France, Spain and Scotland. By HENRY THOMAS BUCKLE. 3 vols. crown 8vo. 24*s.*

Lectures on the History of England from the Earliest Times to the Death of King Edward II. By W. LONGMAN, F.S.A. Maps and Illustrations. 8vo. 15*s.*

History of the Life & Times of Edward III. By W. LONGMAN, F.S.A. With 9 Maps, 8 Plates, and 16 Woodcuts. 2 vols. 8vo. 28*s.*

The Historical Geography of Europe. By EDWARD A. FREEMAN, D.C.L. LL.D. With 65 Maps. 2 vols. 8vo. 31*s.* 6*d.*

History of England under the Duke of Buckingham and Charles I. 1624–1628. By S. R. GARDINER. 2 vols. 8vo. Maps, 24*s.*

The Personal Government of Charles I. from the Death of Buckingham to the Declaration in favour of Ship Money, 1628–1637. By S. R. GARDINER. 2 vols. 8vo. 24*s.*

Memorials of the Civil War between King Charles I. and the Parliament of England as it affected Herefordshire and the Adjacent Counties. By the Rev. J. WEBB, M.A. Edited and completed by the Rev. T. W. WEBB, M.A. 2 vols. 8vo. Illustrations, 42*s.*

Popular History of France, from the Earliest Times to the Death of Louis XIV. By Miss SEWELL. Crown 8vo. Maps, 7*s.* 6*d.*

A Student's Manual of the History of India from the Earliest Period to the Present. By Col. MEADOWS TAYLOR; M.R.A.S. Third Thousand. Crown 8vo. Maps, 7*s.* 6*d.*

Lord Minto in India; Correspondence of the First Earl of Minto, while Governor-General of India, from 1807 to 1814. Edited by his Great-Niece, the COUNTESS of MINTO. Post 8vo. Maps, 12*s.*

Waterloo Lectures; a Study of the Campaign of 1815. By Col. C. C. CHESNEY, R.E. 8vo. 10*s.* 6*d.*

The Oxford Reformers— John Colet, Erasmus, and Thomas More; a History of their Fellow-Work. By F. SEEBOHM. 8vo. 14*s.*

History of the Romans under the Empire. By Dean MERIVALE, D.D. 8 vols. post 8vo. 48*s.*

General History of Rome from B.C. 753 to A.D. 476. By Dean MERIVALE, D.D. Crown 8vo. Maps, price 7*s.* 6*d.*

The Fall of the Roman Republic; a Short History of the Last Century of the Commonwealth. By Dean MERIVALE, D.D. 12mo. 7*s.* 6*d.*

The History of Rome. By WILHELM IHNE. VOLS. I. to III. 8vo. price 45*s.*

Carthage and the Carthaginians. By R. BOSWORTH SMITH, M.A. Second Edition. Maps, Plans, &c. Crown 8vo. 10*s.* 6*d.*

History of Ancient Egypt. By G. RAWLINSON, M.A. With Map and numerous Illustrations. 2 vols. 8vo. price 63*s*.

The Seventh Great Oriental Monarchy; or, a History of the Sassanians. By G. RAWLINSON, M.A. With Map and 95 Illustrations. 8vo. 28*s*.

The History of European Morals from Augustus to Charlemagne. By W. E. H. LECKY, M.A. 2 vols. crown 8vo. 16*s*.

History of the Rise and Influence of the Spirit of Rationalism in Europe. By W. E. H. LECKY, M.A. 2 vols. crown 8vo. 16*s*.

The History of Philosophy, from Thales to Comte. By GEORGE HENRY LEWES. Fifth Edition. 2 vols. 8vo. 32*s*.

A History of Classical Greek Literature. By the Rev. J. P. P. MAHAFFY, M.A. Crown. 8vo. VOL. I. Poets, 7*s*. 6*d*. VOL. II. Prose Writers, 7*s*. 6*d*.

Zeller's Stoics, Epicureans, and Sceptics. Translated by the Rev. O. J. REICHEL, M.A. New Edition revised. Crown 8vo. 15*s*.

Zeller's Socrates & the Socratic Schools. Translated by the Rev. O. J. REICHEL, M.A. Second Edition. Crown 8vo. 10*s*. 6*d*.

Zeller's Plato & the Older Academy. Translated by S. FRANCES ALLEYNE and ALFRED GOODWIN, B.A. Crown 8vo. 18*s*.

Zeller's Pre-Socratic Schools; a History of Greek Philosophy from the Earliest Period to the time of Socrates. Translated by SARAH F. ALLEYNE. 2 vols. crown 8vo. 30*s*.

Zeller's Aristotle and the Elder Peripatetics. Translated by B. F. C. COSTELLOE, Balliol College, Oxford. Crown 8vo. [*In preparation.*

*** The above volume will complete the Authorised English Translation of Dr. ZELLER's Work on the Philosophy of the Greeks.

Epochs of Modern History. Edited by C. COLBECK, M.A.

Church's Beginning of the Middle Ages, 2*s*. 6*d*.
Cox's Crusades, 2*s*. 6*d*.
Creighton's Age of Elizabeth, 2*s*. 6*d*.
Gairdner's Houses of Lancaster and York, 2*s*. 6*d*.
Gardiner's Puritan Revolution, 2*s*. 6*d*.
——— Thirty Years' War, 2*s*. 6*d*.
Hale's Fall of the Stuarts, 2*s*. 6*d*.
Johnson's Normans in Europe, 2*s*. 6*d*.
Longman's Frederic the Great and the Seven Years' War, 2*s*. 6*d*.
Ludlow's War of American Independence, 2*s*. 6*d*.
Morris's Age of Anne, 2*s*. 6*d*.
Seebohm's Protestant Revolution, 2/6.
Stubbs's Early Plantagenets, 2*s*. 6*d*.
Warburton's Edward III. 2*s*. 6*d*.

Epochs of Ancient History. Edited by the Rev. Sir G. W. COX, Bart. M.A. & C. SANKEY, M.A.

Beesly's Gracchi, Marius & Sulla, 2*s*. 6*d*.
Capes's Age of the Antonines, 2*s*. 6*d*.
——— Early Roman Empire, 2*s*. 6*d*.
Cox's Athenian Empire, 2*s*. 6*d*.
——— Greeks & Persians, 2*s*. 6*d*.
Curteis's Macedonian Empire, 2*s*. 6*d*.
Ihne's Rome to its Capture by the Gauls, 2*s*. 6*d*.
Merivale's Roman Triumvirates, 2*s*. 6*d*.
Sankey's Spartan & Theban Supremacies, 2*s*. 6*d*.
Smith's Rome and Carthage, the Punic Wars, 2*s*. 6*d*.

Creighton's Shilling History of England, introductory to 'Epochs of English History.' Fcp. 1*s*.

Epochs of English History. Edited by the Rev. MANDELL CREIGHTON, M.A. Fcp. 8vo. 5*s*.

Browning's Modern England, 1820-1874, 9*d*.
Cordery's Struggle against Absolute Monarchy, 1603-1688, 9*d*.
Creighton's (Mrs.) England a Continental Power, 1066-1216, 9*d*.
Creighton's (Rev. M.) Tudors and the Reformation, 1485-1603, 9*d*.
Rowley's Rise of the People, 1215-1485, price 9*d*.
Rowley's Settlement of the Constitution, 1688-1778, 9*d*.
Tancock's England during the American & European Wars, 1778-1820, 9*d*.
York-Powell's Early England to the Conquest, 1*s*.

The Student's Manual of Ancient History; the Political History, Geography and Social State of the Principal Nations of Antiquity. By W. COOKE TAYLOR, LL.D. Cr. 8vo. 7*s.* 6*d.*

The Student's Manual of Modern History; the Rise and Progress of the Principal European Nations. By W. COOKE TAYLOR, LL.D. Crown 8vo. 7*s.* 6*d.*

BIOGRAPHICAL WORKS.

Reminiscences. By THOMAS CARLYLE. Edited by JAMES ANTHONY FROUDE, M.A. formerly Fellow of Exeter College, Oxford. 2 vols. crown 8vo. 18*s.*

Autobiography. By JOHN STUART MILL. 8vo. 7*s.* 6*d.*

Felix Mendelssohn's Letters, translated by Lady WALLACE. 2 vols. crown 8vo. 5*s.* each.

Memoirs of the Life of Anna Jameson, Author of 'Sacred and Legendary Art' &c. By her Niece, G. MACPHERSON. 8vo. Portrait, 12*s.* 6*d.*

The Life and Letters of Lord Macaulay. By his Nephew, G. OTTO TREVELYAN, M.P.

CABINET EDITION, 2 vols. crown 8vo. 12*s.*
LIBRARY EDITION, 2 vols. 8vo. 36*s.*

William Law, Nonjuror and Mystic, Author of 'A Serious Call to a Devout and Holy Life' &c. a Sketch of his Life, Character, and Opinions. By J. H. OVERTON, M.A. Vicar of Legbourne. 8vo. 15*s.*

The Missionary Secretariat of Henry Venn, B.D. Prebendary of St. Paul's, and Hon. Sec. of the Church Missionary Society. By the Rev. W. KNIGHT, M.A. With Additions by Mr. Venn's Two Sons, and a Portrait. 8vo. 18*s.*

A Dictionary of General Biography. By W. L. R. CATES. Third Edition, revised throughout and completed to the Present Time; with new matter equal to One Hundred pages, comprising nearly Four Hundred Memoirs and Notices of Persons recently deceased. 8vo. 28*s.*

Apologia pro Vitâ Suâ; Being a History of his Religious Opinions by JOHN HENRY NEWMAN, D.D. Crown 8vo. 6*s.*

Biographical Studies. By the late WALTER BAGEHOT, M.A. Fellow of University College, London. Uniform with 'Literary Studies' and 'Economic Studies' by the same Author. 8vo. 12*s.*

Leaders of Public Opinion in Ireland; Swift, Flood, Grattan, O'Connell. By W. E. H. LECKY, M.A. Crown 8vo. 7*s.* 6*d.*

Essays in Ecclesiastical Biography. By the Right Hon. Sir J. STEPHEN, LL.D. Crown 8vo. 7*s.* 6*d.*

Cæsar; a Sketch. By JAMES ANTHONY FROUDE, M.A. formerly Fellow of Exeter College, Oxford. With Portrait and Map. 8vo. 16*s.*

Life of the Duke of Wellington. By the Rev. G. R. GLEIG, M.A. Crown 8vo. Portrait, 6*s.*

Memoirs of Sir Henry Havelock, K.C.B. By JOHN CLARK MARSHMAN. Crown 8vo. 3*s.* 6*d.*

Vicissitudes of Families. By Sir BERNARD BURKE, C.B. Two vols. crown 8vo. 21*s.*

Maunder's Treasury of Biography, reconstructed and in great part re-written, with above 1,600 additional Memoirs by W. L. R. CATES. Fcp. 8vo. 6*s.*

MENTAL and POLITICAL PHILOSOPHY.

Comte's System of Positive Polity, or Treatise upon Sociology. By various Translators. 4 vols. 8vo. £4.

De Tocqueville's Democracy in America, translated by H. REEVE. 2 vols. crown 8vo. 16*s*.

Analysis of the Phenomena of the Human Mind. By JAMES MILL. With Notes, Illustrative and Critical. 2 vols. 8vo. 28*s*.

On Representative Government. By JOHN STUART MILL. Crown 8vo. 2*s*.

On Liberty. By JOHN STUART MILL. Post 8vo. 7*s*. 6*d*. crown 8vo. 1*s*. 4*d*.

Principles of Political Economy. By JOHN STUART MILL. 2 vols. 8vo. 30*s*. or 1 vol. crown 8vo. 5*s*.

Essays on some Unsettled Questions of Political Economy. By JOHN STUART MILL. 8vo. 6*s*. 6*d*.

Utilitarianism. By JOHN STUART MILL. 8vo. 5*s*.

The Subjection of Women. By JOHN STUART MILL. Fourth Edition. Crown 8vo. 6*s*.

Examination of Sir William Hamilton's Philosophy. By JOHN STUART MILL. 8vo. 16*s*.

A System of Logic, Ratiocinative and Inductive. By JOHN STUART MILL. 2 vols. 8vo. 25*s*.

Dissertations and Discussions. By JOHN STUART MILL. 4 vols. 8vo. £2. 7*s*.

The A B C of Philosophy; a Text-Book for Students. By the Rev. T. GRIFFITH, M.A. Prebendary of St. Paul's. Crown 8vo. 5*s*.

A Systematic View of the Science of Jurisprudence. By SHEL-

Path and Goal; a Discussion on the Elements of Civilisation and the Conditions of Happiness. By M. M. KALISCH, Ph.D. M.A. 8vo. price 12*s*. 6*d*.

The Law of Nations considered as Independent Political Communities. By Sir TRAVERS TWISS, D.C.L. 2 vols. 8vo. £1. 13*s*.

A Primer of the English Constitution and Government. By S. AMOS, M.A. Crown 8vo. 6*s*.

Fifty Years of the English Constitution, 1830-1880. By SHELDON AMOS, M.A. Crown 8vo. 10*s*. 6*d*.

Principles of Economical Philosophy. By H. D. MACLEOD, M.A. Second Edition, in 2 vols. VOL. I. 8vo. 15*s*. VOL. II. PART I. 12*s*.

Lord Bacon's Works, collected & edited by R. L. ELLIS, M.A. J. SPEDDING, M.A. and D. D. HEATH. 7 vols. 8vo. £3. 13*s*. 6*d*.

Letters and Life of Francis Bacon, including all his Occasional Works. Collected and edited, with a Commentary, by J. SPEDDING. 7 vols. 8vo. £4. 4*s*.

The Institutes of Justinian; with English Introduction, Translation, and Notes. By T. C. SANDARS, M.A. 8vo. 18*s*.

The Nicomachean Ethics of Aristotle, translated into English by R. WILLIAMS, B.A. Crown 8vo. price 7*s*. 6*d*.

Aristotle's Politics, Books I. III. IV. (VII.) Greek Text, with an English Translation by W. E. BOLLAND, M.A. and Short Essays by A. LANG, M.A. Crown 8vo. 7*s*. 6*d*.

The Politics of Aristotle; Greek Text, with English Notes. By

DICTIONARIES and OTHER BOOKS of REFERENCE.

One-Volume Dictionary of the English Language. By R. G. LATHAM, M.A. M.D. Medium 8vo. 14*s.*

Larger Dictionary of the English Language. By R. G. LATHAM, M.A. M.D. Founded on Johnson's English Dictionary as edited by the Rev. H. J. TODD. 4 vols. 4to. £7.

Roget's Thesaurus of English Words and Phrases, classified and arranged so as to facilitate the expression of Ideas, and assist in Literary Composition. Revised and enlarged by the Author's Son, J. L. ROGET. Crown 8vo. 10*s.* 6*d.*

English Synonymes. By E. J. WHATELY. Edited by R. WHATELY, D.D. Fcp. 8vo. 3*s.*

Handbook of the English Language. By R. G. LATHAM, M.A. M.D. Crown 8vo. 6*s.*

Contanseau's Practical Dictionary of the French and English Languages. Post 8vo. price 7*s.* 6*d.*

Contanseau's Pocket Dictionary, French and English, abridged from the Practical Dictionary by the Author. Square 18mo. 3*s.* 6*d.*

A Practical Dictionary of the German and English Languages. By Rev. W. L. BLACKLEY, M.A. & Dr. C. M. FRIEDLÄNDER. Post 8vo. 7*s.* 6*d.*

A New Pocket Dictionary of the German and English Languages. By F. W. LONGMAN, Ball. Coll. Oxford. Square 18mo. 5*s.*

Becker's Gallus; Roman Scenes of the Time of Augustus. Translated by the Rev. F. METCALFE, M.A. Post 8vo. 7*s.* 6*d.*

Becker's Charicles; Illustrations of the Private Life of the Ancient Greeks. Translated by the Rev. F. METCALFE, M.A. Post 8vo. 7*s.* 6*d.*

A Dictionary of Roman and Greek Antiquities. With 2,000 Woodcuts illustrative of the Arts and Life of the Greeks and Romans. By A. RICH, B.A. Crown 8vo. 7*s.* 6*d.*

A Greek-English Lexicon. By H. G. LIDDELL, D.D. Dean of Christchurch, and R. SCOTT, D.D. Dean of Rochester. Crown 4to. 36*s.*

Liddell & Scott's Lexicon, Greek and English, abridged for Schools. Square 12mo. 7*s.* 6*d.*

An English-Greek Lexicon, containing all the Greek Words used by Writers of good authority. By C. D. YONGE, M.A. 4to. 21*s.* School Abridgment, square 12mo. 8*s.* 6*d.*

A Latin-English Dictionary. By JOHN T. WHITE, D.D. Oxon. and J. E. RIDDLE, M.A. Oxon. Sixth Edition, revised. Quarto 21*s.*

White's College Latin-English Dictionary, for the use of University Students. Royal 8vo. 12*s.*

M'Culloch's Dictionary of Commerce and Commercial Navigation. Re-edited, with a Supplement shewing the Progress of British Commercial Legislation to the Year 1880, by HUGH G. REID. With 11 Maps and 30 Charts. 8vo. 63*s.*

Keith Johnston's General Dictionary of Geography, Descriptive, Physical, Statistical, and Historical; a complete Gazetteer of the World. Medium 8vo. 42*s.*

The Public Schools Atlas of Ancient Geography, in 28 entirely new Coloured Maps. Edited by the Rev. G. BUTLER, M.A. Imperial 8vo. or imperial 4to. 7*s.* 6*d.*

The Public Schools Atlas of Modern Geography, in 31 entirely new Coloured Maps. Edited by the Rev. G. BUTLER, M.A. Uniform, 5*s.*

ASTRONOMY and METEOROLOGY.

Outlines of Astronomy. By Sir J. F. W. HERSCHEL, Bart. M.A. Latest Edition, with Plates and Diagrams. Square crown 8vo. 12*s.*

Essays on Astronomy. A Series of Papers on Planets and Meteors, the Sun and Sun-surrounding Space, Stars and Star Cloudlets. By R. A. PROCTOR, B.A. With 10 Plates and 24 Woodcuts. 8vo. 12*s.*

The Moon; her Motions, Aspects, Scenery, and Physical Condition. By R. A. PROCTOR, B.A. With Plates, Charts, Woodcuts, and Lunar Photographs. Crown 8vo. 10*s.* 6*d.*

The Sun; Ruler, Light, Fire, and Life of the Planetary System. By R. A. PROCTOR, B.A. With Plates & Woodcuts. Crown 8vo. 14*s.*

The Orbs Around Us; a Series of Essays on the Moon & Planets, Meteors & Comets, the Sun & Coloured Pairs of Suns. By R. A. PROCTOR, B.A. With Chart and Diagrams. Crown 8vo. 7*s.* 6*d.*

The Universe of Stars; Presenting Researches into and New Views respecting the Constitution of the Heavens. By R. A. PROCTOR, B.A. Second Edition, with 22 Charts (4 Coloured) and 22 Diagrams. 8vo. price 10*s.* 6*d.*

Other Worlds than Ours; The Plurality of Worlds Studied under the Light of Recent Scientific Researches. By R. A. PROCTOR, B.A. With 14 Illustrations. Cr. 8vo. 10*s.* 6*d.*

Saturn and its System. By R. A. PROCTOR, B.A. 8vo. with 14 Plates, 14*s.*

The Moon, and the Condition and Configurations of its Surface. By E. NEISON, F.R.A.S. With 26 Maps & 5 Plates. Medium 8vo. 31*s.* 6*d.*

Celestial Objects for Common Telescopes. By the Rev. T. W. WEBB, M.A. Fourth Edition, revised and adapted to the Present State of Sidereal Science; Map, Plate, Woodcuts. Crown 8vo. 9*s.*

A New Star Atlas, for the Library, the School, and the Observatory, in 12 Circular Maps (with 2 Index Plates). By R. A. PROCTOR, B.A. Crown 8vo. 5*s.*

Larger Star Atlas, for the Library, in Twelve Circular Maps, with Introduction and 2 Index Plates. By R. A. PROCTOR, B.A. Folio, 15*s.* or Maps only, 12*s.* 6*d.*

Air and Rain; the Beginnings of a Chemical Climatology. By R. A. SMITH, F.R.S. 8vo. 24*s.*

NATURAL HISTORY and PHYSICAL SCIENCE.

Elementary Treatise on Physics, Experimental and Applied, for the use of Colleges and Schools. Translated and edited from GANOT'S *Traité Élémentaire de Physique* (with the Author's sanction) by EDMUND ATKINSON, Ph.D. F.C.S. Professor of Experimental Science, Staff College. Ninth Edition, revised and enlarged; with 4 Coloured Plates and 844 Woodcuts. Large crown 8vo. 15*s.*

Natural Philosophy for General Readers and Young Persons; a Course of Physics divested of Mathematical Formulæ and expressed in the language of daily life. Translated and edited from GANOT'S *Cours de Physique* (with the Author's sanction) by EDMUND ATKINSON, Ph.D. F.C.S. Professor of Experimental Science, Staff College. Fourth Edition, revised; with 2 Plates and 471 Woodcuts. Crown 8vo. 7*s.* 6*d.*

Professor Helmholtz on the Sensations of Tone, as a Physiological Basis for the Theory of Music. Translated by A. J. ELLIS, F.R.S. 8vo. 36*s*.

Professor Helmholtz' Popular Lectures on Scientific Subjects. Translated and edited by EDMUND ATKINSON, Ph.D. F.C.S. Professor of Chemistry &c. Staff College, Sandhurst. FIRST SERIES, with a Preface by Professor TYNDALL, F.R.S. Second Edition, with 51 Woodcuts. Crown 8vo. 7*s*. 6*d*.

Professor Helmholtz' Popular Lectures on Scientific Subjects, SECOND SERIES, on the Origin and Signification of Geometrical Axioms, the relation of Form, Shade, Colour and Harmony of Colour to Painting, the Origin of the Planetary System, &c. Translated by EDMUND ATKINSON, Ph.D. F.C.S. Professor of Chemistry &c. Staff College, Sandhurst. With 17 Woodcuts. Crown 8vo. 7*s*. 6*d*.

Arnott's Elements of Physics or Natural Philosophy. Seventh Edition, edited by A. BAIN, LL.D. and A. S. TAYLOR, M.D. F.R.S. Crown 8vo. Woodcuts, 12*s*. 6*d*.

The Correlation of Physical Forces. By the Hon. Sir W. R. GROVE, F.R.S. &c. Sixth Edition, revised and augmented. 8vo. 15*s*.

A Treatise on Magnetism, General and Terrestrial. By H. LLOYD, D.D. D.C.L. &c. late Provost of Trinity College, Dublin. 8vo. 10*s*. 6*d*.

Elementary Treatise on the Wave-Theory of Light. By H. LLOYD, D.D. D.C.L. &c. late Provost of Trinity College, Dublin. 8vo. price 10*s*. 6*d*.

The Mathematical and other Tracts of the late James M'Cullagh, F.T.C.D. Professor of Natural Philosophy in the University of Dublin. Now first collected, and Edited by the Rev. J. H. JELLETT, B.D. and the Rev. S. HAUGHTON, M.D. F

A Text-Book of Systematic Mineralogy. By H. BAUERMA F.G.S. Associate of the Royal School Mines. With numerous Woodcu Small 8vo. 6*s*.

A Text-Book of Descriptive Mineralogy. In the same Ser. of *Text-Books of Science*, and by t same Author. Small 8vo. Woodcu [*In preparation.*

Fragments of Scienc By JOHN TYNDALL, F.R.S. Sixt Edition, revised and augmented. 2 vol crown 8vo. 16*s*.

Heat a Mode of Motion By JOHN TYNDALL, F.R.S Sixth Edition (Thirteenth Thousand thoroughly revised and enlarge Crown 8vo. 12*s*.

Sound. By JOHN TYNDALL F.R.S. Fourth Edition, includin Recent Researches. [*Nearly ready.*

Contributions to Molecular Physics in the domain o Radiant Heat. By JOHN TYNDALL F.R.S. Plates and Woodcuts. 8vo. 16*s*

Professor Tyndall's Researches on Diamagnetism and Magne-Crystallic Action; including Diamagnetic Polarity. New Edition in preparation.

Professor Tyndall's Lectures on Light, delivered in America in 1872 and 1873. With Portrait, Plate & Diagrams. Crown 8vo. 7*s*. 6*d*.

Professor Tyndall's Lessons in Electricity at the Royal Institution, 1875–6. With 58 Woodcuts. Crown 8vo. 2*s*. 6*d*.

Professor Tyndall's Notes of a Course of Seven Lectures on Electrical Phenomena and Theories, delivered at the Royal Institution. Crown 8vo. 1*s*. sewed, 1*s*. 6*d*. cloth.

Professor Tyndall's Notes of a Course of Nine Lectures on Light, delivered at the Royal Institu-

Text-Books of Science,

Mechanical and Physical, adapted for the use of Artisans and of Students in Public and Science Schools. Small 8vo. with Woodcuts, &c.

Abney's Photography, 3*s.* 6*d.*

Anderson's (Sir John) Strength of Materials, 3*s.* 6*d.*

Armstrong's Organic Chemistry, 3*s.* 6*d.*

Ball's Elements of Astronomy, 6*s.*

Barry's Railway Appliances, 3*s.* 6*d.*

Bauerman's Systematic Mineralogy, 6*s.*

Bloxam's Metals, 3*s.* 6*d.*

Goodeve's Mechanics, 3*s.* 6*d.*

Gore's Electro-Metallurgy, 6*s.*

Griffin's Algebra & Trigonometry, 3/6.

Jenkin's Electricity & Magnetism, 3/6.

Maxwell's Theory of Heat, 3*s.* 6*d.*

Merrifield's Technical Arithmetic, 3*s.* 6*d.*

Miller's Inorganic Chemistry, 3*s.* 6*d.*

Preece & Sivewright's Telegraphy, 3/6.

Rutley's Study of Rocks, 4*s.* 6*d.*

Shelley's Workshop Appliances, 3*s.* 6*d.*

Thomé's Structural and Physiological Botany, 6*s.*

Thorpe's Quantitative Analysis, 4*s.* 6*d.*

Thorpe & Muir's Qualitative Analysis, price 3*s.* 6*d.*

Tilden's Chemical Philosophy, 3*s.* 6*d.*

Unwin's Machine Design, 3*s.* 6*d.*

Watson's Plane & Solid Geometry, 3/6.

Six Lectures on Physical Geography,

delivered in 1876, with some Additions. By the Rev. SAMUEL HAUGHTON, F.R.S. M.D. D.C.L. With 23 Diagrams. 8vo. 15*s.*

An Introduction to the Systematic Zoology and Morphology of Vertebrate Animals.

By A. MACALISTER, M.D. With 28 Diagrams. 8vo. 10*s.* 6*d.*

The Comparative Anatomy and Physiology of the Vertebrate Animals.

By RICHARD OWEN, F.R.S. With 1,472 Woodcuts. 3 vols. 8vo. £3. 13*s.* 6*d.*

Homes without Hands;

a Description of the Habitations of Animals, classed according to their Principle of Construction. By the Rev. J. G. WOOD, M.A. With about 140 Vignettes on Wood. 8vo. 14*s.*

Wood's Strange Dwellings;

a Description of the Habitations of Animals, abridged from 'Homes without Hands.' With Frontispiece and 60 Woodcuts. Crown 8vo. 7*s.* 6*d.*

Wood's Insects at Home;

a Popular Account of British Insects, their Structure, Habits, and Transformations. 8vo. Woodcuts, 14*s.*

Wood's Insects Abroad;

a Popular Account of Foreign Insects, their Structure, Habits, and Transformations. 8vo. Woodcuts, 14*s.*

Wood's Out of Doors;

a Selection of Original Articles on Practical Natural History. With 6 Illustrations. Crown 8vo. 7*s.* 6*d.*

Wood's Bible Animals;

a description of every Living Creature mentioned in the Scriptures, from the Ape to the Coral. With 112 Vignettes. 8vo. 14*s.*

The Sea and its Living Wonders.

By Dr. G. HARTWIG. 8vo. with many Illustrations, 10*s.* 6*d.*

Hartwig's Tropical World.

With about 200 Illustrations. 8vo. 10*s.* 6*d.*

Hartwig's Polar World;

a Description of Man and Nature in the Arctic and Antarctic Regions of the Globe. Maps, Plates & Woodcuts. 8vo. 10*s.* 6*d.*

Hartwig's Subterranean World.

With Maps and Woodcuts. 8vo. 10*s.* 6*d.*

Hartwig's Aerial World;

a Popular Account of the Phenomena and Life of the Atmosphere. Map, Plates, Woodcuts. 8vo. 10*s.* 6*d.*

A Familiar History of Birds.

By E. STANLEY, D.D. New Edition, revised and enlarged, with 160 Woodcuts. Crown 8vo. 6*s.*

Rural Bird Life; Essays on Ornithology, with Instructions for Preserving Objects relating to that Science. By CHARLES DIXON. With Coloured Frontispiece and 44 Woodcuts by G. Pearson. Crown 8vo. 7*s.* 6*d.*

The Note-book of an Amateur Geologist. By JOHN EDWARD LEE, F.G.S. F.S.A. &c. With numerous Woodcuts and 200 Lithographic Plates of Sketches and Sections. 8vo. 21*s.*

Rocks Classified and Described. By BERNHARD VON COTTA. An English Translation, by P. H. LAWRENCE, with English, German, and French Synonymes. Post 8vo. 14*s.*

The Geology of England and Wales; a Concise Account of the Lithological Characters, Leading Fossils, and Economic Products of the Rocks. By H. B. WOODWARD, F.G.S. Crown 8vo. Map & Woodcuts, 14*s.*

Keller's Lake Dwellings of Switzerland, and other Parts of Europe. Translated by JOHN E. LEE, F.S.A. F.G.S. With 206 Illustrations. 2 vols. royal 8vo. 42*s.*

Heer's Primæval World of Switzerland. Edited by JAMES HEYWOOD, M.A. F.R.S. With Map, 19 Plates, & 372 Woodcuts. 2 vols. 8vo. 16*s.*

The Puzzle of Life and How it Has Been Put Together; a Short History of Praehistoric Vegetable and Animal Life on the Earth. By A. NICOLS, F.R.G.S. With 12 Illustrations. Crown 8vo. 3*s.* 6*d.*

The Origin of Civilisation, and the Primitive Condition of Man; Mental and Social Condition of Savages. By Sir J. LUBBOCK, Bart. M.P. F.R.S. 8vo. Woodcuts, 18*s.*

Light Science for Leisu Hours; Familiar Essays on Scient Subjects, Natural Phenomena, By R. A. PROCTOR, B.A. 2 vc crown 8vo. 7*s.* 6*d.* each.

A Dictionary of Scienc Literature, and Art. Re-edited the Rev. Sir G. W. COX, Bart. M. 3 vols. medium 8vo. 63*s.*

Hullah's Course of Le tures on the History of Mode Music. 8vo. 8*s.* 6*d.*

Hullah's Second Cours of Lectures on the Transition Peri of Musical History. 8vo. 10*s.* 6*d.*

Loudon's Encyclopædi of Plants; the Specific Charact Description, Culture, History, &c. all Plants found in Great Britain. Wi 12,000 Woodcuts. 8vo. 42*s.*

De Caisne & Le Maout' Descriptive and Analytical Botan Translated by Mrs. HOOKER; edit and arranged by J. D. HOOKER, M. With 5,500 Woodcuts. Imperial 8v price 31*s.* 6*d.*

Rivers's Orchard-House or, the Cultivation of Fruit Trees und Glass. Sixteenth Edition. Crown 8v with 25 Woodcuts, 5*s.*

The Rose Amateur' Guide. By THOMAS RIVERS. Late Edition. Fcp. 8vo. 4*s.* 6*d.*

Town and Window Gar dening, including the Structure, Habi and Uses of Plants. By Mrs. BUCKTO With 127 Woodcuts. Crown 8vo. 2

Loudon's Encyclopædi of Gardening; the Theory and Pra tice of Horticulture, Floriculture, Arbor culture & Landscape Gardening. Wi 1,000 Woodcuts. 8vo. 21*s.*

CHEMISTRY and PHYSIOLOGY.

Experimental Chemistry for Junior Students. By J. E. REYNOLDS, M.D. F.R.S. Professor of Chemistry, University of Dublin. Part I. Introductory. Fcp. 8vo. 1*s.* 6*d.*

Practical Chemistry; th Principles of Qualitative Analysi By W. A. TILDEN, D.Sc. Lond. F.C. Professor of Chemistry in Mason's Co lege, Birmingham. Fcp. 8vo. 1*s.* 6*d*

Miller's Elements of Chemistry, Theoretical and Practical. Re-edited, with Additions, by H. MACLEOD, F.C.S. 3 vols. 8vo.

PART I. CHEMICAL PHYSICS. 16*s.*

PART II. INORGANIC CHEMISTRY, 24*s.*

PART III. ORGANIC CHEMISTRY, in Two Sections. SECTION I. 31*s.* 6*d.*

Annals of Chemical Medicine; including the Application of Chemistry to Physiology, Pathology, Therapeutics, Pharmacy, Toxicology, and Hygiene. Edited by J. L. W. THUDICHUM, M.D. VOL. I. 8vo. 14*s.*

Health in the House: Twenty-five Lectures on Elementary Physiology in its Application to the Daily Wants of Man and Animals. By Mrs. BUCKTON. Crown 8vo. Woodcuts, 2*s.*

A Dictionary of Chemistry and the Allied Branches of other Sciences. Edited by HENRY WATTS, F.C.S. 8 vols. medium 8vo. £12. 12*s.* 6*d.*

Third **Supplement,** completing the Record of Chemical Discovery to the year 1877. PART II. completion, is now ready, price 50*s.*

Select Methods in Chemical Analysis, chiefly Inorganic. By W. CROOKES, F.R.S. With 22 Woodcuts. Crown 8vo. 12*s.* 6*d.*

The History, Products, and Processes of the Alkali Trade, including the most recent Improvements. By C. T. KINGZETT, F.C.S. With 32 Woodcuts. 8vo. 12s.

Animal Chemistry, or the Relations of Chemistry to Physiology and Pathology: a Manual for Medical Men and Scientific Chemists. By C. T. KINGZETT, F.C.S. 8vo. 18*s.*

The FINE ARTS and ILLUSTRATED EDITIONS.

Notes on Foreign Picture Galleries. By C. L. EASTLAKE. F.R.I.B.A. Keeper of the National Gallery, London. Crown 8vo. fully Illustrated. [*In preparation.*

Vol. I. The Brera Gallery, Milan.
,, II. The Louvre, Paris.
,, III. The Pinacothek, Munich.

In Fairyland; Pictures from the Elf-World. By RICHARD DOYLE. With 16 coloured Plates, containing 36 Designs. Folio, 15*s.*

Lord Macaulay's Lays of Ancient Rome, with Ivry and the Armada. With 41 Wood Engravings by G. Pearson from Original Drawings by J. R. Weguelin. Crown 8vo. 6*s.*

Lord Macaulay's Lays of Ancient Rome. With Ninety Illustrations engraved on Wood from Drawings by G. Scharf. Fcp. 4to. 21*s.* or imperial 16mo. 10*s.* 6*d.*

The Three Cathedrals dedicated to St. Paul in London.

Moore's Lalla Rookh. TENNIEL'S Edition, with 68 Woodcut Illustrations. Crown 8vo. 10*s.* 6*d.*

Moore's Irish Melodies, MACLISE'S Edition, with 161 Steel Plates. Super-royal 8vo. 21*s.*

Lectures on Harmony, delivered at the Royal Institution. By G. A. MACFARREN. 8vo. 12*s.*

Sacred and Legendary Art. By Mrs. JAMESON. 6 vols. square crown 8vo. £5. 15*s.* 6*d.*

Jameson's Legends of the Saints and Martyrs. With 19 Etchings and 187 Woodcuts. 2 vols. 31*s.* 6*d.*

Jameson's Legends of the Monastic Orders. With 11 Etchings and 88 Woodcuts. 1 vol. 21*s.*

Jameson's Legends of the Madonna. With 27 Etchings and 165 Woodcuts. 1 vol. 21*s.*

Jameson's History of the Saviour, His Types and Precursors. Completed by Lady EASTLAKE. With

The Elements of Mechanism. By T. M. GOODEYE, M.A. Barrister-at-Law. New Edition, re-written and enlarged, with 342 Woodcuts. Crown 8vo. 6*s.*

The Amateur Mechanics' Practical Handbook; describing the different Tools required in the Workshop. By A. H. G. HOBSON. With 33 Woodcuts. Crown 8vo. 2*s.* 6*d.*

The Engineer's Valuing Assistant. By H. D. HOSKOLD, Civil and Mining Engineer. 8vo. price 31*s.* 6*d.*

Industrial Chemistry; a Manual for Manufacturers and for Colleges or Technical Schools; a Translation (by Dr. T. H. BARRY) of Stohmann and Engler's German Edition of PAYEN'S 'Précis de Chimie Industrielle;' with Chapters on the Chemistry of the Metals, &c. by B. H. PAUL, Ph.D. With 698 Woodcuts. Medium 8vo. 42*s.*

Gwilt's Encyclopædia of Architecture, with above 1,600 Woodcuts. Revised and extended by W. PAPWORTH. 8vo. 52*s.* 6*d.*

Lathes and Turning, Simple, Mechanical, and Ornamental. By W. H. NORTHCOTT. Second Edition, with 338 Illustrations. 8vo. 18*s.*

The Theory of Strains in Girders and similar Structures, with Observations on the application of Theory to Practice, and Tables of the Strength and other Properties of Materials. By B. B. STONEY, M.A. M. Inst. C.E. Royal 8vo. with 5 Plates and 123 Woodcuts, 36*s.*

Recent Naval Administration; Shipbuilding for the Purposes of War. By T. BRASSEY, M.P. 6 vols. 8vo. with Illustrations by the Chevalier E. de Martino. [*In the press.*

A Treatise on Mills and Millwork. By the late Sir W. FAIRBAIRN, Bart. C.E. Fourth Edition, with 18 Plates and 333 Woodcuts. 1 vol. 8vo. 25*s.*

Useful Information f Engineers. By the late Sir FAIRBAIRN, Bart. C.E. With ma Plates and Woodcuts. 3 vols. cro 8vo. 31*s.* 6*d.*

The Application of Ca and Wrought Iron to Build Purposes. By the late Sir W. FA BAIRN, Bart. C.E. With 6 Plates a 118 Woodcuts. 8vo. 16*s.*

Hints on Househol Taste in Furniture, Upholste and other Details. By C. L. EAS LAKE. Fourth Edition, with 100 Ill trations. Square crown 8vo. 14*s.*

Handbook of Practic Telegraphy. By R. S. CULLE Memb. Inst. C.E. Seventh Editic Plates & Woodcuts. 8vo. 16*s.*

A Treatise on the Stea Engine, in its various applications Mines, Mills, Steam Navigation, Ra ways and Agriculture. By J. BOURN C.E. With Portrait, 37 Plates, a 546 Woodcuts. 4to. 42*s.*

Catechism of the Stea Engine, in its various Applicatio By JOHN BOURNE, C.E. Fcp. 8 Woodcuts, 6*s.*

Handbook of the Stea Engine, a Key to the Author's Ca chism of the Steam Engine. By BOURNE, C.E. Fcp. 8vo. Woodcuts,

Recent Improvements i the Steam Engine. By J. BOURN C.E. Fcp. 8vo. Woodcuts, 6*s.*

Examples of Steam an Gas Engines of the most recent A proved Types as employed in Min Factories, Steam Navigation, Railw and Agriculture, practically describ By JOHN BOURNE, C.E. With Plates and 356 Woodcuts. 4to. 70*s*

Ure's Dictionary of Art Manufactures, and Mines. Seve Edition, re-written and enlarged by HUNT, F.R.S. assisted by numer Contributors. With 2,604 Woodc 4 vols. medium 8vo. £7. 7*s.*

Cresy's Encyclopædia of Civil Engineering, Historical, Theoretical, and Practical. With above 3,000 Woodcuts. 8vo. 25*s.*

Kerl's Practical Treatise on Metallurgy. Adapted from the last German Edition by W. CROOKES, F.R.S. &c. and E. RÖHRIG, Ph.D. 3 vols. 8vo. with 625 Woodcuts. £4. 19*s.*

Ville on Artificial Manures, their Chemical Selection and Scientific Application to Agriculture; a Series of Lectures given at the Experimental Farm at Vincennes. Translated and edited by W. CROOKES, F.R.S. With 31 Plates. 8vo. 21*s.*

Mitchell's Manual of Practical Assaying. Fourth Edition, revised, with the Recent Discoveries incorporated, by W. CROOKES, F.R.S. Crown 8vo. Woodcuts, 31*s.* 6*d.*

The Art of Perfumery, and the Methods of Obtaining the Odours of Plants; the Growth and general Flower Farm System of Raising Fragrant Herbs; with Instructions for the Manufacture of Perfumes for the Handkerchief, Scented Powders, Odorous Vinegars and Salts, Snuff, Dentifrices, Cosmetics, Perfumed Soap, &c. By G. W. S. PIESSE, Ph.D. F.C.S. Fourth Edition, with 96 Woodcuts. Square crown 8vo. 21*s.*

Loudon's Encyclopædia of Gardening; the Theory and Practice of Horticulture, Floriculture, Arboriculture & Landscape Gardening. With 1,000 Woodcuts. 8vo. 21*s.*

Loudon's Encyclopædia of Agriculture; the Laying-out, Improvement, and Management of Landed Property; the Cultivation and Economy of the Productions of Agriculture. With 1,100 Woodcuts. 8vo. 21*s.*

RELIGIOUS and MORAL WORKS.

A Handbook to the Bible, or, Guide to the Study of the Holy Scriptures derived from Ancient Monuments and Modern Exploration. By F. R. CONDER, and Lieut. C. R. CONDER, R.E. Second Edit.; Maps, Plates of Coins, &c. Post 8vo. 7*s.* 6*d.*

A History of the Church of England; Pre-Reformation Period. By the Rev. T. P. BOULTBEE, LL.D. 8vo. 15*s.*

Sketch of the History of the Church of England to the Revolution of 1688. By T. V. SHORT, D.D. Crown 8vo. 7*s.* 6*d.*

The English Church in the Eighteenth Century. By CHARLES J. ABBEY, late Fellow of University College, Oxford; and JOHN H. OVERTON, late Scholar of Lincoln College, Oxford. 2 vols. 8vo. 36*s.*

An Exposition of the 39 Articles, Historical and Doctrinal. By

A Commentary on the 39 Articles, forming an Introduction to the Theology of the Church of England. By the Rev. T. P. BOULTBEE, LL.D. New Edition. Crown 8vo. 6*s.*

Sermons preached mostly in the Chapel of Rugby School by the late T. ARNOLD, D.D. Collective Edition, revised by the Author's Daughter, Mrs. W. E. FORSTER. 6 vols. crown 8vo. 30*s.* or separately, 5*s.* each.

Historical Lectures on the Life of Our Lord Jesus Christ. By C. J. ELLICOTT, D.D. 8vo. 12*s.*

The Eclipse of Faith; or a Visit to a Religious Sceptic. By HENRY ROGERS. Fcp. 8vo. 5*s.*

Defence of the Eclipse of Faith. By H. ROGERS. Fcp. 8vo. 3*s.* 6*d.*

Nature, the Utility of

A Critical and Grammatical Commentary on St. Paul's Epistles.
By C. J. ELLICOTT, D.D. 8vo. Galatians, 8*s.* 6*d.* Ephesians, 8*s.* 6*d.* Pastoral Epistles, 10*s.* 6*d.* Philippians, Colossians, & Philemon, 10*s.* 6*d.* Thessalonians, 7*s.* 6*d.*

Conybeare & Howson's Life and Epistles of St. Paul.
Three Editions, copiously illustrated.

Library Edition, with all the Original Illustrations, Maps, Landscapes on Steel, Woodcuts, &c. 2 vols. 4to. 42*s.*

Intermediate Edition, with a Selection of Maps, Plates, and Woodcuts. 2 vols. square crown 8vo. 21*s.*

Student's Edition, revised and condensed, with 46 Illustrations and Maps. 1 vol. crown 8vo. 7*s.* 6*d.*

Smith's Voyage & Shipwreck of St. Paul;
with Dissertations on the Life and Writings of St. Luke, and the Ships and Navigation of the Ancients. Fourth Edition, revised by the Author's Son; with a Memoir of the Author, a Preface by the BISHOP OF CARLISLE, and all the Original Illustrations. Crown 8vo. 7*s.* 6*d.*

The Angel-Messiah of Buddhists, Essenes, and Christians.
By ERNEST DE BUNSEN. 8vo. 10*s.* 6*d.*

Bible Studies.
By M. M. KALISCH, Ph.D. PART I. *The Prophecies of Balaam.* 8vo. 10*s.* 6*d.* PART II. *The Book of Jonah.* 8vo. price 10*s.* 6*d.*

Historical and Critical Commentary on the Old Testament;
with a New Translation. By M. M. KALISCH, Ph.D. Vol. I. Genesis, 8vo. 18*s.* or adapted for the General Reader, 12*s.* Vol. II. Exodus, 15*s.* or adapted for the General Reader, 12*s.* Vol. III. Leviticus, Part I. 15*s.* or adapted for the General Reader, 8*s.* Vol. IV. Leviticus, Part II. 15*s.* or adapted for the General Reader, 8*s.*

The Four Gospels in Greek,
with Greek-English Lexicon.

Ewald's History of Israe
Translated from the German by J. CARPENTER, M.A. with Preface by MARTINEAU, M.A. 5 vols. 8vo. 63.

Ewald's Antiquities Israel.
Translated from the Germ by H. S. SOLLY, M.A. 8vo. 12*s.* 6

The Types of Genesi
briefly considered as revealing t Development of Human Nature. A. JUKES. Crown 8vo. 7*s.* 6*d.*

The Second Death an the Restitution of all Things;
wi some Preliminary Remarks on t Nature and Inspiration of Holy Scri ture. By A. JUKES. Crown 8vo. 3*s.* 6

The Gospel for the Nineteenth Century.
Fourth Editio 8vo. price 10*s.* 6*d.*

Supernatural Religion
an Inquiry into the Reality of I vine Revelation. Complete Editio thoroughly revised. 3 vols. 8vo. 36*s*

Lectures on the Origi and Growth of Religion,
as illu trated by the Religions of India being the Hibbert Lectures, deliver at the Chapter House, Westminst Abbey, in 1878, by F. MAX MÜLLE K.M. 8vo. 10*s.* 6*d.*

Introduction to the Science of Religion,
Four Lectures d livered at the Royal Institution; wi Essays on False Analogies and t Philosophy of Mythology. By F. MA MÜLLER, K.M. Crown 8vo. 10*s.* 6

Passing Thoughts o Religion.
By Miss SEWELL. Fcp. 8v price 3*s.* 6*d.*

Thoughts for the Ag
By Miss SEWELL. Fcp. 8vo. 3*s.* 6*d.*

Preparation for the Hol Communion;
the Devotions chie from the works of Jeremy Taylor. Miss SEWELL. 32mo. 3*s.*

Private Devotions f Young Persons.
Compiled

Bishop Jeremy Taylor's Entire Works; with Life by Bishop Heber. Revised and corrected by the Rev. C. P. EDEN. 10 vols. £5. 5*s*.

Hymns of Praise and Prayer. Corrected and edited by Rev. JOHN MARTINEAU, LL.D. Crown 8vo. 4*s*. 6*d*. 32mo. 1*s*. 6*d*.

Spiritual Songs for the Sundays and Holidays throughout the Year. By J. S. B. MONSELL, LL.D. Fcp. 8vo. 5*s*. 18mo. 2*s*.

Christ the Consoler; a Book of Comfort for the Sick. By ELLICE HOPKINS. Second Edition. Fcp. 8vo. 2*s*. 6*d*.

Lyra Germanica; Hymns translated from the German by Miss C. WINKWORTH. Fcp. 8vo. 5*s*.

Hours of Thought on Sacred Things; Two Volumes of Sermons. By JAMES MARTINEAU, D.D. LL.D. 2 vols. crown 8vo. 7*s*. 6*d*. each.

Endeavours after the Christian Life; Discourses. By JAMES MARTINEAU, D.D. LL.D. Fifth Edition. Crown 8vo. 7*s*. 6*d*.

The Pentateuch & Book of Joshua Critically Examined. By J. W. COLENSO, D.D. Bishop of Natal. Crown 8vo. 6*s*.

Lectures on the Pentateuch and the Moabite Stone; with Appendices. By J. W. COLENSO, D.D. Bishop of Natal. 8vo. 12*s*.

TRAVELS, VOYAGES, &c.

The Flight of the 'Lapwing'; a Naval Officer's Jottings in China, Formosa, and Japan. By the Hon. H. N. SHORE, R.N. With 2 Illustrations and 2 Maps. 8vo. 15*s*.

Turkish Armenia and Eastern Asia Minor. By the Rev. H. F. TOZER, M.A. F.R.G.S. With Map and 5 Illustrations. 8vo. 16*s*.

Sunshine and Storm in the East, or Cruises to Cyprus and Constantinople. By Mrs. BRASSEY. With 2 Maps and 114 Illustrations engraved on Wood by G. Pearson, chiefly from Drawings by the Hon. A. Y. Bingham; the Cover from an Original Design by Gustave Doré. 8vo. 21*s*.

A Voyage in the 'Sunbeam,' our Home on the Ocean for Eleven Months. By Mrs. BRASSEY. Cheaper Edition, with Map and 65 Wood Engravings. Crown 8vo. 7*s*. 6*d*.

Eight Years in Ceylon. By Sir SAMUEL W. BAKER, M.A. Crown 8vo. Woodcuts, 7*s*. 6*d*.

The Rifle and the Hound in Ceylon. By Sir SAMUEL W. BAKER, M.A. Crown 8vo. Woodcuts, 7*s*. 6*d*.

Sacred Palmlands; or, the Journal of a Spring Tour in Egypt and the Holy Land. By A. G. WELD. Crown 8vo. 7*s*. 6*d*.

One Thousand Miles up the Nile; a Journey through Egypt and Nubia to the Second Cataract. By Miss AMELIA B. EDWARDS. With Facsimiles, &c. and 80 Illustrations engraved on Wood from Drawings by the Author. Imperial 8vo. 42*s*.

Wintering in the Riviera; with Notes of Travel in Italy and France, and Practical Hints to Travellers. By WILLIAM MILLER, S.S.C. Edinburgh. With 12 Illustrations. Post 8vo. 7*s*. 6*d*.

San Remo and the Western Riviera, climatically and medically considered. By A. HILL HASSALL, M.D. Map and Woodcuts. Crown 8vo. 10*s*. 6*d*.

Himalayan and Sub-Himalayan Districts of British India, their Climate, Medical Topography, and Disease Distribution; with reasons for assigning a Malarious Origin to Goître and some other Diseases. By F. N. MACNAMARA, M.D. With Map and Fever Chart. 8vo. 21*s*.

The Alpine Club Map of Switzerland, with parts of the Neighbouring Countries, on the scale of Four Miles to an Inch. Edited by R. C. NICHOLS, F.R.G.S. 4 Sheets in Portfolio, 42*s.* coloured, or 34*s.* uncoloured.

Dr. Rigby's Letters from France, &c. in 1789. Edited by his Daughter, Lady EASTLAKE. Crown 8vo. 10*s.* 6*d.*

The Alpine Guide. By JOHN BALL, M.R.I.A. Post 8vo. with Maps and other Illustrations :—

The Eastern Alps, 10*s.* 6

Central Alps, including a the Oberland District, 7*s.* 6*d.*

Western Alps, includir Mont Blanc, Monte Rosa, Zermatt, Price 6*s.* 6*d.*

On Alpine Travelling an the Geology of the Alps. Price Either of the Three Volumes or Parts the 'Alpine Guide' may be had w this Introduction prefixed, 1*s.* extra.

WORKS of FICTION.

Novels and Tales. By the Right Hon. the EARL of BEACONSFIELD, K.G. The Cabinet Edition. Eleven Volumes, crown 8vo. 6*s.* each.

Endymion, 6*s.*

Lothair, 6*s.*	**Venetia,** 6*s.*
Coningsby, 6*s.*	**Alroy, Ixion, &c.** 6*s.*
Sybil, 6*s.*	**Young Duke &c.** 6*s.*
Tancred, 6*s.*	**Vivian Grey,** 6*s.*

Henrietta Temple, 6*s.*
Contarini Fleming, &c. 6*s.*

Blues and Buffs; a Contested Election and its Results. By ARTHUR MILLS. Crown 8vo. 6*s.*

Yellow Cap, and other Fairy Stories for Children, viz. Rumpty-Dudget, Calladon, and Theeda. By JULIAN HAWTHORNE. Crown 8vo. 6*s.* cloth extra, gilt edges.

The Crookit Meg: a Scottish Story of the Year One. By JOHN SKELTON, LL.D. Advocate, Author of 'Essays in Romance and Studies from Life' (by 'SHIRLEY'). Crown 8vo. 6*s.*

Buried Alive; or, Ten Years of Penal Servitude in Siberia. By FEDOR DOSTOYEFFSKY. Translated from the German by MARIE VON THILO. Post 8vo. 10*s.* 6*d.*

'Apart from its interest as a picture of prison life, *Buried Alive* gives us several curious sketches of Russian life and character. Of course it is of the criminal side, but it seems to agree with what we learn from other sources of other classes.'

Whispers from Fair land. By the Right Hon. E. KNATCHBULL-HUGESSEN, M.P. Wi 9 Illustrations. Crown 8vo. 3*s.* 6*d.*

Higgledy-Piggledy; o Stories for Everybody and Eve body's Children. By the Right Ho E. H. KNATCHBULL-HUGESSEN, M. With 9 Illustrations. Cr. 8vo. 3*s.* 6

Stories and Tales. E ELIZABETH M. SEWELL. Cabir Edition, in Ten Volumes, each contai ing a complete Tale or Story :—

Amy Herbert, 2*s.* 6*d.* **Gertrude,** 2*s.* 6 **The Earl's Daughter,** 2*s.* 6*d.* T **Experience of Life,** 2*s.* 6*d.* **Cle Hall,** 2*s.* 6*d.* **Ivors,** 2*s.* 6*d.* **Kathar Ashton,** 2*s.* 6*d.* **Margaret Perciv** 3*s.* 6*d.* **Laneton Parsonage,** 3*s.* 6 **Ursula,** 3*s.* 6*d.*

The Modern Novelist Library. Each work complete in itse price 2*s.* boards, or 2*s.* 6*d.* cloth :

By Lord BEACONSFIELD.

Lothair.	**Henrietta Temple.**
Coningsby.	**Contarini Fleming.**
Sybil.	**Alroy, Ixion, &c.**
Tancred.	**The Young Duke, &**
Venetia.	**Vivian Grey.**

By ANTHONY TROLLOPE.
Barchester Towers.

By Major WHYTE-MELVILLE.

Digby Grand.
General Bounce.
Kate Coventry.
The Gladiators.
Good for Nothing.
Holmby House.
The Interpreter.
Queen's Maries.

By the Author of 'The Rose Garden.'

Unawares.

By the Author of 'Mlle. Mori.'

The Atelier du Lys.
Mademoiselle Mori.

By Various Writers.

Atherstone Priory.
The Burgomaster's Family.
Elsa and her Vulture.
The Six Sisters of the Valleys.

Novels and Tales by the Right Honourable the Earl of Beaconsfield, K.G. Ten Volumes, crown 8vo. cloth extra, gilt edges, price 30*s.*

POETRY and THE DRAMA.

Poetical Works of Jean Ingelow. New Edition, reprinted, with Additional Matter, from the 23rd and 6th Editions of the two volumes respectively; with 2 Vignettes. 2 vols. fcp. 8vo. 12*s.*

Faust. From the German of GOETHE. By T. E. WEBB, LL.D. one of Her Majesty's Counsel in Ireland; sometime Fellow of Trinity College, now Regius Professor of Laws and Public Orator in the University of Dublin. 8vo. 12*s.* 6*d.*

Goethe's Faust. A New Translation, chiefly in Blank Verse; with a complete Introduction and copious Notes. By JAMES ADEY BIRDS, B.A. F.G.S. Large crown 8vo. 12*s.* 6*d.*

Goethe's Faust. The German Text, with an English Introduction and Notes for the use of Students. By ALBERT M. SELSS, M.A. Ph.D. &c. Professor of German in the University of Dublin. Crown 8vo. 5*s.*

Lays of Ancient Rome; with Ivry and the Armada. By LORD MACAULAY. 16mo. 3*s.* 6*d.*

The Poem of the Cid: a Translation from the Spanish, with Introduction and Notes. By JOHN ORMSBY. Crown 8vo. 5*s.*

Festus, a Poem. By PHILIP JAMES BAILEY. 10th Edition, enlarged & revised. Crown 8vo. 12*s.* 6*d.*

The Iliad of Homer, Homometrically translated by C. B. CAYLEY. 8vo. 12*s.* 6*d.*

The Æneid of Virgil. Translated into English Verse. By J. CONINGTON, M.A. Crown 8vo. 9*s.*

Bowdler's Family Shakspeare. Genuine Edition, in 1 vol. medium 8vo. large type, with 36 Woodcuts, 14*s.* or in 6 vols. fcp. 8vo. 21*s.*

Southey's Poetical Works, with the Author's last Corrections and Additions. Medium 8vo. with Portrait, 14*s.*

RURAL SPORTS, HORSE and CATTLE MANAGEMENT, &c.

Blaine's Encyclopædia of Rural Sports; Complete Accounts, Historical, Practical, and Descriptive, of Hunting, Shooting, Fishing, Racing, &c. With 600 Woodcuts. 8vo. 21*s.*

A Book on Angling; or, Treatise on the Art of Fishing in every branch; including full Illustrated Lists of Salmon Flies. By FRANCIS FRANCIS. Post 8vo. Portrait and Plates, 15*s.*

Wilcocks's Sea-Fisherman: comprising the Chief Methods of Hook and Line Fishing, a glance at Nets, and remarks on Boats and Boating. Post 8vo. Woodcuts, 12*s.* 6*d.*

The Fly-Fisher's Entomology. By ALFRED RONALDS. With 20 Coloured Plates. 8vo. 14*s.*

Horses and Roads; or, How to Keep a Horse Sound on his Legs. By FREE-LANCE. Second Edition. Crown 8vo. 6*s.*

Horses and Riding. By GEORGE NEVILE, M.A. With 31 Illustrations. Crown 8vo. 6*s.*

Youatt on the Horse. Revised and enlarged by W. WATSON, M.R.C.V.S. 8vo. Woodcuts, 7*s.* 6*d.*

Youatt's Work on the Dog. Revised and enlarged. 8vo. Woodcuts, 6*s.*

The Dog in Health and Disease. By STONEHENGE. Third Edition, with 78 Wood Engravings. Square crown 8vo. 7*s.* 6*d.*

The Greyhound. E STONEHENGE. Revised Edition, w 25 Portraits of Greyhounds, Square crown 8vo. 15*s.*

Stables and Stable Fittings. By W. MILES. Imp. 8v with 13 Plates, 15*s.*

The Horse's Foot, an How to keep it Sound. By MILES. Imp. 8vo. Woodcuts, 12*s.* (

A Plain Treatise o Horse-shoeing. By W. MILES. P 8vo. Woodcuts, 2*s.* 6*d.*

Remarks on Horse Teeth, addressed to Purchasers. W. MILES. Post 8vo. 1*s.* 6*d.*

A Treatise on the Diseases of the Ox; being a Manual Bovine Pathology specially adapted the use of Veterinary Practitioners a Students. By J. H. STEEL, M.R.C.V. F.Z.S. With 2 Plates and 116 Woc cuts. 8vo. 15*s.*

WORKS of UTILITY and GENERAL INFORMATION.

Maunder's Biographical Treasury. Latest Edition, reconstructed and partly re-written, with above 1,600 additional Memoirs, by W. L. R. CATES. Fcp. 8vo. 6*s.*

Maunder's Treasury of Natural History; or, Popular Dictionary of Zoology. Revised and corrected Edition. Fcp. 8vo. with 900 Woodcuts, 6*s.*

Maunder's Treasury of Geography, Physical, Historical, Descriptive, and Political. Edited by W. HUGHES, F.R.G.S. With 7 Maps and 16 Plates. Fcp. 8vo. 6*s.*

Maunder's Historical Treasury; Introductory Outlines of Universal History, and Separate Histories of all Nations. Revised by the Rev. Sir G. W. COX, Bart. M.A.

Maunder's Treasury Knowledge and Library of Refe ence; comprising an English Dictic ary and Grammar, Universal Gazette Classical Dictionary, Chronology, Dictionary, Synopsis of the Peerag Useful Tables, &c. Fcp. 8vo. 6*s.*

Maunder's Scientific an Literary Treasury; a Popular E cyclopædia of Science, Literature, a Art. Latest Edition, partly re-writte with above 1,000 New Articles, by Y. JOHNSON. Fcp. 8vo. 6*s.*

The Treasury of Botan or Popular Dictionary of the Vegeta Kingdom; with which is incorporat a Glossary of Botanical Terms. Edit by J. LINDLEY, F.R.S. and T. MOOR F.L.S. With 274 Woodcuts and

The Treasury of Bible Knowledge; being a Dictionary of the Books, Persons, Places, Events, and other Matters of which mention is made in Holy Scripture. By the Rev. J. AYRE, M.A. Maps, Plates & Woodcuts. Fcp. 8vo. 6*s.*

A Practical Treatise on Brewing; with Formulæ for Public Brewers & Instructions for Private Families. By W. BLACK. 8vo. 10*s.* 6*d.*

The Theory of the Modern Scientific Game of Whist. By W. POLE, F.R.S. Twelfth Edition. Fcp. 8vo. 2*s.* 6*d.*

The Correct Card; or, How to Play at Whist; a Whist Catechism. By Major A. CAMPBELL-WALKER, F.R.G.S. Latest Edition. Fcp. 8vo. 2*s.* 6*d.*

The Cabinet Lawyer; a Popular Digest of the Laws of England, Civil, Criminal, and Constitutional. Twenty-Fifth Edition, corrected and extended. Fcp. 8vo. 9*s.*

Chess Openings. By F.W. LONGMAN, Balliol College, Oxford. New Edition. Fcp. 8vo. 2*s.* 6*d.*

Pewtner's Comprehensive Specifier; a Guide to the Practical Specification of every kind of Building-Artificer's Work. Edited by W. YOUNG. Crown 8vo. 6*s.*

Modern Cookery for Private Families, reduced to a System of Easy Practice in a Series of carefully-tested Receipts. By ELIZA ACTON. With 8 Plates and 150 Woodcuts. Fcp. 8vo. 6*s.*

Food and Home Cookery. A Course of Instruction in Practical Cookery and Cleaning, for Children in Elementary Schools. By Mrs. BUCKTON. Woodcuts. Crown 8vo. 2*s.*

The Ventilation of Dwelling Houses and the Utilisation of Waste Heat from Open Fire-Places, &c. By F. EDWARDS, Jun. Second Edition. With numerous Lithographic Plates, comprising 106 Figures. Royal 8vo. 10*s.* 6*d.*

Hints to Mothers on the Management of their Health during the Period of Pregnancy and in the Lying-in Room. By THOMAS BULL, M.D. Fcp. 8vo. 2*s.* 6*d.*

The Maternal Management of Children in Health and Disease. By THOMAS BULL, M.D. Fcp. 8vo. 2*s.* 6*d.*

American Food and Farming. By FINLAY DUN, Special Correspondent for the 'Times.' 8vo. [*In the press.*

The Farm Valuer. By JOHN SCOTT, Land Valuer. Crown 8vo. 5*s.*

Rents and Purchases; or, the Valuation of Landed Property, Woods, Minerals, Buildings, &c. By JOHN SCOTT. Crown 8vo. 6*s.*

Economic Studies. By the late WALTER BAGEHOT, M.A. Fellow of University College, London. Edited by RICHARD HOLT HUTTON. 8vo. 10*s.* 6*d.*

Economics for Beginners By H. D. MACLEOD, M.A. Small crown 8vo. 2*s.* 6*d.*

The Elements of Banking. By H. D. MACLEOD, M.A. Fourth Edition. Crown 8vo. 5*s.*

The Theory and Practice of Banking. By H. D. MACLEOD, M.A. 2 vols. 8vo. 26*s.*

The Resources of Modern Countries; Essays towards an Estimate of the Economic Position of Nations and British Trade Prospects. By ALEX. WILSON. 2 vols. 8vo. 24*s.*

The Patentee's Manual; a Treatise on the Law and Practice of Letters Patent, for the use of Patentees and Inventors. By J. JOHNSON, Barrister-at-Law; and J. H. JOHNSON, Assoc. Inst. C.E. Solicitor and Patent Agent, Lincoln's Inn Fields and Glasgow. Fourth Edition, enlarged. 8vo. price 10*s.* 6*d.*

INDEX.

UK Ltd.

318
0012B/933/P